DK

How to be good at maths

WORKBOOK 1

The **simplest-ever** visual workbook

Produced for DK by
Dynamo Limited
1 Cathedral Court, Southernhay East, Exeter, EX1 1AF

Authors Tim Handley, Linda Glithro
Consultant Paul Broadbent

Senior Editor Ankita Awasthi Tröger
Senior Art Editor Amy Child
Editors Lizzie Munsey,
Catharine Robertson, Ben Ffrancon Davies
Designer Anna Scully
Managing Editor Christine Stroyan
Managing Art Editor Anna Hall
Senior Production Editor Andy Hilliard
Production Editor George Nimmo
Production Controller Sian Cheung
Jacket Design Development Manager Sophia MTT
Jacket Designer Tanya Mehrotra
DTP Designer Rakesh Kumar
Publisher Andrew Macintyre
Associate Publishing Director Liz Wheeler
Art Director Karen Self
Publishing Director Jonathan Metcalf

First published in Great Britain in 2021 by
Dorling Kindersley Limited
20 Vauxhall Bridge Road,
London SW1V 2SA

The authorised representative in the EEA is
Dorling Kindersley Verlag GmbH. Arnulfstr. 124,
80636 Munich, Germany

10 9 8 7 6 5 4 3
003-322111-Oct/2021

A CIP catalogue record for this book
is available from the British Library.
ISBN 978-0-2414-7141-8

Printed and bound in China

www.dk.com

MIX
Paper | Supporting responsible forestry
FSC www.fsc.org FSC™ C018179

This book was made with Forest Stewardship Council™ certified paper – one small step in DK's commitment to a sustainable future.
Learn more at www.dk.com/uk/information/sustainability

Contents

Numbers

Calculating

Measurement

Geometry

Carol Vorderman, one of Britain's best known and loved TV personalities, feels passionately about the value of education. She joined forces with DK in 1999 to become DK's Education Champion and has helped us to build the bestselling *Made Easy* and *How to be Good at* series, which include topics in English, maths, and science and technology. Carol has a degree in engineering from the University of Cambridge, and was awarded an MBE in 2000 for services to broadcasting.

Pages 000–000

The page numbers next to this icon refer to pages in DK's *How to be Good at Maths*.

Number symbols

People have used numbers in their daily lives since the earliest times. We use numbers to count, measure, tell time, and buy or sell things.

DID YOU KNOW?
The Babylonian, Ancient Roman, and Ancient Egyptian number systems did not have a symbol for zero.

Hindu-Arabic	0	1	2	3	4	5	6	7	8	9
Ancient Roman		I	II	III	IV	V	VI	VII	VIII	IX
Babylonian		𒁹	𒈫	𒐈	𒐉	𒐊	𒐋	𒐌	𒐍	𒐎
Ancient Egyptian		𓏺	𓏻	𓏼	𓏽	𓏾	𓏿	𓐀	𓐁	𓐂

Warm-up Colour the Hindu-Arabic symbols in red, the Egyptian symbols in green, the Roman symbols in blue, and the Babylonian symbols in yellow.

7	5	IX	𓐀	6	𒐌
V	3	𒐊	III	𒐈	VII
𓏼	𒐎	VI	𓐂	9	𓏾

1 Use the chart at the top of the page to help you fill in the numbers for each of these symbols.

a IV = 4

b 𒈫 = ☐

c VIII = ☐

d 𓏾 = ☐

e 𒐍 = ☐

f 𓐂 = ☐

g 𒐎 = ☐

h IX = ☐

2

The seven letters I, V, X, L, C, D, and M are put together to make up all of the numbers in the Roman number system:

Ones	I 1	II 2	III 3	IV 4	V 5	VI 6	VII 7	VIII 8	IX 9
Tens	X 10	XX 20	XXX 30	XL 40	L 50	LX 60	LXX 70	LXXX 80	XC 90
Hundreds	C 100	CC 200	CCC 300	CD 400	D 500	DC 600	DCC 700	DCCC 800	CM 900
Thousands	M 1000	MM 2000	MMM 3000	$\overline{IV}$ 4000	$\overline{V}$ 5000	$\overline{VI}$ 6000	$\overline{VII}$ 7000	$\overline{VIII}$ 8000	$\overline{IX}$ 9000

Draw lines to match each Hindu-Arabic number with the correct Roman numeral. Use the chart above to help you.

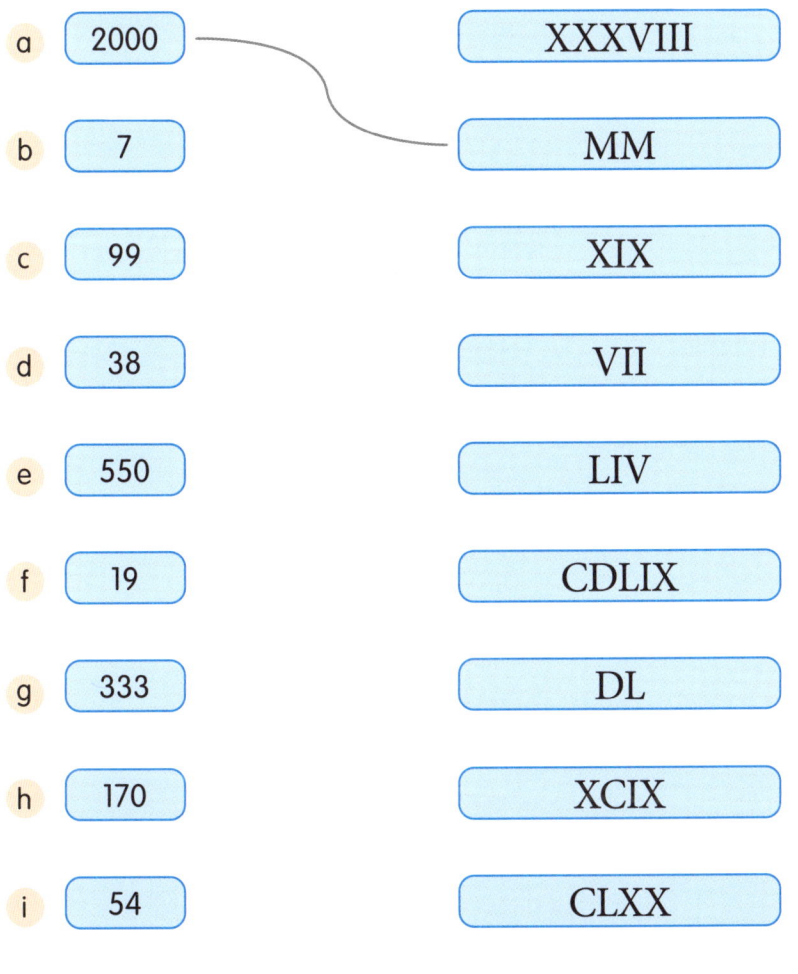

a	2000	XXXVIII
b	7	MM
c	99	XIX
d	38	VII
e	550	LIV
f	19	CDLIX
g	333	DL
h	170	XCIX
i	54	CLXX
j	459	CCCXXXIII

MATHS IN CONTEXT

What year was that?

TV programmes and films often have the year they were made in Roman numerals at the end of the credits. Work out the dates that these imaginary films were made.

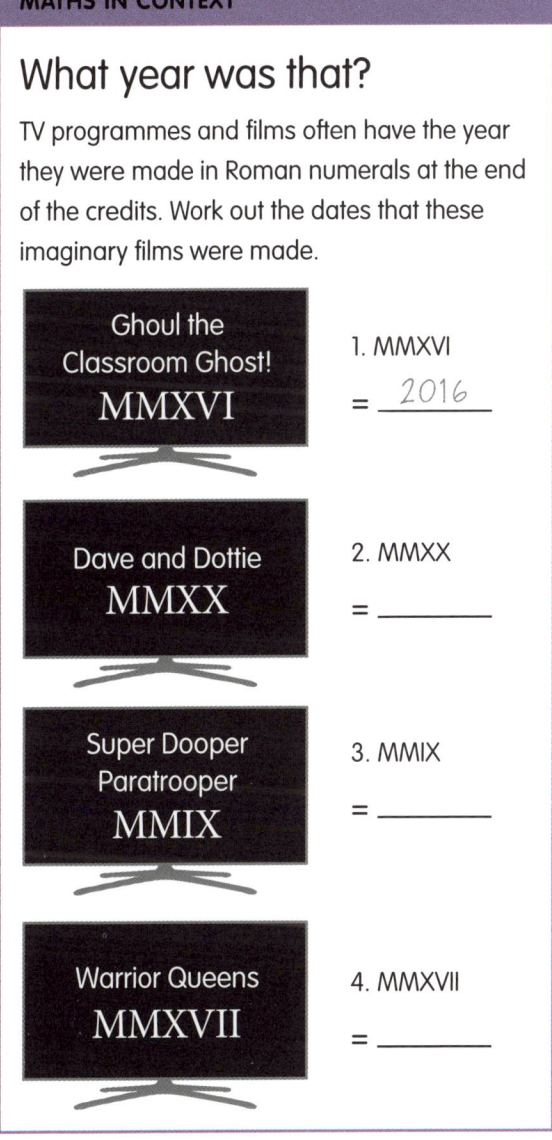

1. MMXVI
= 2016

2. MMXX
= ________

3. MMIX
= ________

4. MMXVII
= ________

Pages 10–11

Place value

In our number system, the amount a digit is worth depends on where it's placed in a number. This is called its place value. For example, the digit 1 is worth 10 in 5610, but 1000 in 1584.

Th	H	T	O
5	6	1	0
1	5	8	4

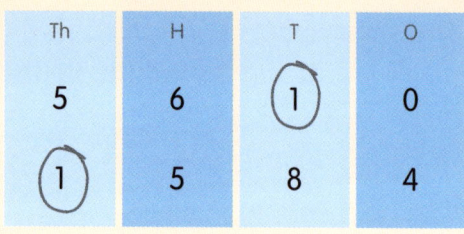

We can work out the value of a digit by using a place value grid.

Warm-up Circle the digit that shows the tens in each number below.

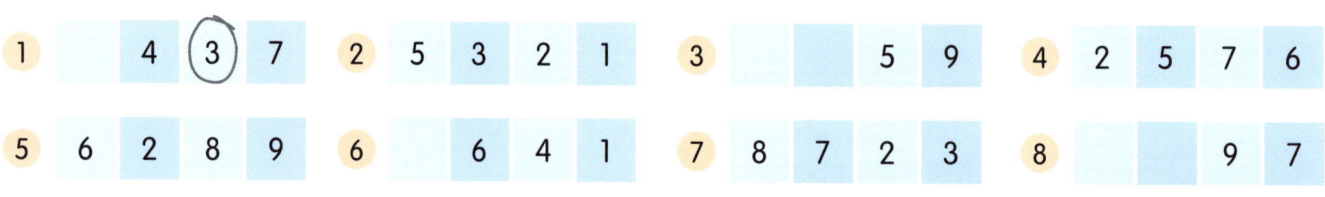

1		4	3	7	2	5	3	2	1	3			5	9	4	2	5	7	6
5	6	2	8	9	6		6	4	1	7	8	7	2	3	8			9	7

1

Fill in how many thousands, hundreds, tens, and ones each of these numbers has.

a 4567 4 thousands 5 hundreds 6 tens 7 ones

b 98 ____ thousands ____ hundreds ____ tens ____ ones

c 2425 ____ thousands ____ hundreds ____ tens ____ ones

d 897 ____ thousands ____ hundreds ____ tens ____ ones

e 3774 ____ thousands ____ hundreds ____ tens ____ ones

f 798 ____ thousands ____ hundreds ____ tens ____ ones

2

These numbers all contain the digit 5, but it has a different value in each of them. Draw lines to match each digit 5 with its correct place value.

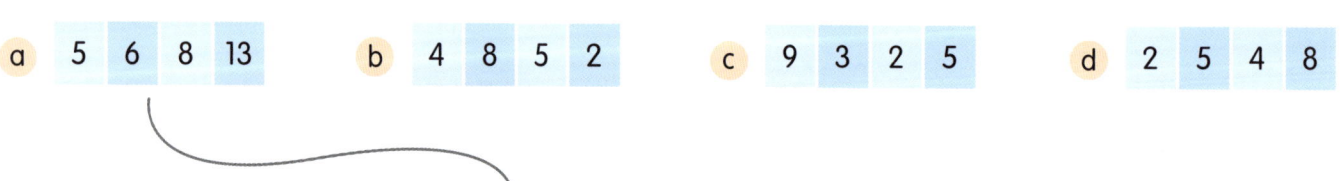

a 5 6 8 13

b 4 8 5 2

c 9 3 2 5

d 2 5 4 8

50

5000

500

5

3 Fill in the number that is being described in each of these sentences.

a This number has 7 tens, 8 ones, 3 thousands, and 2 hundreds. This number is: 3278

b This number has 4 thousands, 9 tens, 8 ones, and 3 hundreds. This number is: ______

c This number has 5 ones, 6 thousands, 8 tens, and 4 hundreds. This number is: ______

d This number has 6 tens, 4 ones, 9 thousands, and 3 hundreds. This number is: ______

e This number has 6 hundreds, 1 ten, 2 ones, and 3 thousands. This number is: ______

f This number has 4 tens, 7 thousands, 0 ones, and 8 hundreds. This number is: ______

g This number has 3 tens, 4 ones, 5 thousands, and 7 hundreds. This number is: ______

h This number has 5 hundreds, 9 ones, 2 tens, and 2 thousands. This number is: ______

4 Use the number box to help you find five different numbers that have the digit 3 in the tens column.

~~380~~ ~~4237~~ 9370 1439 9803 37 3970 5322 31 3128 830 340 2380 5493

a 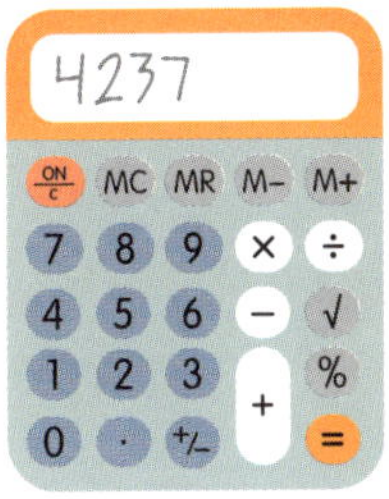

b 

c 

d 

e 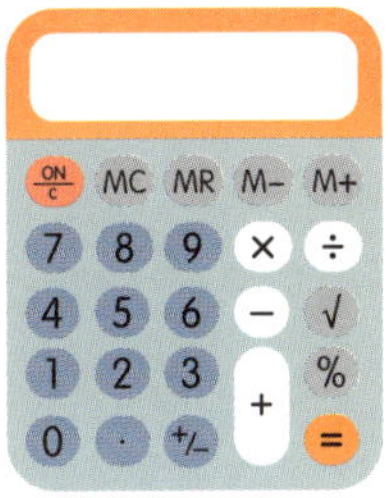

Now use the number box to find five different numbers that have the digit 3 in the hundreds column.

f 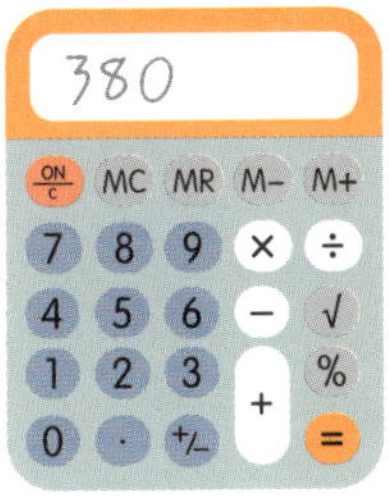

g 

h 

i 

j 

Pages 12–13

Sequences and patterns

A sequence is a set of numbers that follows a pattern or rule. Using the rule lets us work out other numbers in the sequence.

+3 +3 +3 +3

5 8 11 14 17

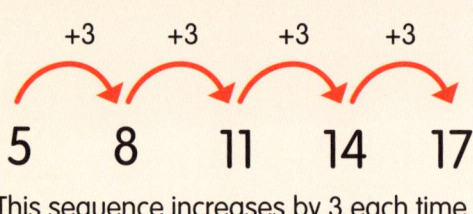

This sequence increases by 3 each time.

Warm-up

Fill in the next two numbers in each of these sequences.

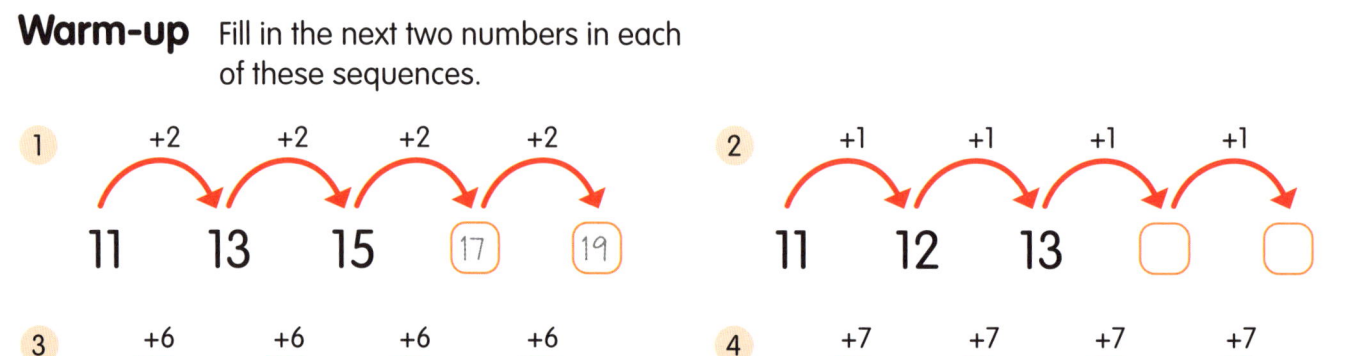

1. +2 +2 +2 +2
   11 13 15 [17] [19]

2. +1 +1 +1 +1
   11 12 13 [ ] [ ]

3. +6 +6 +6 +6
   11 17 23 [ ] [ ]

4. +7 +7 +7 +7
   11 18 25 [ ] [ ]

1

The numbers below follow sequences with subtraction rules. Work out the patterns, then fill in the numbers to complete the sequences.

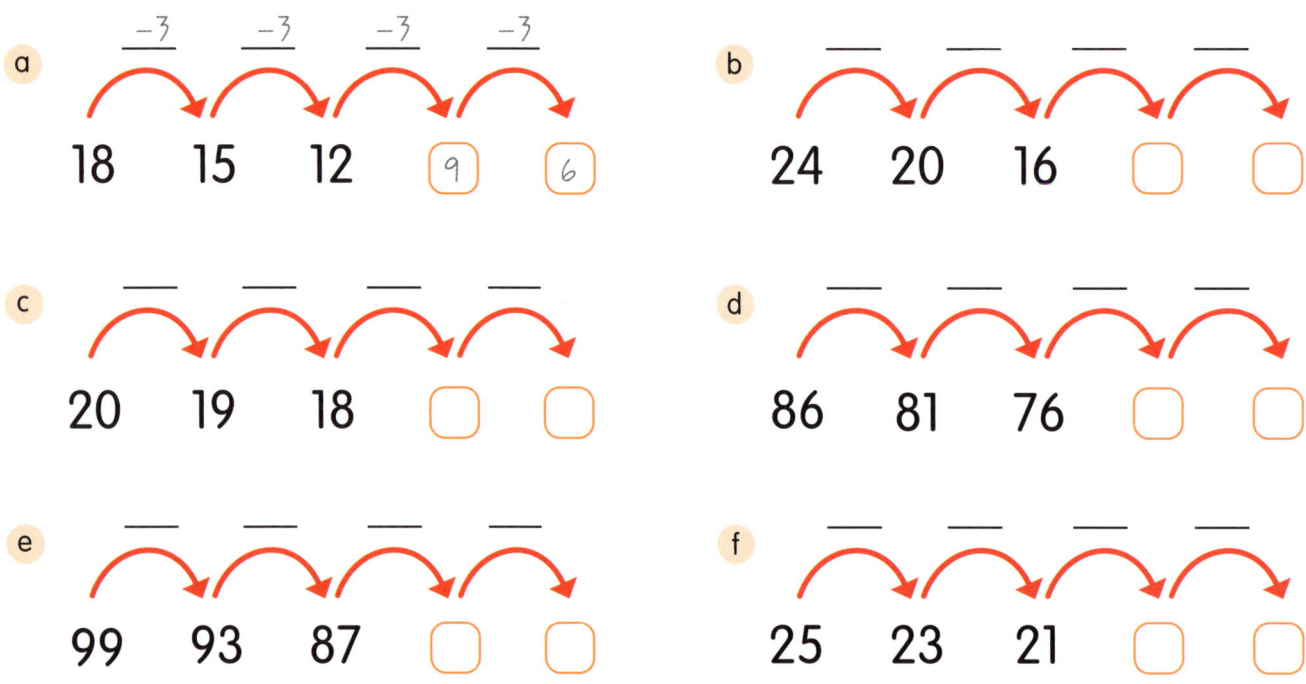

a. [−3] [−3] [−3] [−3]
   18 15 12 [9] [6]

b. ___ ___ ___ ___
   24 20 16 [ ] [ ]

c. ___ ___ ___ ___
   20 19 18 [ ] [ ]

d. ___ ___ ___ ___
   86 81 76 [ ] [ ]

e. ___ ___ ___ ___
   99 93 87 [ ] [ ]

f. ___ ___ ___ ___
   25 23 21 [ ] [ ]

2 Fill in the next two numbers for each sequence. Then complete the sentences to describe each pattern.

a 8, 12, 16, 20, 24, 28, 32 — The pattern is + 4 each time.

b 4, 14, 24, 34, 44, ___, ___ — The pattern is ______ each time.

c 7, 14, 21, 28, 35, ___, ___ — The pattern is ______ each time.

d 4, 7, 10, 13, 16, ___, ___ — The pattern is ______ each time.

3 Write four different sequences of your own. The start number is given to you. Write the rule for each.

a 24, 21, 18, 15, 12, 9 — The rule is −3.

b 30, ___, ___, ___, ___, ___ — The rule is ______.

c 18, ___, ___, ___, ___, ___ — The rule is ______.

d 45, ___, ___, ___, ___, ___ — The rule is ______.

4 Sometimes, a rule can have more than one part. Complete these sequences with two-part patterns.

a Pattern: add 3, then take away 1.

+3, −1, +3, −1

8 → 11 → 10 → 13 → 12

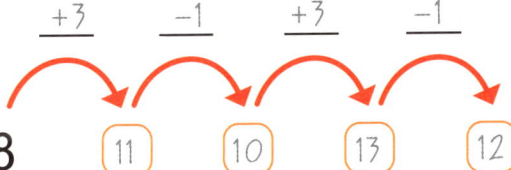

b Pattern: add 8, then take away 3.

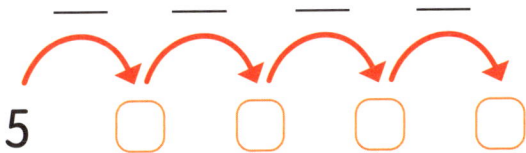

___ ___ ___ ___

5 → ☐ → ☐ → ☐ → ☐

c Pattern: add 5, then take away 2.

___ ___ ___ ___

4 → ☐ → ☐ → ☐ → ☐

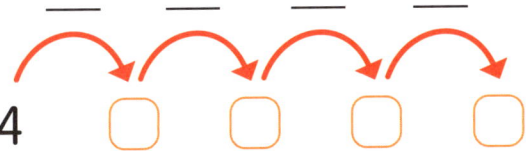

d Pattern: take away 5, then add 4.

___ ___ ___ ___

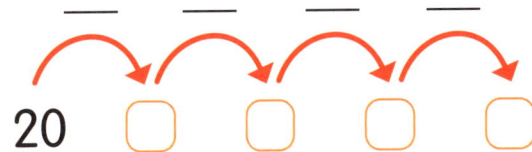

20 → ☐ → ☐ → ☐ → ☐

Pages 14–15

Positive and negative numbers

Positive numbers are all of the numbers that are greater than zero. Negative numbers are less than zero, and they always have a negative sign (–) in front of them, like this: –4.

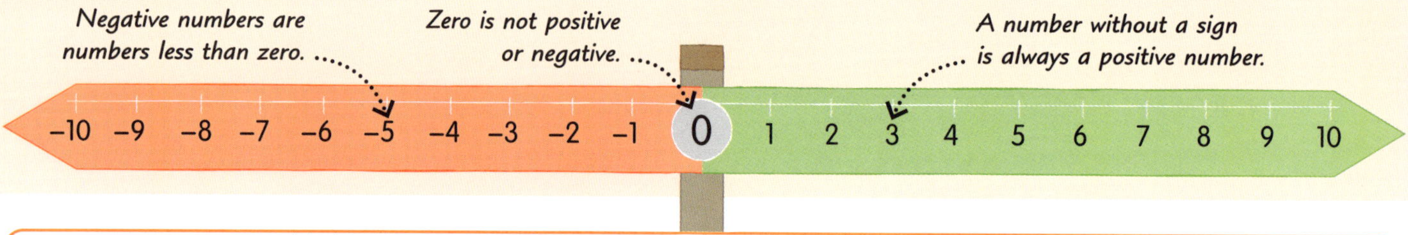

Zero is not positive or negative.
A number without a sign is always a positive number.

Warm-up Fill in the missing numbers on the number lines below.

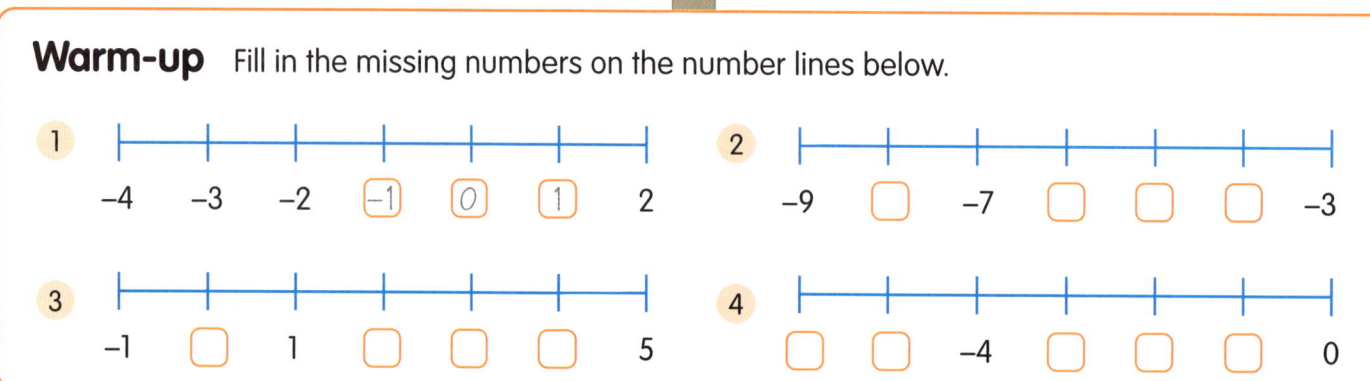

1. –4 –3 –2 [–1] [0] [1] 2

2. –9 [ ] –7 [ ] [ ] [ ] –3

3. –1 [ ] 1 [ ] [ ] [ ] 5

4. [ ] [ ] –4 [ ] [ ] [ ] 0

1 Count back five steps from the number circled on each of the number lines below. Then fill in the number that you land on.

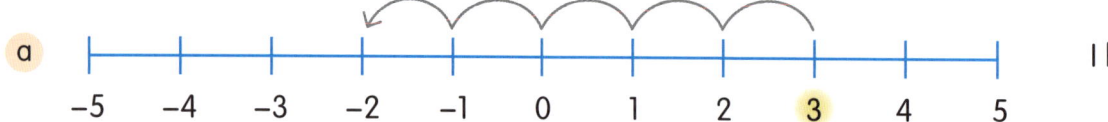

a –5 –4 –3 –2 –1 0 1 2 **3** 4 5 — I landed on –2 .

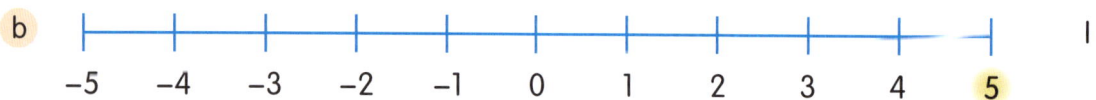

b –5 –4 –3 –2 –1 0 1 2 3 4 **5** — I landed on ______ .

c –5 –4 –3 –2 –1 **0** 1 2 3 4 5 — I landed on ______ .

d –5 –4 –3 –2 –1 0 1 **2** 3 4 5 — I landed on ______ .

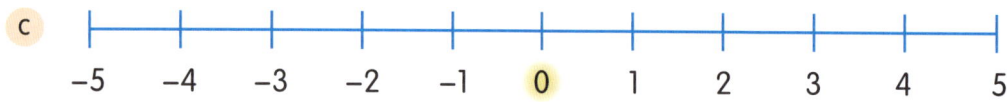

2 Count backwards five times from each number shown.

a 5, 4, 3, 2, 1, 0

b 9, ___, ___, ___, ___, ___

c 3, ___, ___, ___, ___, ___

d 1, ___, ___, ___, ___, ___

e 12, ___, ___, ___, ___, ___

f 7, ___, ___, ___, ___, ___

3 Count backwards five times in 2s.

a 10, 8, 6, 4, 2, 0

b 4, ___, ___, ___, ___, ___

c 3, ___, ___, ___, ___, ___

d 1, ___, ___, ___, ___, ___

e 7, ___, ___, ___, ___, ___

f 9, ___, ___, ___, ___, ___

4 Work out the difference between each pair of numbers, using the number lines to help you.

a The difference between –3 and 2 is 5.

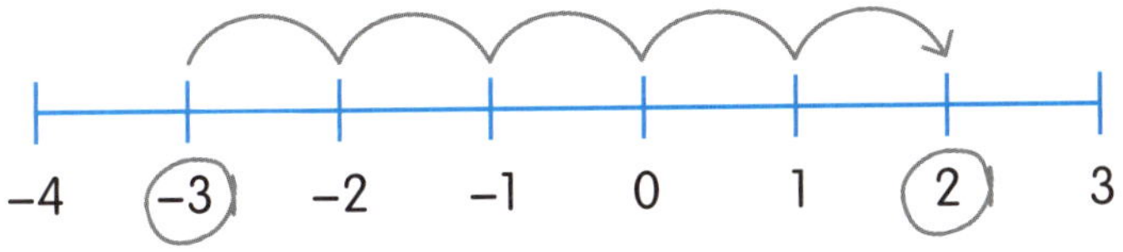

b The difference between 4 and 10 is ___.

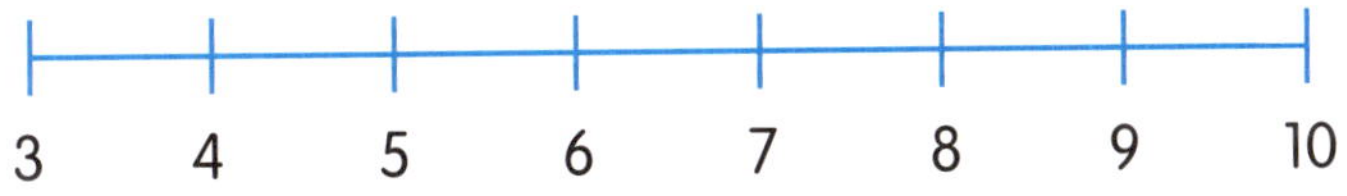

c The difference between –5 and –1 is ___.

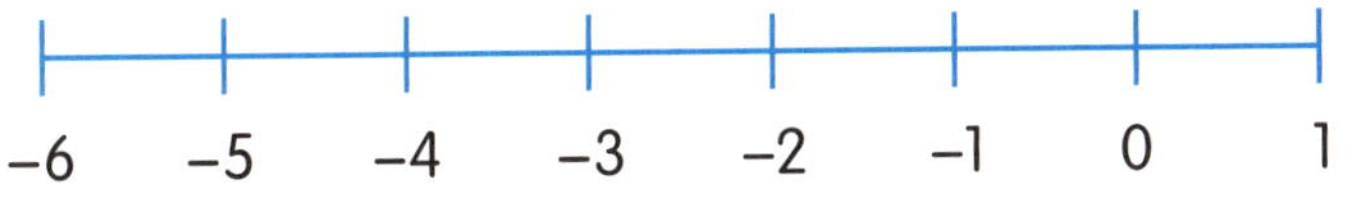

MATHS IN CONTEXT

Getting warmer?

Use the thermometer to find the answers to these word puzzles.

1. The temperature outside at 4am was –4°C. At 10 am, it was 5°C. How much warmer was it at 10am than at 4 am?

It was ______°C warmer.

2. The temperature outside at noon was 5°C. At 8 pm it was –3°C. How much cooler was it at 8 pm than midday?

It was ______°C cooler.

3. The temperature in Greenland was –5°C. In Norway it was 2°C. How much warmer was it in Norway than in Greenland?

It was ______°C warmer.

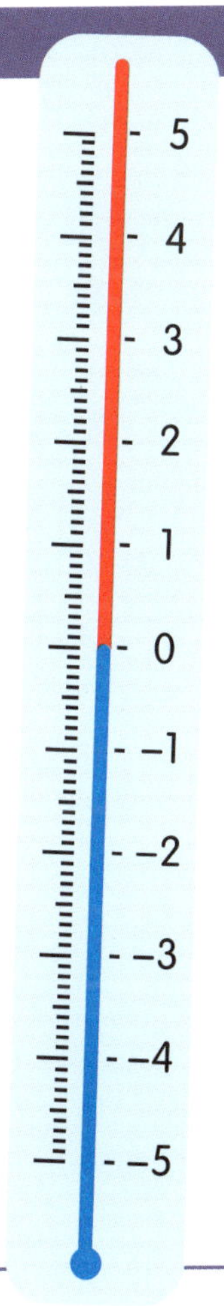

Pages 18–19

Comparing numbers

We can compare numbers to find out if a number is the same as, smaller than, or larger than another number. We sometimes use symbols to help us compare numbers.

= Equal to

> Greater than

< Less than

Warm-up

Circle the greater number in each of the pairs below.

1 305 (350)	2 989 99	3 288 828	4 123 1127
5 46 408	6 674 2674	7 531 513	8 822 82

1 Compare these pairs of numbers by writing less than (<), greater than (>), or equal to (=).

	H	T	O		H	T	O
a	6	8	9	>	6	7	3
b	1	3	7		3	1	7
c		3	3			2	7
d	4	8	5		4	8	4
e	9	3	5		9	3	5
f		4	9			9	4
g	2	2	6		2	6	2

2 Count how many items there are in each set. Then compare the sets by writing less than (<), greater than (>), or equal to (=).

a 10 [>] 8

b ______ [ ] ______

c ______ [ ] ______

d ______ [ ] ______

e ______ [ ] ______

f ______ [ ] ______

3 Fill in the missing numbers to make these comparisons true.

a [6] [5] [3] [8] [=] [6] [5] [3] [8]

b [3] [2] [6] [ ] [>] [3] [2] [6] [8]

c [4] [9] [7] [1] [<] [4] [ ] [7] [3]

Pages 20–21

Ordering numbers

We can compare the size or value of more than two numbers by putting them in order. We use what we know about place value to help us order numbers.

REMEMBER!
"Ascending order" means from smallest to biggest.
"Descending order" means from biggest to smallest.

Warm-up These numbers all contain the same digits, but in different place value order. Order each set of numbers by size, starting with the smallest.

1	12345	54321	45123	23451	43215	31245
	12345	23451	31245	43215	45123	54321
2	9672	2769	7629	6792	9762	2679
3	5298	8259	5289	2985	2958	5928
4	4379	4397	4937	4739	4793	3497

1 Write each set of numbers in ascending order.

a	567	578	568	587	487	487	567	568	578	587
b	127	712	732	237	777					
c	12	1243	123	1289	289					
d	465	4065	6540	1465	64					
e	409	490	491	419	420					

2

Each of these sets of numbers is in descending order. Fill in the missing digits in each number. There is more than one correct answer for each missing digit here.

a	4 7 0 1	4 5 8 9	4 5 6 9	4 5 6 8
b	5 9 □ 3	5 9 8 □	□ 9 5 6	3 9 5 6
c	1 5 □ 6	1 5 □ 6	1 4 3 □	1 4 3 8
d	8 9 □ 3	8 8 7 □	□ 7 8 7	7 7 7 8
e	4 1 □ 4	4 1 2 □	□ 2 4 5	2 3 4 5
f	5 8 □ 2	5 8 0 □	□ 0 1 1	5 0 0 1
g	5 □ 4 5	□ 6 8 9	□ 9 9 9	4 0 □ 3
h	9 □ 6 6	9 8 □ 6	9 □ 7 6	□ 8 7 7

3

Some children are comparing their highest scores on a game.

Evie's score is:	8959
Josh's score is:	8849
Grace's score is:	8961
Elliot's score is:	8843
Naziah's score is:	8943
Colby's score is:	7875

Order the children by their scores, starting with the lowest.

a Colby

b ______

c ______

d ______

e ______

f ______

MATHS IN CONTEXT

Around the world

Use the table to help you answer these questions:

1. Which city is closest to London? Chennai
2. Which city is furthest from London? ______
3. Which city is the third-closest to London? ______
4. Which city is the second-furthest from London? ______

City	Distance from London in kilometres
Durban	9544
Los Angeles	8750
Bangkok	9535
Shanghai	9191
Rio de Janeiro	9272
Chennai	8206

Pages 22–23

Estimating

Sometimes when we are calculating, we don't need to know the exact answer. Instead, we can make an estimate – a sensible guess.

REMEMBER!
Estimating allows us to make a quick guess when calculating the exact answer would take too long.

Warm-up We can estimate without counting by comparing amounts. Write an estimate for each tray of raspberries, then count to check your estimates.

1 My estimate is ____.

Actual number ____.

2 My estimate is ____.

Actual number ____.

3 My estimate is ____.

Actual number ____.

1

Estimate the number of marbles in each jar. Then work out the actual number.

a My estimate is ____.

Actual number ____.

b My estimate is ____.

Actual number ____.

c My estimate is ____.

Actual number ____.

2

Estimate the number of birds by counting how many there are in one row and then multiplying by the number of rows.

a My estimate is ____. Actual number ____.

b My estimate is ____. Actual number ____.

Pages 24–25

Rounding

When we round a number, we change it to another number that is close in value, but is easier to work with or remember.

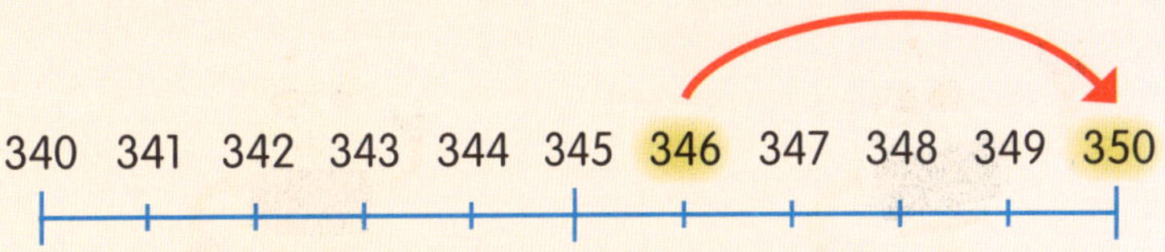

346 rounded to the nearest ten is 350, because 346 is closer to 350 than to 340.

REMEMBER!
When a digit is less than 5, we round down. When it is 5 or more, we round up.

Warm-up Round these numbers to the nearest 10, using the number line to help.

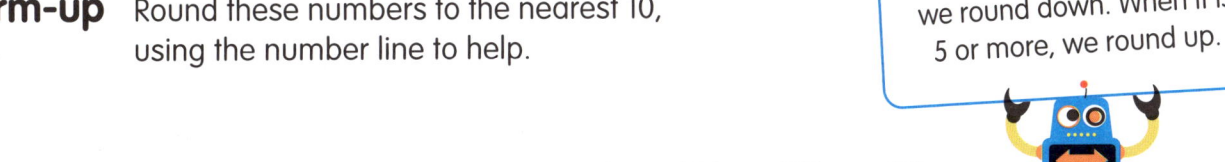

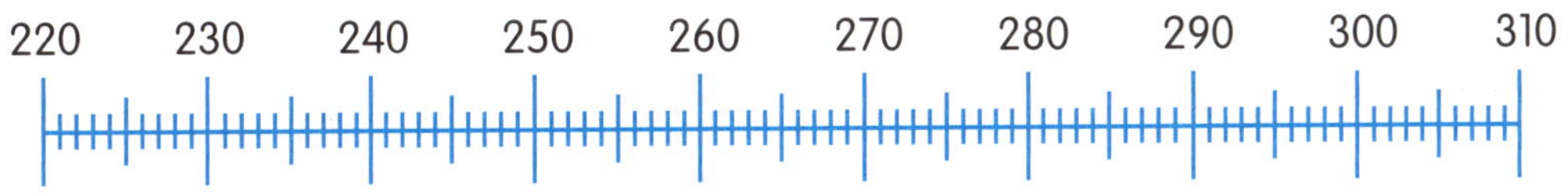

1 243 rounded to the nearest 10 is 240.

2 221 rounded to the nearest 10 is ______ .

3 309 rounded to the nearest 10 is ______ .

4 266 rounded to the nearest 10 is ______ .

1

Answer these questions to help you practise rounding to the nearest 10.

a Circle the four numbers below that round to 560 when rounded to the nearest 10.

565 561 555 559 569 554 558

b Circle the four numbers below that round to 800 when rounded to the nearest 10.

796 804 802 807 794 795 809

c Circle all the numbers below that round to 1000 when rounded to the nearest 10.

997 1010 1001 995 994 1008 1004

d Circle all the numbers below that round to 1500 when rounded to the nearest 10.

1495 1549 1059 1503 1565 1497 1551

2

Answer these questions about rounding.

a What is the largest number that rounds to 560 when rounded to the nearest 10? 564

b What is the smallest number that rounds to 560 when rounded to the nearest 10? ______

c What is the largest number that rounds to 890 when rounded to the nearest 10? ______

d What is the smallest number that rounds to 890 when rounded to the nearest 10? ______

e What is the largest number that rounds to 1000 when rounded to the nearest 10? ______

Pages 26–27

Fractions

A fraction is a part of a whole. We write a fraction as one number over another number. Fractions can either be part of one thing, like half a pizza, or part of a group, like half the students in a class.

$$\frac{1}{4}$$

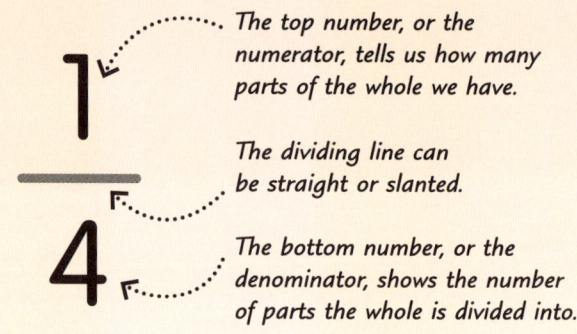

The top number, or the numerator, tells us how many parts of the whole we have.

The dividing line can be straight or slanted.

The bottom number, or the denominator, shows the number of parts the whole is divided into.

Warm-up Circle the fraction shown by the red part of each of these shapes.

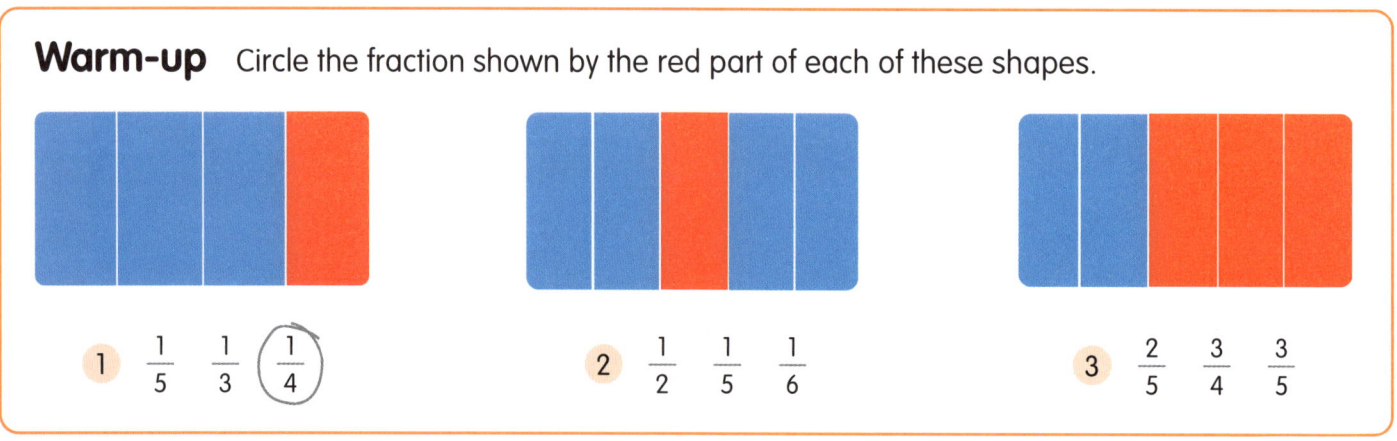

1 $\frac{1}{5}$ $\frac{1}{3}$ $\frac{1}{4}$

2 $\frac{1}{2}$ $\frac{1}{5}$ $\frac{1}{6}$

3 $\frac{2}{5}$ $\frac{3}{4}$ $\frac{3}{5}$

1 Draw lines to match each shape with the correct fraction and fraction word.

a $\frac{1}{4}$ b $\frac{1}{2}$ c $\frac{2}{6}$ d $\frac{1}{6}$ e $\frac{1}{5}$ f $\frac{2}{3}$

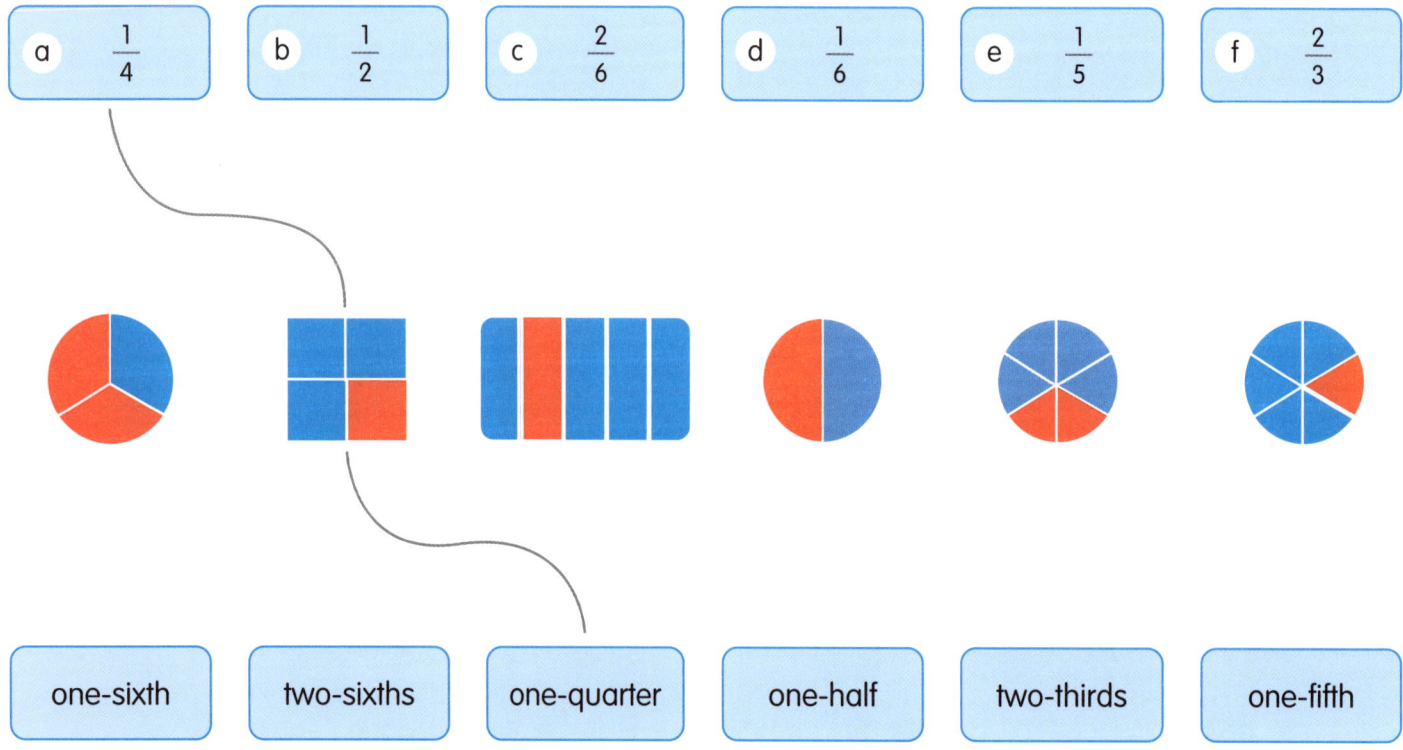

one-sixth two-sixths one-quarter one-half two-thirds one-fifth

2

Look at the pictures below, then fill in the fraction shown by the orange balloons in each group.

a 1/2 ____________

b ____________

c ____________

d ____________

e ____________

f ____________

g ____________

h ____________

3

Colour in the correct number of pizza slices to match each fraction.

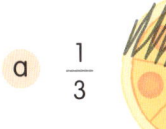

a $\frac{1}{3}$

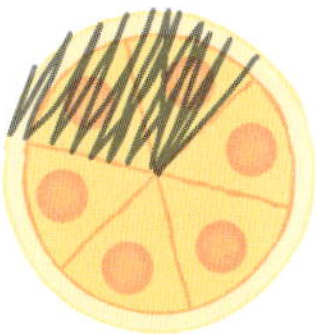

b $\frac{5}{6}$

c $\frac{1}{2}$

d $\frac{4}{6}$

e $\frac{1}{6}$

f $\frac{1}{4}$

g $\frac{2}{6}$

h $\frac{3}{4}$

MATHS IN CONTEXT

Share the cake

Jane cuts a cake into six equal slices. She gives ½ of the cake to her grandparents. The next day Tim eats ⅓ of the remaining cake.

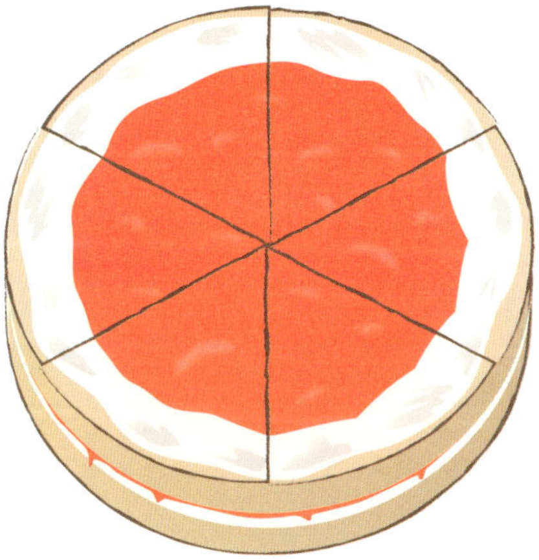

How many slices of cake are left? ____________

Pages 40–41

Equivalent fractions

Fractions can be written in different ways – for example, one-quarter of a pizza is exactly the same amount as two-eighths. We call these equivalent fractions.

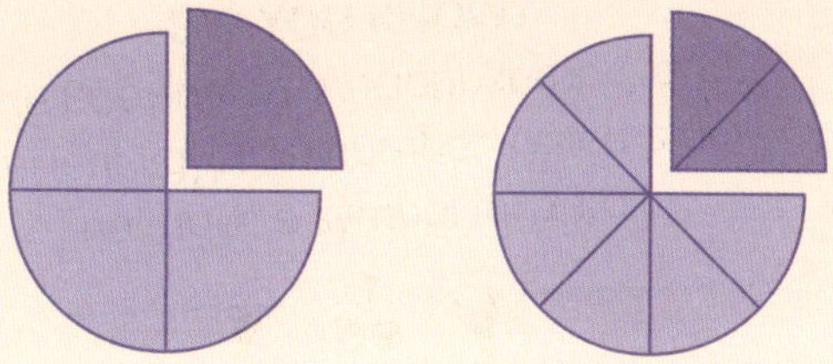

$\frac{1}{4} = \frac{2}{8}$

Warm-up Look at these pairs of images, then fill in the equivalent fractions under each.

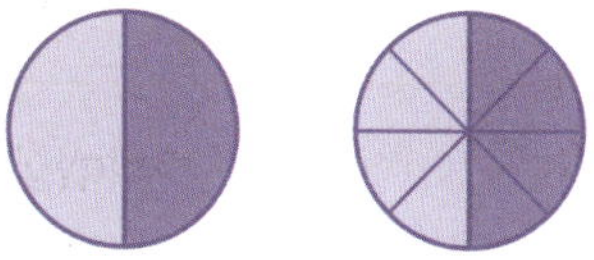

1 $\frac{1}{2} =$ [$\frac{4}{8}$]

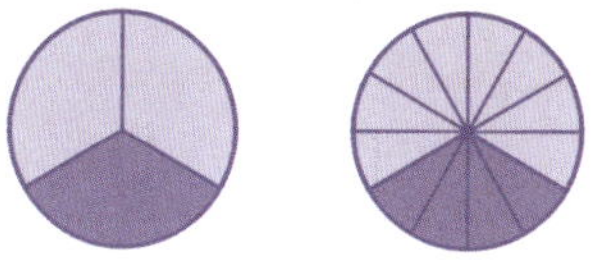

2 $\frac{1}{3} =$ [ ]

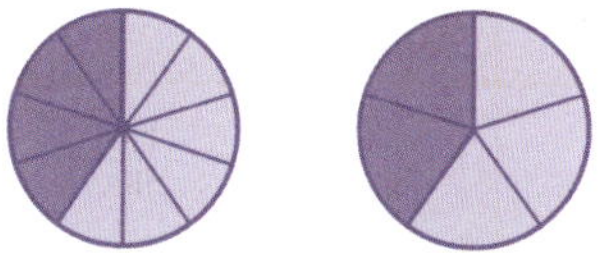

3 $\frac{4}{10} =$ [ ]

1 Fill in the missing fractions on this fraction wall.

1 whole

$\frac{1}{2}$ | $\frac{1}{2}$

$\frac{1}{3}$ | $\frac{1}{3}$ | ___

$\frac{1}{4}$ | $\frac{1}{4}$ | $\frac{1}{4}$ | ___

$\frac{1}{5}$ | $\frac{1}{5}$ | $\frac{1}{5}$ | ___ | ___

$\frac{1}{6}$ | $\frac{1}{6}$ | $\frac{1}{6}$ | $\frac{1}{6}$ | $\frac{1}{6}$ | ___

$\frac{1}{8}$ | $\frac{1}{8}$ | $\frac{1}{8}$ | $\frac{1}{8}$ | $\frac{1}{8}$ | ___ | ___ | ___

$\frac{1}{10}$ | $\frac{1}{10}$ | $\frac{1}{10}$ | $\frac{1}{10}$ | $\frac{1}{10}$ | $\frac{1}{10}$ | $\frac{1}{10}$ | $\frac{1}{10}$ | $\frac{1}{10}$ | ___

$\frac{1}{12}$ | $\frac{1}{12}$ | $\frac{1}{12}$ | $\frac{1}{12}$ | $\frac{1}{12}$ | $\frac{1}{12}$ | $\frac{1}{12}$ | $\frac{1}{12}$ | ___ | ___ | ___ | ___

2

Use the fraction wall from question 1 to help you complete these equivalent fractions.

a $\frac{1}{4}$ is equivalent to $\frac{2}{8}$ and $\frac{3}{12}$

b $\frac{2}{3}$ is equivalent to $\frac{\_}{6}$ and $\frac{\_}{12}$

c $\frac{1}{2}$ is equivalent to $\frac{\_}{4}$ and $\frac{\_}{8}$

d $\frac{3}{5}$ is equivalent to $\frac{\_}{10}$

e $\frac{3}{6}$ is equivalent to $\frac{\_}{8}$ and $\frac{\_}{12}$

f $\frac{4}{8}$ is equivalent to $\frac{\_}{10}$ and $\frac{\_}{2}$

3

Draw lines to match each fraction in the top row with its equivalent fraction below.

a $\frac{3}{9}$ b $\frac{1}{5}$ c $\frac{2}{3}$ d $\frac{1}{2}$ e $\frac{3}{4}$ f $\frac{3}{7}$

$\frac{3}{15}$ $\frac{12}{16}$ $\frac{9}{21}$ $\frac{9}{27}$ $\frac{10}{20}$ $\frac{4}{6}$

4

Fill in an equivalent fraction for each of these fractions.

a $\frac{4}{5} = \frac{8}{10}$

b $\frac{8}{24} =$ ☐

c $\frac{3}{4} =$ ☐

d $\frac{9}{30} =$ ☐

e $\frac{2}{3} =$ ☐

f $\frac{5}{9} =$ ☐

g $\frac{8}{11} =$ ☐

h $\frac{11}{12} =$ ☐

MATHS IN CONTEXT

Pizza time

Rav and Leonie are eating pizza. Shade in the amount each of them has eaten.

Who has eaten more pizza?

____

Rav has eaten ¾ of his pizza.

Leonie has eaten ⅔ of her pizza.

Pages 44–45

Finding a fraction of an amount

To find out what a fraction of a number or an amount is, we divide the amount by the denominator, then multiply the answer by the numerator.

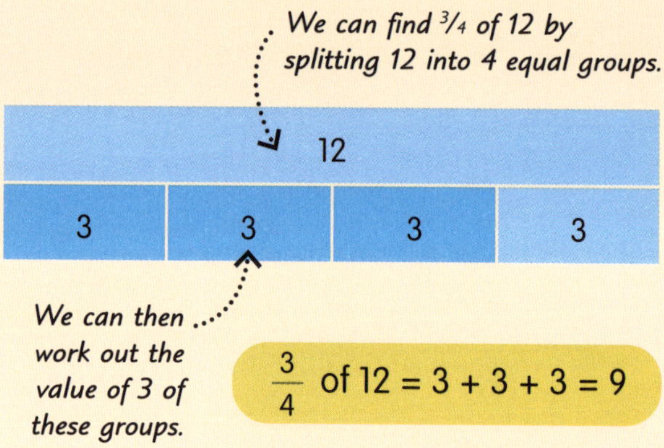

Warm-up Circle ⅓ of each of these sets of items.

1

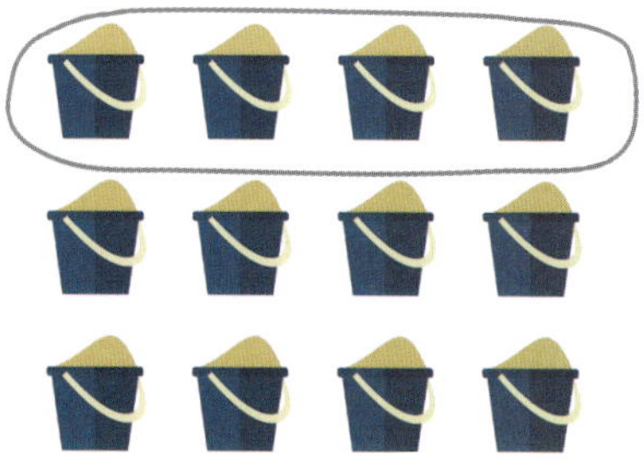

2

3

1 Use the bar models below to help you find the fractions of these amounts.

a $\frac{2}{3}$ of 30 is 20

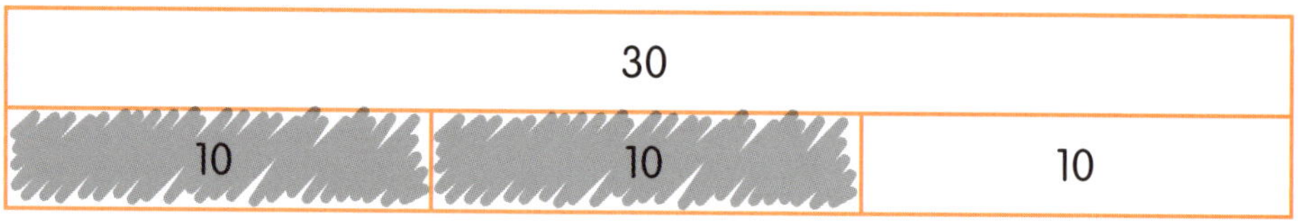

b $\frac{1}{4}$ of 24 is ______

c $\frac{4}{6}$ of 18 is ______

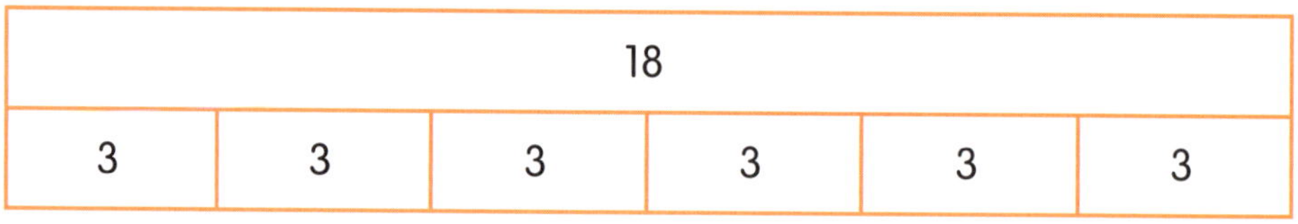

d $\frac{2}{5}$ of 20 is ______

2 Circle the correct answer to complete each of these number sentences.

a $\frac{2}{3}$ of 36 = 12 (24)

b $\frac{3}{4}$ of 48 = 35 36

c $\frac{1}{2}$ of 50 = 20 25

d $\frac{5}{6}$ of 36 = 30 24

e $\frac{3}{5}$ of 45 = 25 27

f $\frac{1}{8}$ of 40 = 4 5

3 Complete these number sentences.

a $\frac{1}{4}$ of 40 = 10

b $\frac{1}{4}$ of ___ = 12

c $\frac{1}{2}$ of ___ = 60

d $\frac{2}{3}$ of 96 = ___

e $\frac{1}{3}$ of ___ = 15

f $\frac{3}{7}$ of 28 = ___

g $\frac{3}{5}$ of 50 = ___

h $\frac{3}{4}$ of ___ = 6

i $\frac{2}{5}$ of ___ = 20

j $\frac{3}{4}$ of 48 = ___

k $\frac{2}{7}$ of ___ = 10

l $\frac{1}{5}$ of 10 = ___

m $\frac{1}{6}$ of 60 = ___

n $\frac{1}{2}$ of ___ = 45

o $\frac{4}{5}$ of ___ = 48

4 How many different fractions questions can you create that have the answer 30?

$\frac{1}{3}$ of 90 = 30

Page 47

Comparing fractions with the same denominators

If fractions have the same denominators, we can compare them by putting the numerators in order.

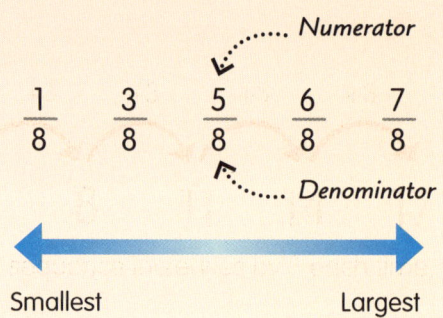

$\frac{1}{8}$ $\frac{3}{8}$ $\frac{5}{8}$ $\frac{6}{8}$ $\frac{7}{8}$

Numerator

Denominator

Smallest ⟷ Largest

Warm-up Circle the bigger fraction in each pair.

1. $\frac{2}{10}$ $\frac{4}{10}$ (circled)
2. $\frac{1}{10}$ $\frac{6}{10}$
3. $\frac{9}{10}$ $\frac{8}{10}$
4. $\frac{5}{10}$ $\frac{3}{10}$
5. $\frac{3}{10}$ $\frac{8}{10}$

1

Order each set of fractions by size, starting with the smallest.

a $\frac{7}{12}$ $\frac{3}{12}$ $\frac{9}{12}$ $\frac{5}{12}$ $\frac{1}{12}$

$\frac{1}{12}$ $\frac{3}{12}$ $\frac{5}{12}$ $\frac{7}{12}$ $\frac{9}{12}$

Smallest ⟷ Largest

b $\frac{4}{18}$ $\frac{2}{18}$ $\frac{12}{18}$ $\frac{6}{18}$ $\frac{3}{18}$

☐ ☐ ☐ ☐ ☐

Smallest ⟷ Largest

c $\frac{17}{20}$ $\frac{7}{20}$ $\frac{1}{20}$ $\frac{19}{20}$ $\frac{9}{20}$

☐ ☐ ☐ ☐ ☐

Smallest ⟷ Largest

2

Compare these fraction pairs by writing less than (<) or greater than (>).

a $\frac{1}{3}$ $<$ $\frac{2}{3}$

b $\frac{5}{6}$ ☐ $\frac{4}{6}$

c $\frac{2}{2}$ ☐ $\frac{1}{2}$

d $\frac{6}{8}$ ☐ $\frac{7}{8}$

e $\frac{1}{4}$ ☐ $\frac{3}{4}$

f $\frac{4}{7}$ ☐ $\frac{6}{7}$

g $\frac{6}{8}$ ☐ $\frac{4}{8}$

h $\frac{2}{3}$ ☐ $\frac{1}{3}$

i $\frac{3}{5}$ ☐ $\frac{2}{5}$

j $\frac{8}{9}$ ☐ $\frac{1}{9}$

k $\frac{8}{10}$ ☐ $\frac{9}{10}$

l $\frac{3}{4}$ ☐ $\frac{2}{4}$

m $\frac{5}{7}$ ☐ $\frac{1}{7}$

n $\frac{5}{6}$ ☐ $\frac{4}{6}$

o $\frac{1}{8}$ ☐ $\frac{8}{8}$

p $\frac{2}{9}$ ☐ $\frac{5}{9}$

Page 48

Comparing unit fractions

Unit fractions are fractions where the numerator is 1. To compare unit fractions, we put their denominators in order.

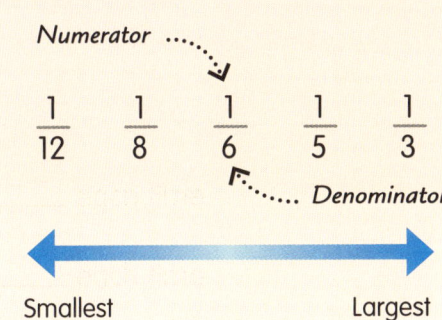

Numerator

$\frac{1}{12}$ $\frac{1}{8}$ $\frac{1}{6}$ $\frac{1}{5}$ $\frac{1}{3}$

Denominator

Smallest ⟷ Largest

Warm-up Order each set of fractions by size, starting with the smallest.

1. $\frac{1}{16}$ $\frac{1}{6}$ $\frac{1}{7}$ $\frac{1}{2}$ $\frac{1}{9}$

$\frac{1}{16}$ $\frac{1}{9}$ $\frac{1}{7}$ $\frac{1}{6}$ $\frac{1}{2}$

Smallest ⟷ Largest

2. $\frac{1}{12}$ $\frac{1}{4}$ $\frac{1}{3}$ $\frac{1}{8}$ $\frac{1}{6}$

☐ ☐ ☐ ☐ ☐

Smallest ⟷ Largest

REMEMBER!
The larger the denominator, the smaller the fraction.

1 Colour in the boxes to show these fractions. Then circle the bigger fraction in each pair.

a. $\frac{1}{3}$ $\frac{1}{4}$

b. $\frac{1}{6}$ $\frac{1}{12}$

c. $\frac{1}{2}$ $\frac{1}{4}$

d. $\frac{1}{12}$ $\frac{1}{2}$

e. $\frac{1}{3}$ $\frac{1}{5}$

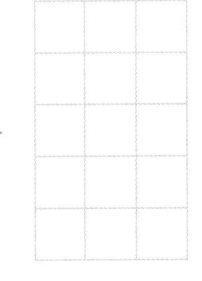

f. $\frac{1}{6}$ $\frac{1}{2}$

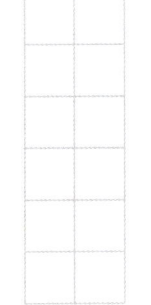

Page 49

Addition

Addition is when we bring two or more numbers or quantities together to make a larger number.

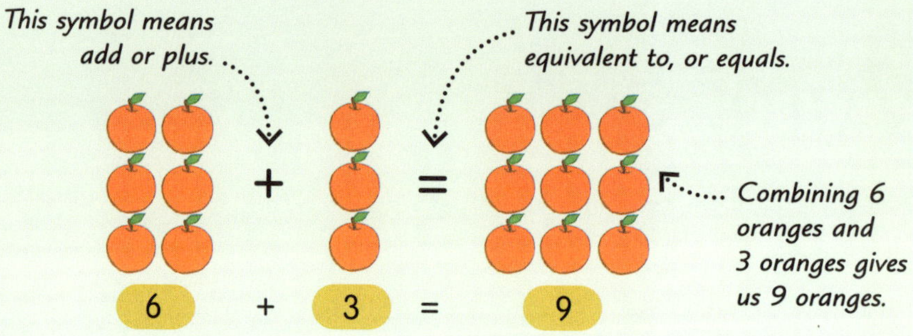
This symbol means add or plus.
This symbol means equivalent to, or equals.
6 + 3 = 9
Combining 6 oranges and 3 oranges gives us 9 oranges.

Warm-up Fill in the numbers for these fruit additions.

1 

5 + 3 = 8

2 

____ + ____ = ____

3 

____ + ____ = ____

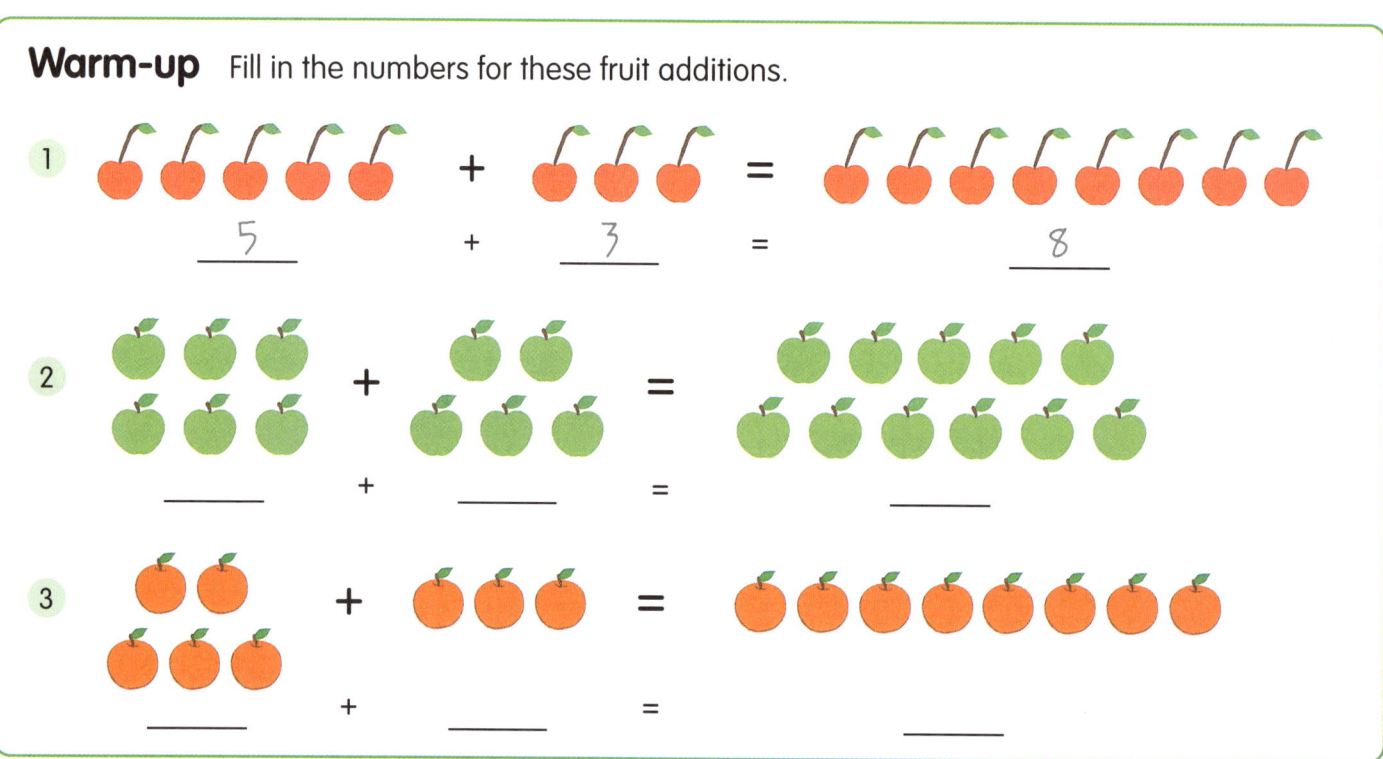

1 Complete these calculations using the counting all method, which means working out the total by counting up the combined units.

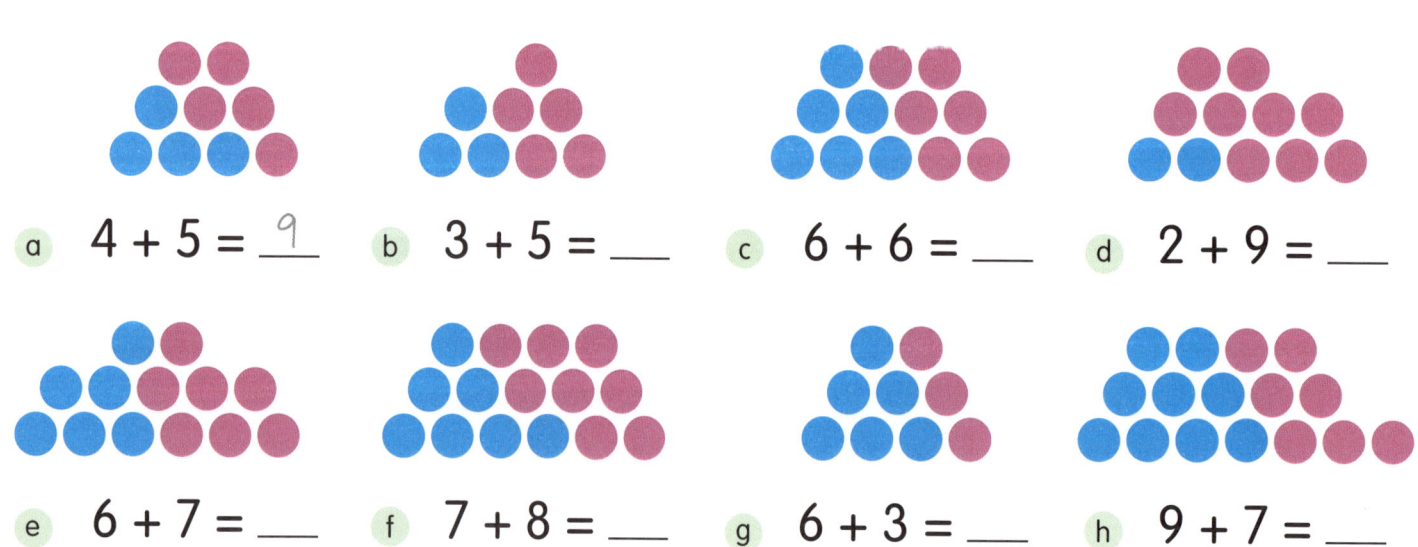

a $4 + 5 =$ 9

b $3 + 5 =$ ____

c $6 + 6 =$ ____

d $2 + 9 =$ ____

e $6 + 7 =$ ____

f $7 + 8 =$ ____

g $6 + 3 =$ ____

h $9 + 7 =$ ____

2 Complete these addition questions by counting on.

a $4 + 3 =$ 7

b $3 + 2 =$ ____

c $5 + 2 =$ ____

d $4 + 1 =$ ____

e $9 + 6 =$ ____

f $7 + 7 =$ ____

g $8 + 6 =$ ____

REMEMBER!
Counting on means counting from the larger number in a series of steps that's equal to the smaller number.

3 Use these counters to help you write nine different addition sums that all add up to 8.

0 1 2 3 4 5 6 7 8

a 2 + 6 = 8
b ____ + ____ = 8
c ____ + ____ = 8
d ____ + ____ = 8
e ____ + ____ = 8
f ____ + ____ = 8
g ____ + ____ = 8
h ____ + ____ = 8
i ____ + ____ = 8

Pages 78–79

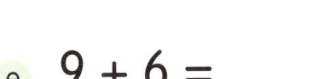

Addition facts

Addition facts are simple calculations that we remember, so that we don't need to work them out each time.

REMEMBER!
Addition facts can also be called number bonds or addition pairs.

Warm-up Fill in the boxes to complete these calculations.

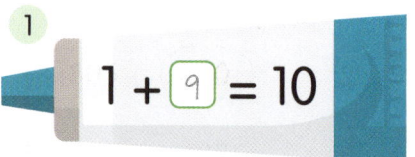

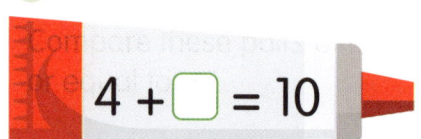

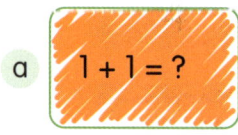

1. 1 + 9 = 10
2. 2 + □ = 10
3. 3 + □ = 10
4. 4 + □ = 10
5. 5 + □ = 10
6. 6 + □ = 10
7. 7 + □ = 10
8. 8 + □ = 10
9. 9 + □ = 10

1 Match each question with the correct answer below, by colouring them in the same colour.

a 1 + 1 = ?
b 2 + 2 = ?
c 3 + 3 = ?
d 4 + 4 = ?
e 5 + 5 = ?
f 6 + 6 = ?
g 7 + 7 = ?
h 8 + 8 = ?
i 9 + 9 = ?
j 10 + 10 = ?

2 20 4 8 14 6 16 10 12 18

2 Circle all of the calculations in this grid that add up to 20.

17 + 3	14 + 3	6 + 14	14 + 6	13 + 7
18 + 3	10 + 10	14 + 8	11 + 5	15 + 8
12 + 9	9 + 11	11 + 9	14 + 7	8 + 12
5 + 15	13 + 8	16 + 4	12 + 8	19 + 2

3 Parts of these calculations have been covered in paint. Use your addition facts to help you fill in the missing numbers.

a 30 + 70 = 100

b ___ + 30 = 90

c 20 + ___ = 80

d 60 + ___ = 100

e 40 + ___ = 70

f 13 + ___ = 73

g 30 + 30 = ___

h 30 + 400 = ___

i 200 + 700 = ___

j ___ + 200 = 300

k 50 + 50 = ___

l 300 + ___ = 800

Page 82

Adding with a number line

We can use number lines to help us add numbers together.

4 + 3 = 7

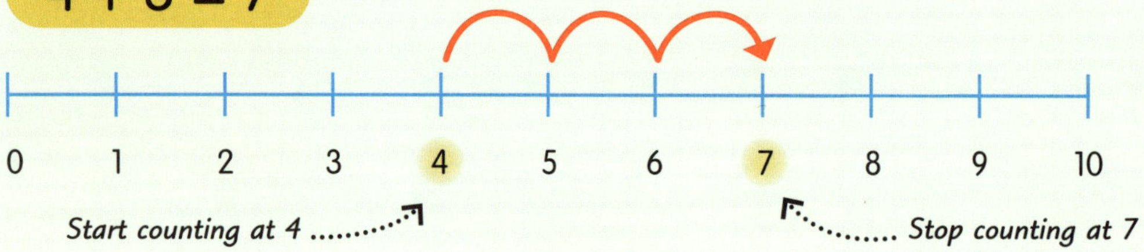

REMEMBER!
We can also make jumps bigger than 1 on the number line. For example, we could make a jump of +2 or +10.

Warm-up Use the number lines to help you add these pairs of numbers together.

1 5 + 6 = 11

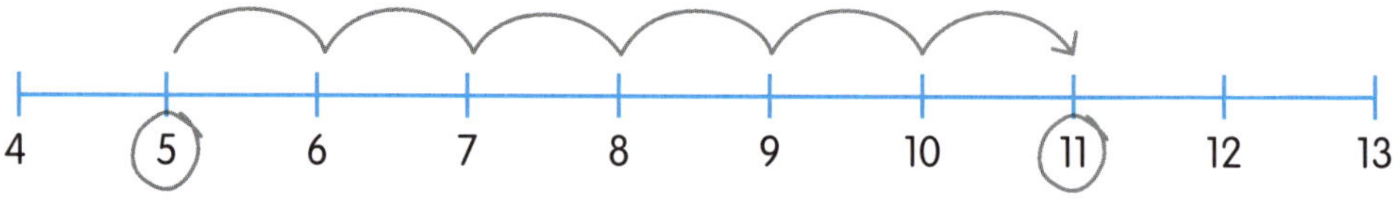

2 1 + 7 = ___

3 12 + 3 = ___

1

Ben is using his addition skills to work out how many children are on his bus. Use this number line to help you answer the questions below.

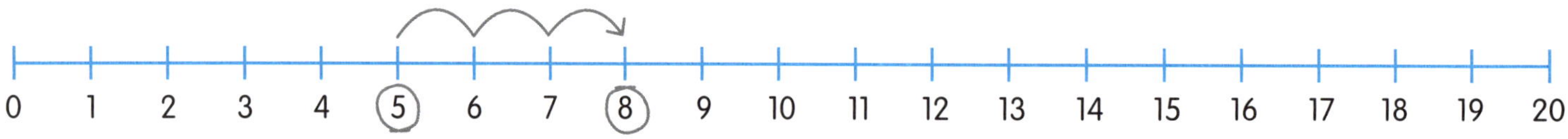

a On Monday, there are 5 children on the bus. 3 more children get on at Ben's stop. How many children are on the bus now?

5 + 3 = 8

b On Tuesday, there are 12 children on the bus. 8 more children get on at Ben's stop. How many children are on the bus now?

___ + ___ = ___

c On Wednesday, there are 3 children on the bus. 13 more children get on at Ben's stop. How many children are on the bus now?

___ + ___ = ___

2 Draw lines to match each addition question with the correct answer. Use the number line to help.

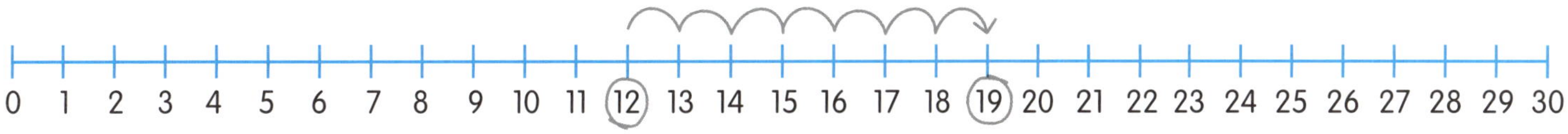

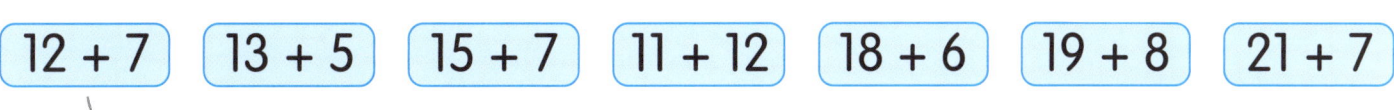

12 + 7	13 + 5	15 + 7	11 + 12	18 + 6	19 + 8	21 + 7
18	22	19	28	24	23	27

3 To calculate larger numbers on a number line, you can make jumps of 10. Use the number lines below to help you complete these additions.

a 40 + 30 = 70

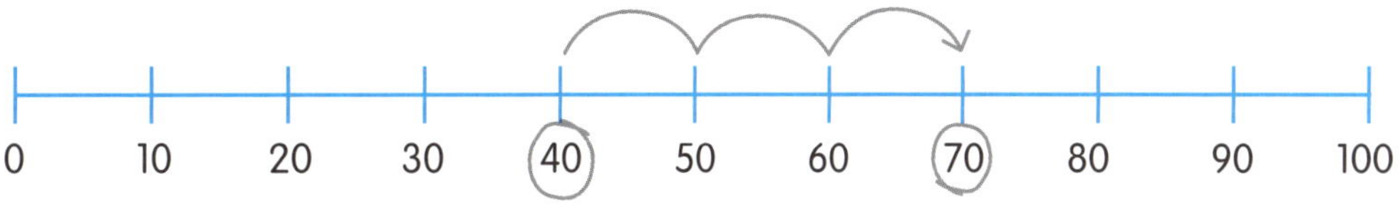

b 30 + 50 = ___

c 10 + 10 = ___

d 20 + 80 = ___

MATHS IN CONTEXT

Pocket money

Shamila has £12. Her grandmother gives her £4, which she puts in her money box. How much money does she have now? Make jumps of 2 on the number line to help you.

£12 + £4 = ___

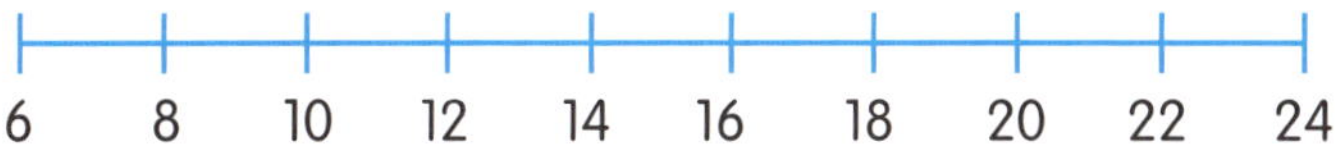

Page 80

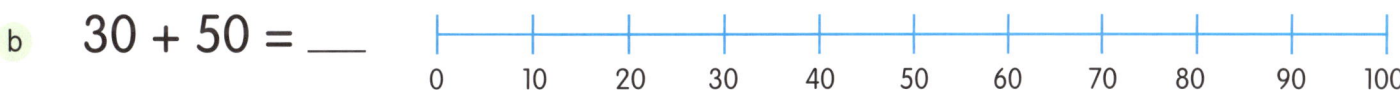

Adding with a number grid

A number grid is useful when adding numbers up to 100. You can do calculations by jumping from square to square. To add 10, jump down one line.

REMEMBER!
A number grid shows the numbers from 1 to 100 in rows of 10.

Warm-up Use the number grids below to help you answer these addition questions.

1 37 + 28 = 65

21	22	23	24	25	26	27	28	29	30
31	32	33	34	35	36	37	38	39	40
41	42	43	44	45	46	47	48	49	50
51	52	53	54	55	56	57	58	59	60
61	62	63	64	65	66	67	68	69	70
71	72	73	74	75	76	77	78	79	80

2 23 + 23 = ______

11	12	13	14	15	16	17	18	19	20
21	22	23	24	25	26	27	28	29	30
31	32	33	34	35	36	37	38	39	40
41	42	43	44	45	46	47	48	49	50
51	52	53	54	55	56	57	58	59	60

3 65 + 16 = ______

51	52	53	54	55	56	57	58	59	60
61	62	63	64	65	66	67	68	69	70
71	72	73	74	75	76	77	78	79	80
81	82	83	84	85	86	87	88	89	90

1 Use the number grid to help you answer these addition questions.

a 45 + 26 = 71

b 17 + 33 = ______

c 79 + 11 = ______

d 32 + 54 = ______

e 53 + 19 = ______

f 23 + 48 = ______

g 64 + 14 = ______

h 81 + 9 = ______

i 28 + 53 = ______

j 37 + 60 = ______

1	2	3	4	5	6	7	8	9	10
11	12	13	14	15	16	17	18	19	20
21	22	23	24	25	26	27	28	29	30
31	32	33	34	35	36	37	38	39	40
41	42	43	44	45	46	47	48	49	50
51	52	53	54	55	56	57	58	59	60
61	62	63	64	65	66	67	68	69	70
71	72	73	74	75	76	77	78	79	80
81	82	83	84	85	86	87	88	89	90
91	92	93	94	95	96	97	98	99	100

2 Use the number grid on the previous page to help you solve these word problems.

a There are 43 cows in a field. The farmer puts 38 more cows in the field. How many cows are there all together?

81 cows

b Ahmed has 15 robots. He gets 24 more for his birthday. How many robots does he have all together?

_____ robots

c There are 12 kiwis in the fruit bowl and 17 in the fridge. How many kiwis are there all together?

_____ kiwis

d Hamish has 5 coins. He earns 4 more coins each day for four days. On day five he earns 8 more coins. How many coins does he have in total?

_____ coins

e Naziah eats 16 raspberries, then 12, then another 6. How many raspberries has she eaten in total?

_____ raspberries

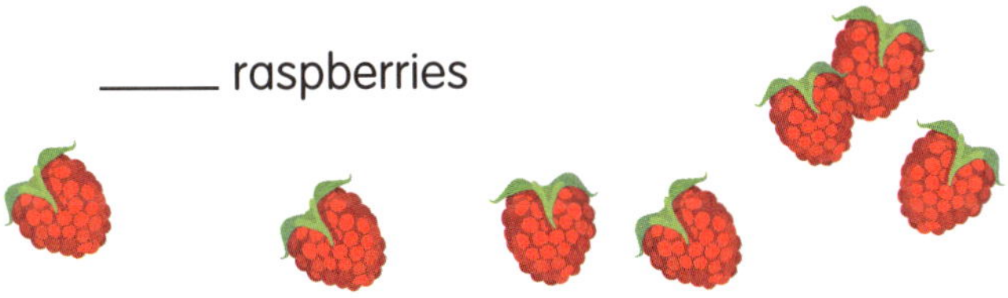

f Rio has 6 books, Mia has 8, and Mimi has 12. How many books do they have all together?

_____ books

3 Use the numbers on these cards to help you fill in the answers to the calculations below. You can use each digit card once only.

4	~~5~~	6	8	3	2	9	3	1	3	4	~~7~~	2	9	2	7

a $36 + 21 =$ 5 7

b $49 + 34 =$ ☐☐

c $11 + 18 =$ ☐☐

d $17 + 29 =$ ☐☐

e $15 + 16 =$ ☐☐

f $39 + 53 =$ ☐☐

g $15 + 3 + 9 =$ ☐☐

h $12 + 17 + 5 =$ ☐☐

Page 81

Partitioning for addition

We can sometimes make adding numbers simpler by splitting them into numbers that are easier to work with, then adding in stages. We call this partitioning.

T	O		T	O		T	O
3	7	+	2	5	=	?	?

Start by adding the tens together and writing the answer to the right of the equals sign.

T	O		T	O		T	O
3	0	+	2	0	=	5	0

Next, add the ones together.

T	O		T	O		T	O
	7	+		5	=	1	2

Finally, recombine the two answers to get the total.

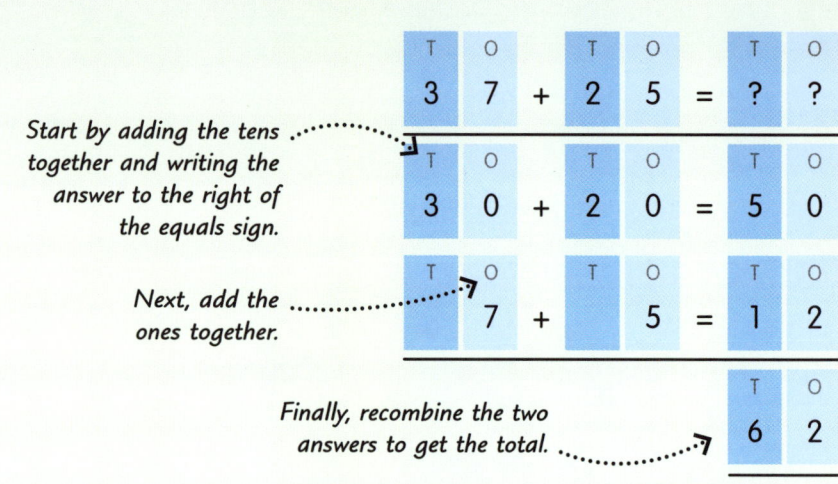

T	O
6	2

Warm-up Use partitioning to help you complete these calculations.

1 23 + 48 = 71

T	O		T	O		T	O
2	0	+	4	0	=	6	0
	3	+		8	=	1	1
						7	1

2 14 + 59 = ____

T	O		T	O		T	O
__	0	+	__	0	=	__	0
__	__	+	__	__	=	__	__
						__	__

3 78 + 13 = ____

T	O		T	O		T	O
__	0	+	__	0	=	__	0
__	__	+	__	__	=	__	__
						__	__

1 Use partitioning to answer these calculations.

a 46 + 23 = 69

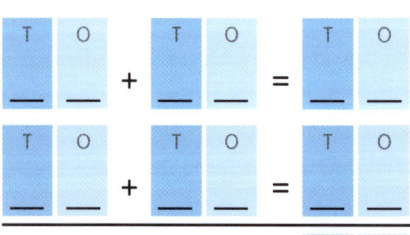

T	O		T	O		T	O
4	0	+	2	0	=	6	0
	6	+		3	=		9
						6	9

b 54 + 24 = ____

T	O		T	O		T	O
__	__	+	__	__	=	__	__
__	__	+	__	__	=	__	__
						__	__

c 39 + 47 = ____

T	O		T	O		T	O
__	__	+	__	__	=	__	__
__	__	+	__	__	=	__	__
						__	__

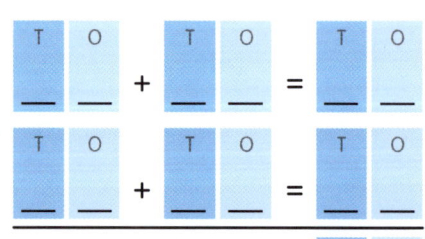

2 Work out the missing digits in these addition calculations.

a 34 + 3 3 = 67

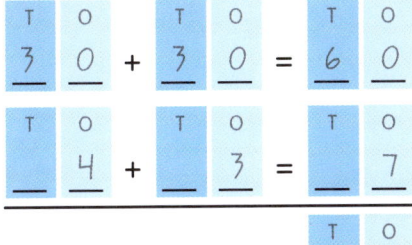

T	O		T	O		T	O
3	0	+	3	0	=	6	0
	4	+		3	=		7
						6	7

b 42 + 3 __ = 79

T	O		T	O		T	O
__	__	+	__	__	=	__	__
__	__	+	__	__	=	__	__
						__	__

c 28 + 38 = __ 6

T	O		T	O		T	O
__	__	+	__	__	=	__	__
__	__	+	__	__	=	__	__
						__	__

3 Use partitioning to help you answer these word problems.

a In the art class, group A have 29 coloured pencils and group B have 32. How many do they have between them?

T	O		T	O		T	O
2	0	+	3	0	=	5	0
	9	+		2	=	1	1
						6	1

61 pencils

b Dev has 67 marbles. He buys 16 more. How many marbles does he have now?

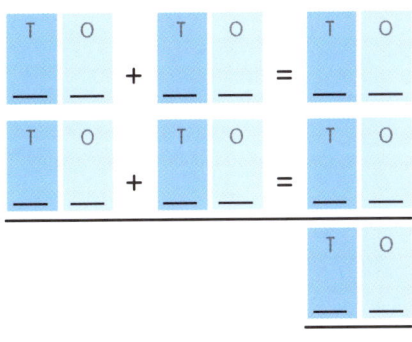

T	O		T	O		T	O
__	__	+	__	__	=	__	__
__	__	+	__	__	=	__	__
						__	__

__ marbles

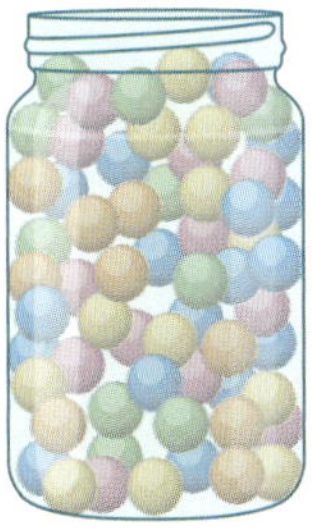

c Elise has 18 balloons and her brother has 19. How many do they have all together?

T	O		T	O		T	O
__	__	+	__	__	=	__	__
__	__	+	__	__	=	__	__
						__	__

__ balloons

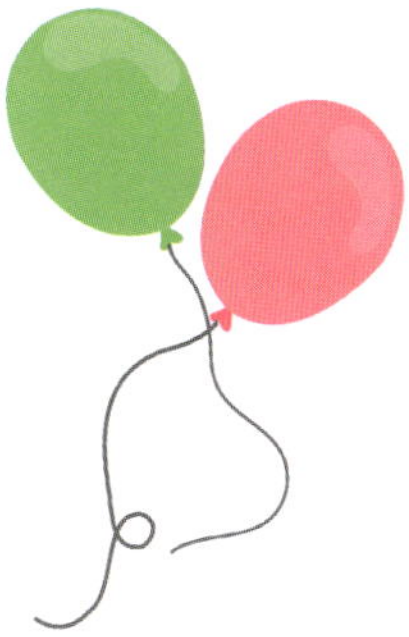

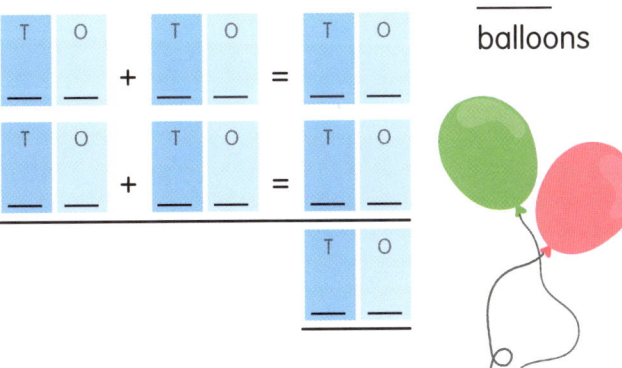

d Ben has 32 yoyos, then adds another 14. How many yoyos does he have now?

T	O		T	O		T	O
__	__	+	__	__	=	__	__
__	__	+	__	__	=	__	__
						__	__

__ yoyos

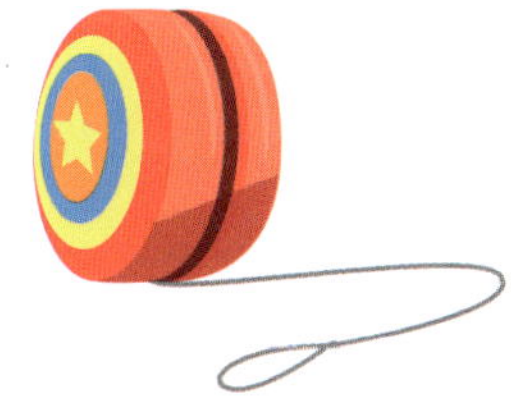

Page 83

Expanded column addition

We can use expanded column addition to help us add together larger numbers. It's important to line up the digits by their place values when using this method.

	H	T	O
	3	8	5
+	1	5	7
		1	2
	1	3	0
+	4	0	0
	5	4	2

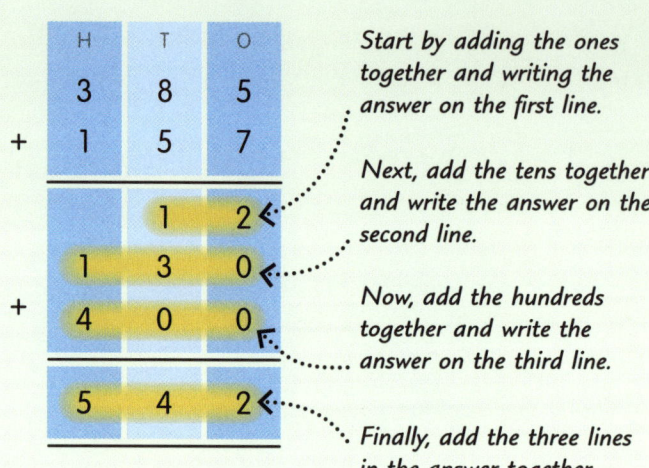

Start by adding the ones together and writing the answer on the first line.

Next, add the tens together and write the answer on the second line.

Now, add the hundreds together and write the answer on the third line.

Finally, add the three lines in the answer together.

Warm-up Complete these addition questions using the expanded column addition method.

1 359 + 432= 791

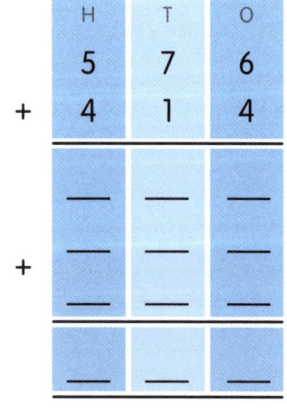

	H	T	O
	3	5	9
+	4	3	2
	___	1	1
	___	8	0
+	7	0	0
	7	9	1

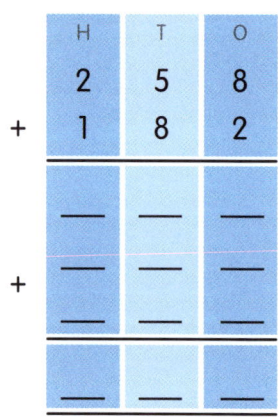

2 258 + 182 = ____

	H	T	O
	2	5	8
+	1	8	2
	___	___	___
	___	___	___
+	___	___	___
	___	___	___

3 621 + 251 = ____

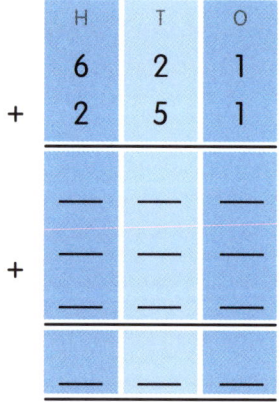

	H	T	O
	6	2	1
+	2	5	1
	___	___	___
	___	___	___
+	___	___	___
	___	___	___

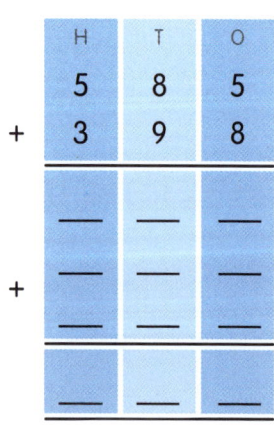

4 576 + 414 = ____

	H	T	O
	5	7	6
+	4	1	4
	___	___	___
	___	___	___
+	___	___	___
	___	___	___

5 585 + 398 = ____

	H	T	O
	5	8	5
+	3	9	8
	___	___	___
	___	___	___
+	___	___	___
	___	___	___

6 321 + 456 = ____

	H	T	O
	3	2	1
+	4	5	6
	___	___	___
	___	___	___
+	___	___	___
	___	___	___

1 Work out these calculations, then draw lines to match each one with the correct answer.

a

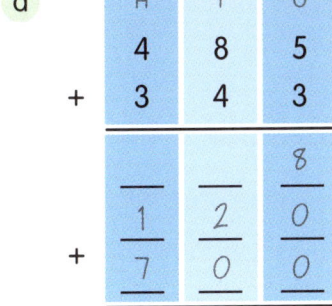

	H	T	O
	4	8	5
+	3	4	3
			8
	1	2	0
+	7	0	0

b

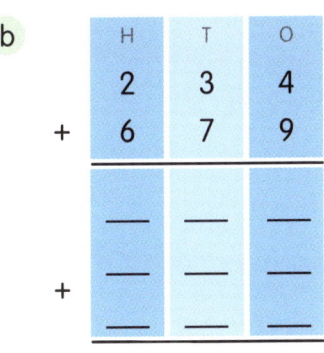

	H	T	O
	2	3	4
+	6	7	9
	___	___	___
	___	___	___
+	___	___	___

c

	H	T	O
	1	8	3
+	4	3	8
	___	___	___
	___	___	___
+	___	___	___

621 828 913

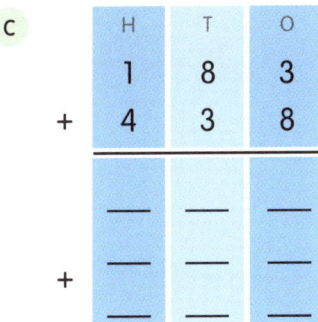

2 There are six different ways of adding these numbers together. Use the expanded column method to help you find them all.

57 42

145 328

a 57 + 42 = 99

b ______ + ______ = ______

c ______ + ______ = ______

d ______ + ______ = ______

e ______ + ______ = ______

f ______ + ______ = ______

MATHS IN CONTEXT

Running times

1. Marie runs 225 m at break time, and 467 m at lunch time. How many metres has she run in total?

______ + ______ = ______ m

2. Khensani ran 342 m more than Marie. How many metres has Khensani run?

______ + ______ = ______ m

3. Joel ran 189 m more than Khensani. How many metres has Joel run?

______ + ______ = ______ m

Pages 84–85

Column addition

Once you are confident at expanded column addition you can use this method, which is quicker and more compact. With column addition, we record the total of each column all on one line.

2586 + 1434 = ?

	Th	H	T	O
	$^{1}2$	$^{1}5$	$^{1}8$	6
+	1	4	3	4
	4	0	1	0

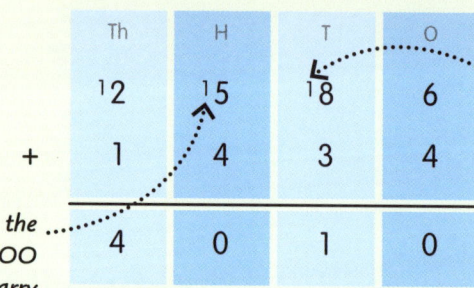

The total in the ones column is 10 or more, so carry this over to the tens column.

The total in the tens column is 100 or more, so carry this over to the hundreds column.

Warm-up Use the column addition method to solve these calculations.

1

	H	T	O
	$^{1}4$	$^{1}5$	6
+	3	6	5
	8	2	1

2

	H	T	O
	4	5	8
+	2	8	4
	___	___	___

3

	H	T	O
	5	6	7
+	3	4	5
	___	___	___

1 Fill in the answers to complete these column additions.

a

	Th	H	T	O
		4	8	3
+		4	5	8
	___	9	4	1

b

	Th	H	T	O
	1	3	6	2
+		6	7	4
	___	___	___	___

c

	Th	H	T	O
		8	6	2
+		3	9	2
	___	___	___	___

d

	Th	H	T	O
	1	8	7	3
+		9	2	6
	___	___	___	___

2

Millie has made cupcakes for a charity bake sale. She baked 148 cupcakes on Monday. On Tuesday, she baked 273 more than she did on Monday. Use column addition to help you answer these questions.

a How many cupcakes did Millie bake on Tuesday?

	H	T	O
	$^{1}2$	$^{1}7$	3
+	1	4	8
	4	2	1

b How many cupcakes did Millie bake in total on Monday and Tuesday?

	H	T	O
	___	___	___
+	___	___	___
	___	___	___

c Millie baked 237 on Wednesday. How many did she bake in total by the end of Wednesday?

	H	T	O
	___	___	___
+	___	___	___
	___	___	___

3

Work out which numbers are missing from these column additions.

a

	Th	H	T	O
		$^{1}8$	$^{1}4$	8
+		5	6	7
	1	4	1	5

b

	Th	H	T	O
	1	___	2	4
+		7	___	8
	2	0	8	___

c

	Th	H	T	O
		___	8	2
+		3	9	___
		8	___	2

d

	Th	H	T	O
		9	___	6
+		8	7	___
	1	___	2	3

e

	Th	H	T	O
		7	___	3
+		6	4	___
	___	3	7	8

f

	Th	H	T	O
	1	3	4	___
+		8	___	9
	2	___	9	8

Pages 86–87

Shopkeeper's addition

People who work in shops often count up in their heads to work out how much change to give their customers. This method of subtraction is called shopkeeper's addition and we can use it to calculate any subtractions involving money.

£10.00 – £3.57 = ?

Add up to the nearest 10p. → £3.57 + £0.03 = £3.60

Add up to the nearest pound. → £3.60 + £0.40 = £4.00

Add up to the original amount. → £4.00 + £6.00 = £10.00

Add together the totals in this column. → £6.43

£10.00 – £3.57 = £6.43

Warm-up Use shopkeeper's addition to work out these calculations.

1 £10.00 – £6.55 = £3.45

£6.55	+	£0.05	=	£6.60
£6.60	+	£0.40	=	£7.00
£7.00	+	£3.00	=	£10.00

2 £25.00 – £11.23 = ______

£11.23	+	______	=	£11.30
£11.30	+	______	=	______
______	+	______	=	£25.00

3 £13.00 – £8.74 = ______

£8.74	+	______	=	£8.80
£8.80	+	______	=	______
______	+	______	=	£13.00

4 £7.00 – £3.65 = ______

£3.65	+	______	=	______
______	+	______	=	______
______	+	______	=	£7.00

1 Use shopkeeper's addition to help you answer these questions.

a £18.00 – £3.46 = £14.54

£3.46 + £0.04 = £3.50

£3.50 + £0.50 = £4.00

£4.00 + £14.00 = £18.00

b £29.00 – £13.18 = ______

______ + ______ = ______

______ + ______ = ______

______ + ______ = ______

c £11.22 – £4.36 = ______

______ + ______ = ______

______ + ______ = ______

______ + ______ = ______

2 If you paid with a £20 note, how much change would you get for each of these bags of shopping? Try calculating the answers in your head using shopkeeper's addition.

a Change = £6.25

b Change = ______

c Change = ______

d Change = ______

e Change = ______

f Change = ______

3 Use shopkeeper's addition to help you circle the correct answer to each calculation.

a £17.00 – £6.46 = ?	£9.54	£10.54	£10.44	£9.40
b £23.50 – £9.32 = ?	£12.18	£14.18	£12.08	£9.08
c £11.63 – £4.94 = ?	£4.69	£5.69	£6.69	£7.69
d £12.85 – £3.29 = ?	£9.56	£9.54	£10.56	£9.64
e £11.32 – £9.07 = ?	£2.75	£5.25	£3.25	£2.25

MATHS IN CONTEXT

Going shopping

Amir buys these three items. He pays with a £20 note. How much change will he get? You will first need to work out how much Amir's shopping costs all together.

Change = ______

Page 93

Subtraction

Subtraction is the opposite of addition. It can be thought of as counting back from a number (taking away), or as finding the difference between two numbers.

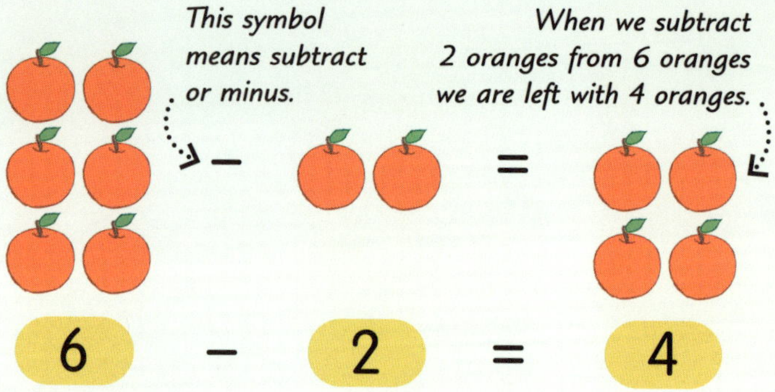
This symbol means subtract or minus.
When we subtract 2 oranges from 6 oranges we are left with 4 oranges.
6 – 2 = 4

Warm-up Write down how many circles there are in each group. Then work out the answers to these subtraction calculations.

1 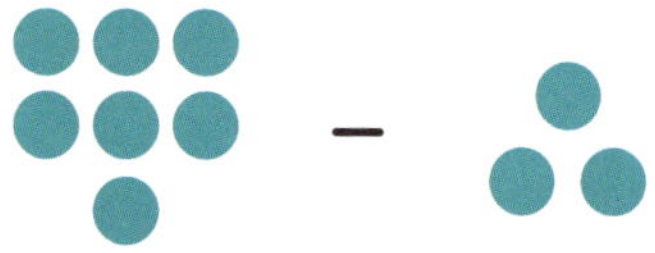

7 – 3 = 4

2 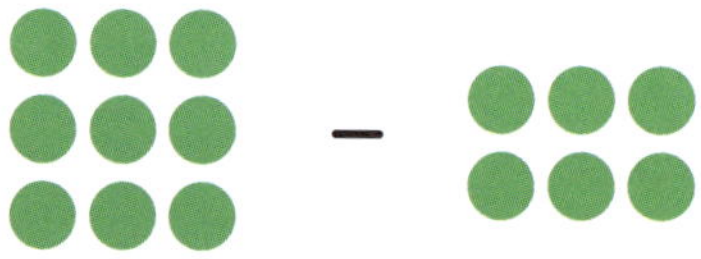

___ – ___ = ___

3 

___ – ___ = ___

4 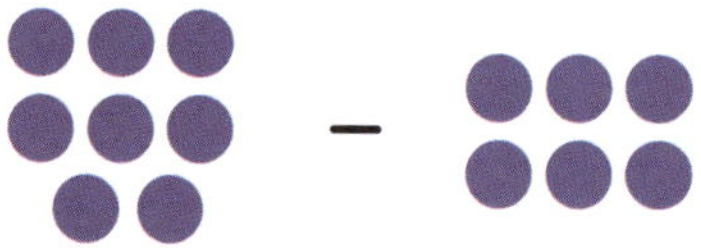

___ – ___ = ___

1

Count back along the number line below to help you answer these subtraction calculations.

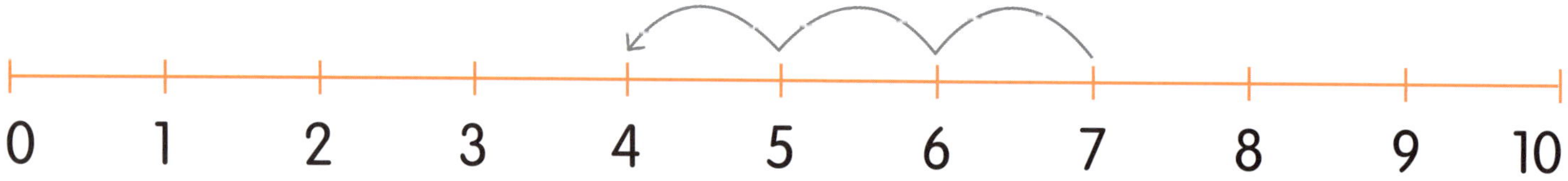
0 1 2 3 4 5 6 7 8 9 10

a 7 – 3 = 4

b 9 – 6 = ___

c 8 – 3 = ___

d 6 – 5 = ___

e 4 – 4 = ___

f 10 – 8 = ___

g 9 – 2 = ___

h 7 – 6 = ___

i 5 – 1 = ___

2 Amara is picking apples. Draw how many apples are left on each tree after Amara has visited it, then fill in the answers below.

Amara picked 5 apples on Wednesday.

a There are 4 apples left.

Amara picked 7 apples on Monday.

b There are ____ apples left.

Amara picked 4 apples on Tuesday.

c There are ____ apples left.

Amara picked 3 apples on Thursday.

d There are ____ apples left.

Amara picked 2 apples on Saturday.

e There are ____ apples left.

Amara picked 10 apples on Friday.

f There are ____ apples left.

MATHS IN CONTEXT

Pet food

1. Andrew gives his rabbit 8 carrots.
If it eats 5 of them, how many carrots will be left?

There will be ____ carrots left.

2. Mia's hamster has 9 pieces of cucumber.
If it eats 3 of them, how many pieces will be left?

There will be ____ pieces of cucumber left.

Pages 88–89

Subtraction facts

Subtraction facts are simple calculations that we remember, so that we don't need to work them out each time. Once you have learned them, you'll be able to apply them to other calculations.

REMEMBER!
Subtraction facts are the inverse (opposite) of the addition facts that we looked at on pages 34–35.

Warm-up Fill in your answers in the triangles to show which number is left when you subtract these numbers from 10.

1 10 – 1 = 9 2 10 – 2 = 3 10 – 3 =

4 10 – 4 = 5 10 – 5 = 6 10 – 6 =

7 10 – 7 = 8 10 – 8 = 9 10 – 9 =

1 Use your subtraction facts to help you fill in the missing numbers in these calculations. Look for doubles to help you.

a 20 – 10 = 10 b 24 – ___ = 12 c 12 – ___ = 6

d 2 – ___ = 1 e 16 – ___ = 8 f 14 – ___ = 7

g 28 – ___ = 14 h 18 – ___ = 9 i 4 – ___ = 2

j 10 – ___ = 5 k 30 – ___ = 15 l 22 – ___ = 11

m 8 – ___ = 4 n 6 – ___ = 3 o 26 – ___ = 13

2 Fill in the two related subtraction calculations for each addition fact below.

a 6 + 4 = 10

10 – 6 = 4 | 10 – 4 = 6

b 2 + 7 = 9

___ – ___ = ___ | ___ – ___ = ___

c 12 + 3 = 15

___ – ___ = ___ | ___ – ___ = ___

d 5 + 8 = 13

___ – ___ = ___ | ___ – ___ = ___

e 4 + 3 = 7

___ – ___ = ___ | ___ – ___ = ___

f 9 + 11 = 20

___ – ___ = ___ | ___ – ___ = ___

g 10 + 5 = 15

___ – ___ = ___ | ___ – ___ = ___

h 8 + 3 = 11

___ – ___ = ___ | ___ – ___ = ___

3 Use your number facts to help you work out which numbers are missing from these subtractions.

a 100 – 40 = 60

b 60 – 10 =

c 80 – 70 =

d 90 – 50 =

e 110 – 80 =

f 60 – 30 =

g 100 – 90 =

h 30 – 20 =

i 70 – 60 =

j 50 – 30 =

k 120 – 80 =

l 90 – 40 =

Page 90

Subtracting with a number line

To help us subtract larger numbers, we can count up or back on a number line using our partitioning skills.

145 – 89 = 56

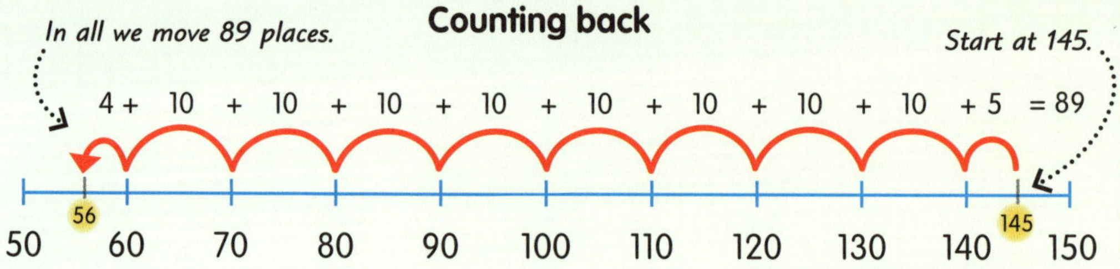

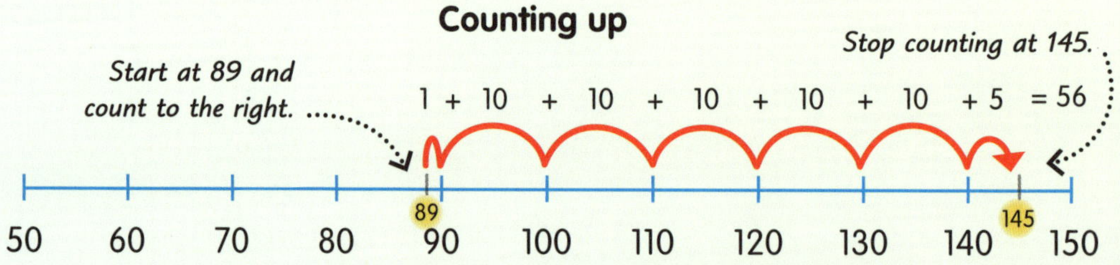

Warm-up Use the number lines below to help you answer these subtraction calculations, counting up or back as instructed.

1. Count back 87 – 29 = 58

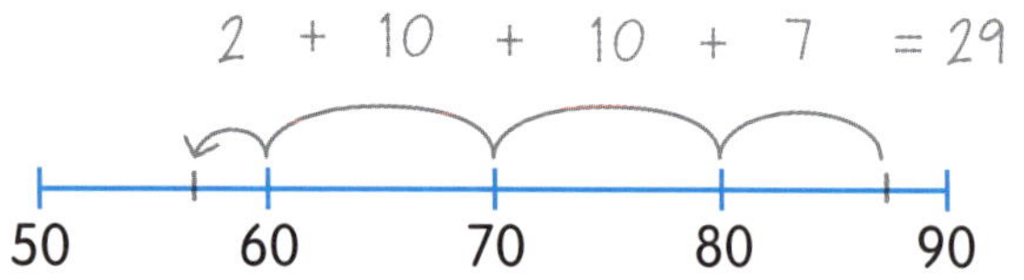

2. Count up 138 – 99 = ____

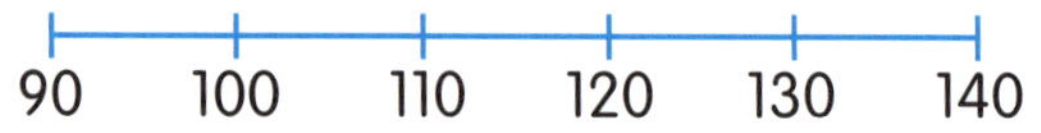

3. Count up 63 – 37 = ____

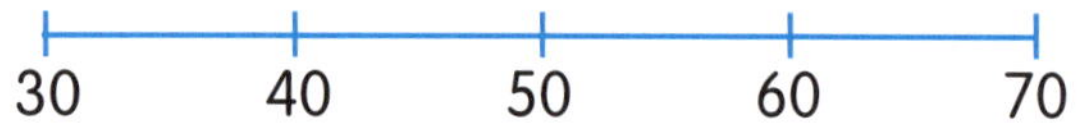

4. Count back 24 – 11 = ____

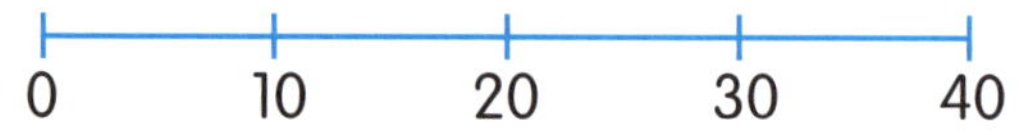

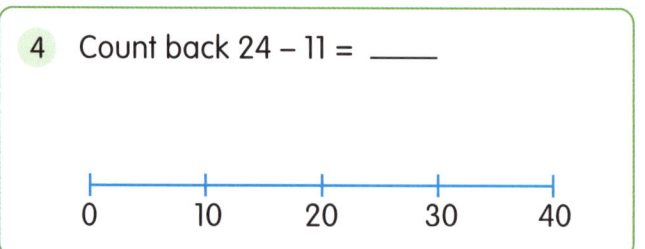

5. Count back 103 – 46 = ____

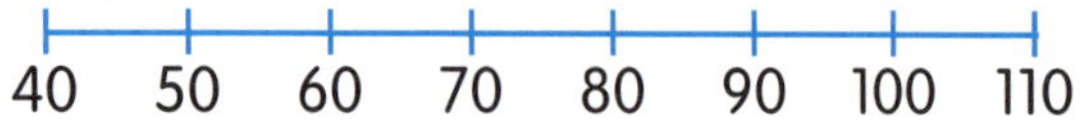

6. Count up 154 – 108 = ____

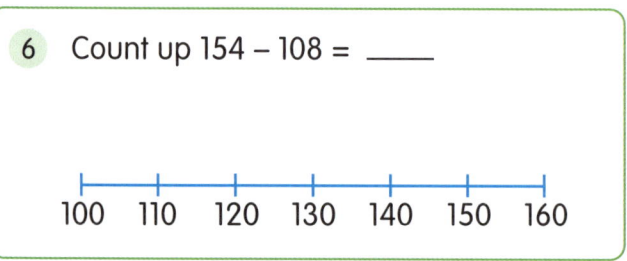

1 Use the blank number lines below to help you solve these subtraction questions. Remember, always put the number you are taking away from on the right of the number line.

a 167 – 102 = 65

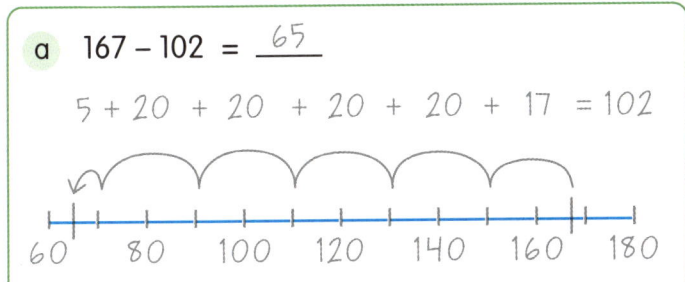

5 + 20 + 20 + 20 + 20 + 17 = 102

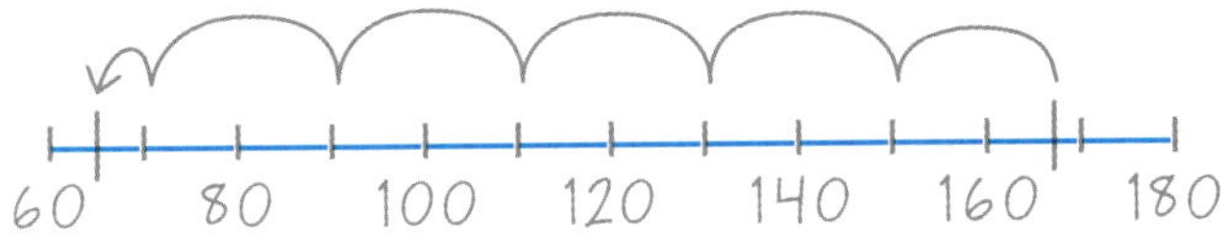

b 456 – 173 = ____

c 676 – 527 = ____

d 124 – 98 = ____

e 287 – 178 = ____

f 534 – 265 = ____

2 Use the number line below to help you answer these word problems. Remember to include the units in your answers.

a There are 148 g of chocolate buttons in a packet. Elise eats 56 g of them. How many grams of chocolate buttons are left?

92 g

b Elliot is given £145 for his birthday. He spends £76 on a model train. How much money does he have left?

____

Page 92

Partitioning for subtraction

We can subtract numbers more easily by splitting them into other numbers that are simpler to work with. We then subtract them in stages. This is called partitioning for subtraction.

62 – 35 = ?

T	O		T	O		T	O
6	2	–	3	5	=	?	?
6	2	–	3	0	=	3	2
3	2	–		5	=	2	7

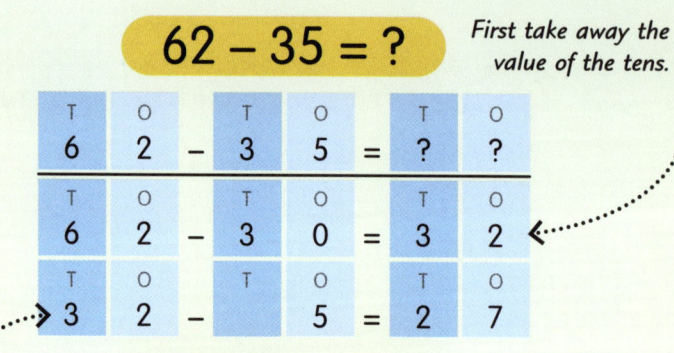

First take away the value of the tens.

Put the answer to the first subtraction here, then take away the value of the ones.

62 – 35 = 27

Warm-up Use partitioning to help you answer these subtraction calculations.

1 78 – 34 = ?

T	O		T	O		T	O
7	8	–	3	0	=	4	8
4	8	–		4	=	4	4

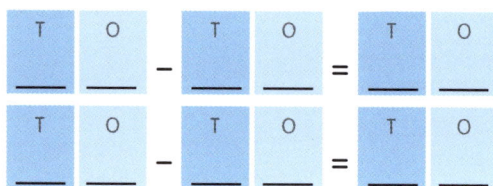

78 – 34 = 44

2 38 – 29 = ?

T	O		T	O		T	O
		–			=		
		–			=		

38 – 29 = ____

3 93 – 47 = ?

T	O		T	O		T	O
		–			=		
		–			=		

93 – 47 – ____

4 26 – 19 = ?

T	O		T	O		T	O
		–			=		
		–			=		

26 – 19 = ____

1 Use partitioning to help you answer these subtraction calculations. Use the space below for your workings.

a 83 – 21 = 62

83 – 20 = 63
63 – 1 = 62
83 – 21 = 62

b 76 – 17 = ____

c 25 – 13 = ____

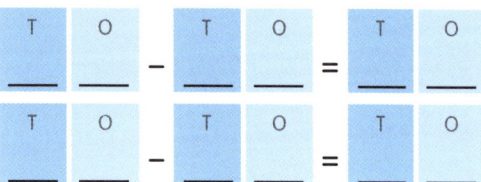

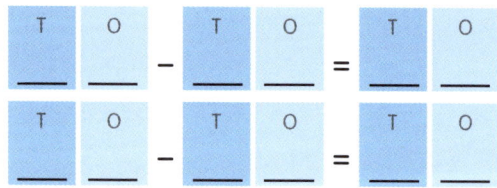

d 98 – 76 = ____

2 Use partitioning to help you answer these subtraction questions.

a 79 – 16 = 63

b 26 – 18 = ____

c 87 – 38 = ____

d 54 – 34 = ____

e 63 – 45 = ____

f 92 – 28 = ____

g 98 – 89 = ____

h 82 – 71 = ____

i 34 – 14 = ____

j 77 – 18 = ____

k 62 – 22 = ____

l 45 – 29 = ____

3 Use partitioning to work out the parts of these calculations that have been covered by leaves.

a 87 – 2[5] = 62

b 73 – 4__ = 24

c 36 – 1__ = 24

d 64 – __3 = 31

e 49 – 23 = __6

f 67 – 22 = __5

g __4 – 18 = 76

h __9 – 14 = 85

i __3 – 16 = 37

MATHS IN CONTEXT

Birds in the tree

There were 67 birds nesting in a tree. 43 of the birds flew away. How many were left in the tree? Use partitioning to help you work out the answer.

________ birds were left in the tree.

Page 91

Expanded column subtraction

We can use expanded column subtraction to find the difference between numbers that have more than two digits.

385 – 157 = ?

	H	T	O	
	3	8	5	
–	1	5	7	
			3	160
		4	0	200
	1	0	0	300
+		8	5	385
	2	2	8	

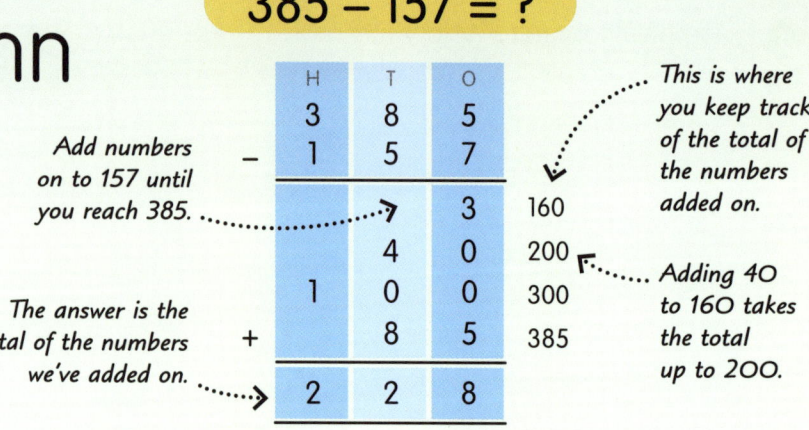

Add numbers on to 157 until you reach 385.

The answer is the total of the numbers we've added on.

This is where you keep track of the total of the numbers added on.

Adding 40 to 160 takes the total up to 200.

Warm-up

Using the expanded column subtraction method, fill in the missing digits in these subtraction questions.

1

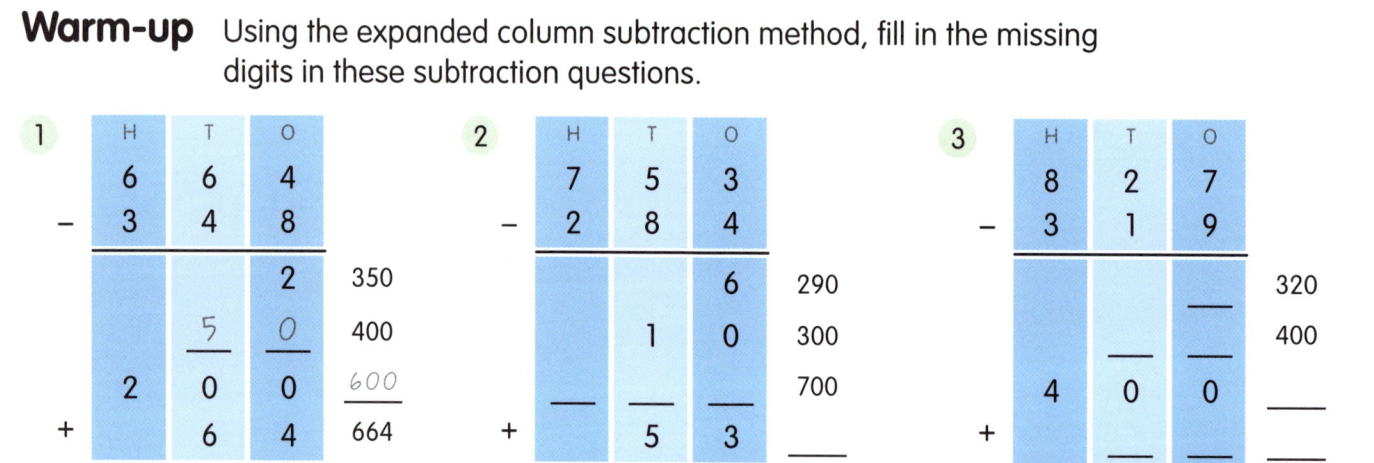

	H	T	O	
	6	6	4	
–	3	4	8	
			2	350
		5	0	400
	2	0	0	600
+		6	4	664
	3	1	6	

2

	H	T	O	
	7	5	3	
–	2	8	4	
			6	290
		1	0	300
	___	___	___	700
+		5	3	___
	___	___	___	

3

	H	T	O	
	8	2	7	
–	3	1	9	
			___	320
		___	___	400
	4	0	0	___
+		___	___	___
	5	0	8	

1 Use the expanded method of column subtraction to solve these subtraction questions. Not all lines need a digit.

a 456 – 176 = 280

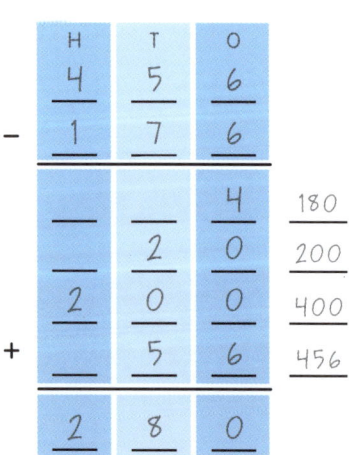

	H	T	O	
	4	5	6	
–	1	7	6	
	___	___	4	180
	___	2	0	200
	2	0	0	400
+	___	5	6	456
	2	8	0	

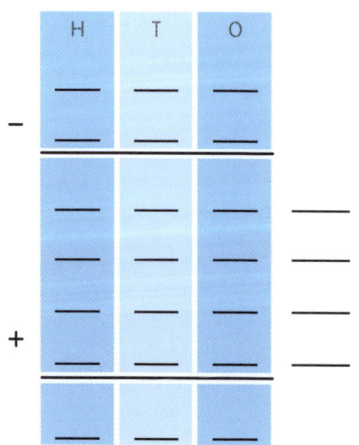

b 787 – 642 = ______

	H	T	O	
	___	___	___	
–	___	___	___	
	___	___	___	___
	___	___	___	___
	___	___	___	___
+	___	___	___	___
	___	___	___	

c 485 – 343 = ______

	H	T	O	
	___	___	___	
–	___	___	___	
	___	___	___	___
	___	___	___	___
	___	___	___	___
+	___	___	___	___
	___	___	___	

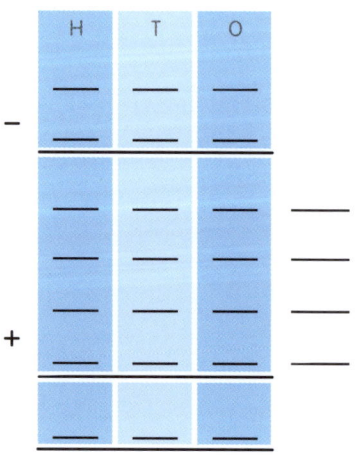

2 Solve these word problems using the expanded column subtraction method. Not all lines will need a digit.

a Greta buys a bag of hamster food that weighs 757 g. Her hamster eats 324 g of food.

	H	T	O	
	7	5	7	
−	3	2	4	
			6	330
		7	0	400
	3	0	0	700
+		5	7	757
	4	3	3	

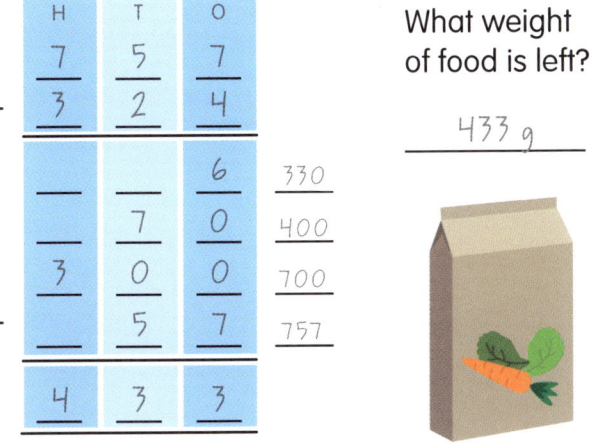

What weight of food is left? 433 g

b Luka has £657 in his savings account. Kristof has £872.

	H	T	O	
−				
+				

How much more money does Kristof have? ______

c Mia scores 576 on a computer game. Leon scores 332.

	H	T	O	
−				
+				

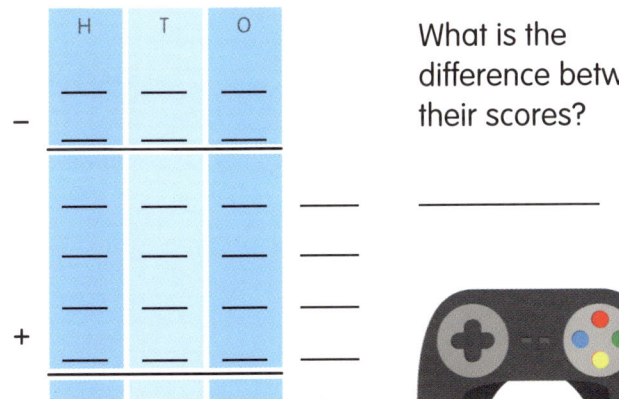

What is the difference between their scores? ______

d Ling takes 375 apples to sell at the market. He sells 189 apples.

	H	T	O	
−				
+				

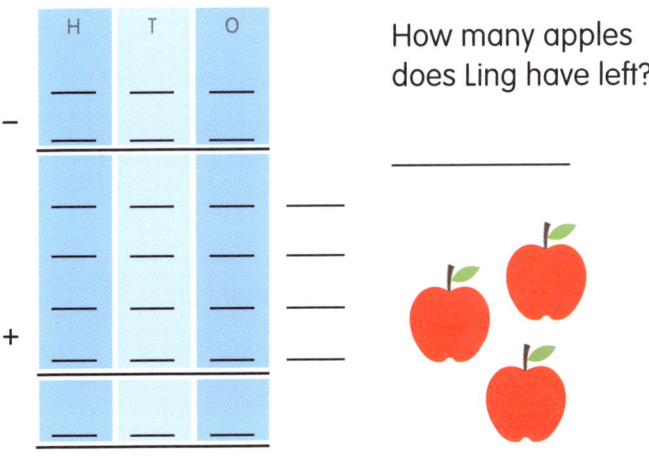

How many apples does Ling have left? ______

3 Draw lines to match each subtraction calculation with the correct answer.

a 678 – 363 b 676 – 383 c 687 – 398 d 874 – 542

293 315 347 289 392 393 332 305

e 893 – 501 f 695 – 348 g 611 – 306 h 680 – 287

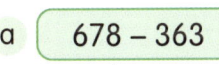

Pages 94–95

Column subtraction

Column subtraction is an even quicker way of subtracting large numbers than expanded column subtraction.

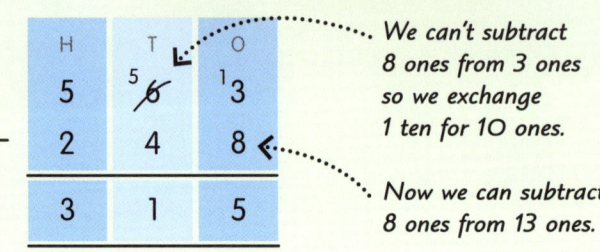

563 – 248 = ?

	H	T	O
	5	5 ~~6~~	1 3
–	2	4	8
	3	1	5

We can't subtract 8 ones from 3 ones so we exchange 1 ten for 10 ones.

Now we can subtract 8 ones from 13 ones.

Warm-up Answer these column subtraction questions. You will only need to exchange numbers with another column once in each calculation.

1

	H	T	O
	8	6 ~~7~~	1 2
–	3	6	8
	5	0	4

2

	H	T	O
	9	4	8
–	2	5	6
	___	___	___

3

	H	T	O
	3	4	2
–	1	2	7
	___	___	___

4

	H	T	O
	5	4	3
–	2	7	6
	___	___	___

1 Answer the subtraction questions below about the heights of these buildings.

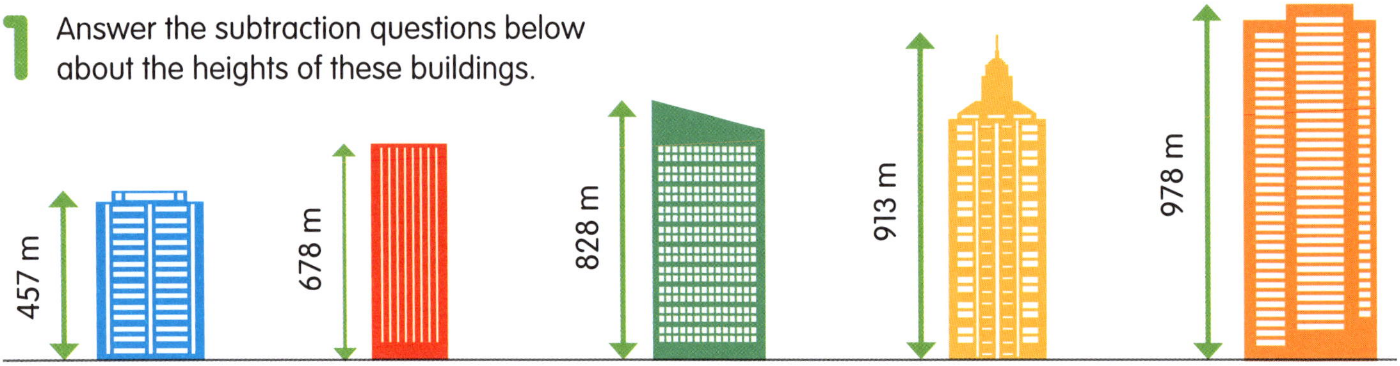

a How much taller is the red building than the blue building?

	H	T	O
	6	7	8
–	4	5	7
	2	2	1

221 m

b How much taller is the yellow building than the blue building?

	H	T	O
	___	___	___
–	___	___	___
	___	___	___

_____ m

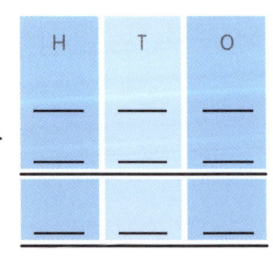

c How much taller is the green building than the blue building?

	H	T	O
	___	___	___
–	___	___	___
	___	___	___

_____ m

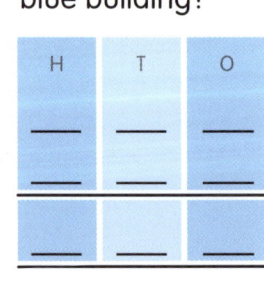

d How much taller is the orange building than the second tallest?

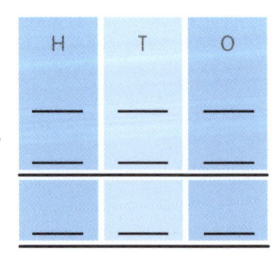

	H	T	O
	___	___	___
–	___	___	___
	___	___	___

_____ m

2

Fill in the answers to these column subtraction calculations. You may need to exchange numbers with other columns more than once in each calculation.

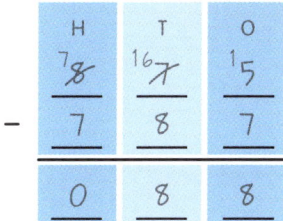

a 875 – 787 = 88

	H	T	O
	7 ~~8~~	16 ~~7~~	15
–	7	8	7
	0	8	8

b 523 – 179 = ___

	H	T	O
	___	___	___
–	___	___	___
	___	___	___

c 614 – 309 = ___

	H	T	O
	___	___	___
–	___	___	___
	___	___	___

d 437 – 259 = ___

	H	T	O
	___	___	___
–	___	___	___
	___	___	___

e 843 – 568 = ___

	H	T	O
	___	___	___
–	___	___	___
	___	___	___

f 711 – 117 = ___

	H	T	O
	___	___	___
–	___	___	___
	___	___	___

g 953 – 949 = ___

	H	T	O
	___	___	___
–	___	___	___
	___	___	___

h 478 – 384 = ___

	H	T	O
	___	___	___
–	___	___	___
	___	___	___

i 398 – 126 = ___

	H	T	O
	___	___	___
–	___	___	___
	___	___	___

3

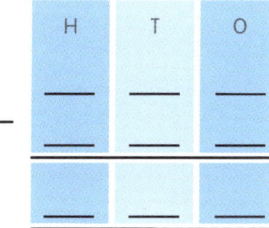

Work out the missing digits in these column subtraction calculations.

a

	H	T	O
	8	6 ~~7~~	16
–	2	5	7
	6	1	9

b

	H	T	O
	6	7	3
–	4	___	5
	1	9	___

c

	H	T	O
	___	6	3
–	1	___	8
	3	0	5

d

	H	T	O
	___	3	7
–	4	___	3
	4	5	___

e

	H	T	O
	6	7	7
–	5	2	___
	1	___	6

f

	H	T	O
	4	2	9
–	1	___	0
	2	8	___

g

	H	T	O
	___	9	4
–	1	___	8
	6	3	6

h

	H	T	O
	___	7	4
–	4	___	5
	1	8	___

Pages 96–97

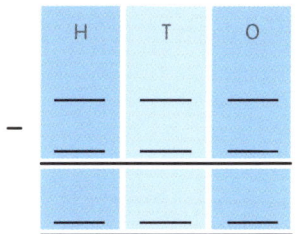

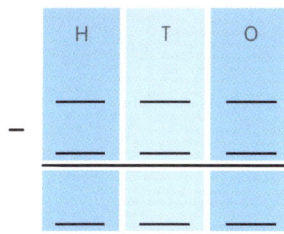

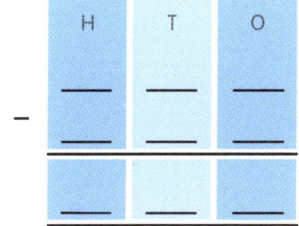

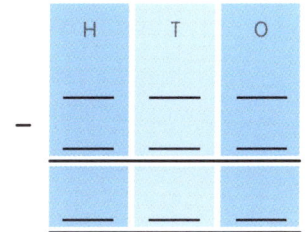

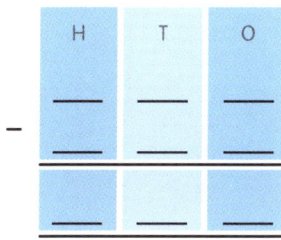

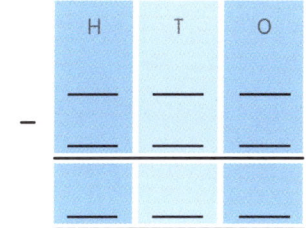

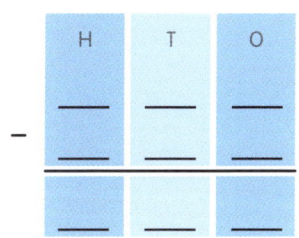

Multiplication

Multiplication can be thought of as repeated addition. Or, it can be seen as putting together lots of quantities of the same size.

3
3
3 +
$3 \times 3 = 9$

Warm-up Fill in the multiplication calculation shown in each picture.

1

5 +
5 +
5 =
5 x 3 = 15

2

___ +
___ +
___ =
___ x ___ = ___

3

___ +
___ +
___ +
___ =
___ x ___ = ___

4

___ +
___ +
___ +
___ =
___ x ___ = ___

1 Complete each calculation for the pictures below.

a 4 + 4 + 4 = 12

therefore 4 x 3 = 12

b ___ + ___ + ___ + ___ = ___

therefore ___ x ___ = ___

c ___ + ___ = ___

therefore ___ x ___ = ___

2

Draw a set of shapes to show each multiplication question.
Then fill in the answers to the calculations.

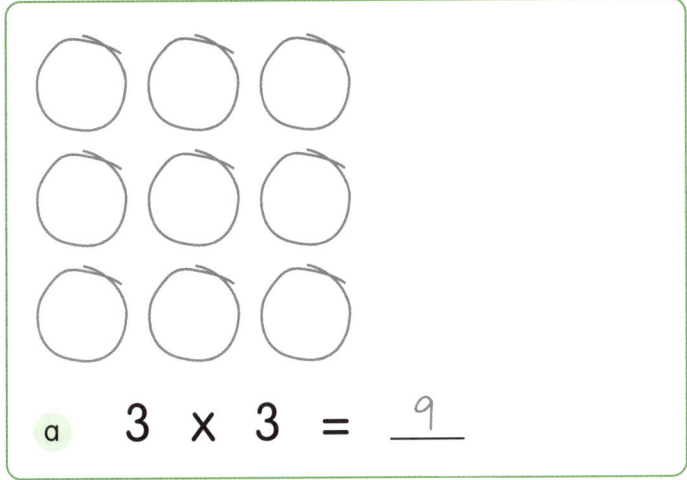

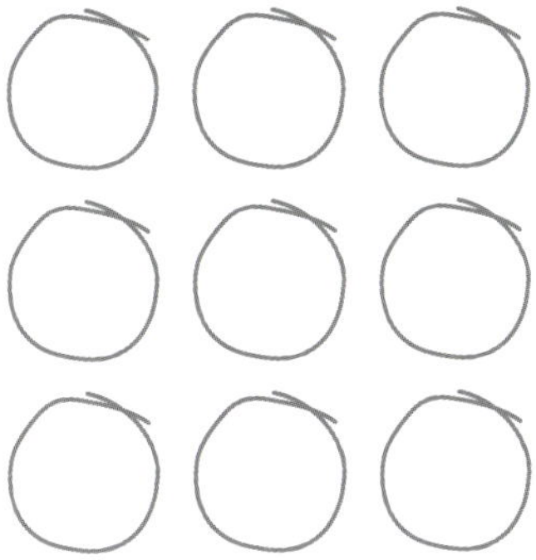

a 3 x 3 = 9

b 7 x 2 = ___

c 3 x 4 = ___

d 6 x 3 = ___

3

Draw lines to match each multiplication statement with the correct repeated addition statement.

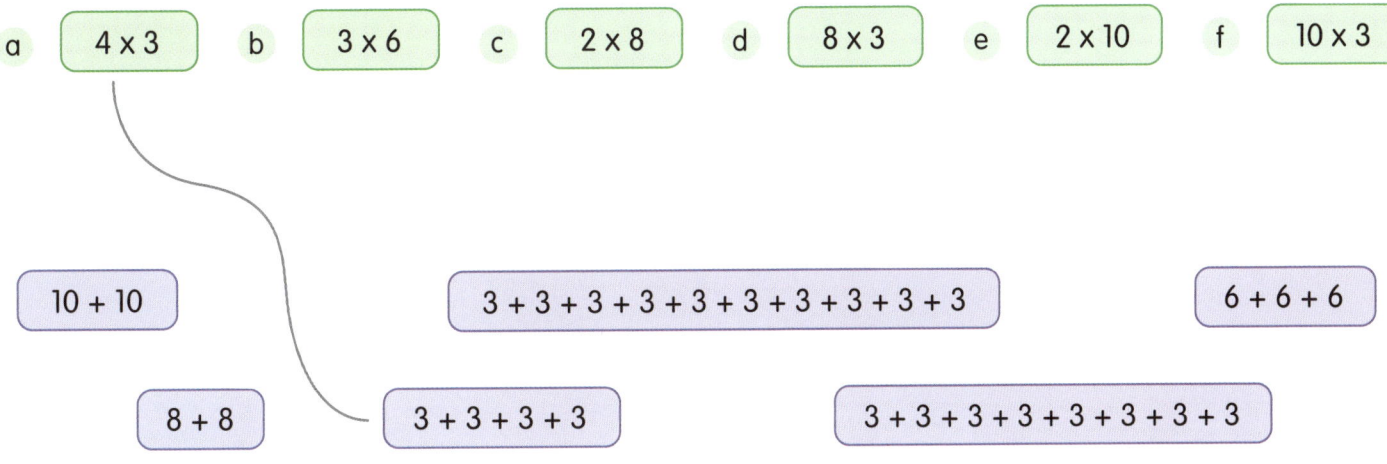

a 4 x 3 b 3 x 6 c 2 x 8 d 8 x 3 e 2 x 10 f 10 x 3

10 + 10

3 + 3 + 3 + 3 + 3 + 3 + 3 + 3 + 3 + 3

6 + 6 + 6

8 + 8

3 + 3 + 3 + 3

3 + 3 + 3 + 3 + 3 + 3 + 3 + 3

Pages 98–99

Counting in multiples

When a whole number is multiplied by another whole number, the result is called a multiple. Counting in multiples helps us do multiplication calculations.

This number line shows the first few multiples of 7.

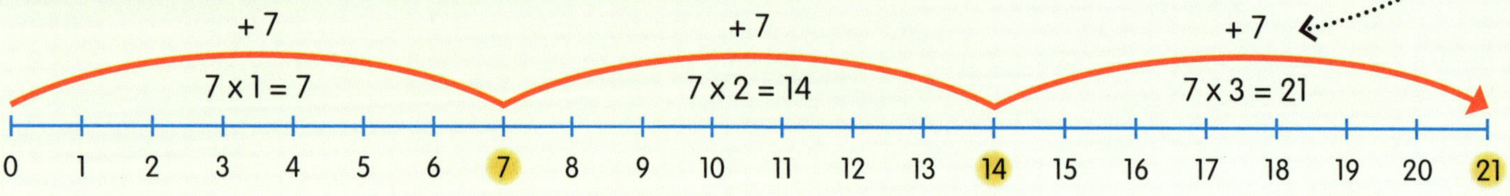

Warm-up Draw arrows above these number lines to show how to count these multiples.

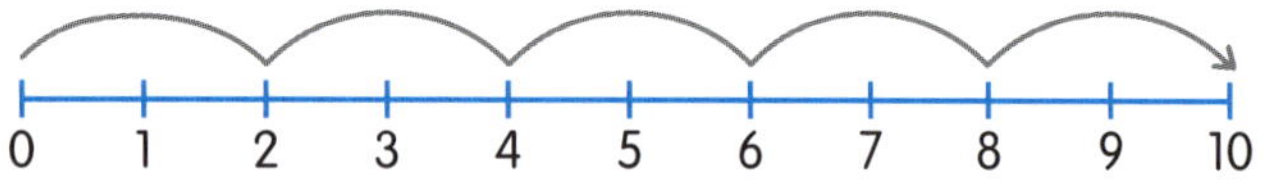

1 Count in 2s from 0.

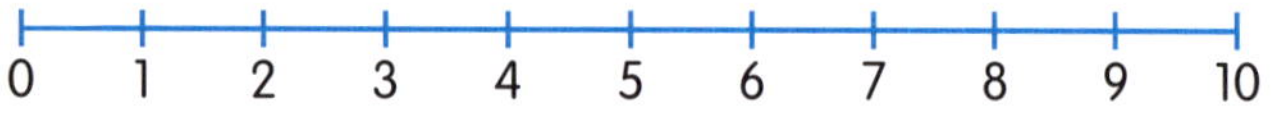

2 Count in 4s from 0.

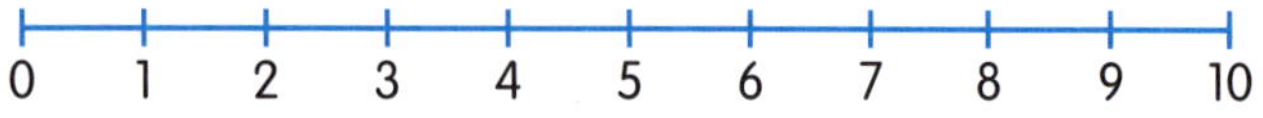

3 Count in 3s from 0.

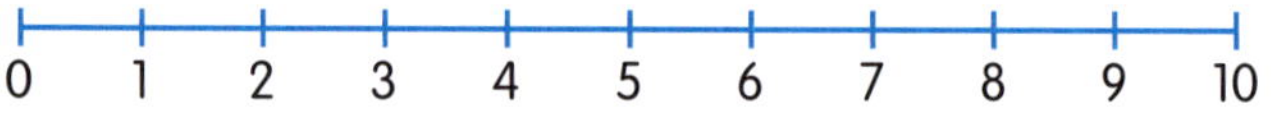

4 Count in 5s from 0.

1

Use the number lines below to help you work out these multiplication statements.

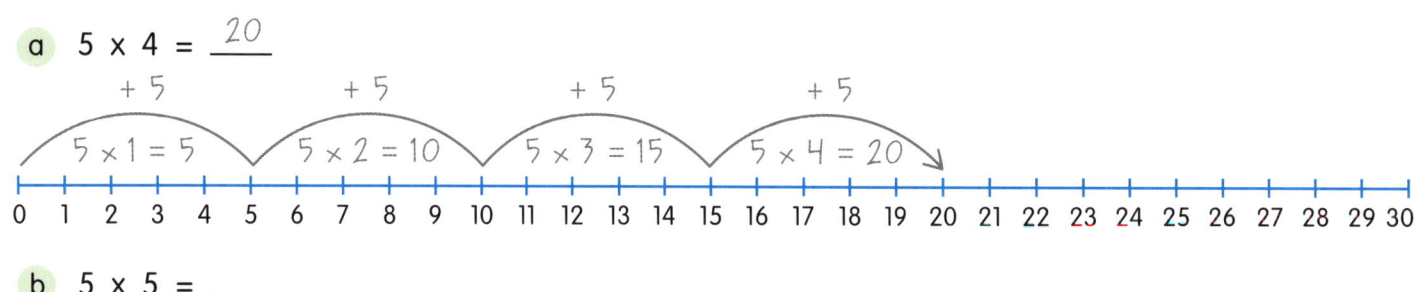

a 5 x 4 = 20

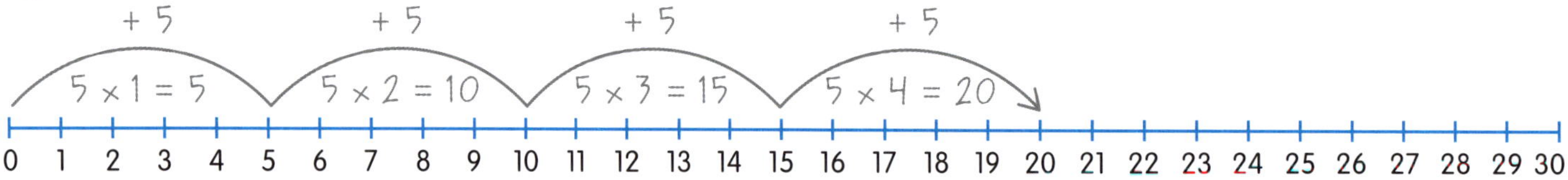

b 5 x 5 = ____

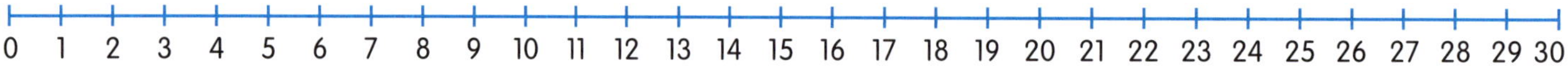

c 4 x 6 = ____

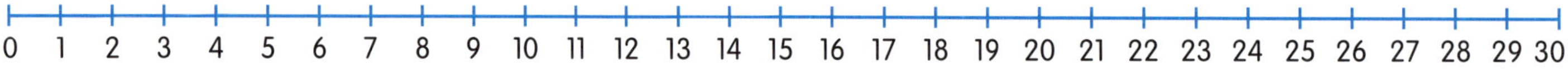

2 Use the number lines below to help you solve these problems.

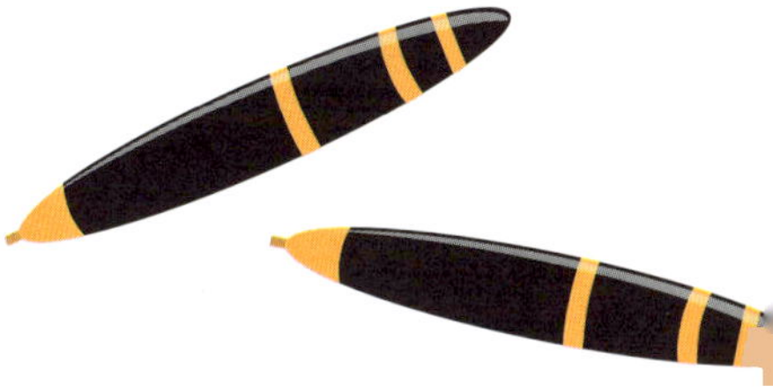

a Mrs Greyling buys 5 packs of pens. There are 6 pens in each pack.
How many pens are there all together?

5 x 6 = 30 There are 30 pens all together.

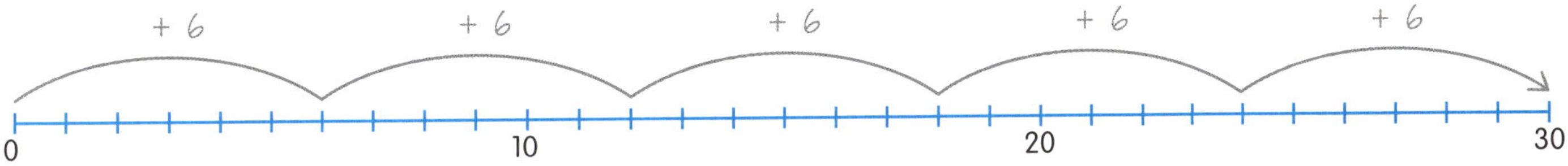

b Adam has 5 days of school until his birthday. He has 7 lessons each day.
How many lessons are there before Adam's birthday?

____ x ____ = ____ There are _____ lessons before Adam's birthday.

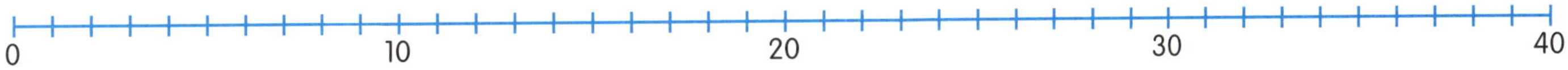

c Samir has 2 boxes with 8 balls in. He is given 1 more box that also has 8 balls in it.
How many balls does Samir have all together?

____ x ____ = ____ Samir has _____ balls all together.

d Naziah buys 8 packs of pencils. Each pack has 8 pencils in it. She already had 1 pack at home. How many pencils does she have in total?

____ x ____ = ____ Naziah has _____ pencils all together.

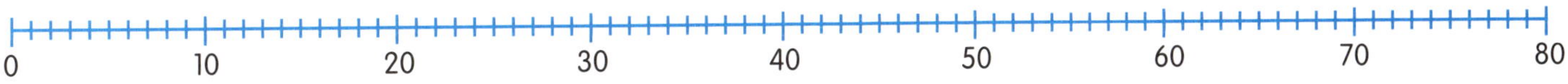

Pages 102–103

Multiplication tables

Multiplication tables are lists of multiplication facts about a particular number. Once you know them, you'll find them very useful when you are doing other calculations.

REMEMBER!
It is useful to memorize your multiplication tables up to 12.

Warm-up Fill in the missing numbers in these multiplication tables.

1

6x table				
6	x	0	=	0
6	x	1	=	6
6	x	___	=	12
6	x	3	=	18
6	x	4	=	___
6	x	___	=	30
6	x	6	=	___
6	x	7	=	42
6	x	8	=	___
6	x	___	=	54
6	x	10	=	60
6	x	11	=	___
6	x	___	=	72

2

7x table				
7	x	0	=	0
7	x	1	=	___
7	x	2	=	14
7	x	___	=	___
7	x	4	=	28
7	x	5	=	___
7	x	6	=	42
7	x	___	=	49
7	x	8	=	___
7	x	9	=	63
7	x	10	=	___
7	x	11	=	___
7	x	___	=	84

3

12x table				
12	x	0	=	0
12	x	1	=	___
12	x	___	=	24
12	x	3	=	___
12	x	4	=	___
12	x	___	=	60
12	x	6	=	72
12	x	7	=	___
12	x	8	=	___
12	x	9	=	108
12	x	10	=	___
12	x	11	=	132
12	x	12	=	___

1 Draw lines to match each multiplication calculation with the correct answer.

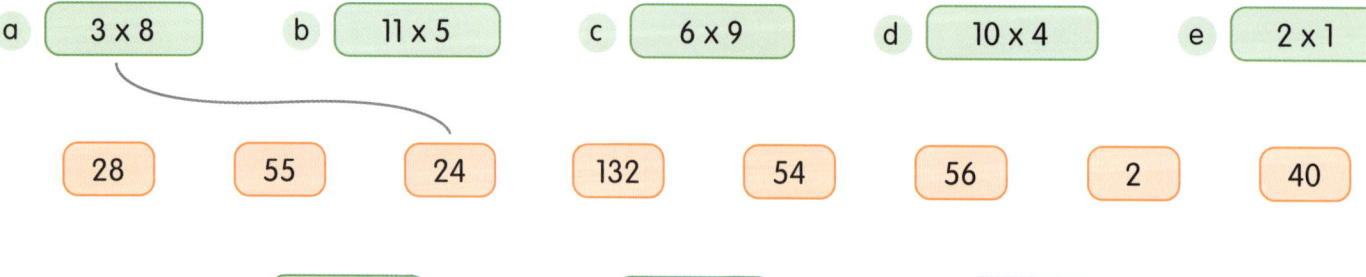

a 3 x 8   b 11 x 5   c 6 x 9   d 10 x 4   e 2 x 1

28   55   24   132   54   56   2   40

f 4 x 7   g 7 x 8   h 12 x 11

2 Use your multiplication tables to help you answer these calculations.

a Omar has 4 bowls, each with 9 raspberries in. How many raspberries does he have in total?

4 x 9 = 36 raspberries.

b Tammy has 3 bowls, each with 5 bananas in. How many bananas does she have in total?

____ x ____ = ____ bananas.

c Rishi has 8 bowls, each with 8 spinach leaves in. How many leaves does he have in total?

____ x ____ = ____ leaves.

d Ephraim has 5 bowls, each with 11 kiwis in. How many kiwis does he have in total?

____ x ____ = ____ kiwis.

e Lucy has 3 bowls, each with 12 avocados in. How many avocados does she have in total?

____ x ____ = ____ avocados.

f Javier has 6 bowls, each with 7 slices of cucumber in. How many slices does he have in total?

____ x ____ = ____ slices.

3 Circle the correct answer to each multiplication calculation.

a	7 x 11	=	76	77 (circled)	78
b	3 x 4	=	12	13	14
c	5 x 12	=	158	59	60
d	8 x 6	=	148	48	50
e	12 x 0	=	10	0	12
f	2 x 9	=	19	18	27
g	10 x 6	=	158	59	60
h	1 x 10	=	110	100	10

MATHS IN CONTEXT

How many pencils?

There are 12 children in Mrs Rahman's class, and each child needs 6 pencils. There are 11 children in Mr Mack's class, and each child needs 7 pencils.

How many pencils do the children need all together?

Total = ______ pencils

Pages 104–105

The multiplication grid

We can arrange all the numbers in the multiplication tables in a grid called a multiplication grid. The factors appear along the top of the grid and down the sides, and the answers are in the middle.

Warm-up Fill in the missing numbers in this multiplication grid.

x	1	2	3	4	5	6	7	8	9	10	11	12
1	1	2	3	4	5	6	___	___	___	10	11	12
2	2	4	6	8	10	___	14	___	18	20	___	24
3	___	___	___	12	15	18	___	24	___	30	33	36
4	4	8	___	___	___	24	28	32	___	___	44	48
5	5	10	15	20	25	___	35	40	___	50	55	60
6	6	___	___	24	30	___	42	48	54	___	66	72
7	7	14	___	___	35	42	___	56	63	___	77	___
8	8	16	___	32	40	48	___	64	___	___	88	___
9	9	18	___	___	___	___	63	72	81	___	99	108
10	10	20	30	___	___	60	70	___	90	___	110	120
11	11	___	___	___	55	66	77	___	99	110	___	132
12	12	___	___	___	60	72	84	96	108	120	___	___

1

Use the multiplication grid in the warm-up to help you fill in the answers to these questions.

a 4 x 6 = 24
b 5 x 5 = ___
c 10 x 7 = ___
d 3 x 11 = ___
e 1 x 3 = ___
f 9 x 2 = ___
g 12 x 9 = ___
h 5 x 12 = ___

2

Use the multiplication grid to help you find the numbers that are hidden under these paint spots.

a 8 x 2 = 16
b 4 x ___ = 16
c ___ x 1 = 7
d 2 x 6 = ___
e 3 x ___ = 27
f ___ x 5 = 40
g 7 x 8 = ___
h 9 x 4 = ___

3

Write out these multiplication questions in digits. You can use the multiplication grid in the warm-up to help you.

a Ted has collected 9 coins, each worth 5p. How much money does he have in total?

9 x 5 = 45 p

b Naziah eats 12 cherries every day for 7 days. How many cherries does she eat all together?

___ x ___ = ___ cherries

c Sami has 3 rabbits. Each rabbit eats 8 carrots every week. How many carrots do all of her rabbits eat in a week?

___ x ___ = ___ carrots

MATHS IN CONTEXT

Sticker time

Mia has 7 packets, each with 4 stickers inside.
Aron has 3 packets, each with 9 stickers inside.
Who has the greater number of stickers?

________ has the greater number of stickers.

Page 106

Multiplication patterns and strategies

Learning multiplication patterns and simple strategies can help you learn your multiplication tables.

REMEMBER!
You will find it useful to learn these patterns and strategies by heart.

Warm-up Fill in an example for each of the multiplication strategies below.

To multiply	How to do it	Example
x 2	Double the number.	1 4 x 2 = 4 + 4 = 8
x 4	Double the number, then double it again.	2 ______
x 5	Multiply by 10 then halve the result.	3 ______
x 9	Multiply the original number by 10, then subtract the original number from the answer.	4 ______
x 11	Write the digit twice, once in the tens place and once in the ones place.	5 ______
x 12	Multiply the original number by 10, then multiply it by 2, then add the two answers.	6 ______

1 Use the strategies in the warm-up to help you fill in the missing numbers in these sentences.

a 12 x 2 = 24 because 12 + 12 = 24

b 7 x 4 = ____ because double ____ = ____ and double ____ = ____

c 5 x 12 = ____ because 10 x 12 = ____ and half of ____ = ____

d 8 x 9 = ____ because 10 x ____ = ____ and ____ – ____ = ____

2 Complete these multiplication calculations. Then explain how you solved each question.

a 4 x 3 = 12 I solved this by doubling 3, then doubling the answer again

b 6 x 12 = ____ I solved this by ____________________

c 2 x 9 = ____ I solved this by ____________________

d 7 x 4 = ____ I solved this by ____________________

e 5 x 7 = ____ I solved this by ____________________

f 8 x 12 = ____ I solved this by ____________________

3 Colour in the correct answer for each of these multiplication calculations.

a 2 x 21 =	36	42	86	92	96
b 5 x 13 =	63	64	65	68	72
c 12 x 15 =	130	140	150	160	180
d 4 x 14 =	54	56	65	74	76
e 5 x 18 =	110	112	90	100	102
f 4 x 16 =	34	44	54	64	74
g 24 x 9 =	206	126	226	216	26

Page 107

Expanded short multiplication

You can use expanded short multiplication when one of the numbers has more than one digit. This method involves writing the numbers out in columns.

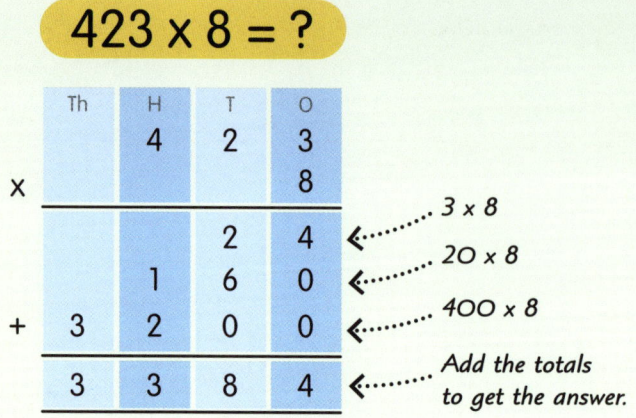

423 x 8 = ?

	Th	H	T	O	
		4	2	3	
x				8	
			2	4	*3 x 8*
		1	6	0	*20 x 8*
+	3	2	0	0	*400 x 8*
	3	3	8	4	*Add the totals to get the answer.*

Warm-up Fill in the missing digits in these expanded short multiplications.

1

	Th	H	T	O
		8	7	6
x				3
			1	8
	___	2	1	0
+	2	4	0	0
	2	6	2	8

2

	Th	H	T	O
		4	5	7
x				4
			___	___
		2	0	0
+	1	6	0	0
	___	___	___	___

3

	Th	H	T	O
		1	2	0
x				9
				0
		___	___	___
+		9	0	0
	___	___	___	___

4

	Th	H	T	O
		3	7	2
x				6
			1	2
		___	___	___
+	1	8	0	0
	___	___	___	___

5

	Th	H	T	O
		5	2	6
x				8
			4	8
		1	6	0
+	___	___	___	___
	___	___	___	___

6

	Th	H	T	O
		2	8	4
x				5
			___	___
		4	0	0
+	1	0	0	0
	___	___	___	___

7

	Th	H	T	O
		9	5	1
x				7
				7
		___	___	___
+	6	3	0	0
	___	___	___	___

8

	Th	H	T	O
		6	0	7
x				2
			1	4
			0	0
+	___	___	___	___
	___	___	___	___

9

	Th	H	T	O
		7	6	4
x				9
			___	___
		5	4	0
+	6	3	0	0
	___	___	___	___

1 Answer these multiplication questions using the expanded short multiplication method.

a

	Th	H	T	O
		7	5	3
x				5
	___	___	1	5
	___	2	5	0
+	3	5	0	0
	3	7	6	5

b

	Th	H	T	O
		3	6	4
x				9
	___	___	___	___
	___	___	___	___
+	___	___	___	___
	___	___	___	___

c

	Th	H	T	O
		4	5	2
x				7
	___	___	___	___
	___	___	___	___
+	___	___	___	___
	___	___	___	___

2 Use the expanded short multiplication method to help you solve these questions.

a Class 3 are selling tickets for their play. Tickets cost £7 each and they have sold 132. How much money has the class collected?

	Th	H	T	O
	___	1	3	2
x	___	___	___	7
	___	___	1	4
	___	2	1	0
+	___	7	0	0
	___	9	2	4

= £ 924

b A doctor's surgery has space to see 287 people in 1 day. How many people can be seen in 5 days?

	Th	H	T	O
	___	___	___	___
x	___	___	___	___
	___	___	___	___
	___	___	___	___
+	___	___	___	___
	___	___	___	___

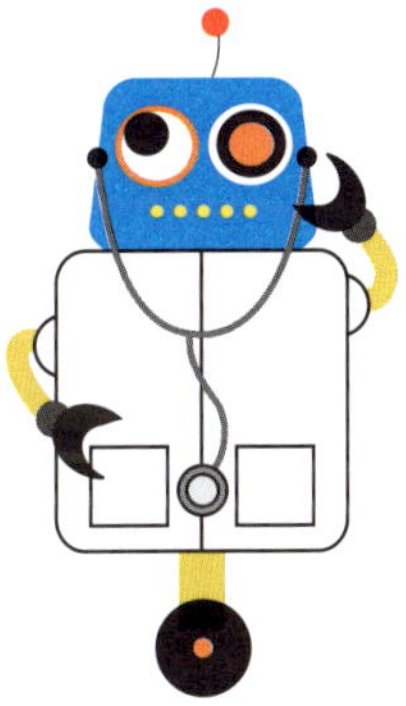

= ______ people

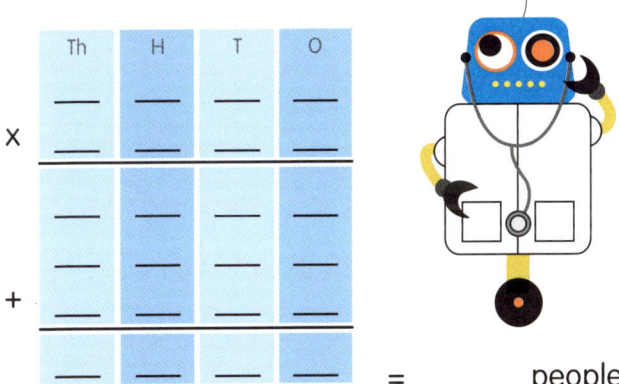

c There are 357 g of cornflakes in a box. How many grams of cornflakes are there in 8 boxes?

	Th	H	T	O
	___	___	___	___
x	___	___	___	___
	___	___	___	___
	___	___	___	___
+	___	___	___	___
	___	___	___	___

= ______ grams

d Josie has 129 marbles in a jar. How many marbles does she have in 9 jars?

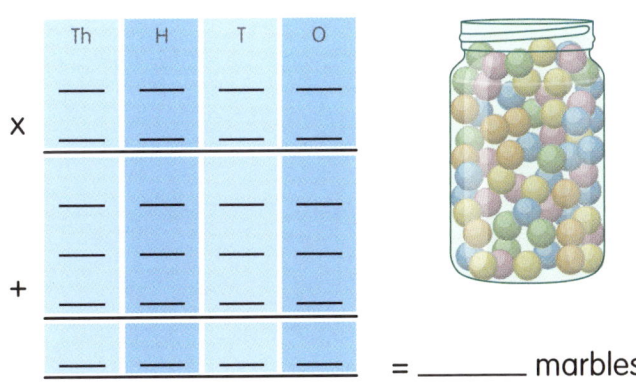

	Th	H	T	O
	___	___	___	___
x	___	___	___	___
	___	___	___	___
	___	___	___	___
+	___	___	___	___
	___	___	___	___

= ______ marbles

Pages 114–115

Short multiplication

This method is quicker than expanded short multiplication. Instead of writing the ones, tens, and hundreds on separate lines and adding them up, we put them all on one line.

Multiply 5 ones by 4 ones.

	Th	H	T	O
		6	²9	5
x				4
				0

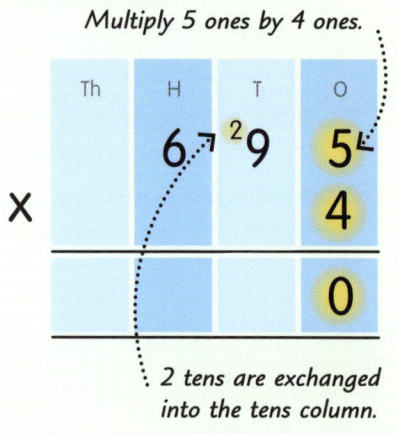

2 tens are exchanged into the tens column.

Multiply 9 tens by 4 ones.

	Th	H	T	O
		³6	²9	5
x				4
			8	0

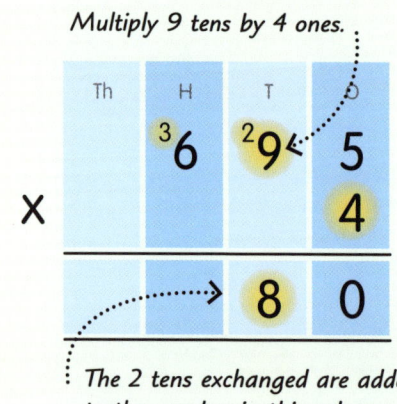

The 2 tens exchanged are added to the number in this column.

Multiply 6 hundreds by 4 ones.

	Th	H	T	O
		³6	²9	5
x				4
	2	7	8	0

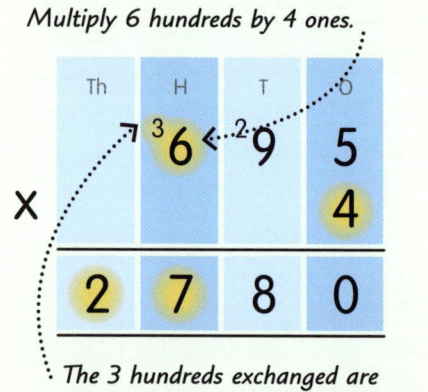

The 3 hundreds exchanged are added to the number in this column.

Warm-up Solve these calculations using the short multiplication method.

1

	Th	H	T	O
		²5	²6	8
x				3
	1	7	0	4

2

	Th	H	T	O
		8	4	3
x				4
	___	___	___	___

3

	Th	H	T	O
		3	4	7
x				5
	___	___	___	___

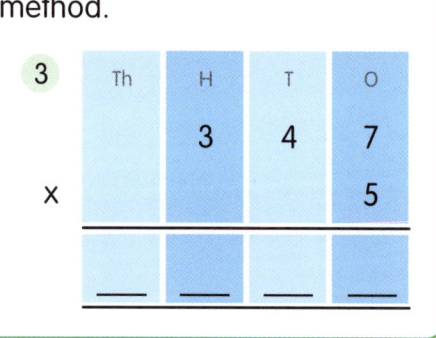

1 Circle the correct answer to each multiplication calculation. Use the short multiplication method use the spaces below for your workings.

a 684 x 5

4320 (3420) 3402

```
  ⁴6 ²8 4
×       5
  3 4 2 0
```

b 854 x 3

2562 2652 2526

c 984 x 6

5940 5904 5804

d 387 x 9

3483 2483 3487

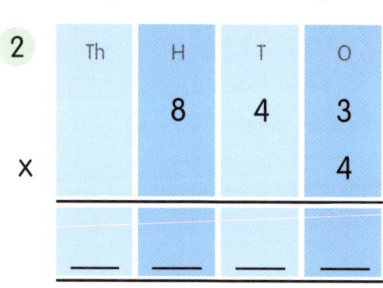

2 Solve these word problems using the short multiplication method.

a Max spends 136 minutes on his tablet each day. How many minutes does he spend on his tablet in 5 days?

= 680 minutes

	Th	H	T	O
		1 (carry 1)	3 (carry 3)	6
x				5
	___	6	8	0

b Ronan's hamster eats 167 g of food each day. How much food does it eat in 1 week?

= ______ grams

	Th	H	T	O
		___	___	___
x				___
	___	___	___	___

c There are 6 grapes on each bunch, and a shop has 345 bunches. How many grapes are there all together?

= ______ grapes

	Th	H	T	O
		___	___	___
x				___
	___	___	___	___

3 Work out the missing digits, then fill them in below.

a

	Th	H	T	O
		8 (carry 3)	6 (carry 2)	4
x				6
	5	1	8	4

b

	Th	H	T	O
		___	8	6
x				___
	5	2	7	4

c

	Th	H	T	O
		9	___	4
x				8
	___	6	3	___

d

	Th	H	T	O
		9	___	3
x				2
	___	8	8	___

e

	Th	H	T	O
		8	___	6
x				7
	___	___	3	2

f

	Th	H	T	O
		5	3	___
x				9
	___	8	3	3

g

	Th	H	T	O
		8	6	___
x				5
	___	3	4	5

h

	Th	H	T	O
		4	___	2
x				6
	___	___	3	2

i

	Th	H	T	O
		5	3	___
x				4
	___	1	4	4

Pages 116–117

Division

Division is splitting a number into equal parts, or finding out how many times one number fits into another number. It doesn't always work out exactly – sometimes there's a bit left over.

Here are 12 apples split into 3 groups of 4.

Count the groups. 12 divided by 3 is 4.
We write this as 12 ÷ 3 = 4.

Warm-up Draw circles round these apples to group them into twos. Count the groups and complete the calculations below.

1 8 grouped in 2s
= 4 groups
8 ÷ 2 = 4

2 12 grouped in 2s
= ____ groups
12 ÷ 2 = ____

3 10 grouped in 2s
= ____ groups
10 ÷ 2 = ____

MATHS IN CONTEXT

Sporting chance

The tennis club needs to order 30 new balls and 20 new rackets.

The balls come in packs of four. How many packs do they need to buy? Will there be any extra?

____

The rackets come in pairs. How many pairs do they need to buy?

____

1 Draw lines to match each calculation with the correct answer in the middle. There are two calculations for each answer, one on each side.

a	20 ÷ 5	3	40 ÷ 8
b	16 ÷ 2	4	27 ÷ 9
c	9 ÷ 3	5	32 ÷ 4
d	21 ÷ 3	6	16 ÷ 4
e	50 ÷ 10	7	42 ÷ 6
f	24 ÷ 4	8	48 ÷ 8

2 Complete these calculations to show that division is the opposite of multiplication.

a $3 \times 4 =$ 12

$12 \div 4 =$ 3

b $5 \times 3 =$ ______

$15 \div 3 =$ ______

c $5 \times 4 =$ ______

$20 \div 4 =$ ______

d $8 \times 2 =$ ______

$16 \div 2 =$ ______

e $5 \times 2 =$ ______

$10 \div 2 =$ ______

f $4 \times 4 =$ ______

$16 \div 4 =$ ______

g $9 \times 3 =$ ______

$27 \div 3 =$ ______

h $6 \times 4 =$ ______

$24 \div 4 =$ ______

i $7 \times 3 =$ ______

$21 \div 3 =$ ______

j $3 \times 3 =$ ______

$9 \div 3 =$ ______

k $5 \times 8 =$ ______

$40 \div 5 =$ ______

REMEMBER!
Not all numbers can be divided equally. If anything is left over, it's called the remainder.

3 Divide the oranges between the robots. Remember to include the remainder in your answers.

a $13 \div 3 =$ 4 r1

b $10 \div 4 =$ ______

c $12 \div 5 =$ ______

d $11 \div 2 =$ ______

e $6 \div 3 =$ ______

f $14 \div 6 =$ ______

Pages 128–129

Dividing with multiples

We can use number lines to see how many times one number (the divisor) fits into another (the dividend). The division is easier if you jump forward in multiples of the divisor.

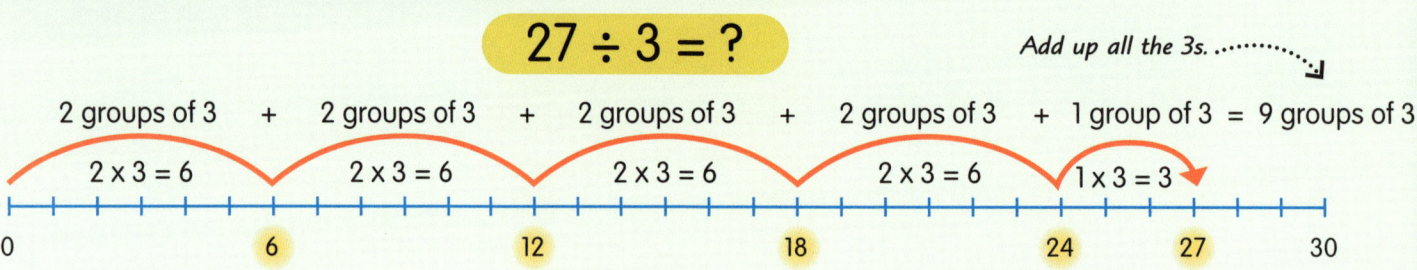

27 ÷ 3 = ?

Add up all the 3s.

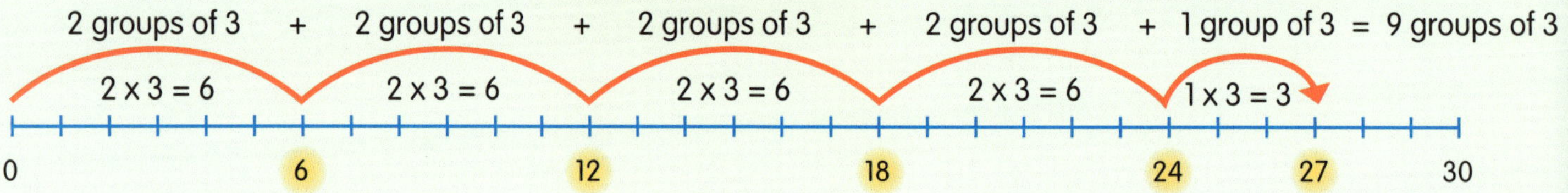

Warm-up Answer these division questions using the number lines below.

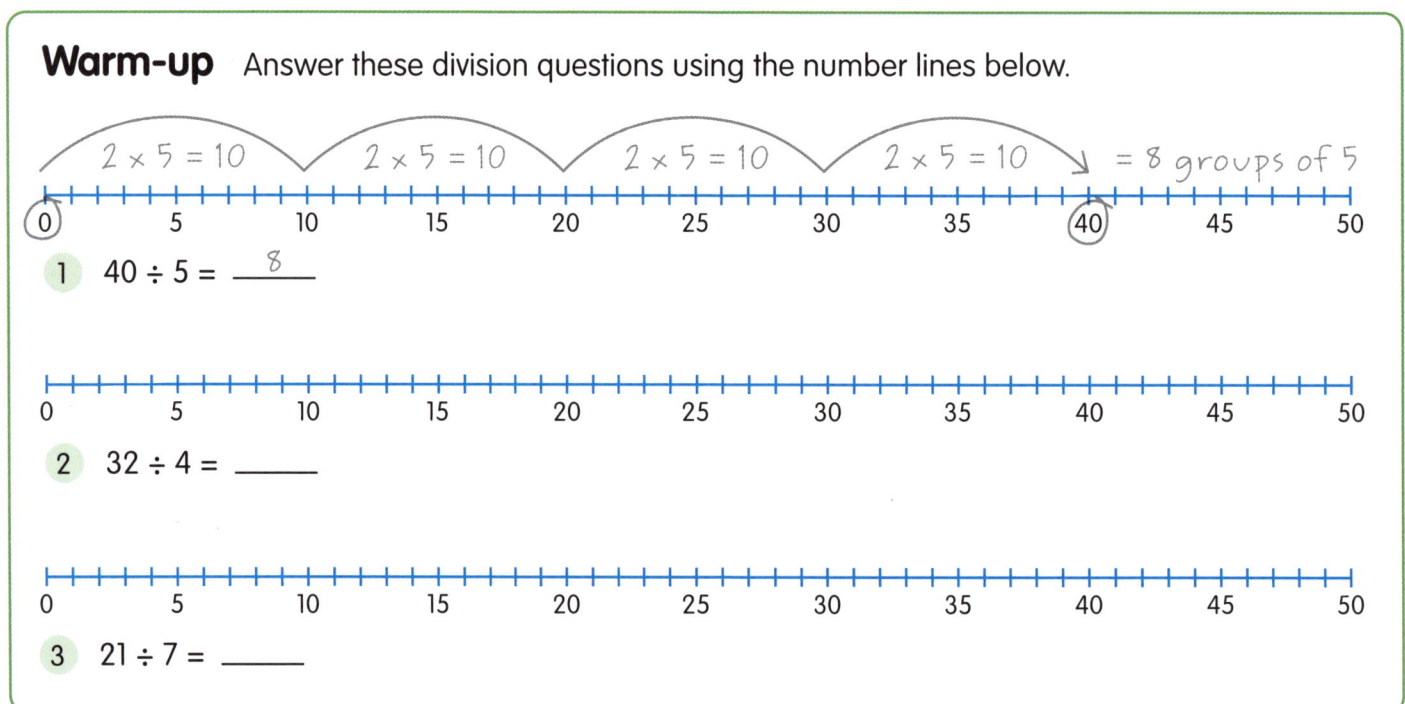

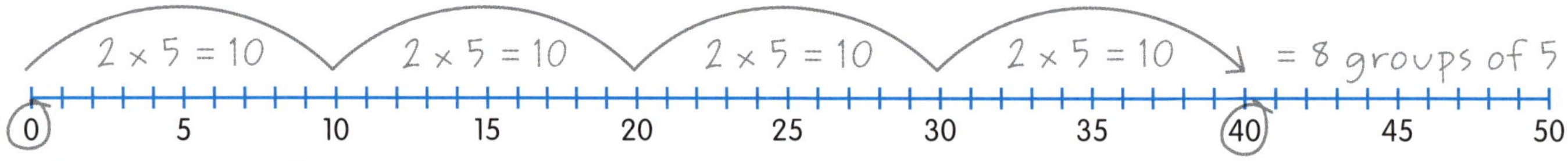

1 40 ÷ 5 = 8

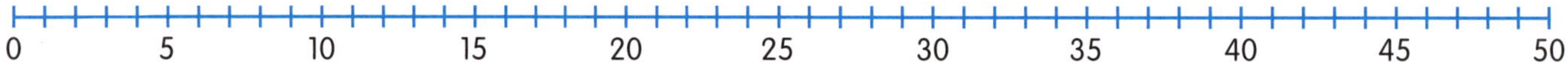

2 32 ÷ 4 = ____

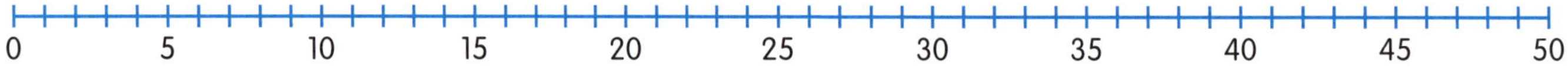

3 21 ÷ 7 = ____

1

Answer these division calculations using the number lines. Each one has a remainder.

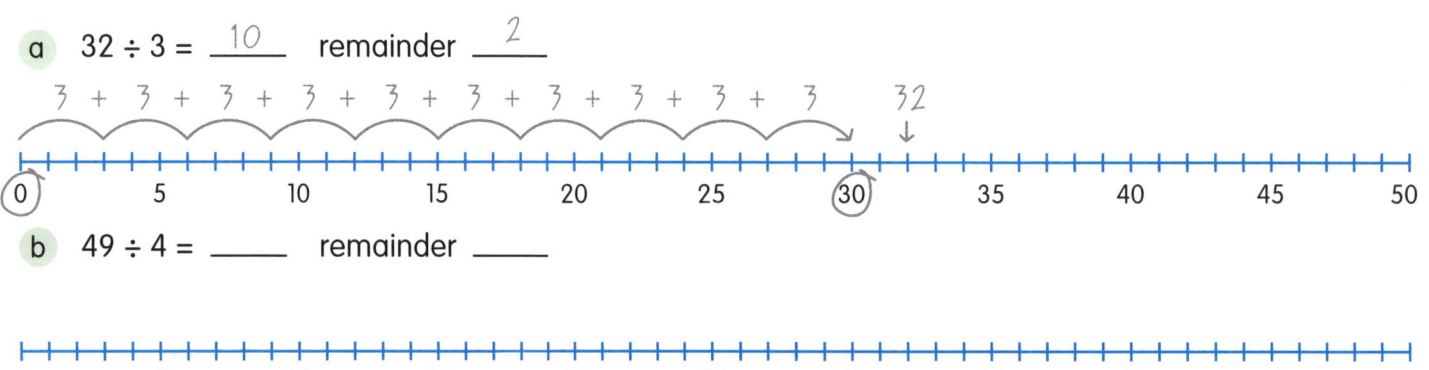

a 32 ÷ 3 = 10 remainder 2

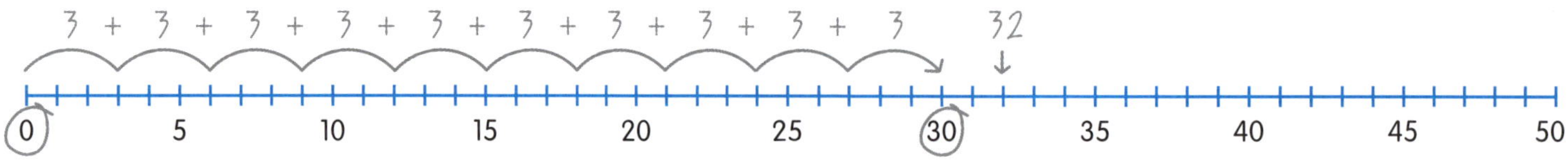

b 49 ÷ 4 = ____ remainder ____

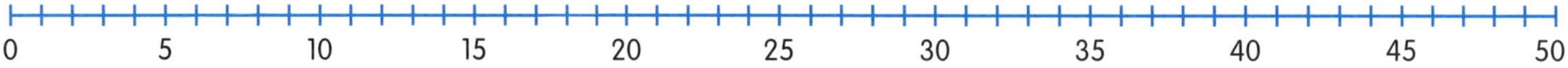

2

Use the number line to help you work out which four of these calculations are wrong. Then fill in those calculations with the correct answers below.

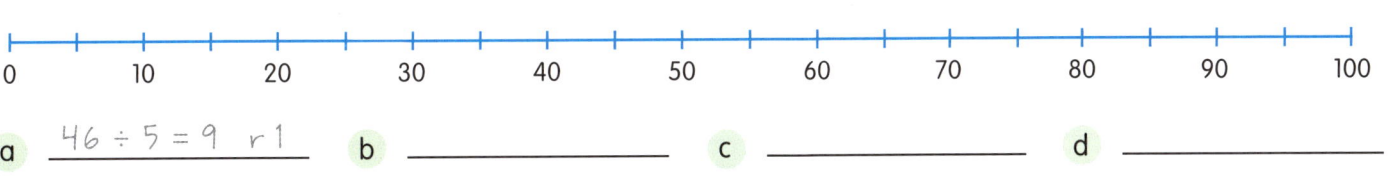

46 ÷ 5 = 9	56 ÷ 4 = 14	88 ÷ 8 = 11	63 ÷ 3 = 21
74 ÷ 4 = 19	72 ÷ 6 = 12	56 ÷ 6 = 9	36 ÷ 3 = 11

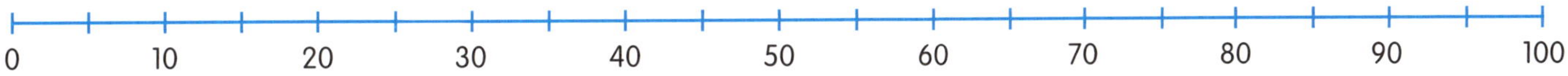

a 46 ÷ 5 = 9 r 1 b ________ c ________ d ________

3

Use the number lines to help you solve these problems.

a Helen's hens lay 132 eggs a week. Eggs are sold in boxes of 6. How many full boxes can Helen make each week? = 22 boxes

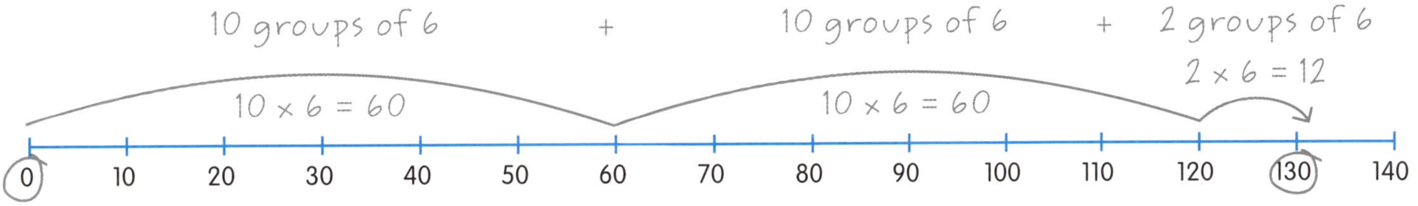

b Year 4 are going by taxi to a bowling alley. Each taxi seats 5 children and there are 42 children in Year 4. How many taxis do they need? = ______ taxis

c Kai is selling biscuits in bags of 6 for charity. He has made 157 biscuits. How many bags can he make? = ______ bags

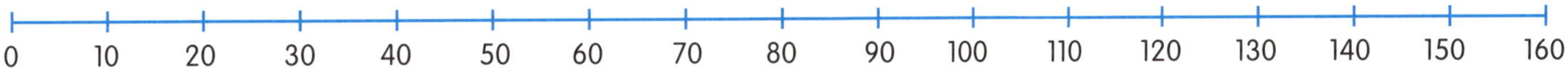

Page 130

Division tables

Division tables are very similar to multiplication tables. In fact, division tables are the opposite – or inverse – of multiplication tables. You can use these tables to help you with division calculations.

Warm-up Fill in the missing numbers in these division tables.

1

6÷ table				
6	÷	6	=	1
12	÷	6	=	2
___	÷	6	=	3
24	÷	6	=	___
30	÷	6	=	5
36	÷	6	=	___
___	÷	6	=	7
48	÷	6	=	___
___	÷	6	=	9
60	÷	6	=	___
66	÷	6	=	11
___	÷	6	=	12

2

9÷ table				
9	÷	9	=	1
___	÷	9	=	2
27	÷	9	=	___
___	÷	9	=	4
___	÷	9	=	5
54	÷	9	=	___
___	÷	9	=	7
72	÷	9	=	___
81	÷	9	=	9
___	÷	9	=	10
99	÷	9	=	___
108	÷	9	=	___

3

11÷ table				
___	÷	11	=	1
___	÷	11	=	2
33	÷	11	=	___
44	÷	11	=	___
55	÷	11	=	5
___	÷	11	=	6
77	÷	11	=	___
___	÷	11	=	8
99	÷	11	=	9
110	÷	11	=	___
___	÷	11	=	11
132	÷	11	=	12

1 Draw lines to match each division calculation with the correct answer.

a 8 ÷ 4 b 77 ÷ 7 c 72 ÷ 12 d 15 ÷ 3 e 24 ÷ 6

4 11 2 12 5 6 7 3

f 60 ÷ 5 g 24 ÷ 8 h 35 ÷ 5

2 Use your division tables to help you answer these calculations.

a A farmer has 48 horses and 8 bales of hay. How many bales will each horse get?

48 ÷ 8 = 6 bales

b Adil has 108 sweets to share between himself and his 9 friends. How many sweets will each child get?

____ ÷ ____ = ____ sweets

c A builder has 144 bricks to build a wall. There need to be 12 bricks per row in her wall. How many rows can she make?

____ ÷ ____ = ____ rows

d Maisie has 20 balloons and wants to tie them to the 4 door handles in her house. How many balloons will be on each door handle?

____ ÷ ____ = ____ balloons

e There are 49 bananas to share between 7 children. How many bananas will each child get?

____ ÷ ____ = ____ bananas

f Destiny has 18 yoyos to share between herself and her 6 friends. How many yoyos will each child get?

____ ÷ ____ = ____ yoyos

3 Circle the correct answer to each division calculation.

a	60 ÷ 10 =	4	5	(6)
b	12 ÷ 3 =	4	5	6
c	54 ÷ 6 =	7	8	9
d	28 ÷ 4 =	7	8	9
e	72 ÷ 8 =	9	10	11
f	99 ÷ 9 =	9	10	11
g	24 ÷ 2 =	8	10	12
h	35 ÷ 7 =	5	6	7

MATHS IN CONTEXT

How many cakes?

Class 4 are making cakes with cherries on top.

1. Gemma has 96 cherries and she puts 12 cherries on each of her cakes. How many cakes does she have?

______ cakes.

2. Albie has 66 cherries and he puts 6 cherries on each of his cakes. How many cakes does he have?

______ cakes.

Pages 132–133

The division grid

The division grid is exactly the same as the multiplication grid on page 62. The numbers in the middle are the dividends – the numbers we want to divide. The numbers along the top and down the left side are divisors and quotients.

Warm-up Use the division grid to help you answer these calculations.

1. 36 ÷ 3 = 12
2. 45 ÷ 5 = ____
3. 44 ÷ 4 = ____
4. 63 ÷ 9 = ____
5. 48 ÷ 6 = ____
6. 81 ÷ 9 = ____
7. 49 ÷ 7 = ____
8. 64 ÷ 8 = ____
9. 72 ÷ 9 = ____
10. 121 ÷ 11 = ____
11. 96 ÷ 8 = ____
12. 108 ÷ 12 = ____

÷	1	2	3	4	5	6	7	8	9	10	11	12
1	1	2	3	4	5	6	7	8	9	10	11	12
2	2	4	6	8	10	12	14	16	18	20	22	24
3	3	6	9	12	15	18	21	24	27	30	33	36
4	4	8	12	16	20	24	28	32	36	40	44	48
5	5	10	15	20	25	30	35	40	45	50	55	60
6	6	12	18	24	30	36	42	48	54	60	66	72
7	7	14	21	28	35	42	49	56	63	70	77	84
8	8	16	24	32	40	48	56	64	72	80	88	96
9	9	18	27	36	45	54	63	72	81	90	99	108
10	10	20	30	40	50	60	70	80	90	100	110	120
11	11	22	33	44	55	66	77	88	99	110	121	132
12	12	24	36	48	60	72	84	96	108	120	132	144

1

Use the division grid above to help you fill in the missing digits in these calculations.

a 64 ÷ 8 = 8

b 30 ÷ 5 = ____

c 70 ÷ ____ = 10

d 33 ÷ ____ = 3

e ____ ÷ 9 = 6

f ____ ÷ 2 = 9

g ____ ÷ 9 = 4

h 132 ÷ 11 = ____

2 Draw lines to match each division calculation with the correct answer.

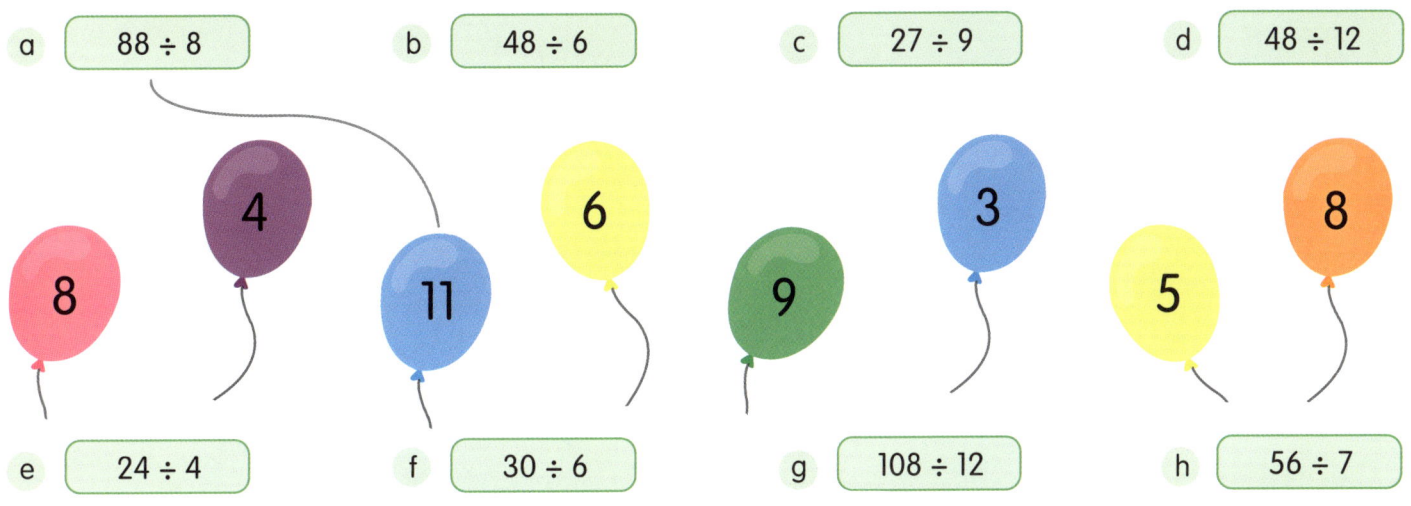

a 88 ÷ 8 b 48 ÷ 6 c 27 ÷ 9 d 48 ÷ 12

e 24 ÷ 4 f 30 ÷ 6 g 108 ÷ 12 h 56 ÷ 7

3 Write out these word problems in numbers, then use the division grid to help you work out the answers.

a Sami has 3 dogs and together they eat 18 tins of food each week. How many tins does each dog eat per week?

18 ÷ 3 = 6 tins

b Anna has collected 55p in 5p coins. How many coins does she have in total?

____ ÷ ____ = ____ coins

c Farmer Giles wants to know how many chickens he has. Each chicken has laid 4 eggs. He counts 48 eggs. How many chickens does he have?

____ ÷ ____ = ____ chickens

d Dougie has 56 chocolates. He shares them between himself and 7 friends. How many chocolates does each person get?

____ ÷ ____ = ____ chocolates

e Sanam has 108 stickers. She will stick 9 stickers on each page of a book. How many pages does she need?

____ ÷ ____ = ____ pages

Page 131

Partitioning for division

When we divide a number that has two or more digits, it can be helpful to partition it into smaller numbers.

288 ÷ 8 = ?

288

280 | 8

280 ÷ 8 = 35

8 ÷ 8 = 1

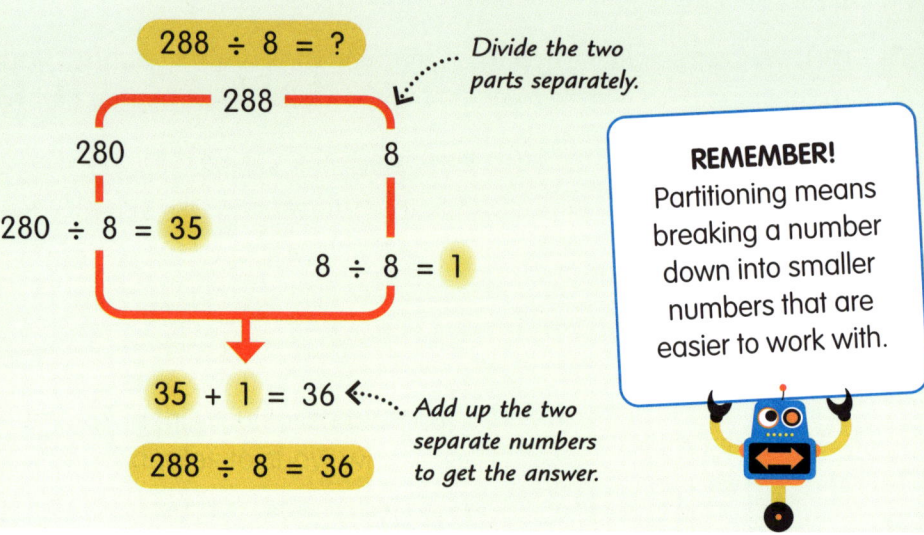

Divide the two parts separately.

35 + 1 = 36

Add up the two separate numbers to get the answer.

288 ÷ 8 = 36

REMEMBER!
Partitioning means breaking a number down into smaller numbers that are easier to work with.

Warm-up

Fill in the gaps in these examples of dividing by partitioning.

1. 144 ÷ 6 = ?

144

120 | 24

120 ÷ 6 = 20

24 ÷ 6 = 4

20 + 4 = 24

144 ÷ 6 = 24

2. 170 ÷ 5 = ?

170

___ | 20

___ ÷ 5 = ___

20 ÷ 5 = 4

___ + 4 = ___

170 ÷ 5 = ___

3. 126 ÷ 3 = ?

126

120 | ___

120 ÷ 3 = ___

___ ÷ 3 = ___

___ + ___ = ___

126 ÷ 3 = ___

4. 264 ÷ 8 = ?

264

___ | 24

___ ÷ 8 = ___

24 ÷ 8 = ___

___ + ___ = ___

264 ÷ 8 = ___

REMEMBER!
Make sure both your partitioned numbers are divisible by the number you are dividing by.

1

Use the partitioning method for division to solve these word problems. Make sure both your partitioned numbers are divisible by the number you are dividing by.

a A photographer prints 176 photographs for his album. Each page has 8 photographs. How many pages are used all together?

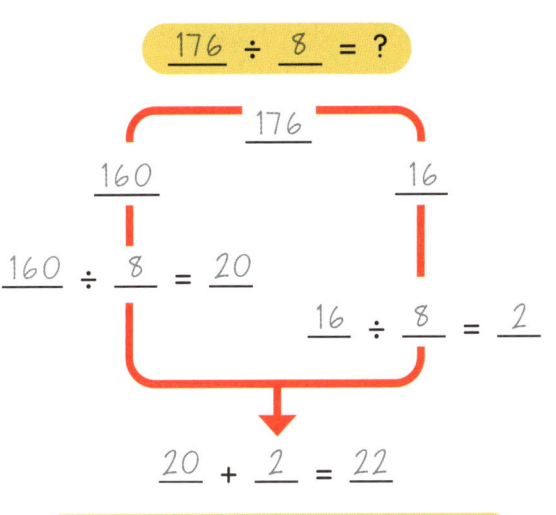

176 ÷ 8 = ?

176

160 | 16

160 ÷ 8 = 20

16 ÷ 8 = 2

20 + 2 = 22

176 ÷ 8 = 22 pages

b At the supermarket apples are sold in packs of 7. How many packs of apples can be made using 189 apples?

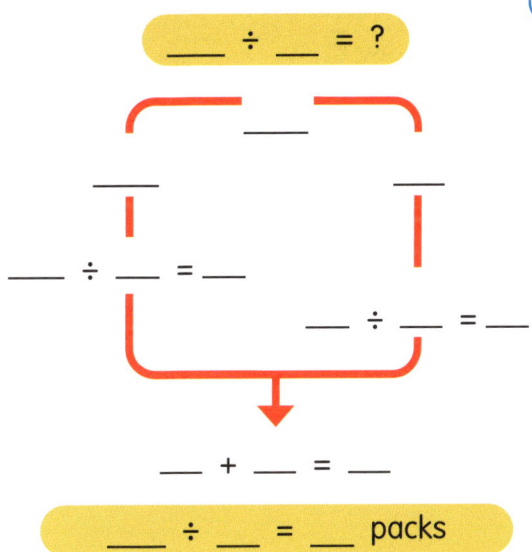

___ ÷ ___ = ?

___

___ | ___

___ ÷ ___ = ___

___ ÷ ___ = ___

___ + ___ = ___

___ ÷ ___ = ___ packs

c A collection of 207 rugby balls is divided equally between 9 bags. How many rugby balls are in each bag?

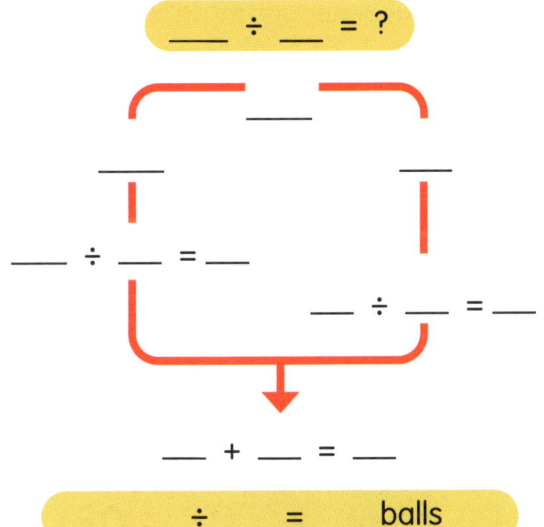

___ ÷ ___ = ?

___

___ | ___

___ ÷ ___ = ___

___ ÷ ___ = ___

___ + ___ = ___

___ ÷ ___ = ___ balls

d 184 pencils are stored on shelves in the art room. There are 8 pencils per shelf. How many shelves are needed to store all 184 pencils?

___ ÷ ___ = ?

___

___ | ___

___ ÷ ___ = ___

___ ÷ ___ = ___

___ + ___ = ___

___ ÷ ___ = ___ shelves

Pages 138–139

Expanded short division

Expanded short division is a method to use when the number you are dividing by (the divisor) is a single digit. You can subtract multiples – or "chunks" – of the divisor to find the answer.

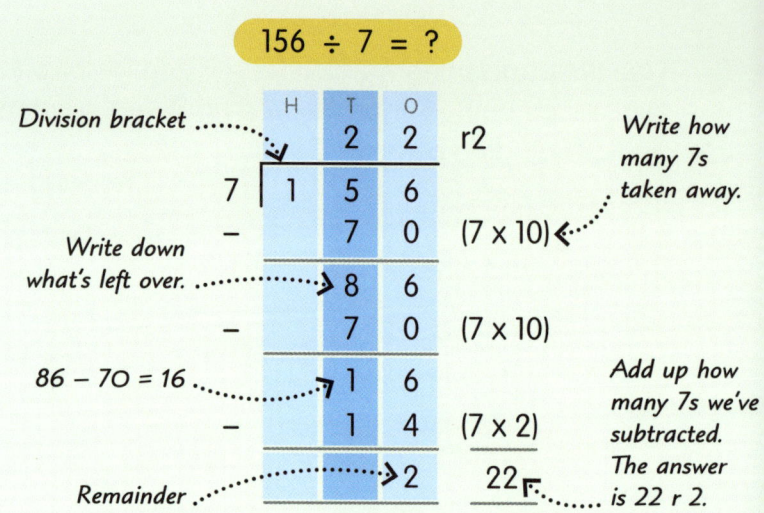

156 ÷ 7 = ?

	H	T	O	
		2	2	r2
7	1	5	6	
–		7	0	(7 x 10)
		8	6	
–		7	0	(7 x 10)
		1	6	
–		1	4	(7 x 2)
			2	22

Division bracket

Write how many 7s taken away.

Write down what's left over.

86 – 70 = 16

Add up how many 7s we've subtracted. The answer is 22 r 2.

Remainder

Warm-up Fill in the missing numbers in these expanded short divisions. None of the answers has a remainder.

1

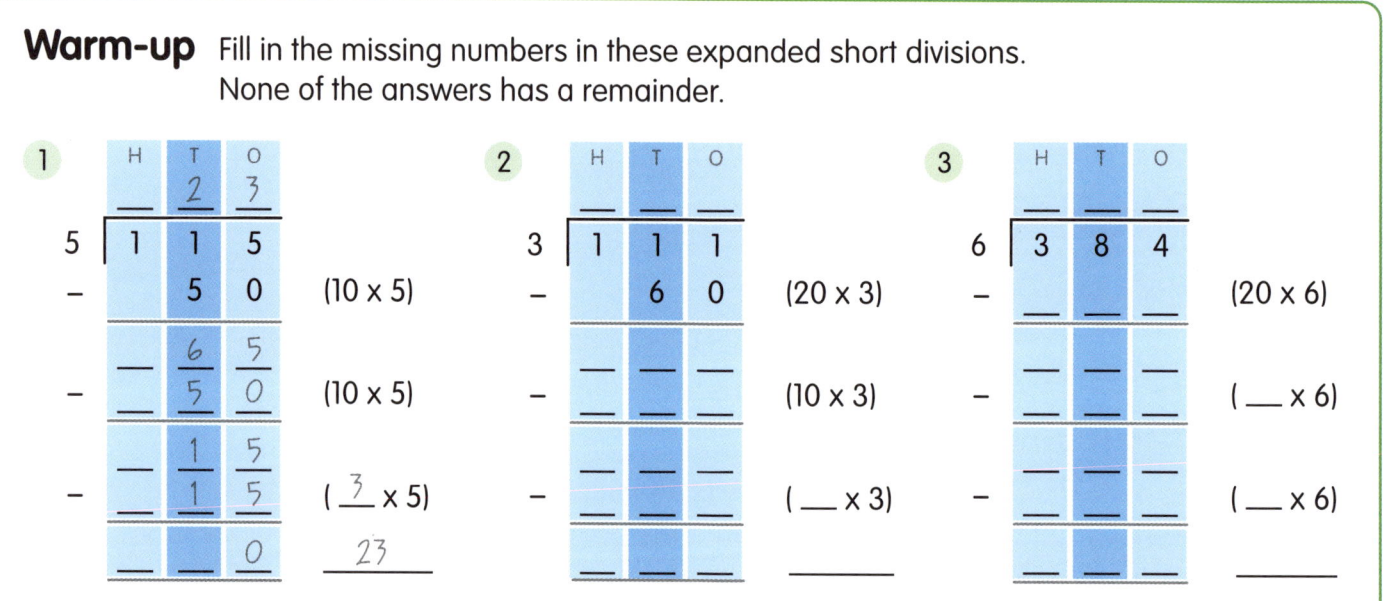

	H	T	O	
	__	2	3	
5	1	1	5	
–		5	0	(10 x 5)
	__	6	5	
–	__	5	0	(10 x 5)
	__	1	5	
–	__	1	5	(3 x 5)
	__	__	0	23

2

	H	T	O	
	__	__	__	
3	1	1	1	
–		6	0	(20 x 3)
	__	__	__	
–	__	__	__	(10 x 3)
	__	__	__	
–	__	__	__	(__ x 3)
	__	__	__	______

3

	H	T	O	
	__	__	__	
6	3	8	4	
–	__	__	__	(20 x 6)
	__	__	__	
–	__	__	__	(__ x 6)
	__	__	__	
–	__	__	__	(__ x 6)
	__	__	__	______

1

Fill in the missing numbers in these expanded short divisions. Each answer will have a remainder.

a

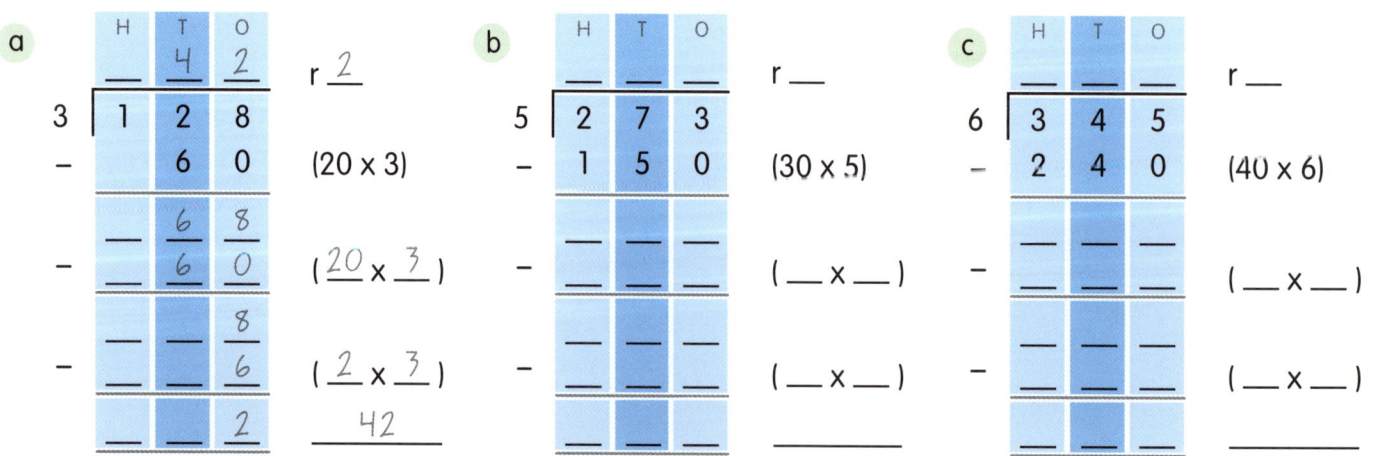

	H	T	O	
	__	4	2	r 2
3	1	2	8	
–		6	0	(20 x 3)
	__	6	8	
–	__	6	0	(20 x 3)
	__	__	8	
–	__	__	6	(2 x 3)
	__	__	2	42

b

	H	T	O	
	__	__	__	r __
5	2	7	3	
–	1	5	0	(30 x 5)
	__	__	__	
–	__	__	__	(__ x __)
	__	__	__	
–	__	__	__	(__ x __)
	__	__	__	______

c

	H	T	O	
	__	__	__	r __
6	3	4	5	
–	2	4	0	(40 x 6)
	__	__	__	
–	__	__	__	(__ x __)
	__	__	__	
–	__	__	__	(__ x __)
	__	__	__	______

2
Draw lines to match each division question with the correct answer.
Use the expanded short division spaces below for your workings.

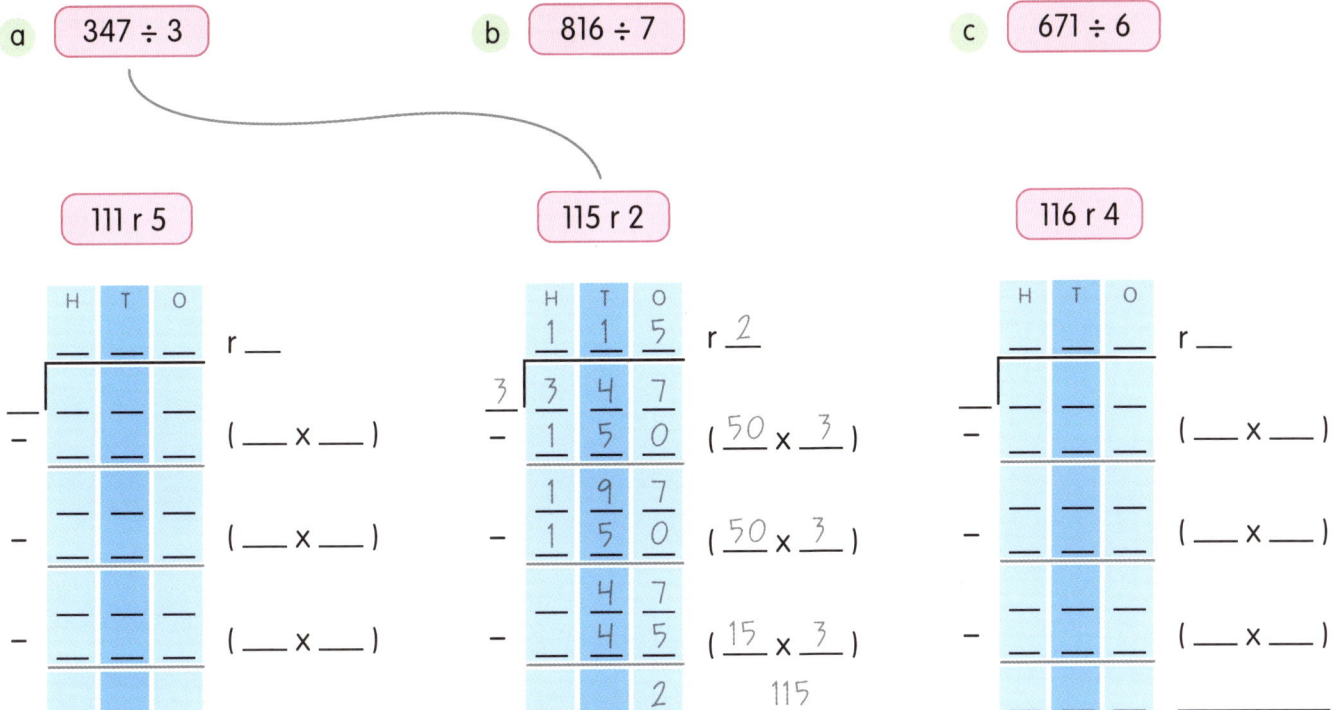

a 347 ÷ 3 b 816 ÷ 7 c 671 ÷ 6

111 r 5 115 r 2 116 r 4

	H	T	O	
	_	_	_	r _
_	_	_	_	
−	_	_	_	(_ x _)
	_	_	_	
−	_	_	_	(_ x _)
	_	_	_	
−	_	_	_	(_ x _)
	_	_	_	___

	H	T	O	
	1	1	5	r 2
3	3	4	7	
−	1	5	0	(50 x 3)
	1	9	7	
−	1	5	0	(50 x 3)
	_	4	7	
−	_	4	5	(15 x 3)
	_	_	2	115

	H	T	O	
	_	_	_	r _
_	_	_	_	
−	_	_	_	(_ x _)
	_	_	_	
−	_	_	_	(_ x _)
	_	_	_	
−	_	_	_	(_ x _)
	_	_	_	___

3
Each robot has answered a division question, but they have forgotten to write down the remainders. Fill in the missing remainders below.
Use the space below each robot for your workings.

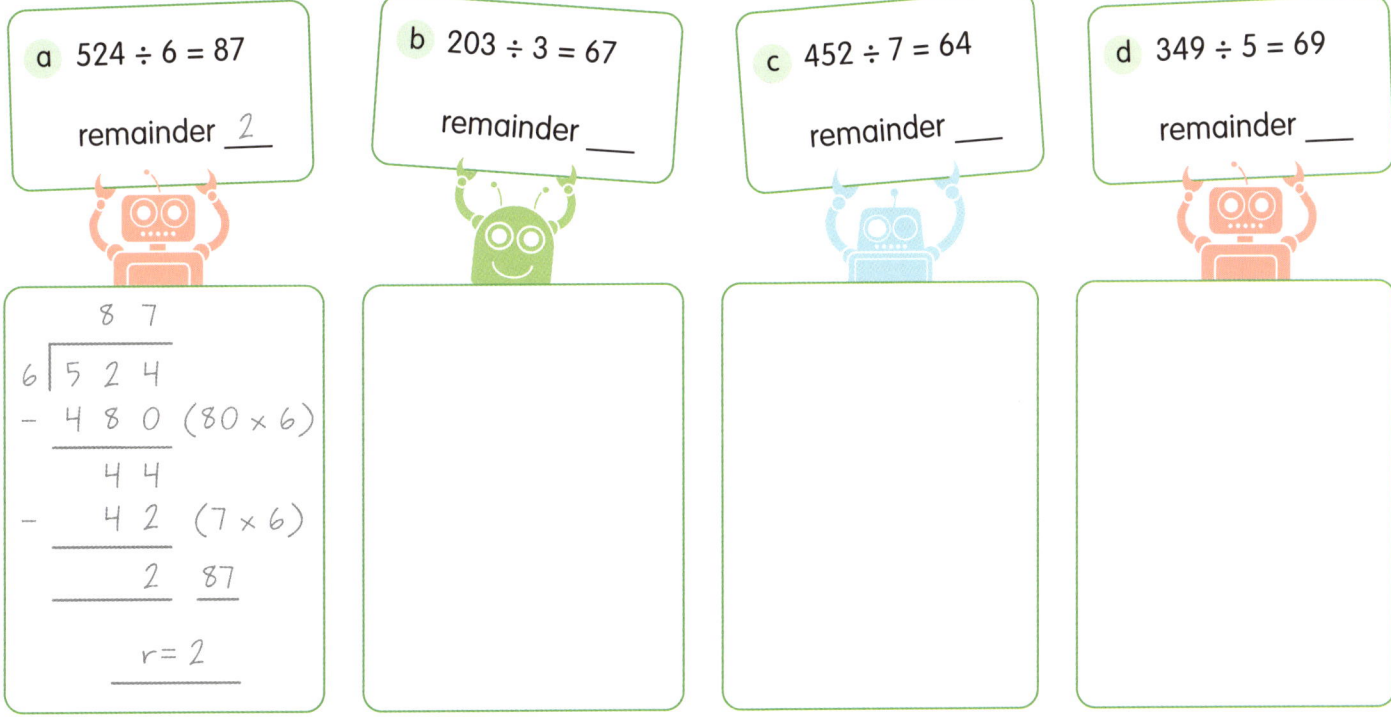

a 524 ÷ 6 = 87
remainder 2

b 203 ÷ 3 = 67
remainder ___

c 452 ÷ 7 = 64
remainder ___

d 349 ÷ 5 = 69
remainder ___

Workings (a):

```
     8 7
6 | 5 2 4
 − 4 8 0  (80 × 6)
     4 4
 −   4 2  (7 × 6)
       2   87

   r = 2
```

Pages 140–141

Short division

When the divisor is a single digit we can also use the short division method. We exchange numbers that are left over to the next column.

$167 \div 7 = ?$

This calculation can be answered using the short division method.

	H	T	O	
		2	3	r 6
7	1	${}^{1}6$	${}^{2}7$	

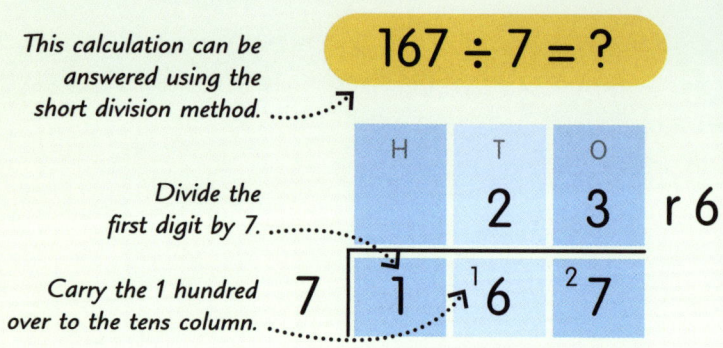

Divide the first digit by 7.

Carry the 1 hundred over to the tens column.

Warm-up Use the short division method to solve these calculations.

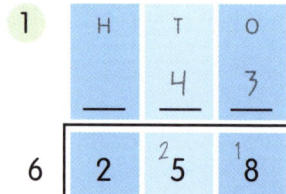

1

	H	T	O
	___	4	3
6	2	${}^{2}5$	${}^{1}8$

2

	H	T	O
	___	___	___
9	2	5	2

3

	H	T	O
	___	___	___
4	3	3	6

4

	H	T	O
	___	___	___
5	3	9	5

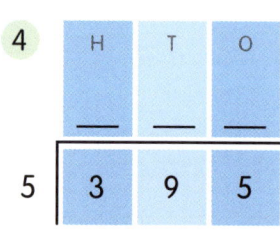

1 Colour the T-shirt that contains the correct answer for each calculation. Use the short division method to help you find the answers.

a $216 \div 6 =$	35	36	37	38
b $196 \div 7 =$	26	27	28	29
c $765 \div 9 =$	82	83	84	85
d $413 \div 7 =$	57	58	59	60
e $344 \div 8 =$	41	42	43	44

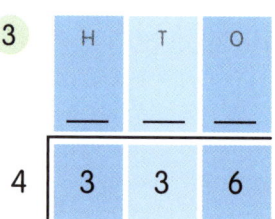

2 Use the short division method to help you find the answers to these questions.

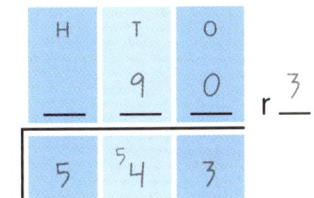

a $543 \div 6 =$ 90 r 3

	H	T	O	
	___	9	0	r 3
6	5	⁵4	3	

b $862 \div 7 =$ ___ r ___

	H	T	O	
	___	___	___	r ___
___	___	___	___	

c $174 \div 4 =$ ___ r ___

	H	T	O	
	___	___	___	r ___
___	___	___	___	

d $623 \div 8 =$ ___ r ___

	H	T	O	
	___	___	___	r ___
___	___	___	___	

e $194 \div 5 =$ ___ r ___

	H	T	O	
	___	___	___	r ___
___	___	___	___	

f $214 \div 4 =$ ___ r ___

	H	T	O	
	___	___	___	r ___
___	___	___	___	

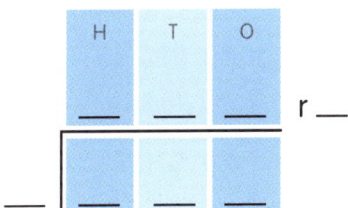

3 Compare these division statements by writing less than (<), greater than (>), or equal to (=).

a $96 \div 8$ [=] $72 \div 6$

b $95 \div 5$ [ ] $147 \div 3$

c $328 \div 8$ [ ] $294 \div 7$

d $189 \div 3$ [ ] $366 \div 6$

e $504 \div 7$ [ ] $432 \div 6$

f $54 \div 3$ [ ] $144 \div 6$

g $128 \div 8$ [ ] $52 \div 4$

h $156 \div 4$ [ ] $228 \div 6$

i $84 \div 6$ [ ] $105 \div 7$

j $72 \div 3$ [ ] $96 \div 2$

k $95 \div 5$ [ ] $171 \div 9$

l $104 \div 8$ [ ] $210 \div 2$

MATHS IN CONTEXT

How much ribbon?

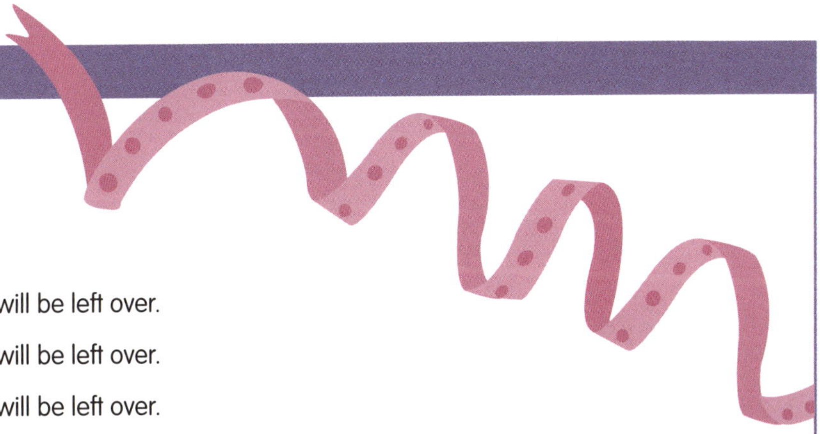

Ebony has a piece of ribbon that is 932 cm long.
Complete the sentences below.

1. If the ribbon is cut into 4 equal pieces ______ cm will be left over.
2. If the ribbon is cut into 6 equal pieces ______ cm will be left over.
3. If the ribbon is cut into 7 equal pieces ______ cm will be left over.
4. If the ribbon is cut into 9 equal pieces ______ cm will be left over.

Pages 142–143

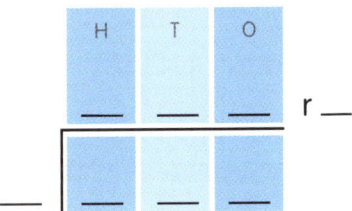

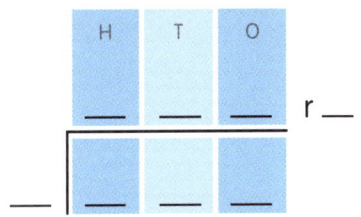

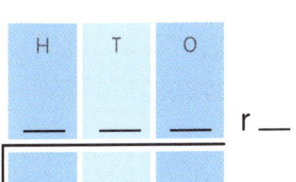

Arithmetic laws

Whenever we're calculating, it helps to remember the commutative and distributive arithmetic laws. These are useful when we're working on a calculation with several parts.

REMEMBER!
When we add or multiply two numbers together, the answer is the same regardless of the order of the numbers. For example: 3 x 2 = 6 and 2 x 3 = 6. This is called the commutative law.

Warm-up Draw a set of dots to show that these multiplication sums have the same answers whichever way you choose to multiply them.

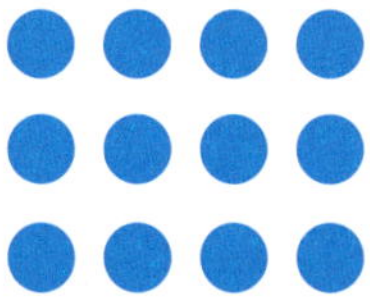

1 4 x 3 = 12 3 x 4 = 12

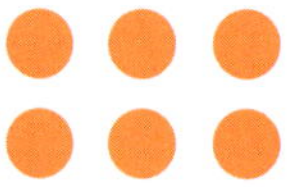

2 3 x 2 = 6 ___ x ___ = 6

3 3 x 5 = 15 ___ x ___ = 15

4 3 x 6 = 18 ___ x ___ = 18

1

The commutative law means you can multiply two numbers together in any order. Use the commutative law to help you fill in the linked multiplications for the calculations below.

a 4 x 6 = 24	6 x 4 = 24	b 1 x 2 = ___	___ x ___ = ___
c 6 x 7 = ___	___ x ___ = ___	d 4 x 9 = ___	___ x ___ = ___
e 9 x 1 = ___	___ x ___ = ___	f 3 x 5 = ___	___ x ___ = ___
g 5 x 6 = ___	___ x ___ = ___	h 7 x 8 = ___	___ x ___ = ___
i 8 x 3 = ___	___ x ___ = ___	j 9 x 6 = ___	___ x ___ = ___

2 Use the distributive law to help you find the answers to these calculations.

a 15 x 6 = (10 x 6) + (5 x 6)
= 60 + 30
= 90

b 24 x 5 = (____ x 5) + (____ x 5)
= ____ + ____
= ____

c 13 x 9 = (____ x 9) + (____ x 9)
= ____ + ____
= ____

d 18 x 4 = (____ x 4) + (____ x 4)
= ____ + ____
= ____

e 21 x 2 = (____ x 2) + (____ x 2)
= ____ + ____
= ____

f 27 x 8 = (____ x 8) + (____ x 8)
= ____ + ____
= ____

g 36 x 3 = (____ x 3) + (____ x 3)
= ____ + ____
= ____

h 46 x 8 = (____ x 8) + (____ x 8)
= ____ + ____
= ____

REMEMBER!
Multiplying a number by some numbers added together will give the same answer as multiplying each number separately. This is the distributive law, and it helps us to break down large or difficult multiplication sums into ones that are easier to work out.

3 Use your knowledge of the arithmetic laws to complete these statements.

a 8 x 4 = 32 using the commutative law is the same as 4 x 8 = 32

b 27 x 3 = ______ using the commutative law is the same as ____________

c 7 x 6 = ______ using the commutative law is the same as ____________

d 2 x 9 = ______ using the commutative law is the same as ____________

e 19 x 7 = ______ using the distributive law is the same as ____________

f 22 x 4 = ______ using the distributive law is the same as ____________

g 12 x 4 = ______ using the distributive law is the same as ____________

h 9 x 8 = ______ using the commutative law is the same as ____________

i 28 x 9 = ______ using the distributive law is the same as ____________

Pages 154–155

Length

Length is the distance between two points. Length, width, height, and distance can all be measured using the same units. We can also convert between different units of length.

REMEMBER!
There are 10 millimetres (mm) in 1 centimetre (cm) and 100 cm in 1 metre (m).

Warm-up Use a ruler to measure the length or height of each of these lines.

1 

Length = 14 cm

2 

Length = ____ cm

3 

Length = ____ cm

4 Height = ____ cm

5 Height = ____ cm

1

Fill in which unit you would use to measure each of these things. You can use mm, cm, m, or km.

a The length of an ant would be measured in mm .

b The height of a door would be measured in _____ .

c The height of a building would be measured in _____ .

d The distance between my door and the end of the road would be measured in _____ .

e The distance between two cities would be measured in _____ .

f The distance between two countries would be measured in _____ .

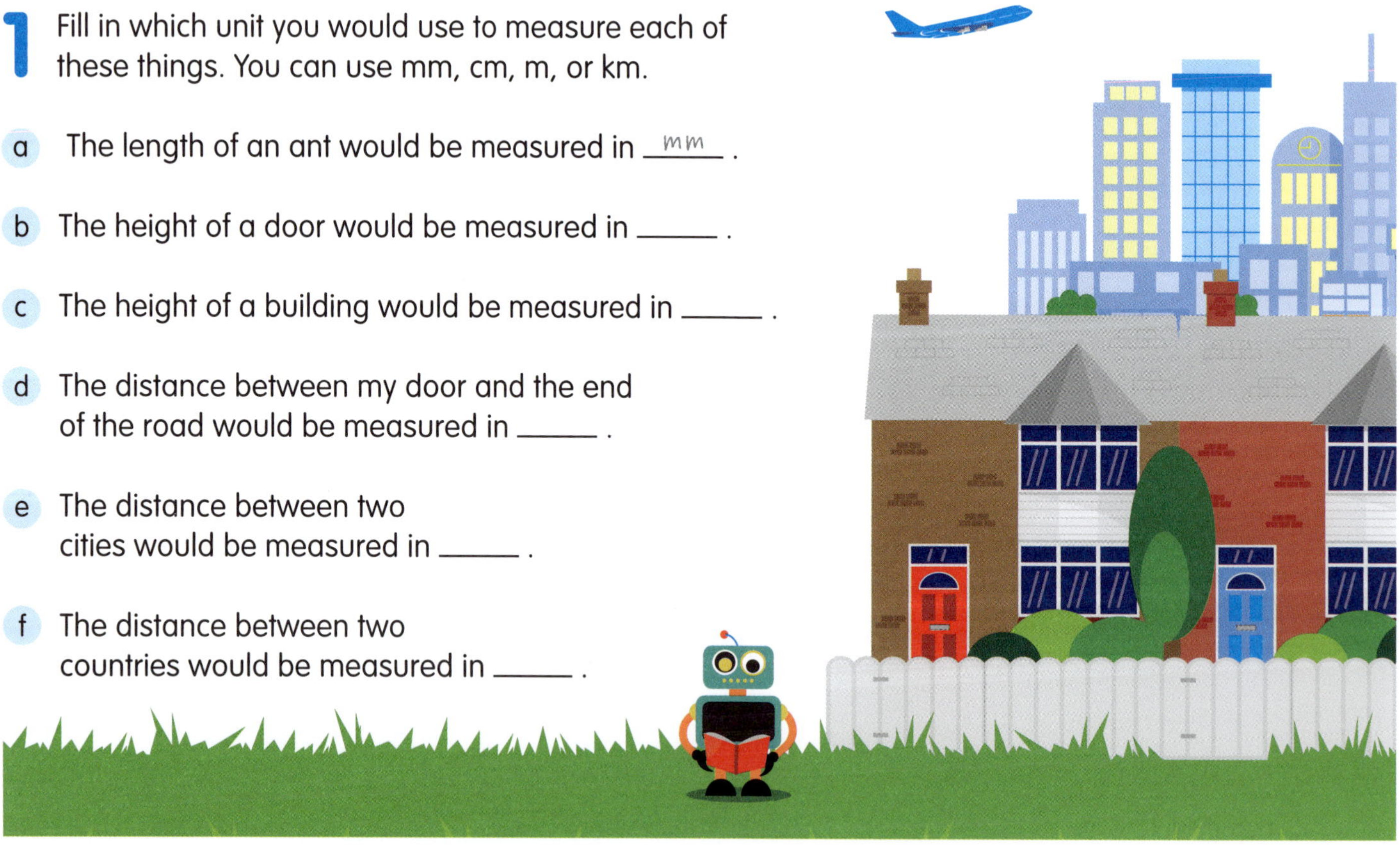

2 Convert these units of length.

a 2 m → x 100 → = 200 cm

b 260 mm → ÷ 10 → = ______ cm

c 130 cm → ÷ 100 → = ______ m

d 17 cm → x 10 → = ______ mm

e 40 mm → ÷ 10 → = ______ cm

f 7 m → x 1000 → = ______ mm

g 28 cm → x 10 → = ______ mm

h 3800 cm → ÷ 100 → = ______ m

3 Order these lengths by size, starting with the shortest.

380 mm	380 cm	~~3 mm~~	320 cm	34 m
3 mm	______	______	______	______

4 Some of these measurements describe the same lengths, but are written using different units of measurement. Colour the pairs of matching lengths in the same colour.

3 m	3 cm	90 mm	800 cm	30 mm
7000 mm	2 m	800 mm	24 cm	8 m
9 m	80 cm	240 mm	4 m	200 cm
400 cm	9 cm	7 m	300cm	900 cm

Pages 160–161

Perimeter

Perimeter is the distance around the edge of a shape. To find a shape's perimeter, we add up the lengths of all of its sides.

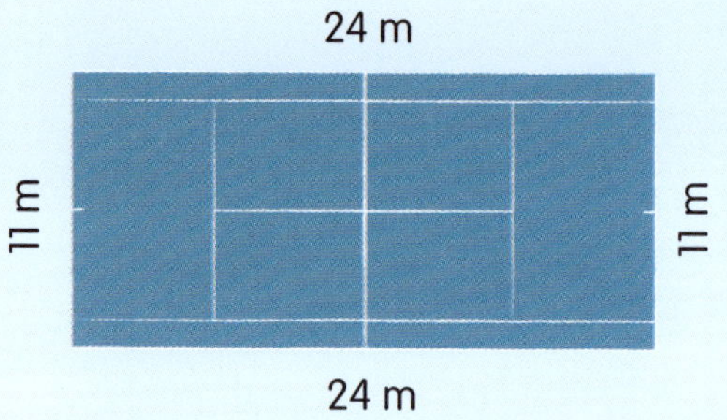

The perimeter of this tennis court is 11 m + 24 m + 11 m + 24 m = 70 m.

Warm-up Measure the perimeter of these shapes, using a ruler.

1 Perimeter = 12 cm

3 cm + 3 cm + 3 cm + 3 cm = 12 cm

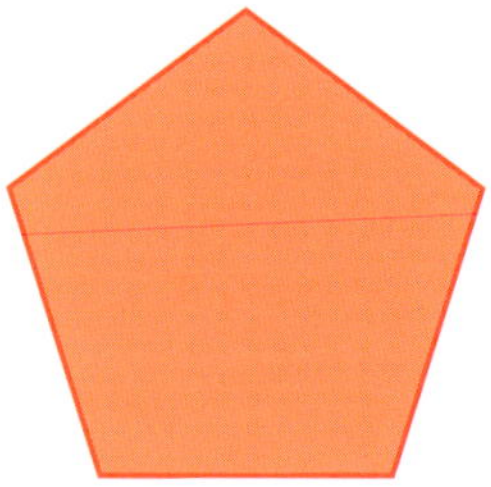

2 Perimeter = ___ cm

___ cm + ___ cm + ___ cm + ___ cm + ___ cm = ___ cm

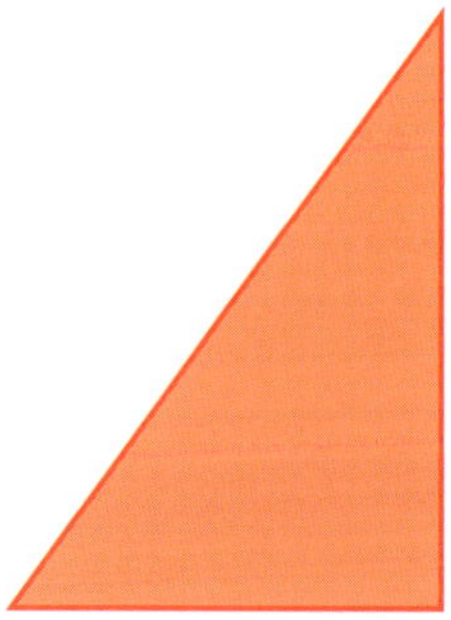

3 Perimeter = ___ cm

___ cm + ___ cm + ___ cm = ___ cm

1 Calculate the perimeter of these fields. They are not drawn to scale.

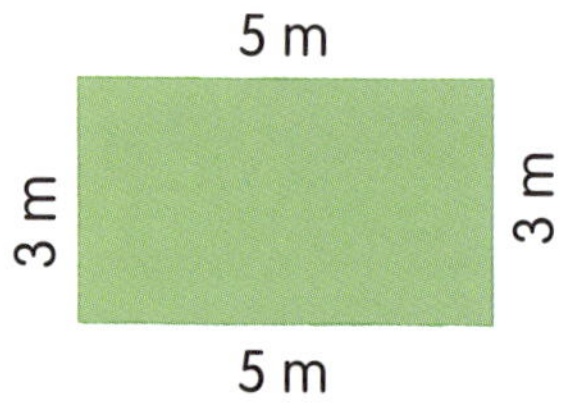

a Perimeter = 16 m

5 m + 3 m + 5 m + 3 m = 16 m

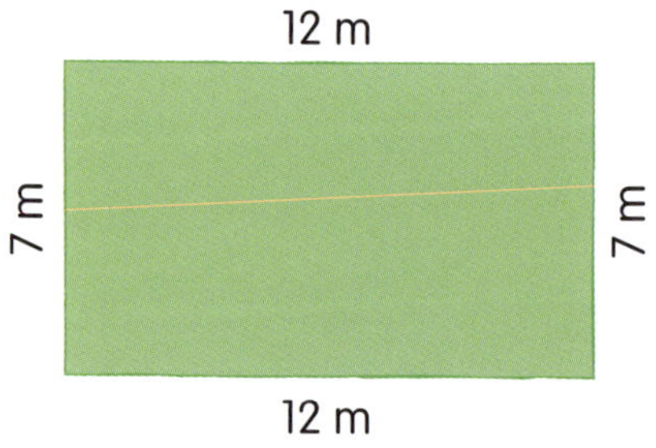

b Perimeter = ___ m

___ m + ___ m + ___ m + ___ m = ___ m

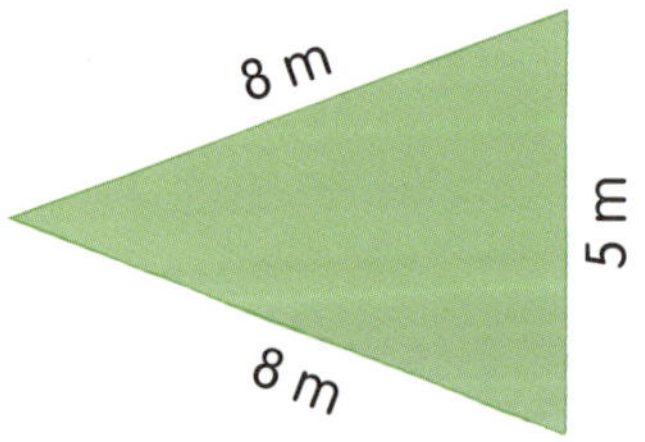

c Perimeter = ___ m

___ m + ___ m + ___ m = ___ m

2 Calculate the perimeters of these shapes. They are not drawn to scale.

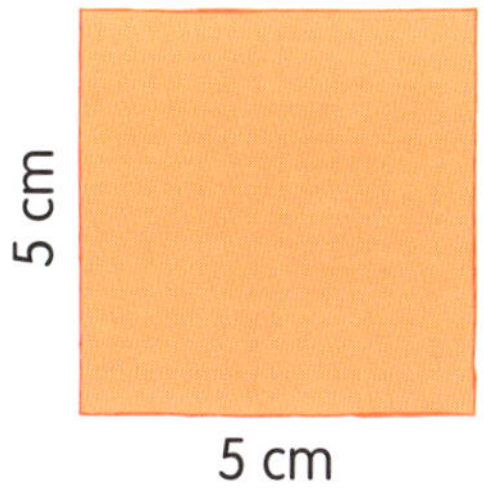

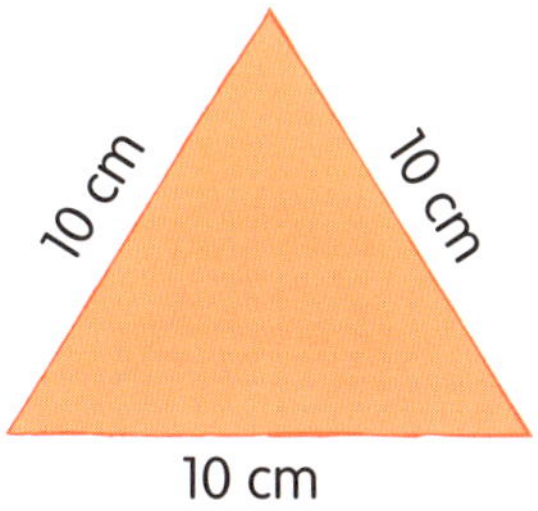

a Perimeter = 20 cm

5 cm + 5 cm + 5 cm + 5 cm = 20 cm

b Perimeter = ___ cm

___ cm + ___ cm + ___ cm = ___ cm

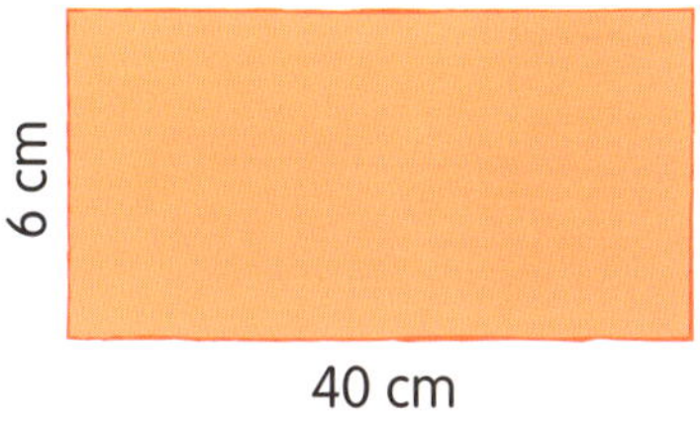

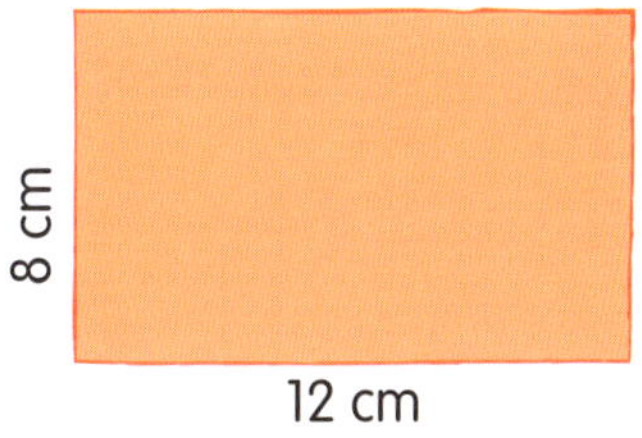

c Perimeter = ___ cm

___ cm + ___ cm + ___ cm + ___ cm = ___ cm

d Perimeter = ___ cm

___ cm + ___ cm + ___ cm + ___ cm = ___ cm

3 A forest is rectangular, with a perimeter of 24 m. Fill in all the possible dimensions of the forest.

a Length = 1 m Width = 11 m

b Length = ___ m Width = ___ m

c Length = ___ m Width = ___ m

d Length = ___ m Width = ___ m

e Length = ___ m Width = ___ m

f Length = ___ m Width = ___ m

g Length = ___ m Width = ___ m

h Length = ___ m Width = ___ m

i Length = ___ m Width = ___ m

j Length = ___ m Width = ___ m

k Length = ___ m Width = ___ m

Pages 164-165

Area

The amount of space enclosed inside a 2D shape is called its area. We can measure area using units called square units – these are based on the units we use for length.

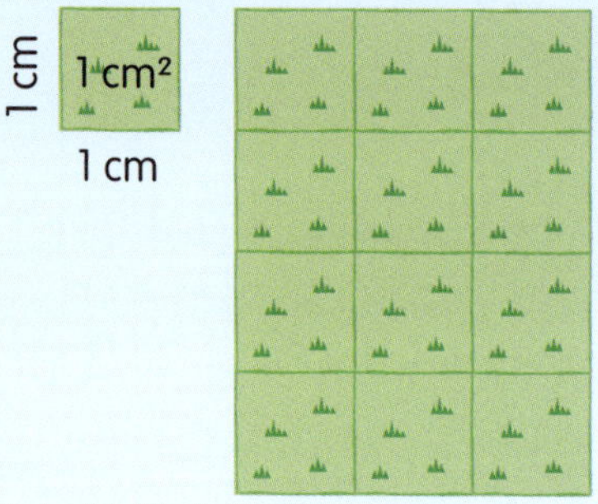

Area = 12 cm²

REMEMBER!
We can find the area of a shape by dividing it into square units, then counting the number of squares.

Warm-up Count the squares, then fill in the area of each shape. Each square has a side length of 1 cm.

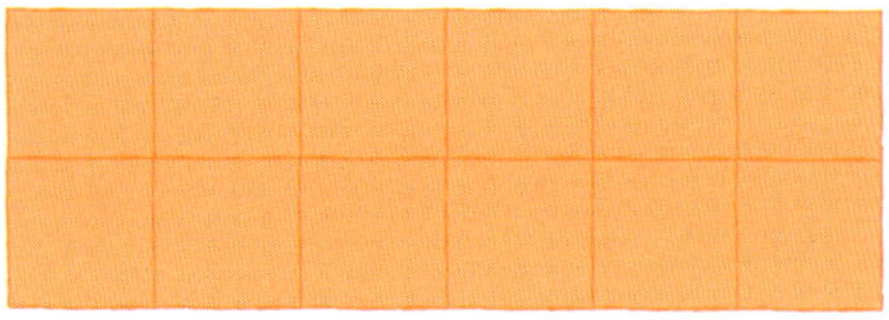

1 Area = 12 cm²

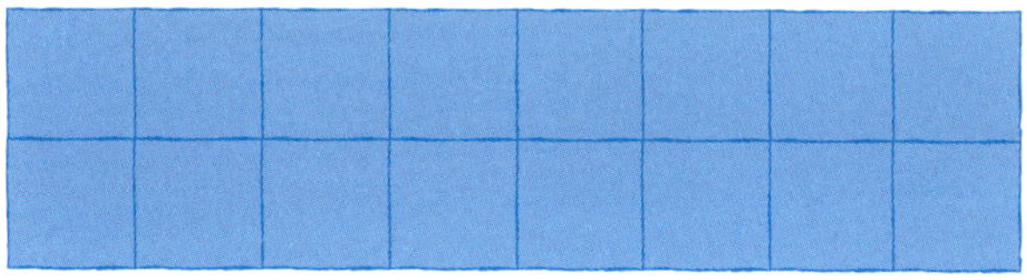

2 Area = ___ cm²

3 Area = ___ cm²

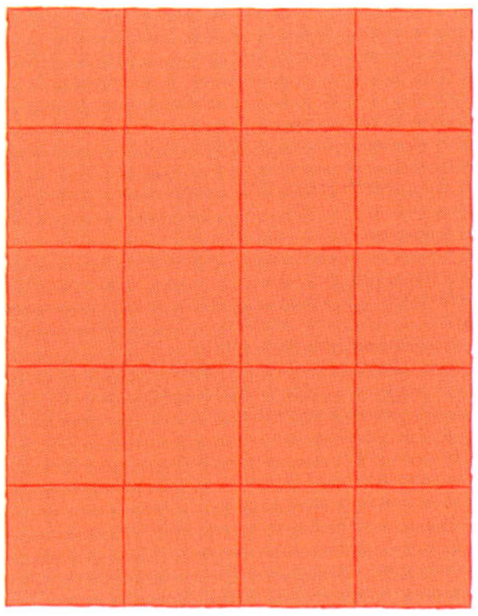

4 Area = ___ cm²

1 Count the squares in these unusual shapes to work out their areas. Each square has a side length of 1 cm.

a Area = 10 cm²

b Area = ___ cm²

c Area = ___ cm²

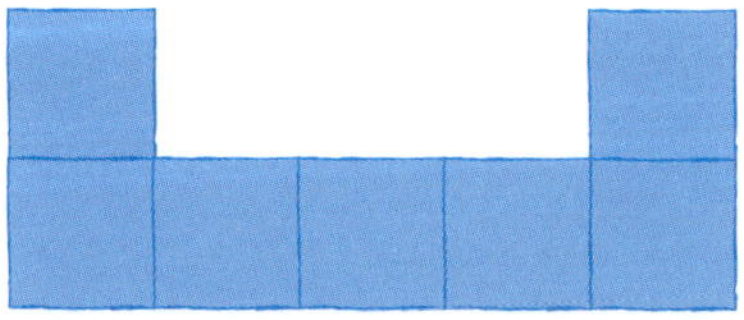

d Area = ___ cm²

e Area = ___ cm²

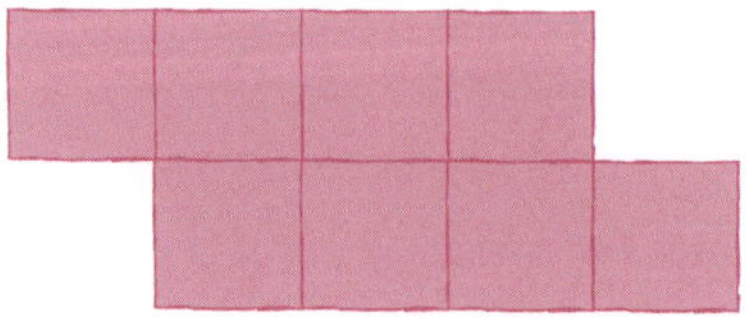

f Area = ___ cm²

2

Here are some designs for kitchen tiles. Add up the number of tiles of each colour.

a
Blue tiles: 4 squares
Red tiles: 6 squares
White tiles: 8 squares

b
Blue tiles: ___ squares
Red tiles: ___ squares
White tiles: ___ squares

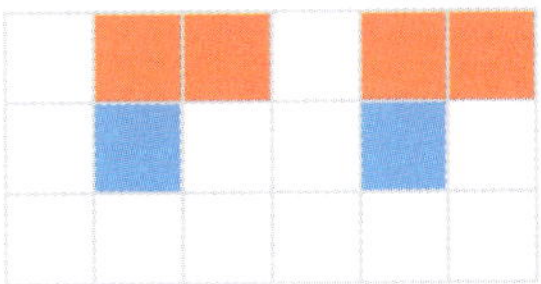

c
Blue tiles: ___ squares
Red tiles: ___ squares
White tiles: ___ squares

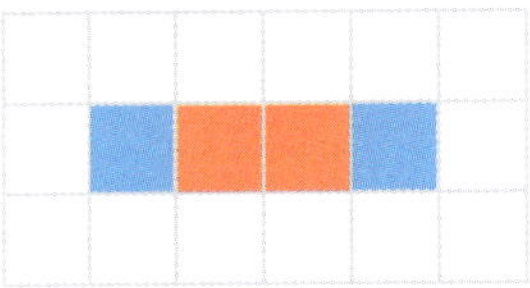

d
Blue tiles: ___ squares
Red tiles: ___ squares
White tiles: ___ squares

e
Blue tiles: ___ squares
Red tiles: ___ squares
White tiles: ___ squares

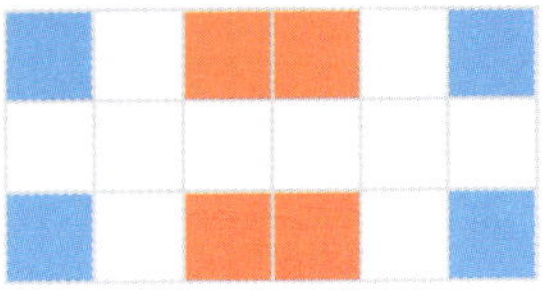

f
Blue tiles: ___ squares
Red tiles: ___ squares
White tiles: ___ squares

3

Draw a different shape in each grid below. Each square in the grids measures 1 cm². Give each shape an area of 6 cm².

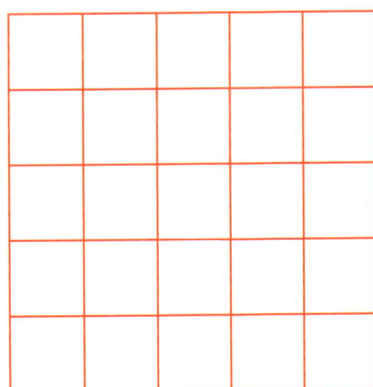

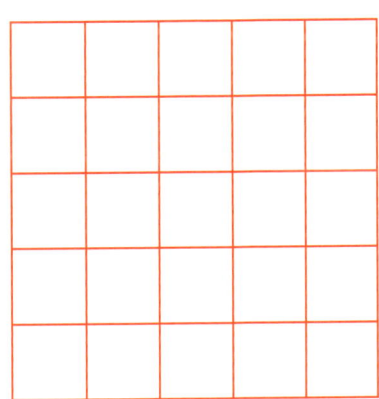

a

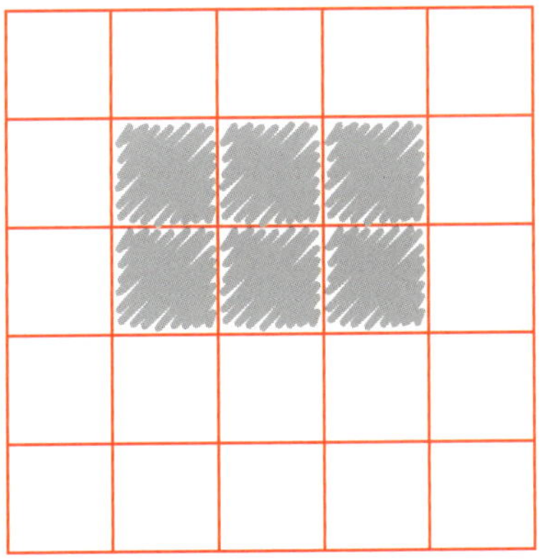

b

c

d

e

f

Page 168

Estimating area

Finding the areas of shapes that are not squares or rectangles may seem tricky. But we can draw a grid, then combine the number of completely full squares and partly full squares to estimate the area.

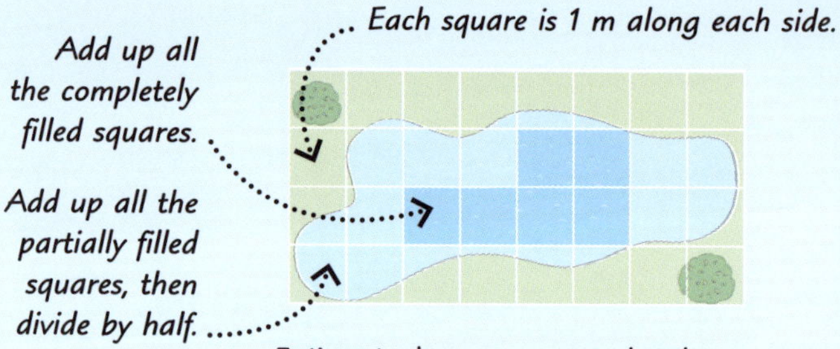
Each square is 1 m along each side.
Add up all the completely filled squares.
Add up all the partially filled squares, then divide by half.

Estimated area = completely + half the partially filled squares = 16 m².

Warm-up Estimate the area of these ponds. Each square is 1 m².

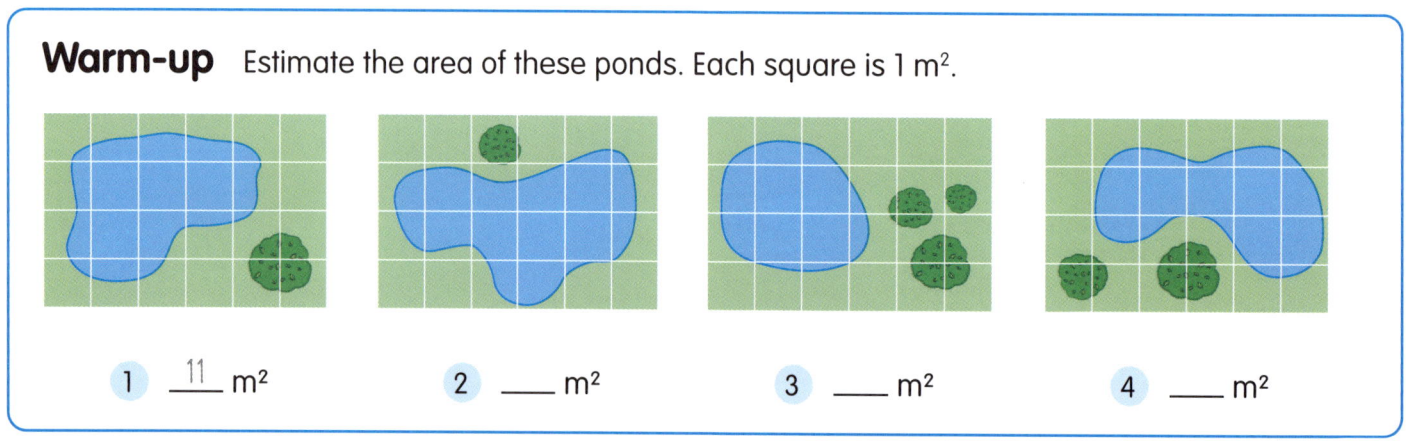

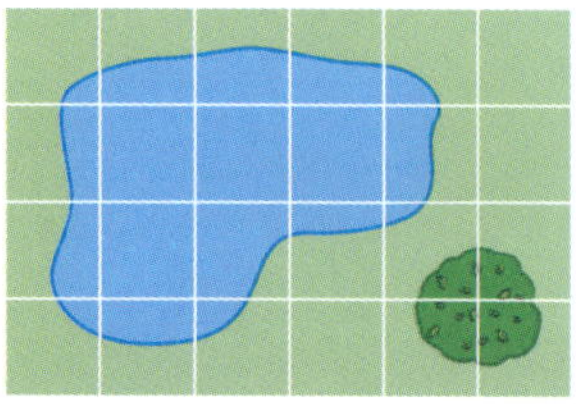
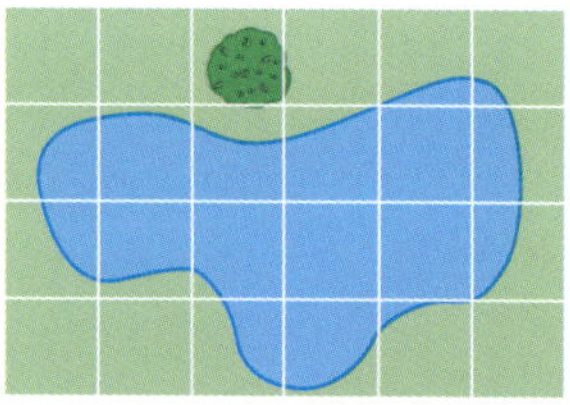
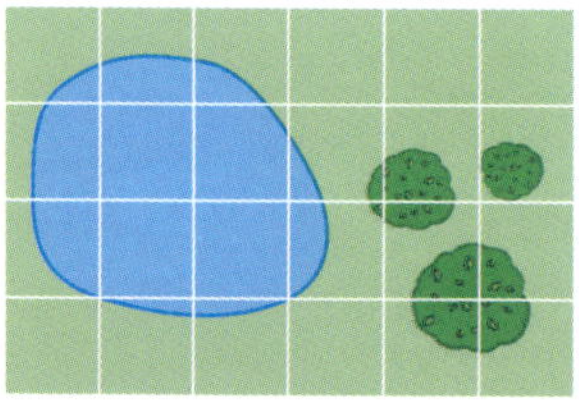
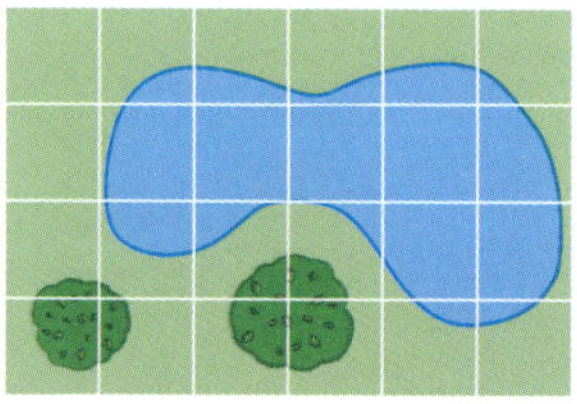

1 __11__ m²   2 ____ m²   3 ____ m²   4 ____ m²

1 Estimate the areas of these rectangles.
Each square is 1 cm².

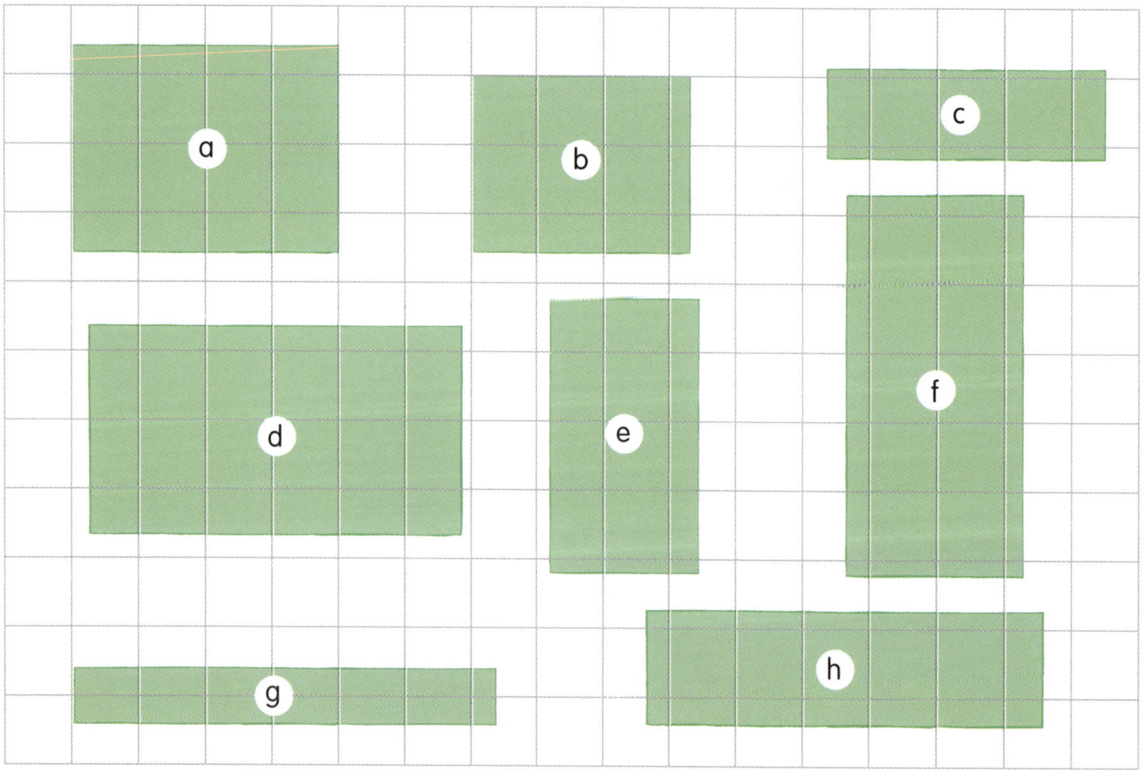
a
b
c
d
e
f
g
h

a = __12__ cm²
b = ____ cm²
c = ____ cm²
d = ____ cm²
e = ____ cm²
f = ____ cm²
g = ____ cm²
h = ____ cm²

2 Draw paint splodges on the grids below to match the areas given. Each square is 1 cm^2. Your splodges must not have straight edges.

a Estimated area of paint splodge = 20 cm^2

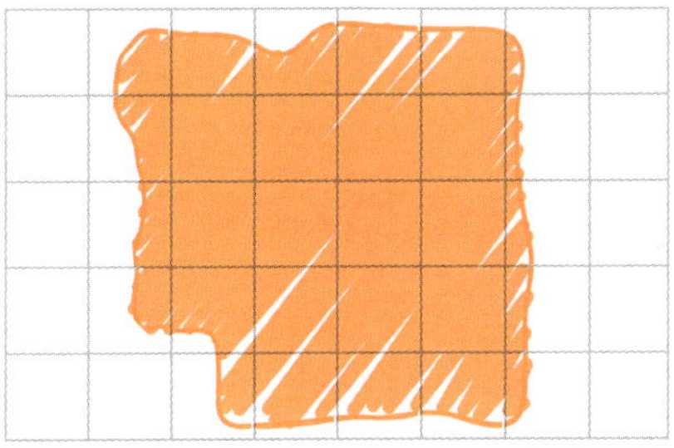

b Estimated area of paint splodge = 19 cm^2

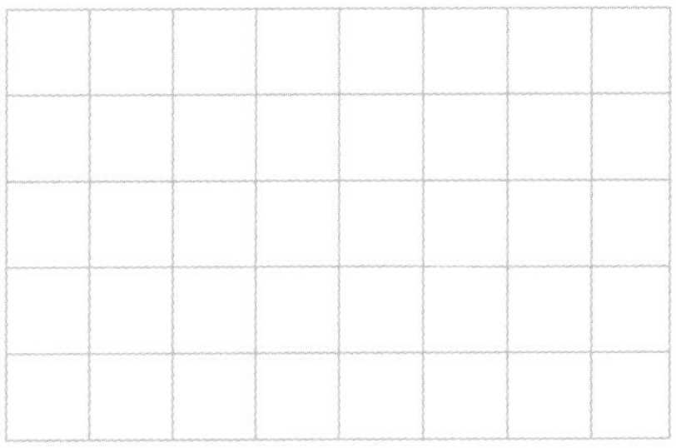

c Estimated area of paint splodge = 28 cm^2

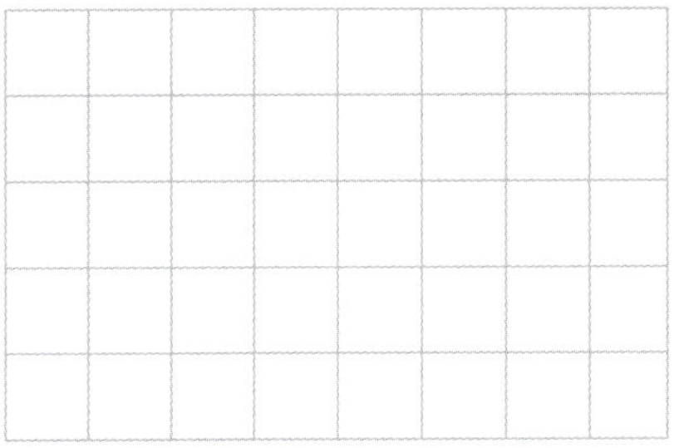

d Estimated area of paint splodge = 13 cm^2

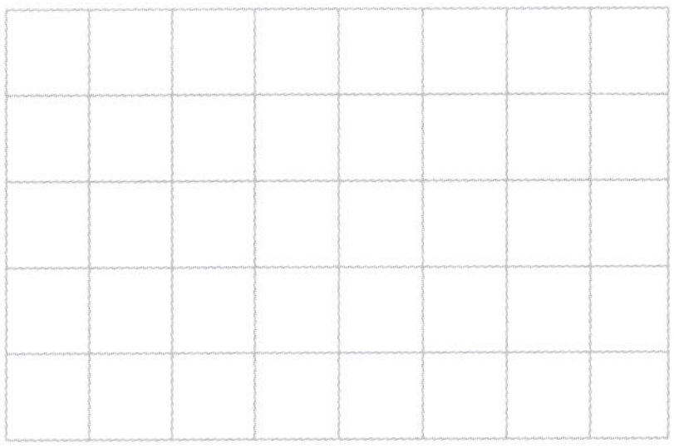

3 Estimate the areas of these craters. Each square is 1 m^2.

a Estimated area of crater = 14 m^2

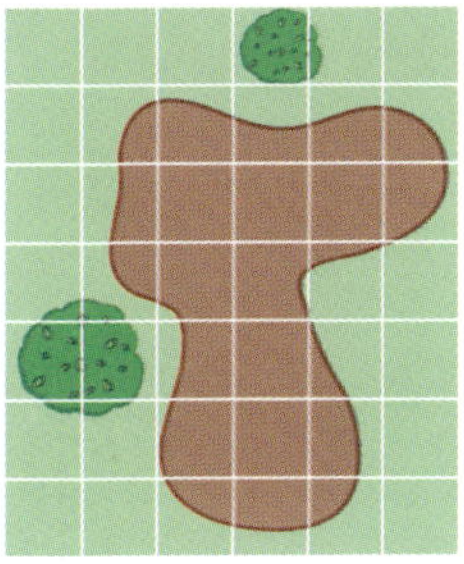

b Estimated area of crater = ______ m^2

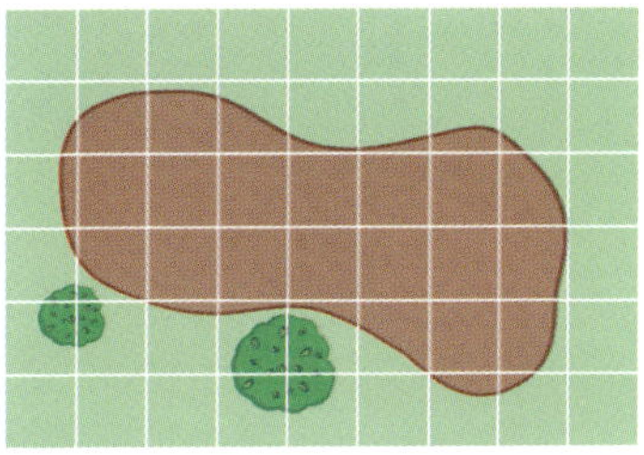

c Estimated area of crater = ______ m^2

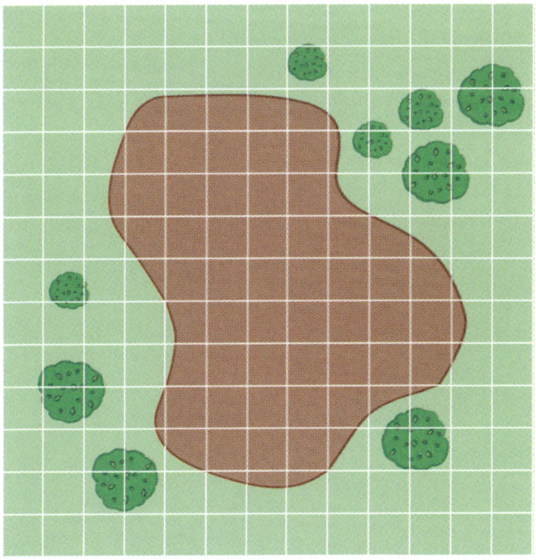

d Estimated area of crater = ______ m^2

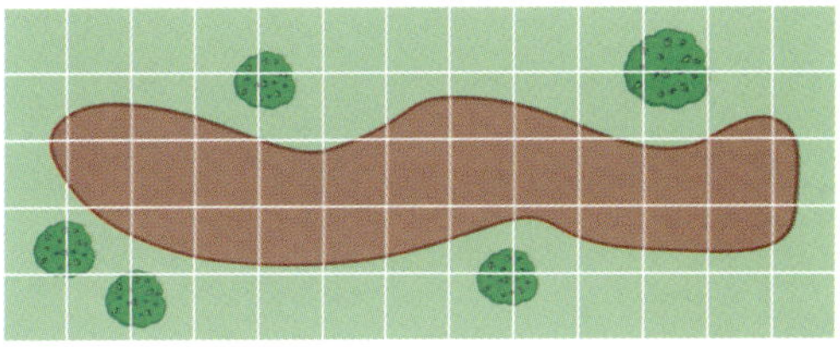

Page 169

Capacity

Capacity is the amount of space inside a shape or container. It can be used to describe how much liquid a container can hold.

Warm-up Two of the units used to measure capacity are millilitres (ml) and litres. Write the capacity of each object below.

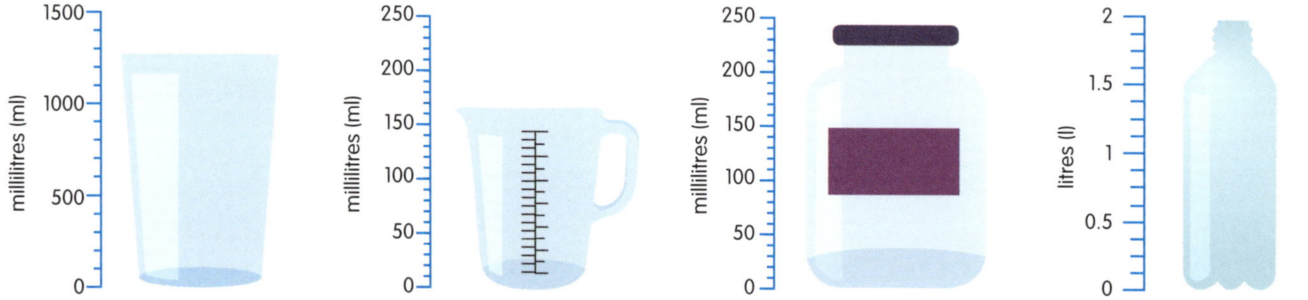

1 1250 ml   2 ______ ml   3 ______ ml   4 ______ litres

1 Look at these containers and think about what their capacity might be. Then label them from 1 to 6, with 1 being the object with the smallest capacity.

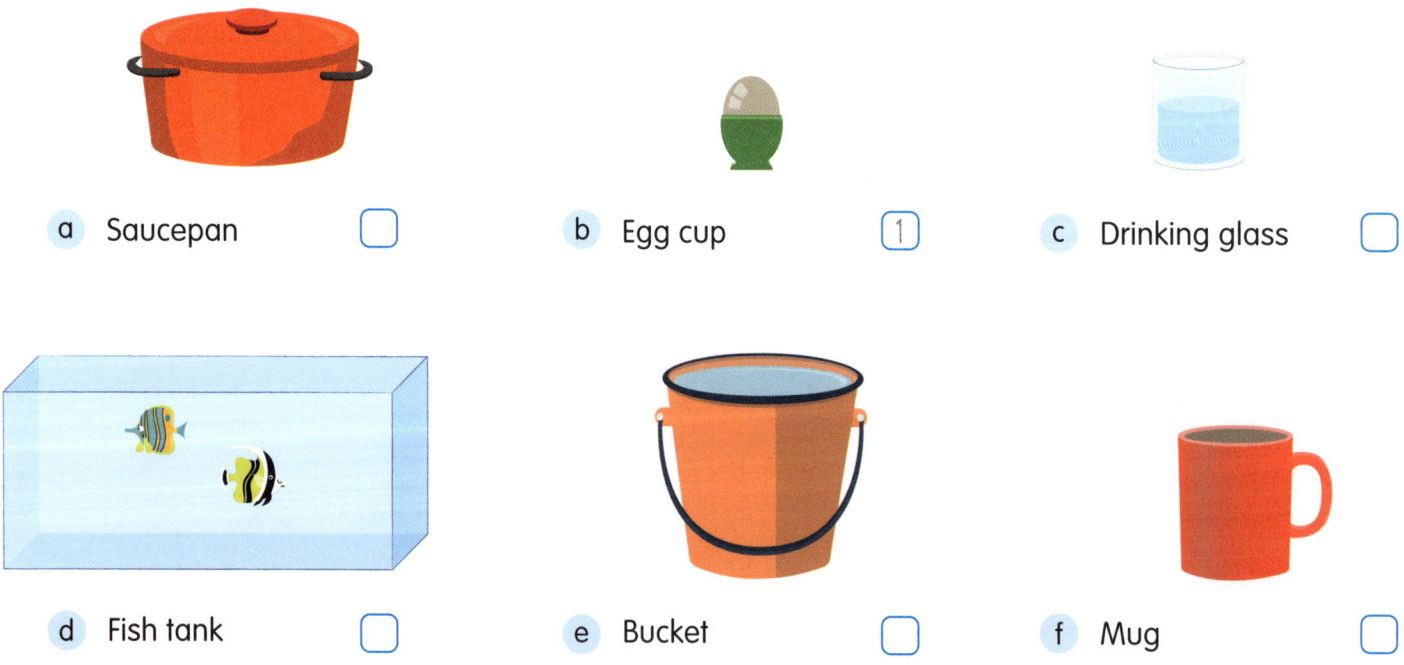

a Saucepan ☐

b Egg cup 1

c Drinking glass ☐

d Fish tank ☐

e Bucket ☐

f Mug ☐

Page 178

Volume

Volume is a measure of how big something is in three dimensions. Adding and subtracting liquid volumes works just like other calculations.

REMEMBER!
We measure liquid volume in millilitres (ml) or litres, just like capacity.
1 litre = 1000 ml.

Warm-up How much liquid is in each container?

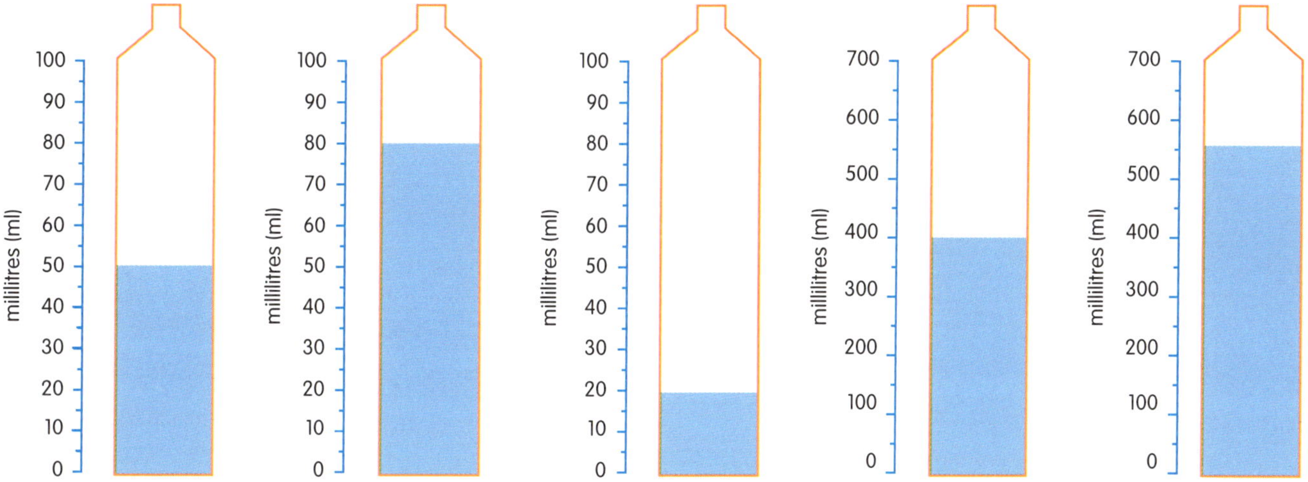

1 __50__ ml 2 ______ ml 3 ______ ml 4 ______ ml 5 ______ ml

1

Draw a line on each container to show where the liquid will come to.

a 700 ml b 450 ml c 325 ml

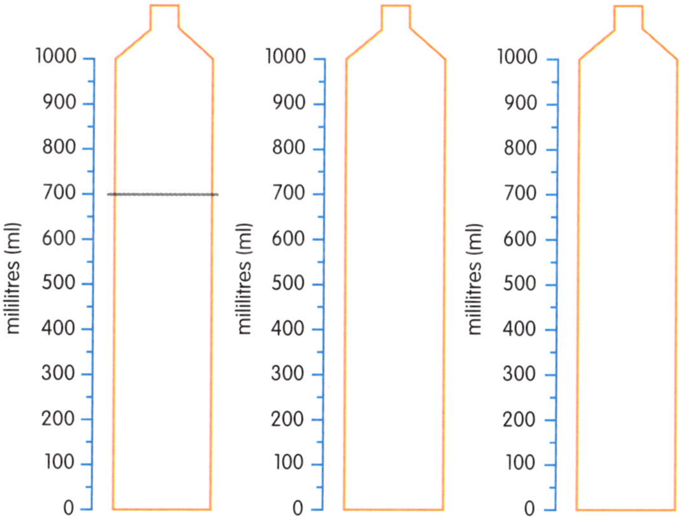

MATHS IN CONTEXT

Recipe measurements

Zak needs to measure out 60 ml of lemon juice for a recipe. He has a teaspoon that holds 5 ml and a tablespoon that holds 15 ml. He needs to use a combination of teaspoon and tablespoon volumes to make up the 60 ml he needs.

Work out five different combinations that Zak could use to measure 60 ml of lemon juice.

1. __12__ teaspoons and __0__ tablespoons
2. ____ teaspoons and ____ tablespoons
3. ____ teaspoons and ____ tablespoons
4. ____ teaspoons and ____ tablespoons
5. ____ teaspoons and ____ tablespoons

Page 179

Mass

Mass is the amount of matter contained inside an object. We measure mass in metric units called milligrams (mg), grams (g), kilograms (kg), and tonnes.

REMEMBER!
There are 1000 mg in 1 g, 1000 g in 1 kg, and 1000 kg in 1 tonne.

Warm-up Fill in the mass of each of these objects.

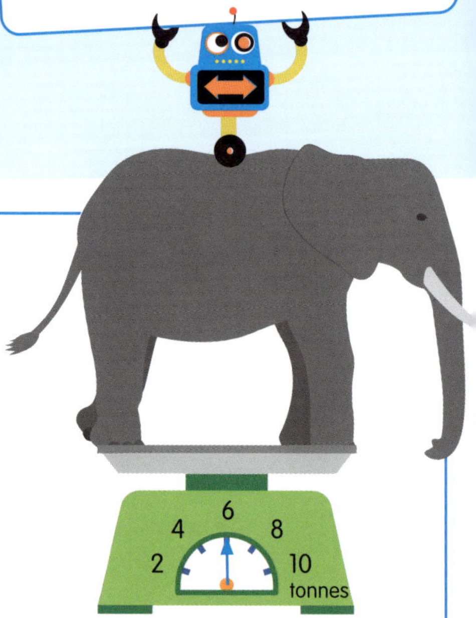

1 Mass = 150 g
2 Mass = ____ g
3 Mass = ____ kg
4 Mass = ____ tonnes

1

Number each set of objects from 1 to 5, with 1 being the object with the smallest mass.

a
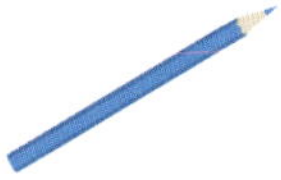 1
 5
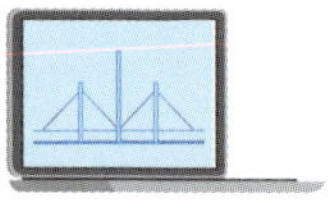 3
 2
 4

b
 ____
 ____
 ____
 ____
 ____

c
 ____
 ____
 ____
 ____
 ____

d
 ____
 ____
 ____
 ____
 ____

2 Draw lines to match each item with the label showing its estimated mass.

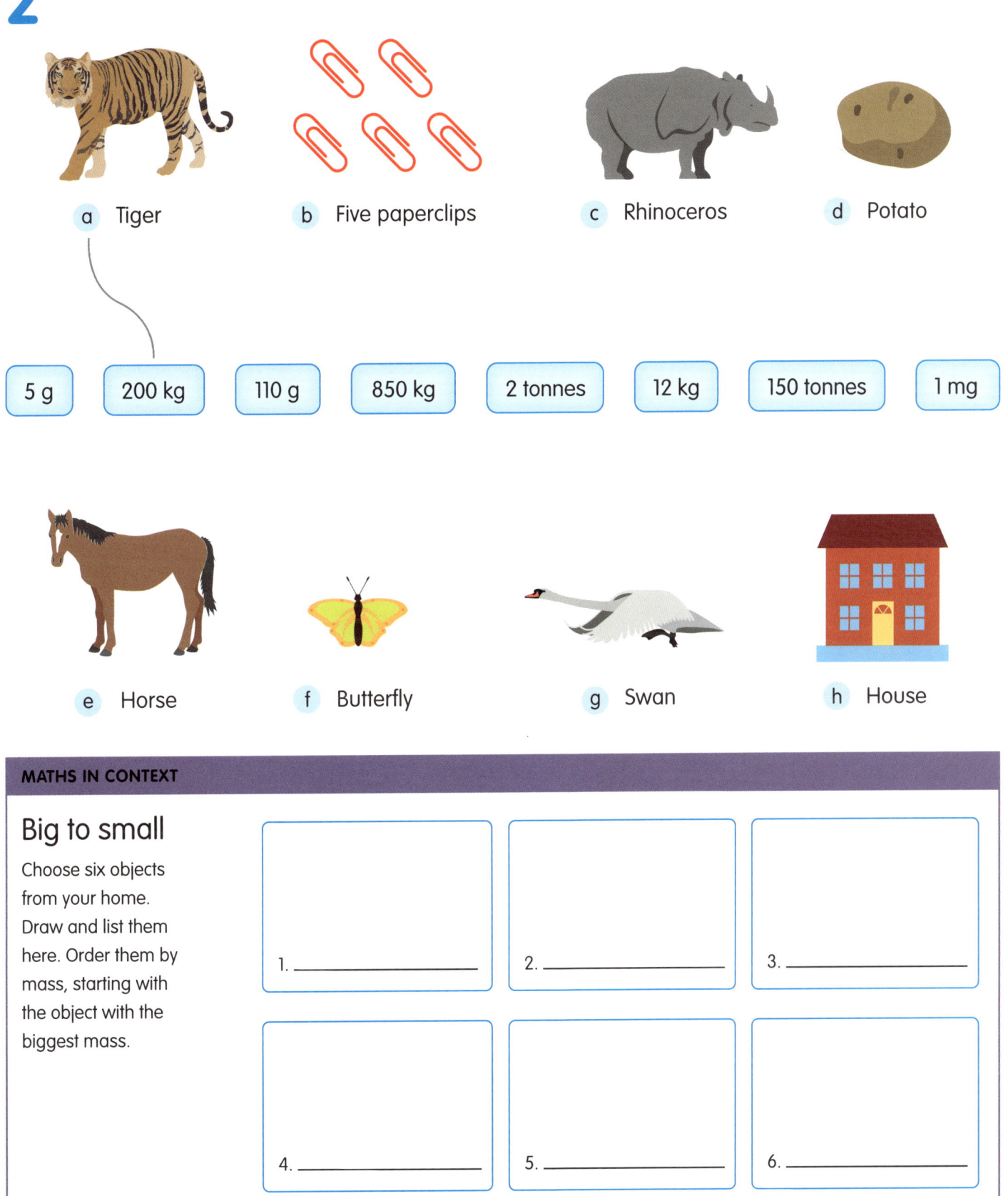

a Tiger

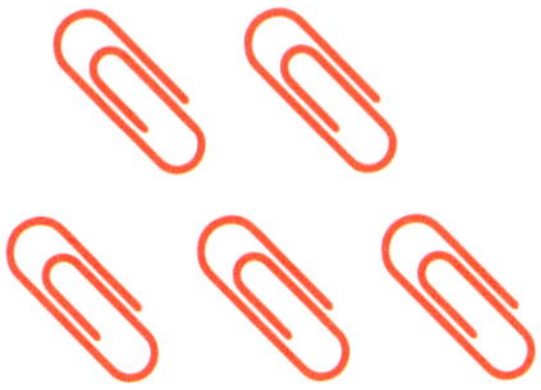

b Five paperclips

c Rhinoceros

d Potato

5 g	200 kg	110 g	850 kg	2 tonnes	12 kg	150 tonnes	1 mg

e Horse

f Butterfly

g Swan

h House

MATHS IN CONTEXT

Big to small

Choose six objects from your home. Draw and list them here. Order them by mass, starting with the object with the biggest mass.

1. ____________________

2. ____________________

3. ____________________

4. ____________________

5. ____________________

6. ____________________

Page 182

Calculating with mass

We can calculate with mass in the same way that we do with other measurements. As long as the masses are in the same units, we can simply add, subtract, multiply, or divide them.

Warm-up Mike is a chef, and is preparing meals for the week for his café. Look at his lists below and calculate the total mass of ingredients for each day's meals.

Monday	
potatoes	11 kg
chicken	20 kg
peas	2 kg
carrots	3 kg

Tuesday	
pasta	10 kg
cheese	5 kg
tomatoes	3 kg
onions	2 kg

Wednesday	
fish fingers	12 kg
chips	13 kg
broccoli	2 kg
sauce	1 kg

Thursday	
bread	6 kg
tuna	12 kg
mayonnaise	2 kg
lettuce	2 kg

Friday	
potatoes	20 kg
baked beans	5 kg
cheese	8 kg
tuna	6 kg

11 + 20 + 2 + 3 ______ ______ ______ ______

1 = 36 kg 2 = ____ kg 3 = ____ kg 4 = ____ kg 5 = ____ kg

1 Use the pictures below to help you complete these sentences about mass.

3 kg

1 g

12 g

445 g

8 kg

2 kg

a The total mass of the cat and the flower is

3000 + 12 = 3012 g.

b The total mass of the butterfly, the flower, and the milk carton is

____________ = ______ g.

c The difference between the mass of the bicycle and the butterfly is

____________ = ______ g.

d The mass of all 6 objects is

____________ = ______ kg.

2 Use the key to help you draw the weights needed to balance the scales for each object or set of objects shown below.

Key 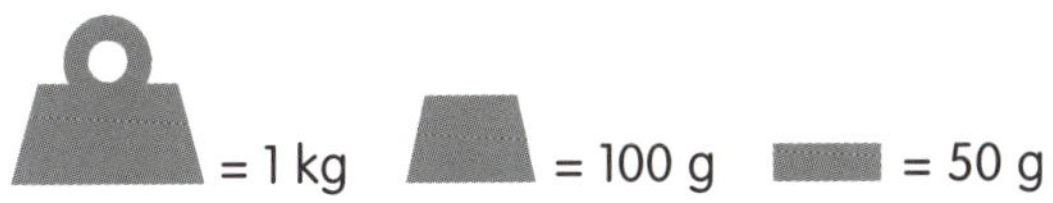

a 

b 

c 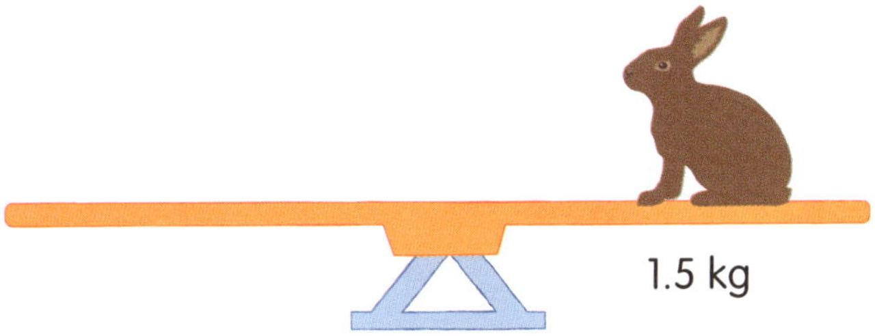

d 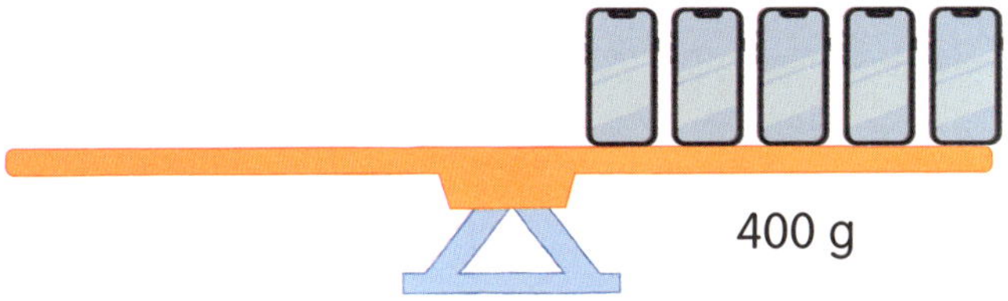

e 

f 

3 Calculate the combined mass of the weights shown in each pair below.

a Total mass = 3100 g

b Total mass = ______ g

c Total mass = ______ g

d Total mass = ______ g

Pages 184–185

Telling the time

We measure time so that we can organize our lives. We use seconds, minutes, hours, days, weeks, months, and years to measure time, and we read the time using clocks.

Both these clocks show half past 9.

Warm-up Write down the time shown on each of these clocks.

1 The time is 7 o'clock

2 The time is ______

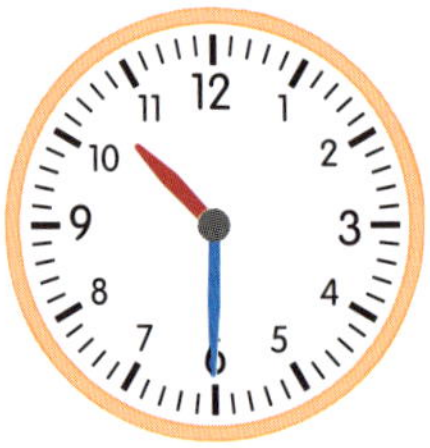

3 The time is ______

4 The time is ______

5 The time is ______

1 Draw lines to match each clock face with the correct time.

a 

b 

c 

quarter to 1

quarter past 1

quarter to 7

quarter past 8

quarter past 7

quarter to 8

d 

e 

f 

2 Draw hands on these analogue clocks to make them match the times given on the digital clocks.

a  18:30

b  08:10

c  21:40

d  19:25

e  10:35

f  11:55

3 Order these clocks by the time they show, starting with the one that shows the earliest time in the day.

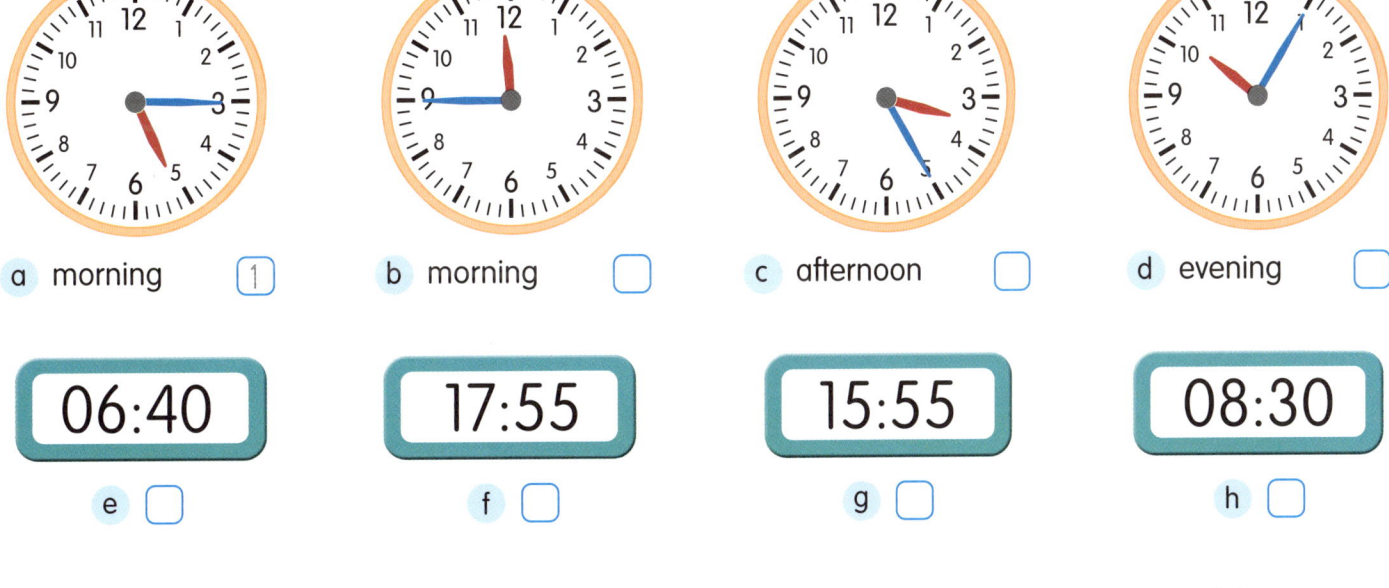

a morning [1]

b morning [ ]

c afternoon [ ]

d evening [ ]

06:40

e [ ]

17:55

f [ ]

15:55

g [ ]

08:30

h [ ]

Pages 192–193

Calculating with time

You can add, subtract, multiply, or divide any amount of time. As with other measurements, you just need to make sure that the numbers are in the same units.

REMEMBER!
There are 60 minutes in 1 hour, and 60 seconds in 1 minute.

Warm-up

Use the number line to help you work out the differences between these times.

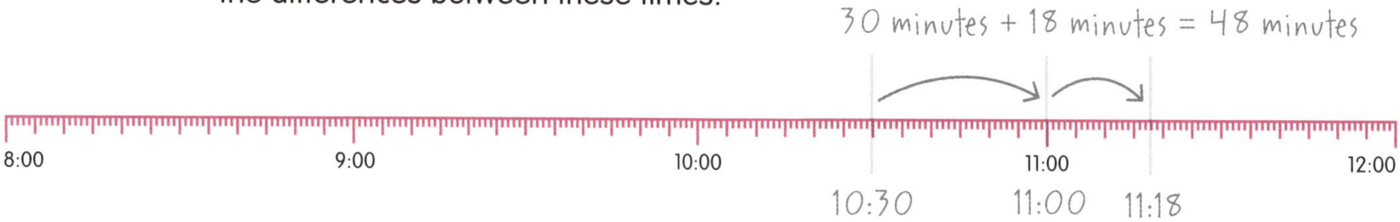

1. 10:30 and 11:18 = 48 minutes
2. 8:35 and 9:45 = _____ minutes
3. 9:45 and 10:35 = _____ minutes
4. 10:30 and 11:55 = _____ minutes
5. 8:50 and 9:35 = _____ minutes
6. 8:40 and 10:00 = _____ minutes

1 These clocks show when children leave home and when they arrive at school. Fill in how long each child's journey to school takes.

Child	Left home	Arrived at school	Journey time
a Mia			20 minutes
c Evie			_____ minutes
e Abbas			_____ minutes

Child	Left home	Arrived at school	Journey time
b Kaya			_____ minutes
d Josh			_____ minutes
f Tam			_____ minutes

2 Work out what the new time will be for each of these questions below.

a The time is: **08:45**

35 minutes pass. The new time is: 09:20

b The time is: **09:20**

45 minutes pass. The new time is: __ : __

c The time is: **10:55**

55 minutes pass. The new time is: __ : __

d The time is: **15:45**

1 hour and 10 minutes pass. The new time is: __ : __

e The time is: **17:55**

2 hours and 25 minutes pass. The new time is: __ : __

f The time is: **20:05**

3 hours and 34 minutes pass. The new time is: __ : __

g The time is: **21:12**

36 minutes pass. The new time is: __ : __

h The time is: **22:13**

1 hour and 26 minutes pass. The new time is: __ : __

MATHS IN CONTEXT

Gemma's day

1. Gemma woke up at 6:30am and she ate breakfast 1 hour 10 minutes later. What time did she eat breakfast?

7 : 4 0 am

2. Gemma left for school at 8:20am and arrived at 8:45 am. How long did her journey take? ______ minutes

3. Gemma started school at 8:55am and had a morning break at 10:45am. How many minutes were there between the start of school and morning break? ______ minutes

4. Gemma's afternoon lessons started at 1:05pm and lasted for 2 hours 15 minutes. What time did her afternoon lessons finish?

__ : __ __ pm

5. Gemma started her homework at 4:05pm and it took her 45 minutes. What time did she finish her homework?

__ : __ __ pm

Pages 196–197

Dates

We measure time in seconds, minutes, and hours. For periods of time that are longer than 24 hours, we can also measure time in units called days, weeks, months, and years.

REMEMBER!
Every four years we have a leap year. A leap year has one more day than a non-leap year.

Warm-up Use the numbers in the box below to help you complete these sentences.

52 365 ~~7~~ 12 28 366 31

1 There are __7__ days in a week and ______ days in a year that is not a leap year.

2 In a leap year, there are ______ days.

3 There are ______ weeks in a year.

4 There are ______ months in a year, and between ______ and ______ days in a month.

1 Use the words in the word box to help you complete the charts showing how many days there are in each month.

~~January~~ February March April May June July
August September October November December

a **28 days**
(29 days in a leap year)

______

______

______

______

______

______

b **30 days**

______

______

______

______

______

______

c **31 days**

January

______

______

______

______

______

2 Use the calendar to help you answer the questions below.

July

M	T	W	T	F	S	S
				1	2	3
4	5	6	7	8	9	10
11	12	13	14	15	16	17
18	19	20	21	22	23	24
25	26	27	28	29	30	31

a How many days are there in July? 31

b What day of the week is 22 July? ______

c How many Saturdays are there in July? ______

d What day of the week is 13 July? ______

e What day of the week is 30 June? ______

f How many Thursdays are there in July? ______

g What day of the week is 1 August? ______

h What day of the week is 27 June? ______

3 Draw lines to match each statement with the correct month. Some statements have two answers, and some answers may be used more than once.

a This month has the fewest number of days.

b This month is in summer.

c This month is in autumn.

d These months have the most days.

e These months have 30 days.

October

February

January

June

April

MATHS IN CONTEXT

Nadia's school holidays

Use this information about Nadia's school holidays to help you answer the questions.

Nadia's December school holiday lasts 3 weeks. Her summer holiday lasts 8 weeks. She has 14 days off in May. Nadia will attend primary school for 7 years.

1. How many days is she off school in December? 21
2. How many days is she off school in the summer? ______
3. How many weeks is she off in May? ______
4. How many months is she at her primary school? ______

Pages 194–195

Money

Understanding money lets us work out how much something costs, and how much change we should get in a shop. Different countries use different currencies (systems of money). In the UK, we use pounds (£) and pence (p).

REMEMBER!
100 pence is the same as 1 pound. We can say that £1 = 100p.

Warm-up Order these items by price by writing the numbers 1 to 5 in the boxes, with 1 being the cheapest.

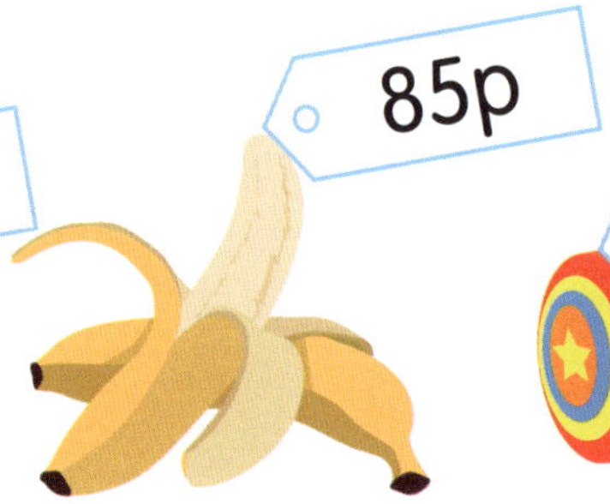

1 ☐ 2 ☐ 1 3 ☐ 4 ☐ 5 ☐

1

Calculate the total cost of each person's shopping.

a Jimmy bought 2 cupcakes and an avocado. £1.65 + £1.65 + 65p = £3.95

b Shareen bought a pumpkin and some cookies. ____________

c Eric bought some flowers and a cupcake. ____________

d Ali bought 3 pumpkins and 3 avocados. ____________

2 Compare the prices of these pairs of items by writing less than (<), greater than (>), or equal to (=).

a   £1.78   < £2.05

b   £5.03   ☐ £5.13

c   £0.98   ☐ 65p

d   £3.05   ☐ 205p

e   255p   ☐ £2.55

f   £10.50 ☐ 105p

3 Fill in the missing values in the tables below.

Pence (p)	Pounds (£)
450p	a £4.50
b _____	£3.05
825p	c _____
d _____	£3.25
e _____	£5.60
1250p	f _____
g _____	£10.60
h _____	£12.00
i _____	£2.86
601p	j _____
k _____	£1.94
1761p	l _____
287p	m _____
n _____	£18.19

4 Draw lines to match each value on the left with an equivalent total on the right.

a   £6.65   £4.30 + £5.11 + 60p

b   £10.01   £3 + 80p + 40p

c   £4.20   £2 + £3 + £1.65

📖 Page 198

Using money

In the UK, our money is made up of eight different coins: 1p, 2p, 5p, 10p, 20p, 50p, £1, and £2. We also use four different notes: £5, £10, £20, and £50. We can combine these coins and notes to make any amount of money we like.

Warm-up Add up the coins shown below and fill in the totals.

1  = 92p

2  = ______

3  = ______

4 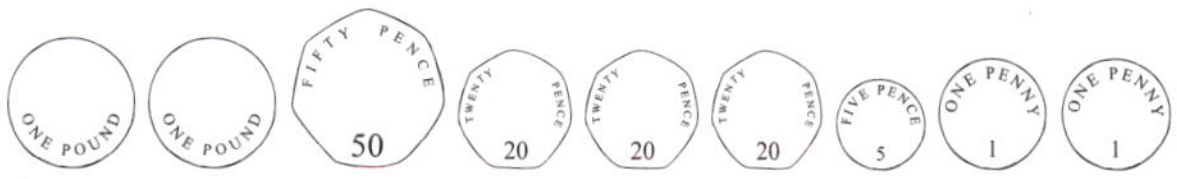 = ______

1

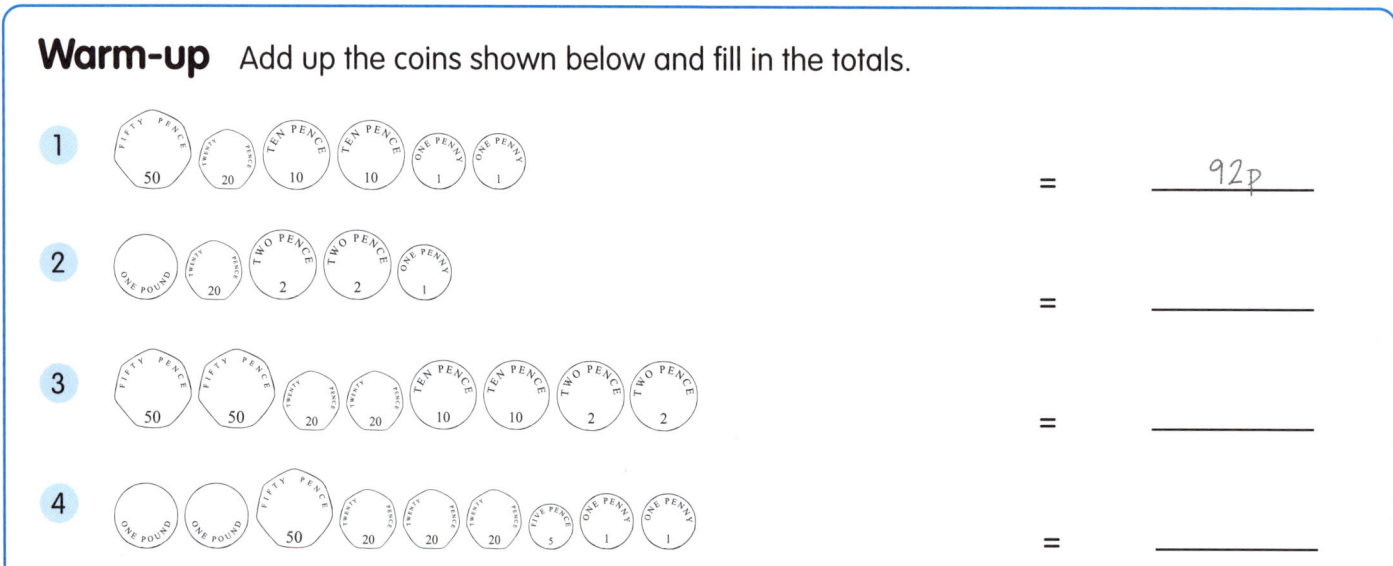

Draw lines to match each set of coins and notes with the correct total.

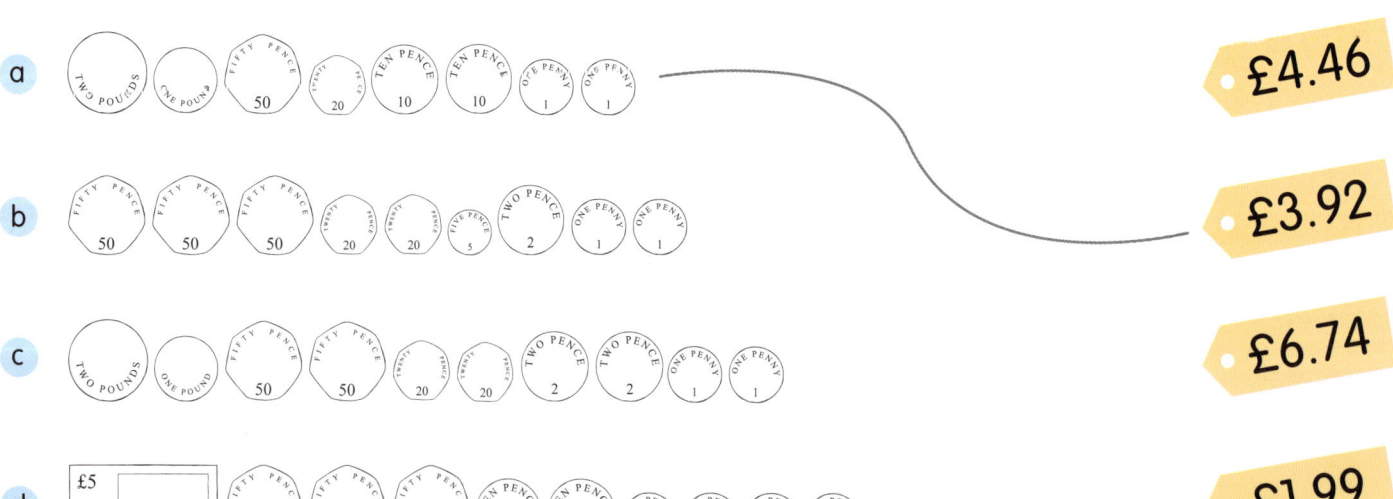

a 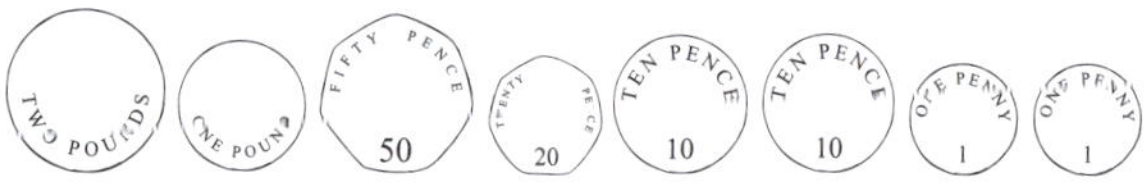

b 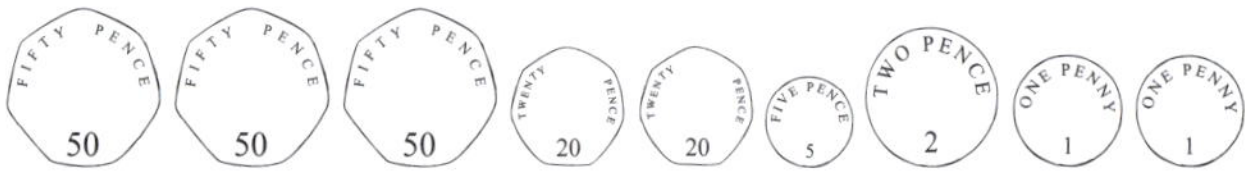

c 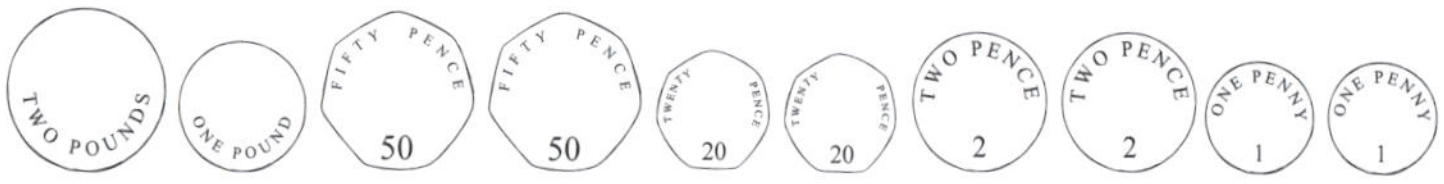

d 

£4.46

£3.92

£6.74

£1.99

2 Work out what each child has saved by adding up their coins and notes, then compare the total amounts by writing less than (<), greater than (>), or equal to (=).

a 

<

b 

☐

c 

☐

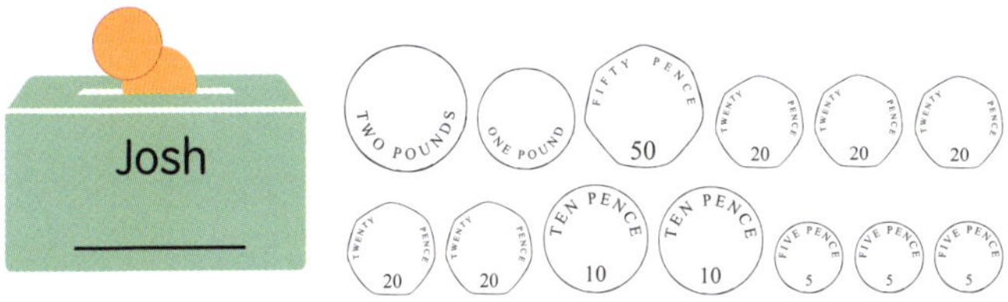

d 

☐

MATHS IN CONTEXT

Combine the coins

Tamara has £2.52 in her purse. She has fewer than 10 coins. Draw or write three combinations of coins that Tamara could have to make the total £2.52.

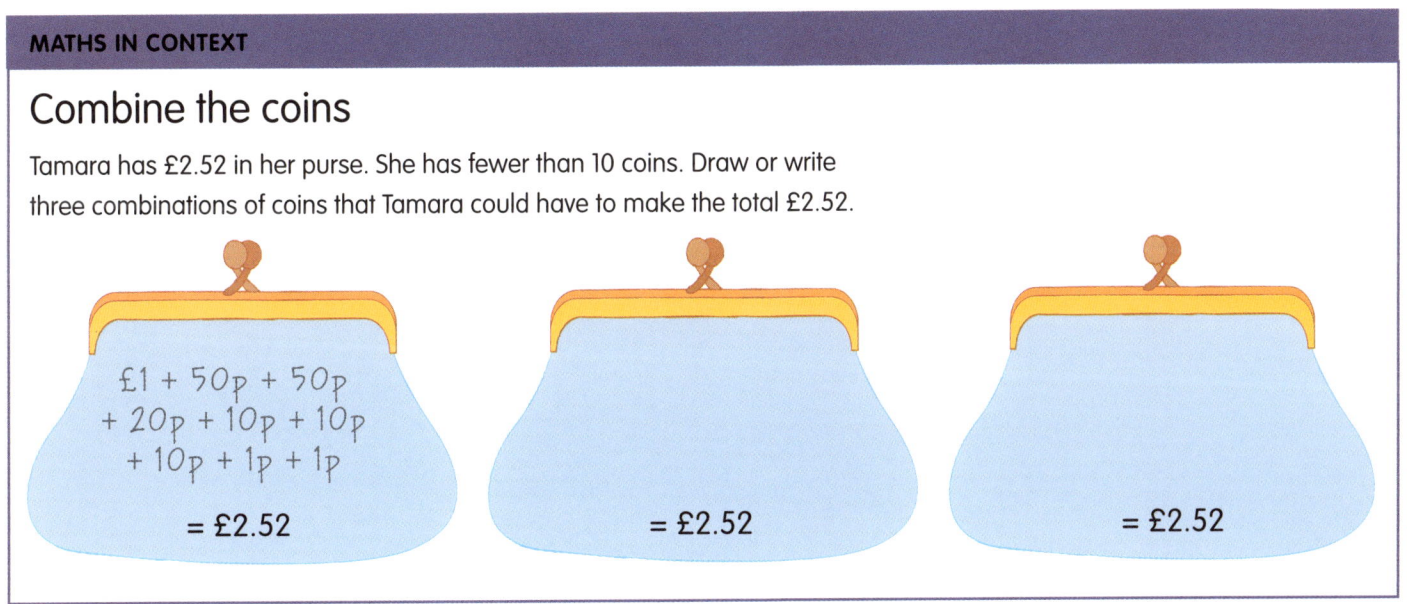

Page 199

What is a line?

A line joins two points together. In geometry, lines can be either straight or curved.
A line has a length that can be measured.

REMEMBER!
Lines are one-dimensional. They have length but no thickness.

Warm-up Measure the lengths of these lines. You can use a piece of string to help you measure the curved lines.

1 length = 6 cm

2 length = ___ cm

3 length = ___ cm

4 length = ___ cm

1

Measure these pairs of lines and fill in which is the longest in each pair.

a The ___red___ line is the longest.

b The ________ line is the longest.

c The ________ line is the longest.

d The ________ line is the longest.

e The ________ line is the longest.

f The ________ line is the longest.

Page 204

Horizontal and vertical lines

A line joins two points together. Horizontal lines go from side to side – they are level like the horizon. Vertical lines go straight up and down, like lamp posts or walls.

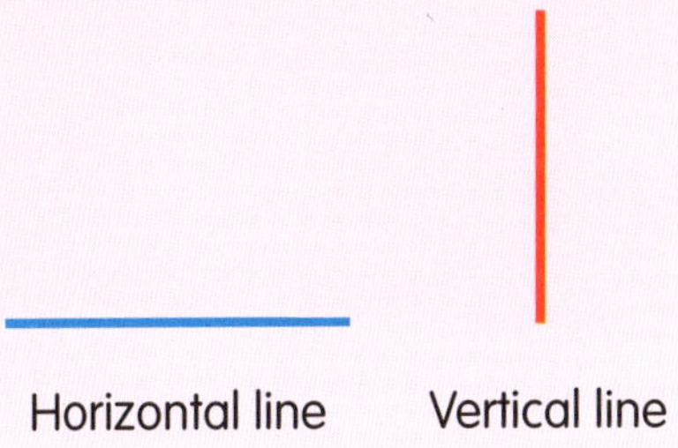

Warm-up

1 Draw in the five missing horizontal lines in blue.

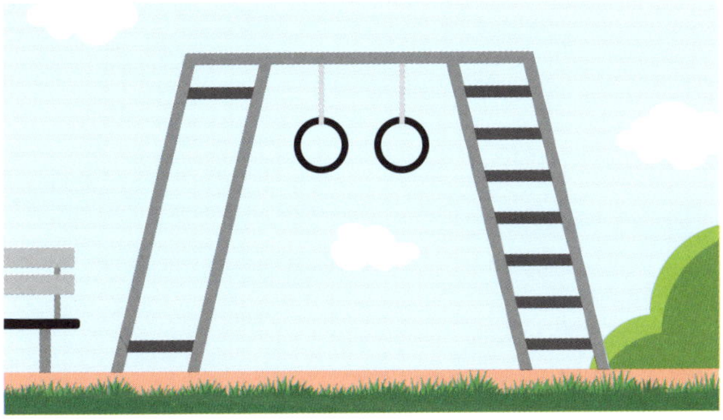

2 Draw in the five missing vertical lines in red.

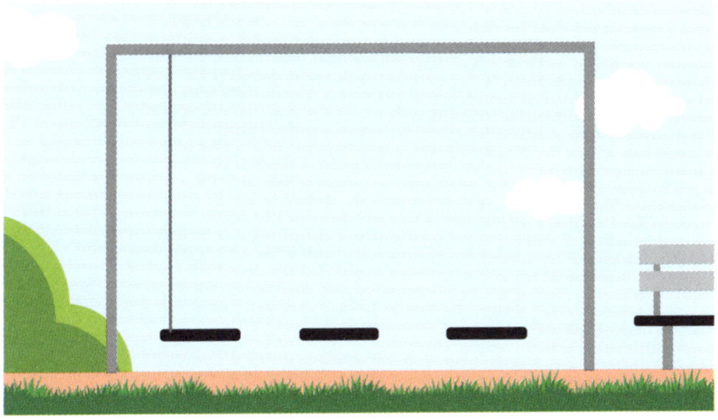

1 Look at the picture below. Draw over the horizontal lines in blue and the vertical lines in red.

Now count the number of horizonal and vertical lines.

There are _____ horizontal lines and _____ vertical lines.

Page 205

Diagonal lines

A diagonal line is neither vertical nor horizontal. Instead, it is a straight line that slants up or down. Another name for a diagonal line is an oblique line.

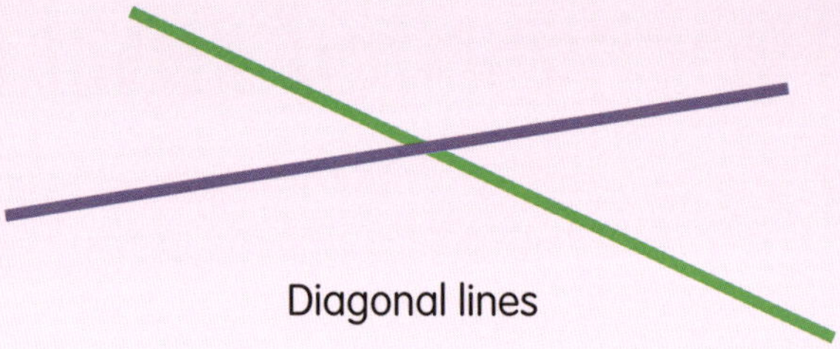

Diagonal lines

Warm-up Join all the dots below together using only diagonal lines. Make sure that each dot is joined diagonally to at least one other dot.

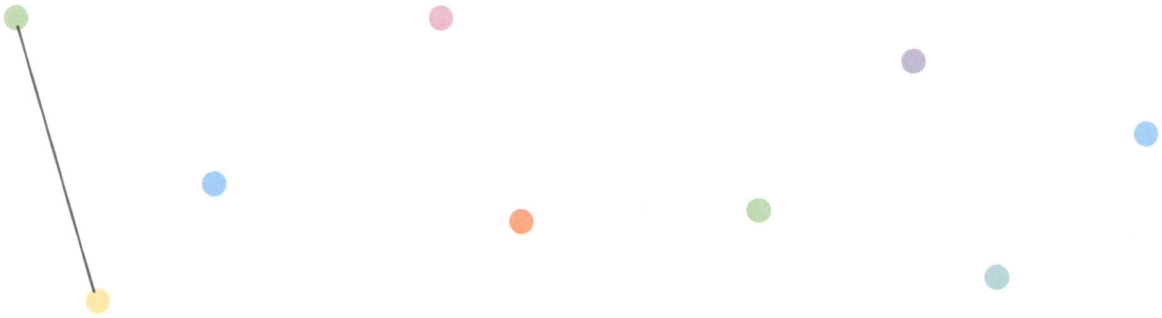

1 Fill in the number of diagonal, vertical, and horizontal lines that each of these shapes has.

REMEMBER!
You looked at horizontal and vertical lines on the previous page.

a

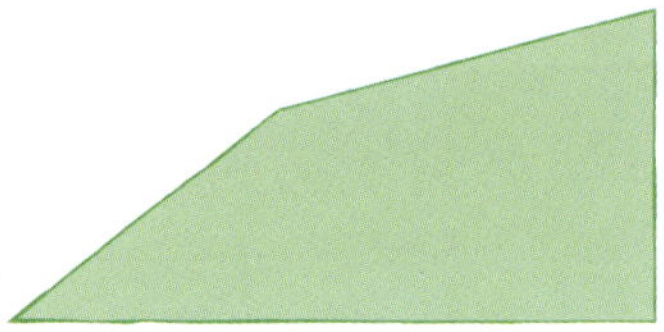

Diagonal lines = 2
Horizontal lines = 1
Vertical lines = 1

b

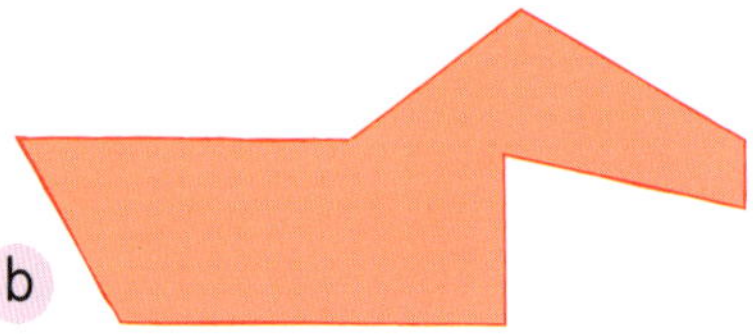

Diagonal lines = ___
Horizontal lines = ___
Vertical lines = ___

c

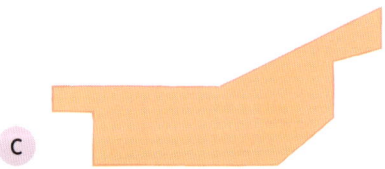

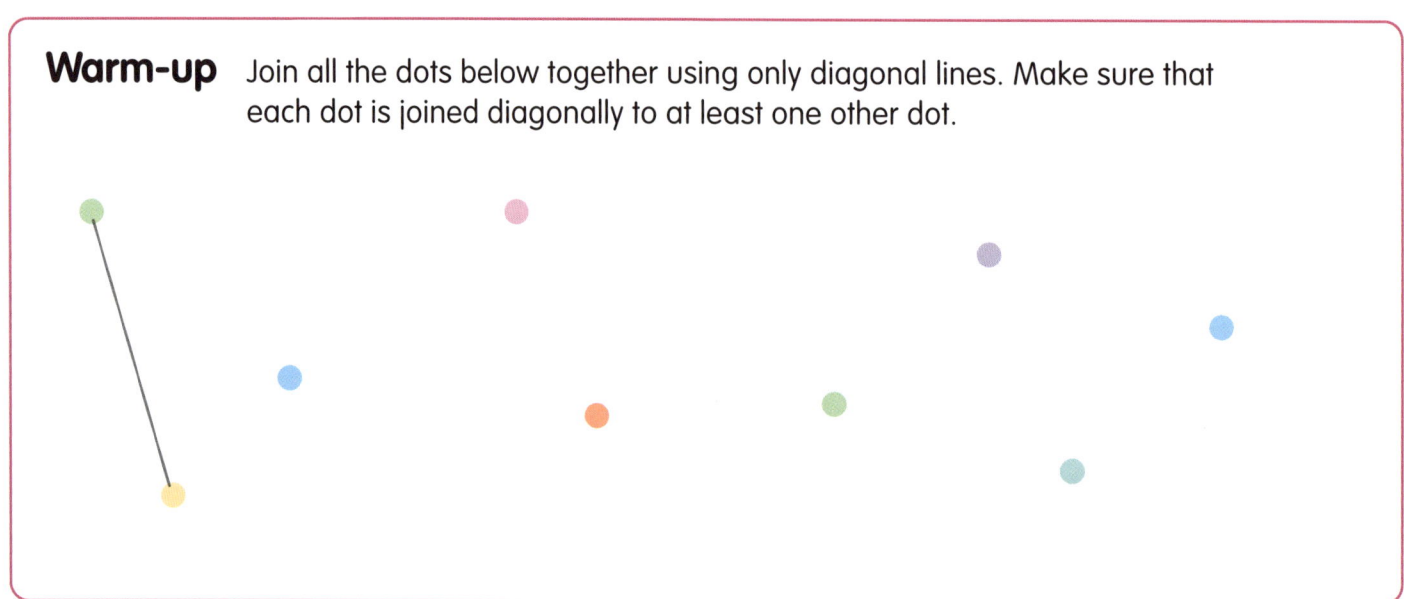

Diagonal lines = ___
Horizontal lines = ___
Vertical lines = ___

d

Diagonal lines = ___
Horizontal lines = ___
Vertical lines = ___

e

Diagonal lines = ___
Horizontal lines = ___
Vertical lines = ___

2 Draw diagonal lines to join all the corners of these shapes. Some of these shapes have more than one correct answer.

a 

b 

c 

d 

e 

f 

3 Compare the number of diagonal lines in each pair of shapes by writing less than (<), greater than (>), or equal to (=) to.

a 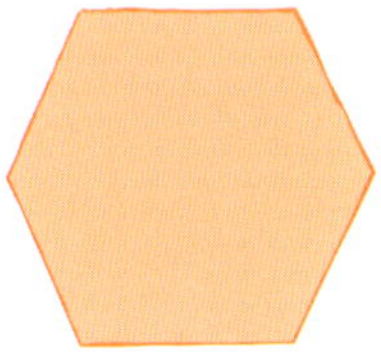 > 

b 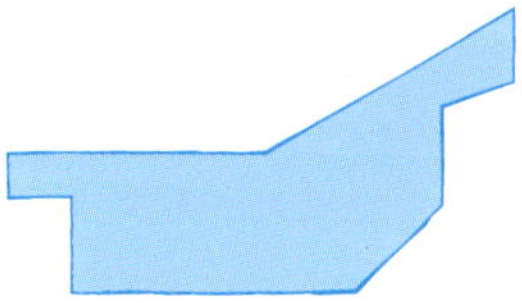 ☐ 

c 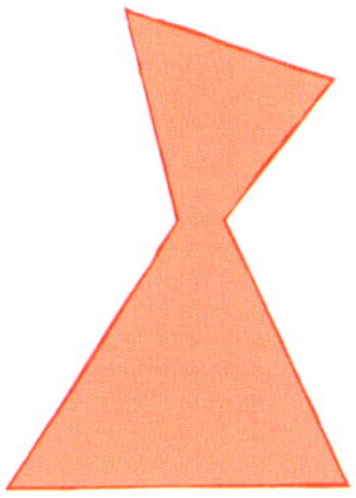 ☐ 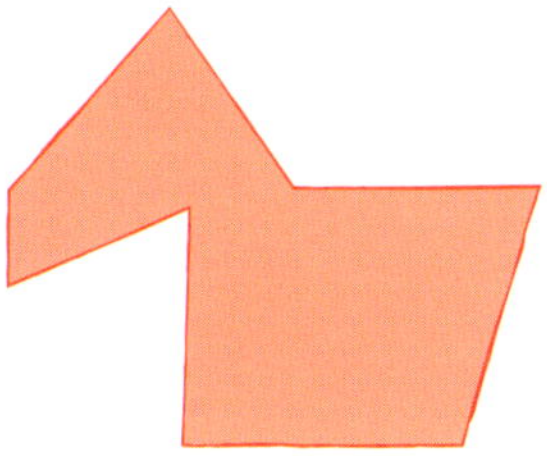

d 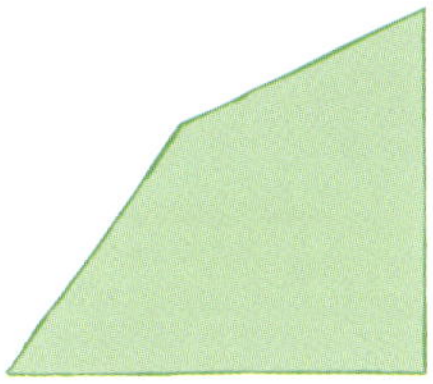 ☐ 

e  ☐ 

f  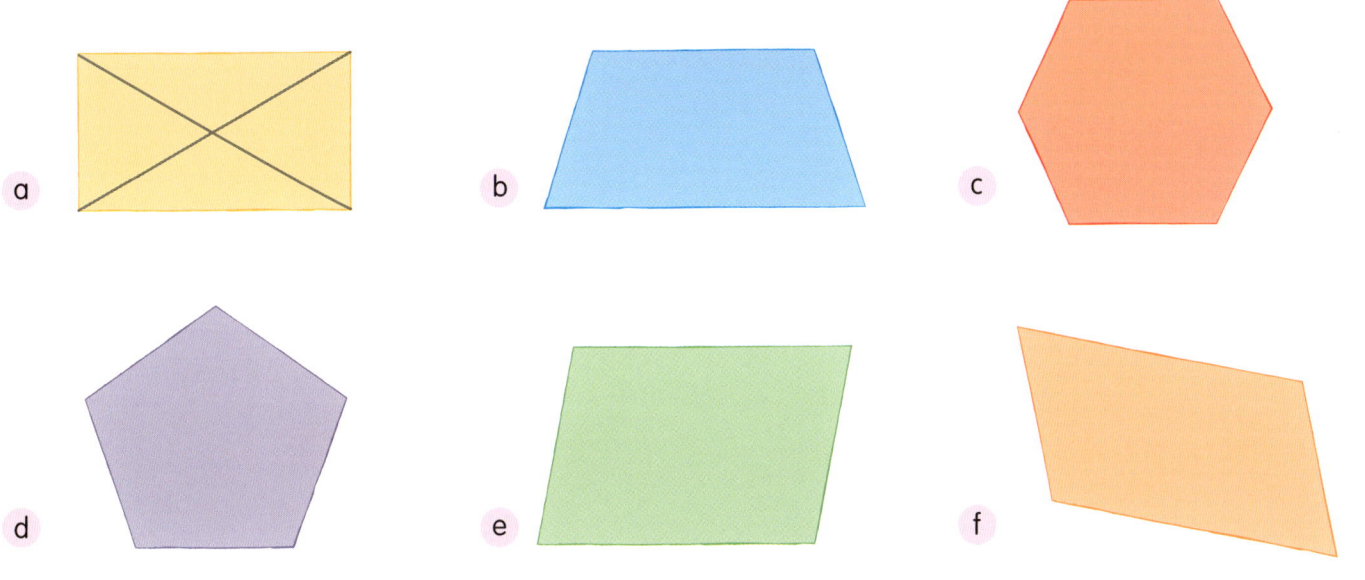 ☐ 

Pages 206–207

Parallel lines

Parallel lines are lines that are exactly the same distance from each other all along their lengths. Parallel lines always come in sets of two or more.

Straight parallel lines

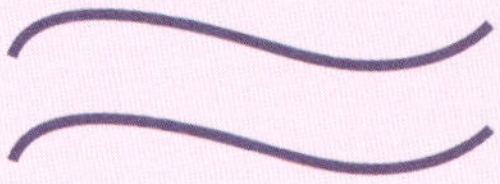

Wavy parallel lines

Warm-up Tick the pairs below that show parallel lines.

1 ☑ 

2 ☐ 

3 ☐ 

4 ☐ 

5 ☐ 

6 ☐ 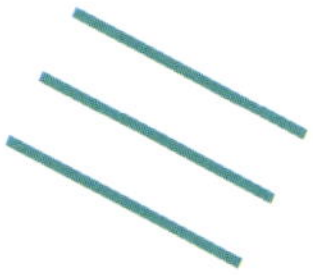

1 Draw a line that is parallel to each of the lines below.

a 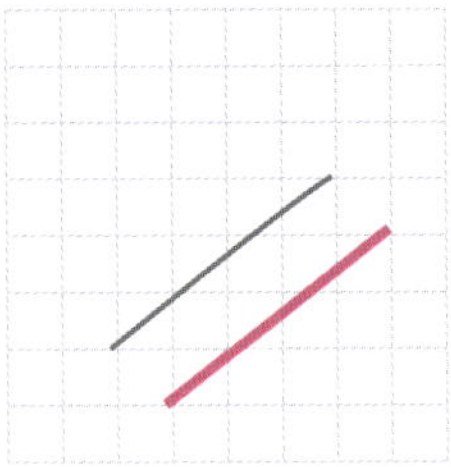

b 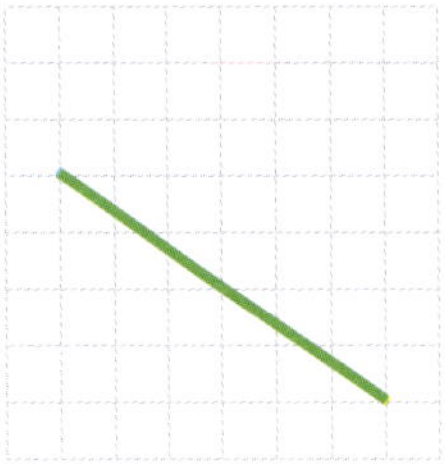

c 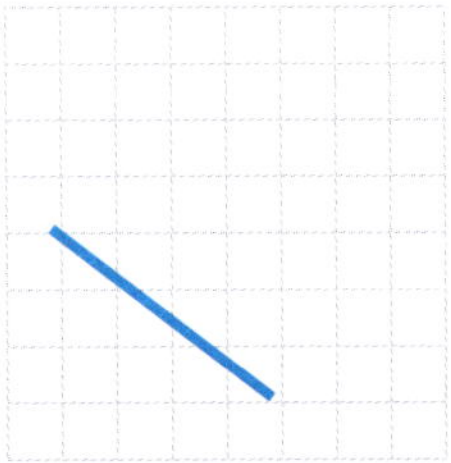

d 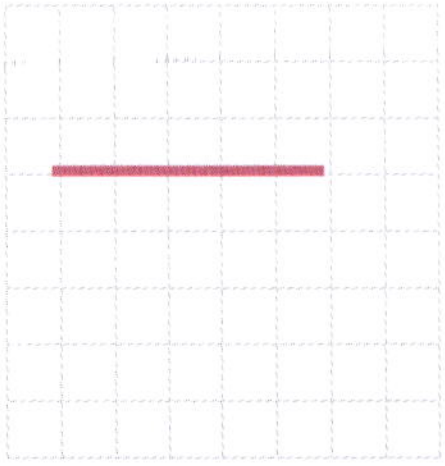

e 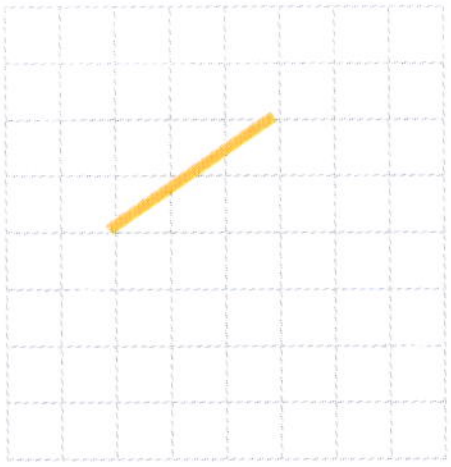

f 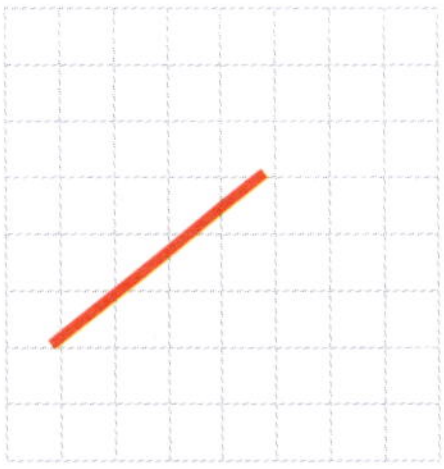

2 Fill in how many pairs of parallel lines there are in each of these shapes.

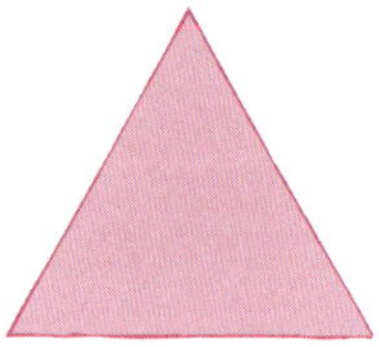

a There are 0 pairs of parallel lines in this triangle.

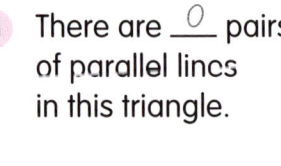

b There are ___ pairs of parallel lines in this rhombus.

c There are ___ pairs of parallel lines in this pentagon.

d There are ___ pairs of parallel lines in this square.

Pages 208–209

Perpendicular lines

Perpendicular lines are lines that are at right angles to each other. They always come in pairs.

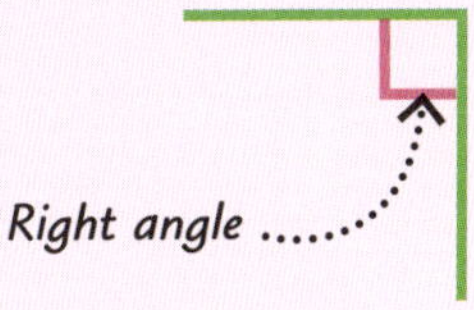

These green lines are perpendicular to each other.

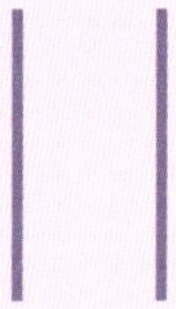

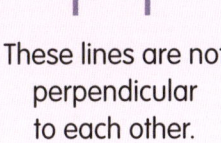

These lines are not perpendicular to each other.

Warm-up Draw a line that is perpendicular to each of the lines below.

1
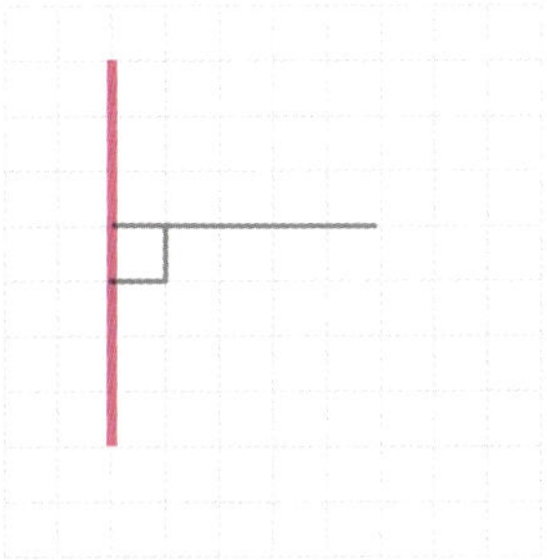

2

3
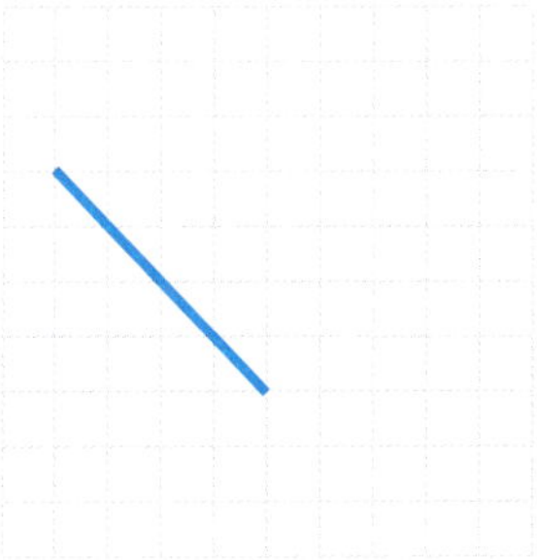

1 Colour in the shapes that have perpendicular lines.

a
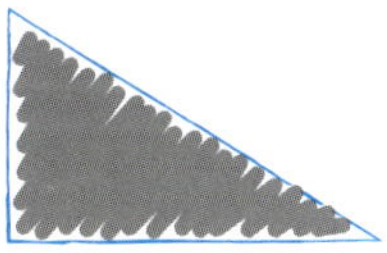

b
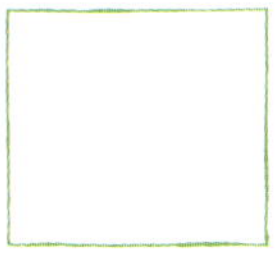

c

d
 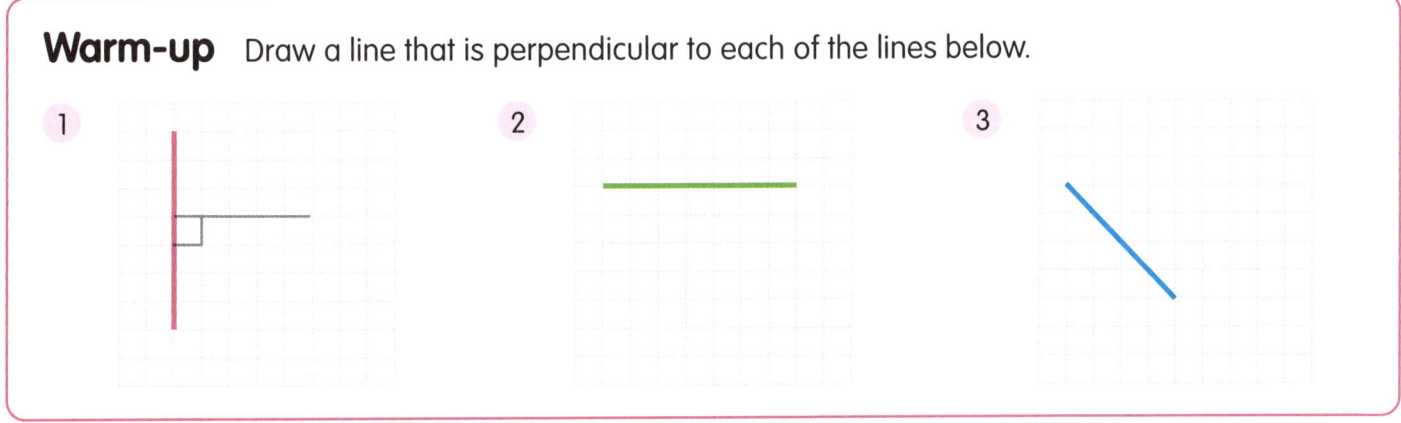

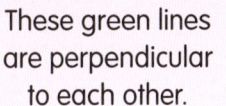

e

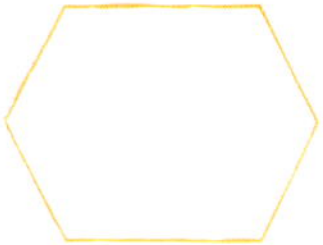

2 Circle the perpendicular lines on this row of houses, then draw in another house using at least five pairs of perpendicular lines.

Pages 210–211

2D shapes

2D means "two-dimensional". 2D shapes have length and height, or length and width, but they do not have thickness or depth. 2D shapes are flat, like the shapes that we draw on paper or on a computer screen.

Polygons are 2D shapes that have three or more straight sides and angles.

This is a polygon.

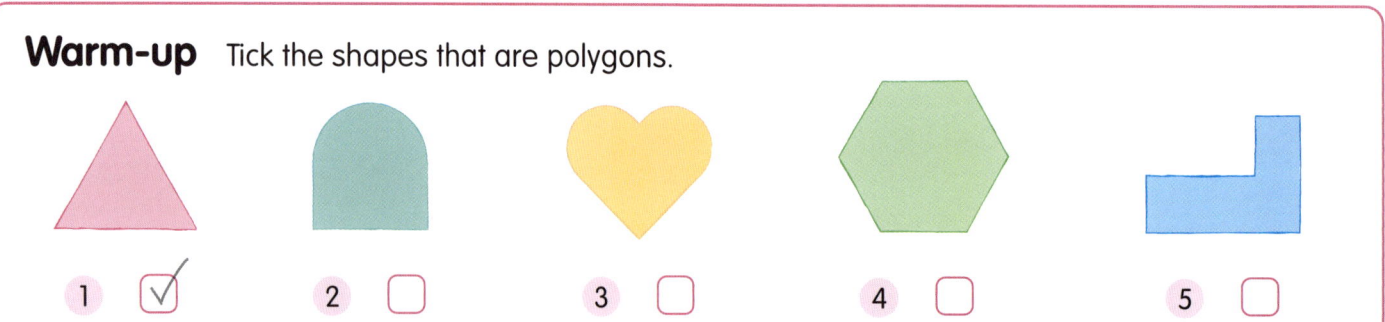

This is not a polygon.

Warm-up Tick the shapes that are polygons.

1 ☑ 2 ☐ 3 ☐ 4 ☐ 5 ☐

1

Count and then colour in all the 2D shapes you can find in this picture.

There are _____ 2D shapes in this picture.

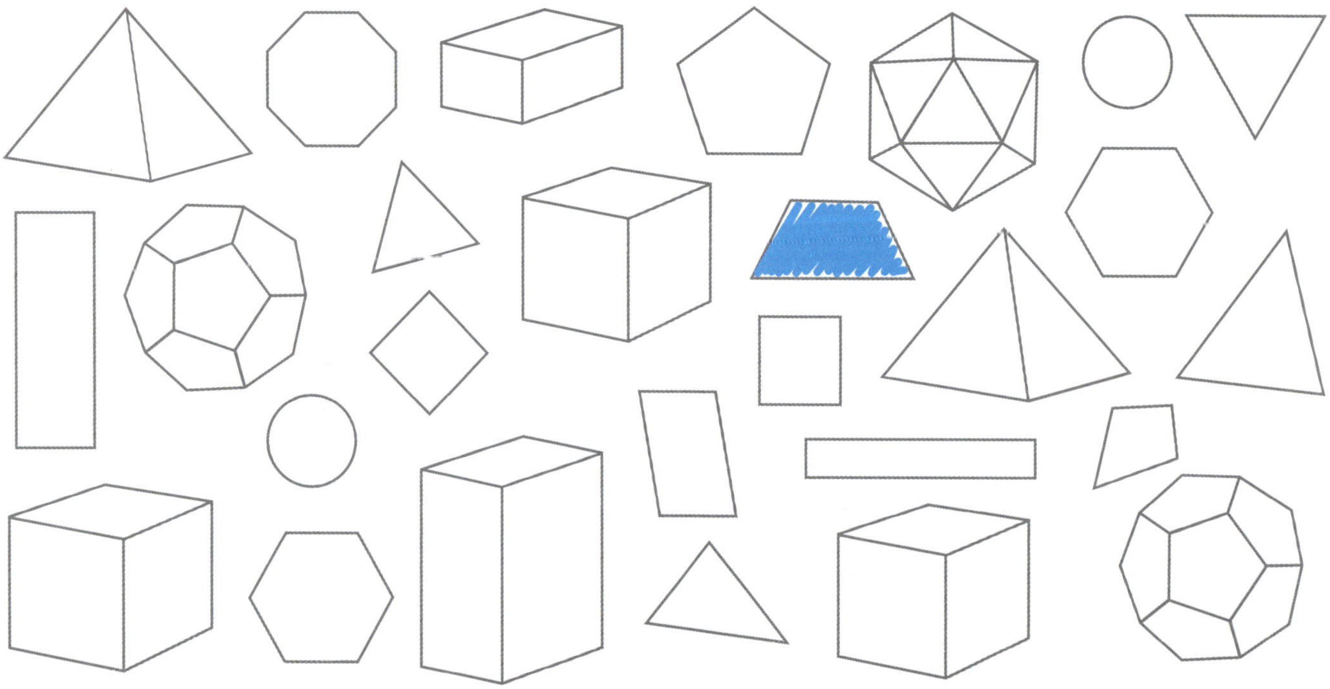

2 Fill in the numbers to describe each of these 2D shapes.

a This shape has _4_ sides, _2 pairs_ of parallel lines, and _2 pairs_ of perpendicular lines.

b This shape has ____ sides, ________ of parallel lines, and ________ of perpendicular lines.

c This shape has ____ sides, ________ of parallel lines, and ________ of perpendicular lines.

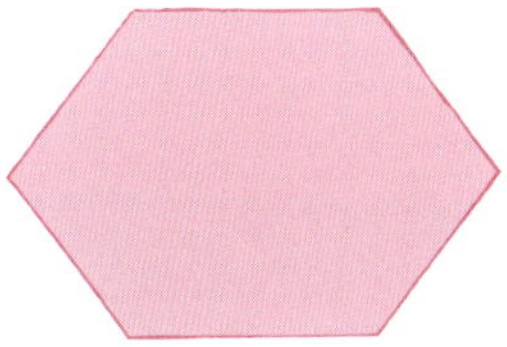

d This shape has ____ sides, ________ of parallel lines, and ________ of perpendicular lines.

3 Draw 2D shapes to match each of these descriptions below.

a This shape has 4 sides of the same length, and has 2 pairs of parallel sides:

b This shape has 3 sides, none of which are perpendicular or parallel:

c This shape has 4 sides; opposing sides are the same length as each other, but a different length from the other 2 sides:

d This shape has 6 sides; all 3 pairs are perpendicular and parallel.

Page 212

Regular and irregular polygons

A polygon is a 2D shape that has three or more straight sides and three or more angles. Polygons can be regular or irregular.

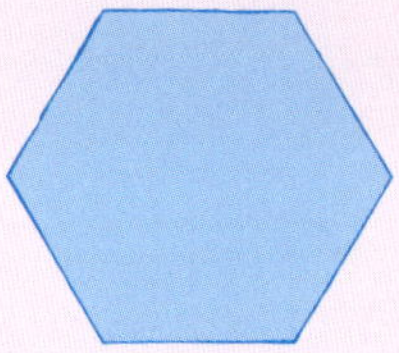

This hexagon is a regular polygon – all six sides are the same length and all the angles are equal.

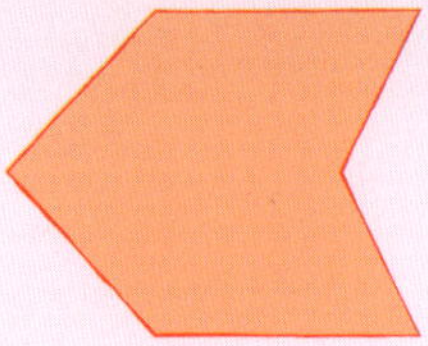

This hexagon is an irregular polygon – the six sides vary in length and th angles are different sizes

Warm-up Look at these shapes. Colour the regular polygons blue and the irregular polygons red.

1 

2 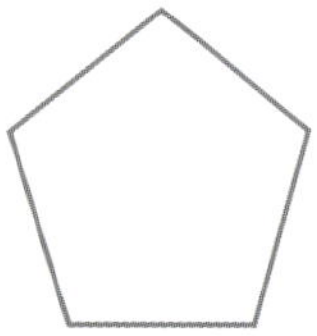

3 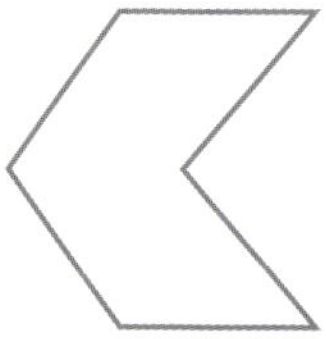

4 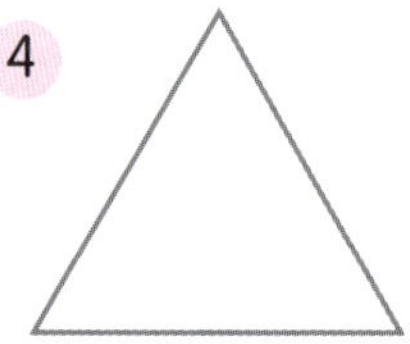

5 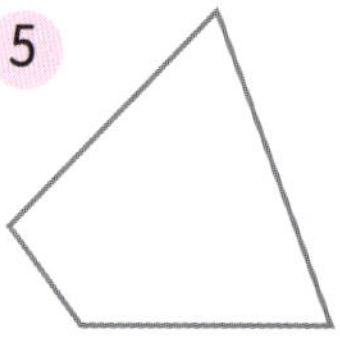

1 Draw lines to match each statement with the shape it describes.

This shape is an irregular polygon with 4 sides.	This shape is a regular polygon with 4 sides.	This shape is a regular polygon with 5 sides.	This shape is an irregular polygon with 7 sides.

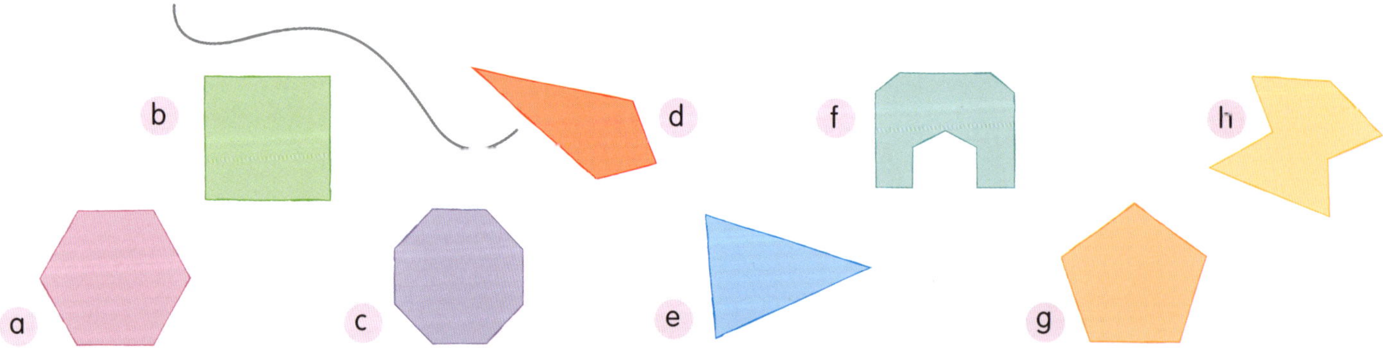

This shape is an irregular polygon with 3 sides.	This shape is a regular polygon with 6 sides.	This shape is a regular polygon with 8 sides.	This shape is an irregular polygon with 11 sides.

2 Draw shapes to match each of these descriptions below.

a A regular polygon with 8 sides:

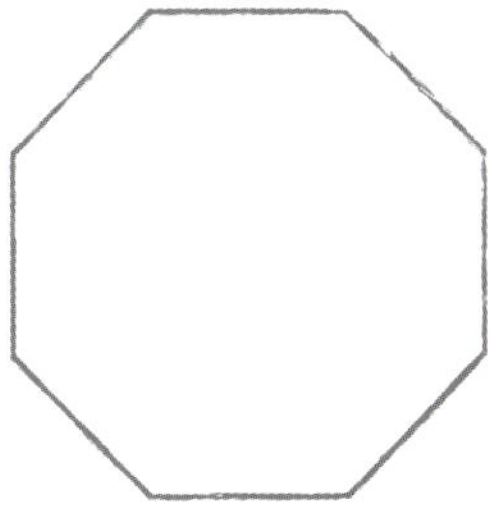

b An irregular polygon with 8 sides:

c A regular polygon with 3 sides:

d An irregular polygon with 3 sides:

e A regular polygon with 5 sides:

f An irregular polygon with 5 sides:

g A regular polygon with 4 sides:

h An irregular polygon with 4 sides:

Page 213

Triangles

A triangle is a type of polygon. It has three straight sides, three angles, and three vertices.

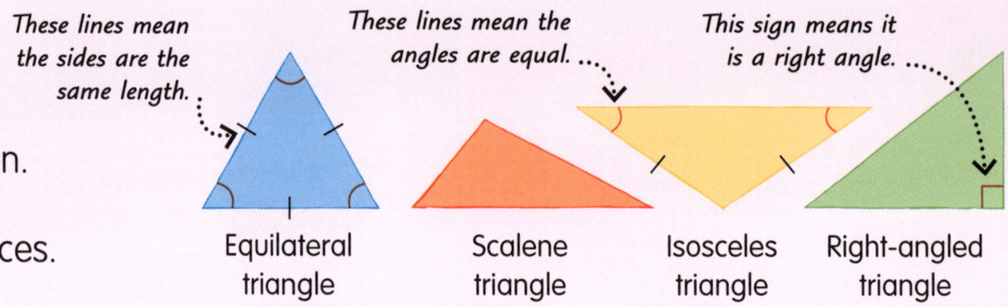
These lines mean the sides are the same length.
These lines mean the angles are equal.
This sign means it is a right angle.
Equilateral triangle
Scalene triangle
Isosceles triangle
Right-angled triangle

Warm-up Use the words in the word box to help you label each part of the triangle.

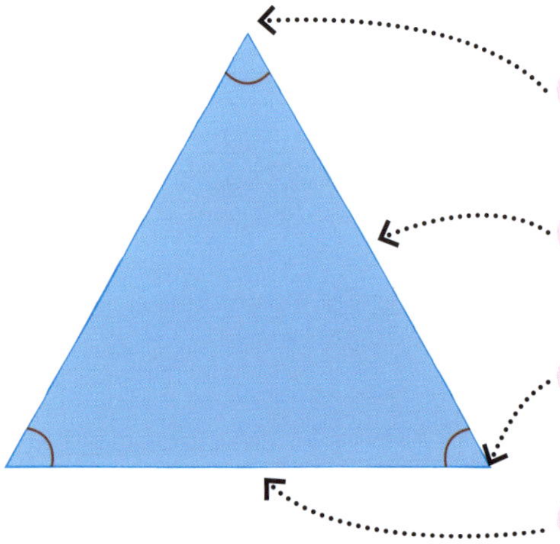

1 apex

2 ______

3 ______

4 ______

side	base
vertex	~~apex~~

Now write the name of the triangle below.

5 ______________

1

Draw lines to match each triangle with the correct label.

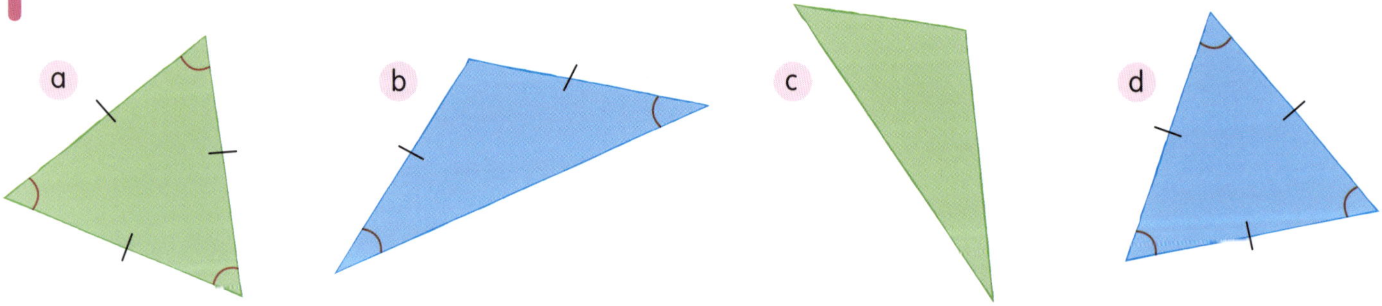
a
b
c
d

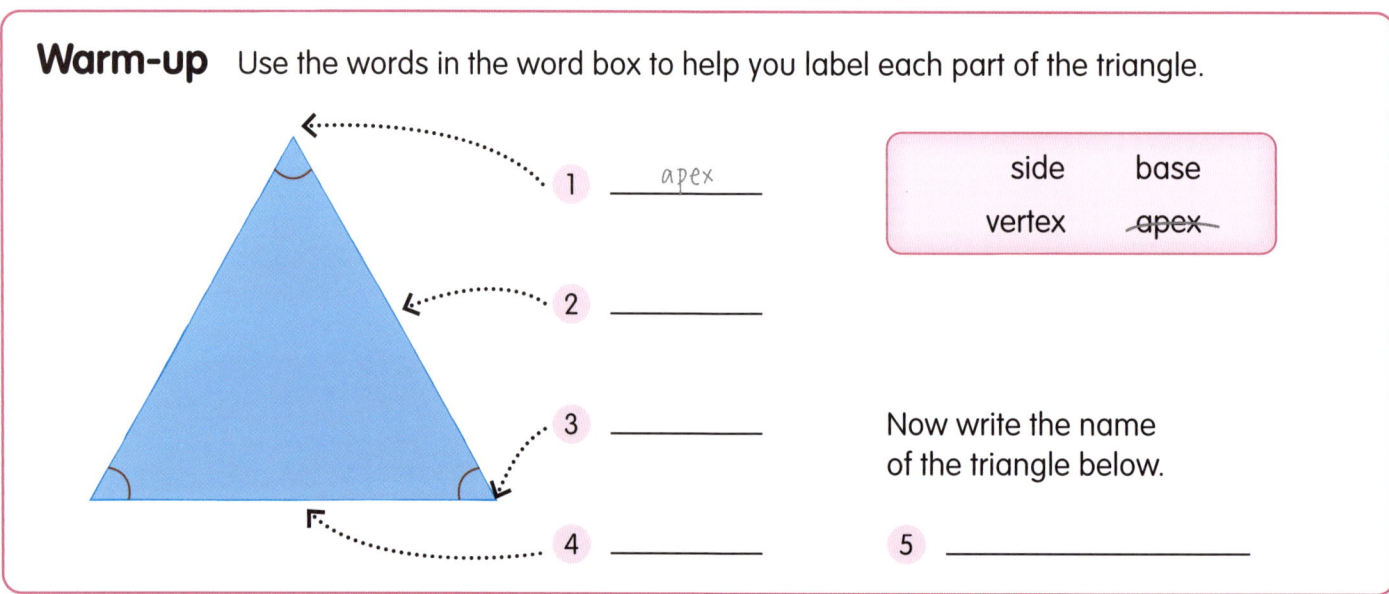

scalene triangle | right-angled triangle | equilateral triangle | isosceles triangle

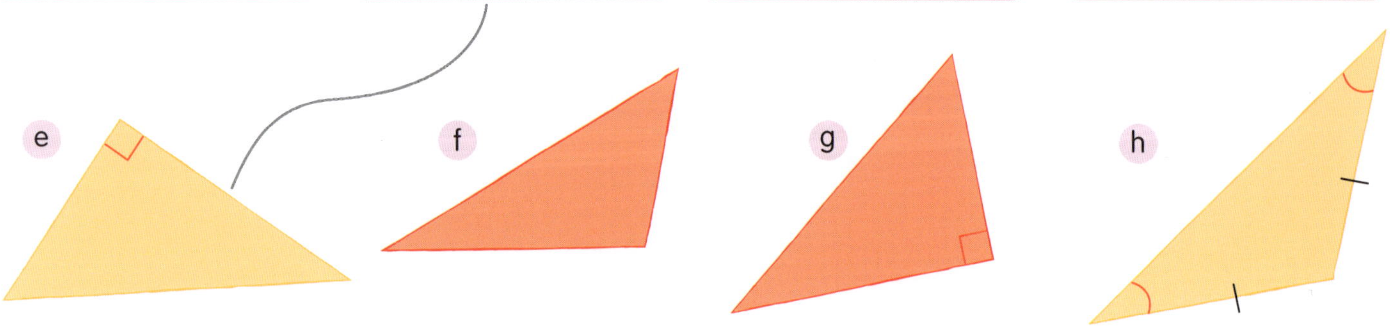
e
f
g
h

2

Look at these three coloured triangles. Colour in the remaining triangles blue, yellow, or red to show which triangle they are congruent with.

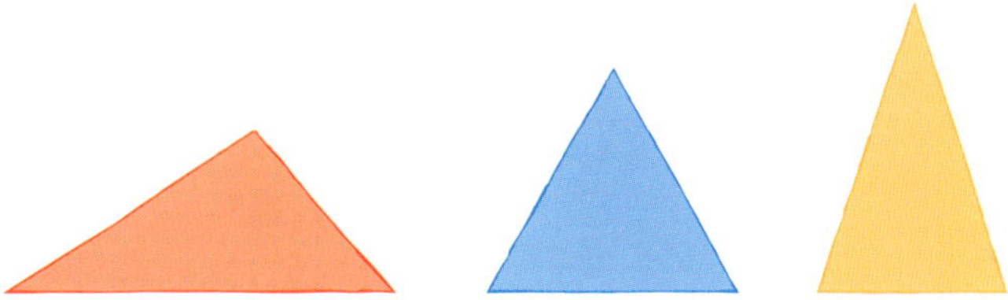

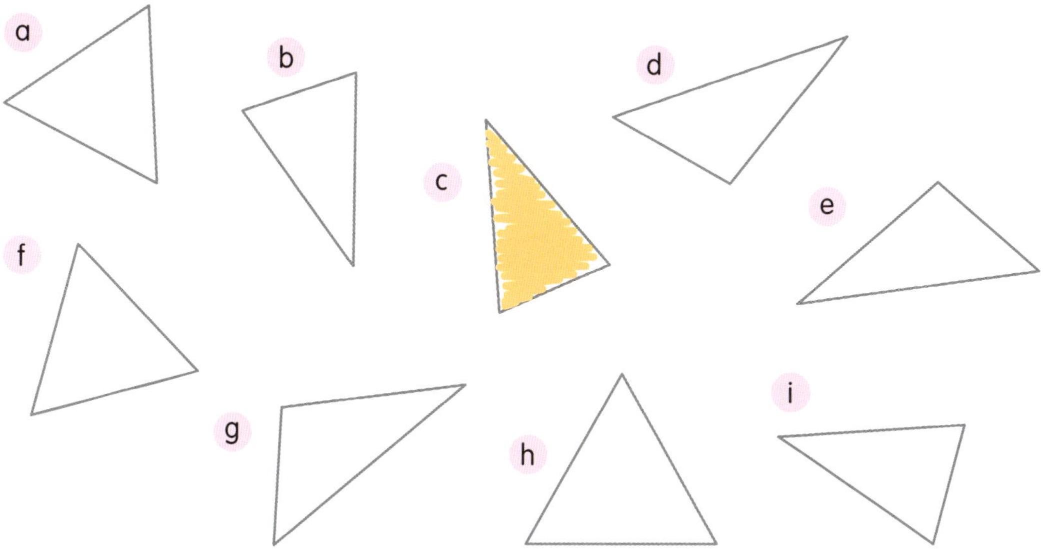

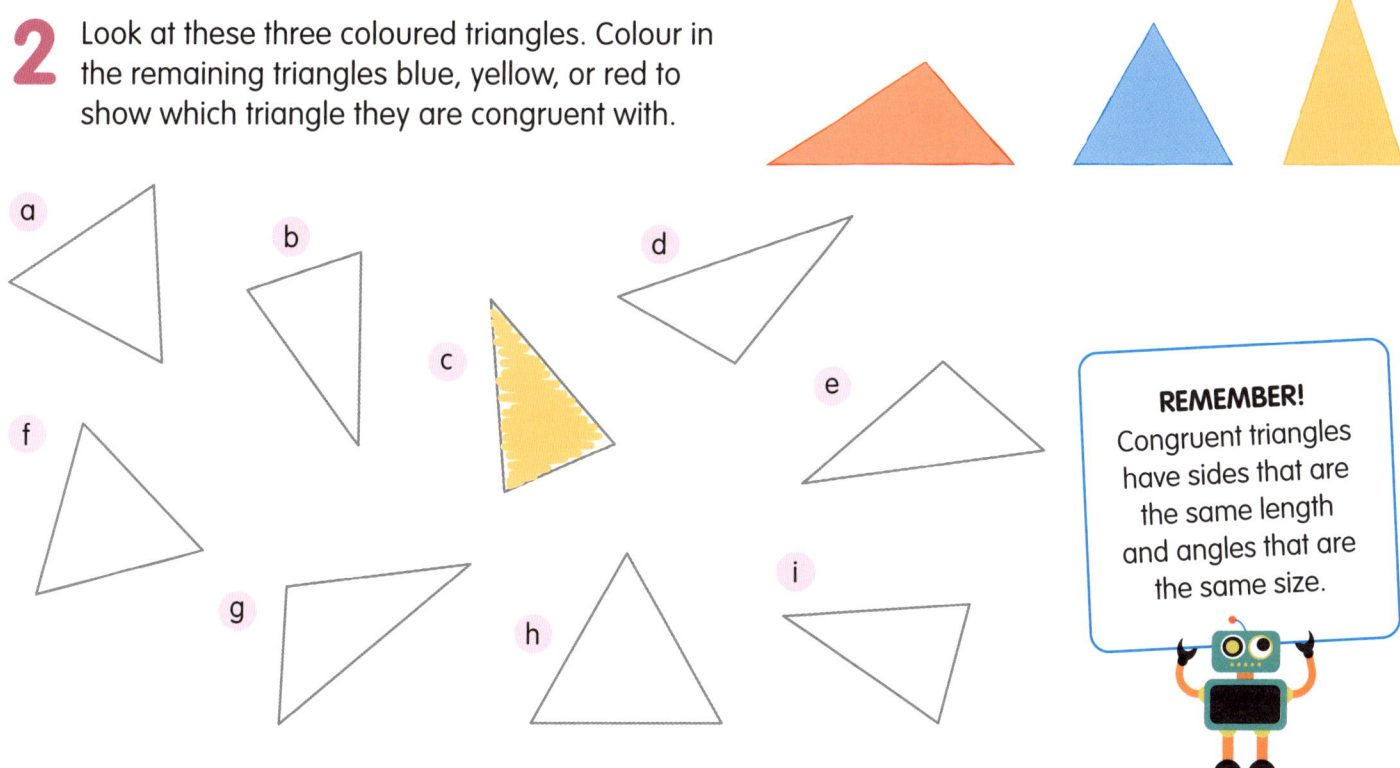

REMEMBER!
Congruent triangles have sides that are the same length and angles that are the same size.

3

Draw triangles to match each of these descriptions below. You will need to use a ruler.

a An equilateral triangle with sides that are 3 cm long:

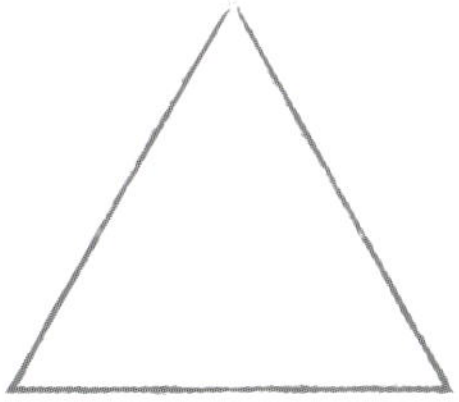

b An isosceles triangle with one side that is 6 cm long:

c An isosceles triangle with two sides that are 3 cm long:

d A scalene triangle with one side that is 4 cm long:

Pages 214–215

Quadrilaterals

A quadrilateral is a shape that has four straight sides, four vertices, and four angles. They always have straight sides.

These shapes are all quadrilaterals.

Warm-up Tick the shapes that are quadrilaterals.

1 ☑

2 ☐

3 ☐

4 ☐

5 ☐

6 ☐

7 ☐

8 ☐

9 ☐

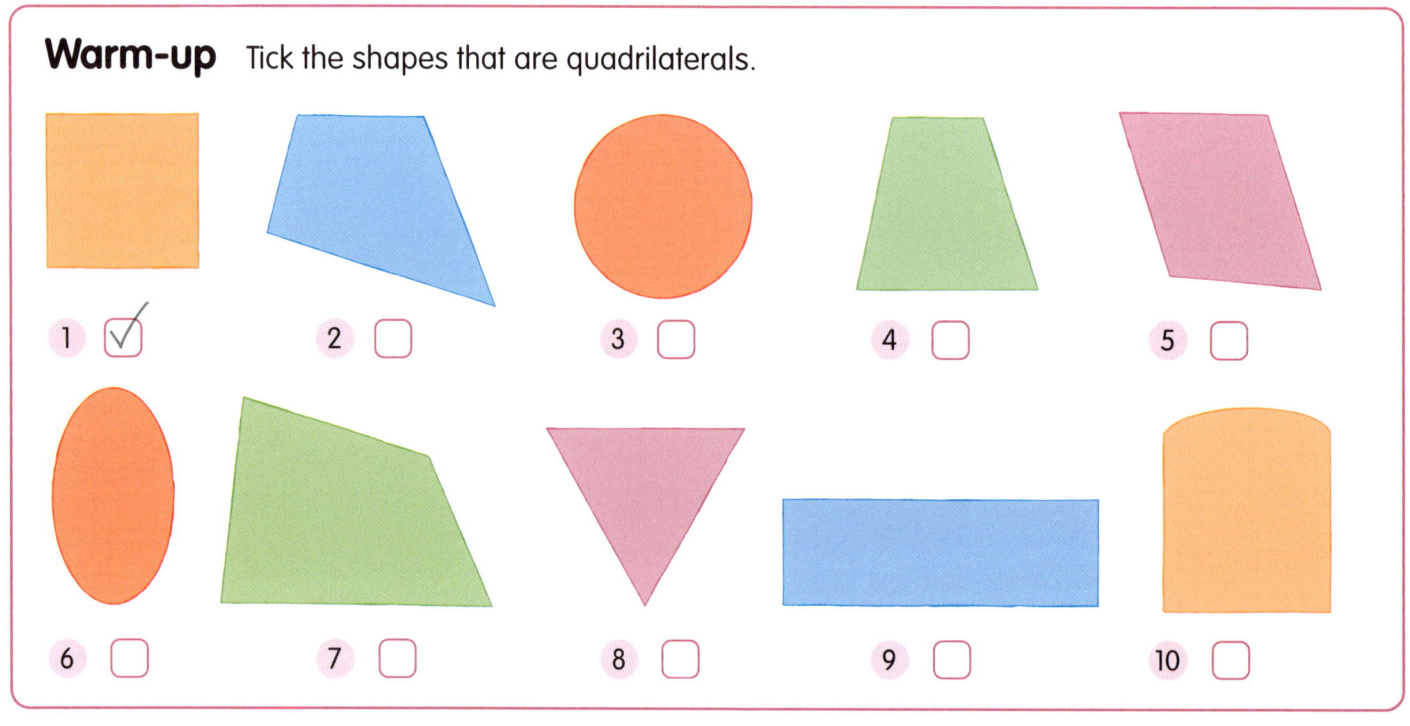

10 ☐

1 Circle the quadrilaterals in this picture. How many are there?

There are ______________ quadrilaterals in the picture.

2 Use the words in the word box to help you label these shapes.

a kite

b ____________

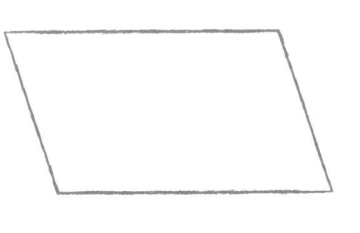

c ____________

d ____________

e ____________

f ____________

rhombus
rectangle
parallelogram
square
~~kite~~
trapezium

3 Draw quadrilaterals to match each of these descriptions below.

a This shape has two sets of parallel sides; its opposite sides and opposite angles are equal:

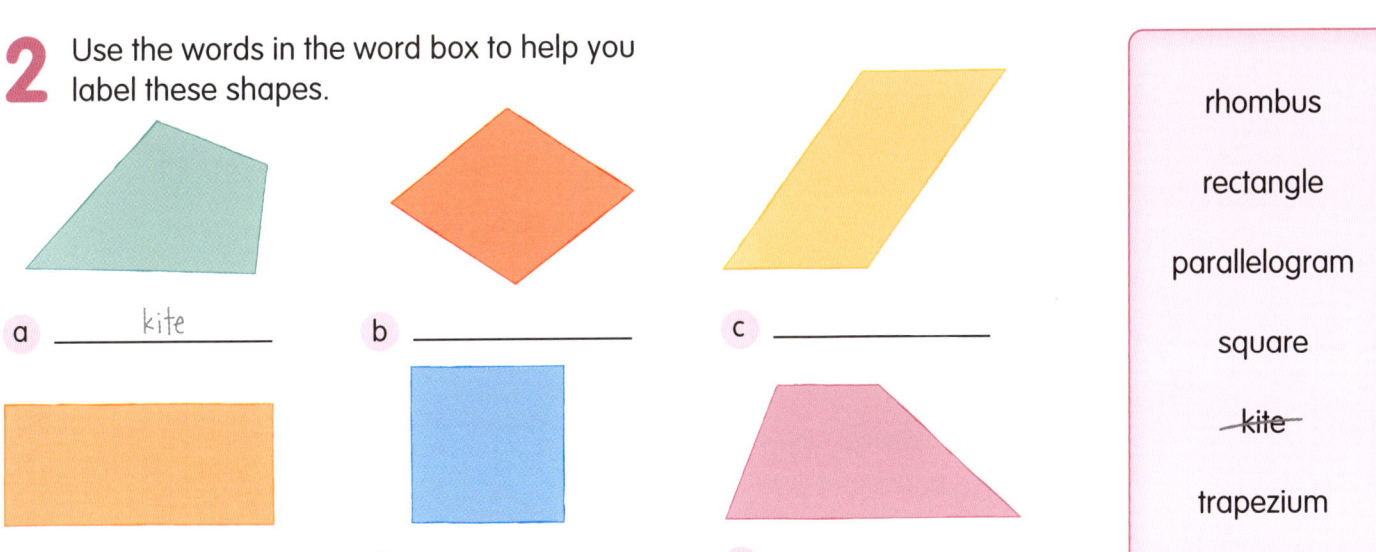

b This shape has four sides, but only one pair of parallel sides:

c This shape has four angles that are all right angles:

d This shape has two pairs of equal, adjacent sides:

e This shape has sides of equal length; its opposite sides are parallel, and its opposite angles are equal:

f This shape has four sides that are all different lengths:

Pages 216–217

Naming polygons

Polygons are named for the number of sides and angles they have. Most polygon names come from the Greek words for different numbers.

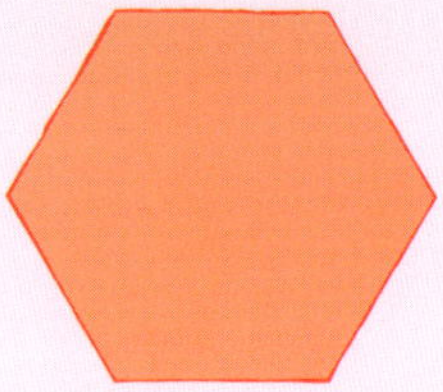
Regular hexagon

Irregular hexagon

Warm-up Fill in the names of these regular polygons.

1 pentagon

2 ______________

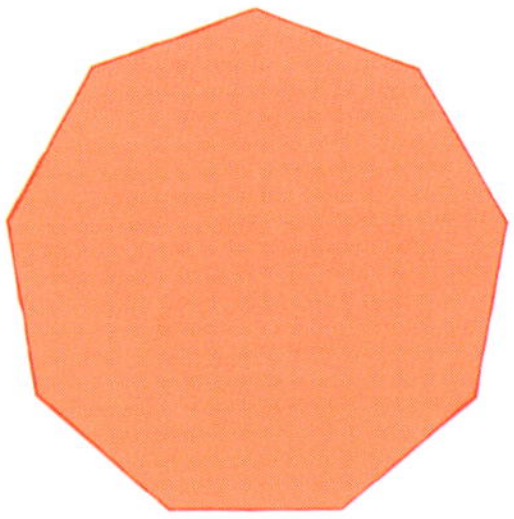
3 ______________

4 ______________

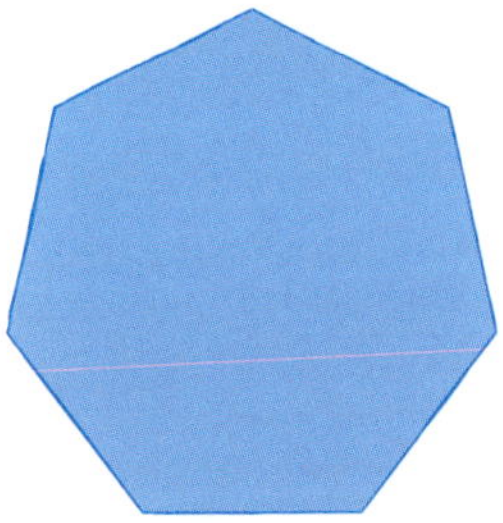
5 ______________

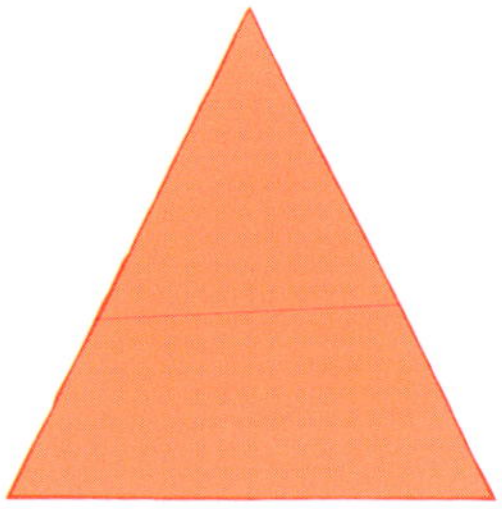
6 ______________

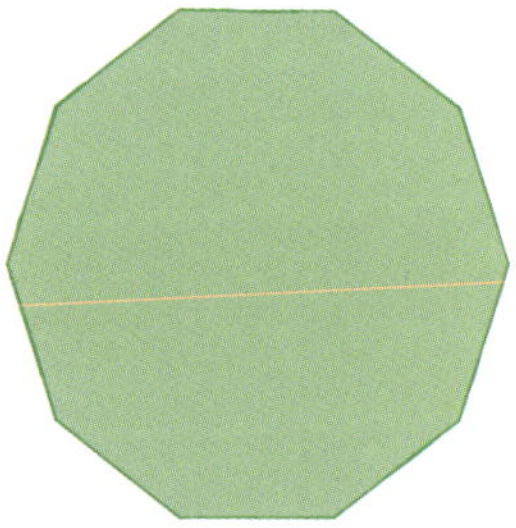
7 ______________

8 ______________

1 Use the words in the word box to help you complete these sentences describing different polygons.

a A quadrilateral is a polygon that has 4 sides and 4 angles.

b A polygon that has 8 sides and 8 angles is called ______________ .

c A dodecagon is a polygon that has 12 sides and ______________ .

d An icosagon is a polygon that has ______________ and ______________ .

e A polygon that has 10 sides and 10 angles is called ______________ .

a decagon
20 angles
~~4 sides~~
an octagon
12 angles
20 sides

2

Draw shapes to match each of these descriptions below.

a A regular triangle:

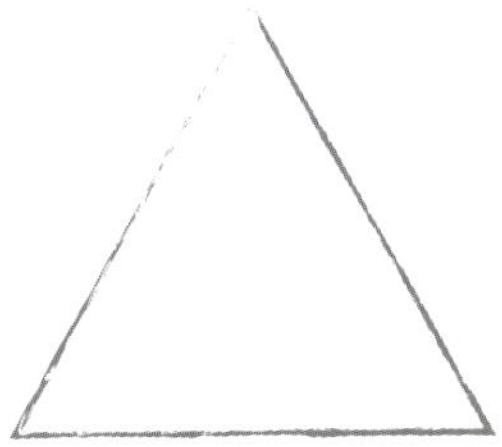

b A regular quadrilateral:

c A regular hexagon:

d A regular pentagon:

e An irregular octagon:

f An irregular quadrilateral:

3

Label each of these partly hidden shapes with its name.
Four of these shapes are regular polygons.

a regular quadrilateral

b ____________

c ____________

d ____________

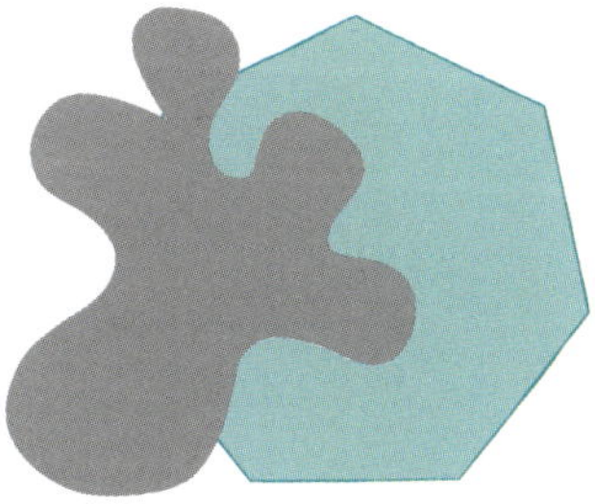

e ____________

f ____________

Pages 218–219

3D shapes

3D means three-dimensional. 3D shapes have three dimensions: length, width, and height. 3D shapes can be solid, like a lump of rock, or hollow, like a football.

REMEMBER!
3D shapes have edges, vertices, and faces.

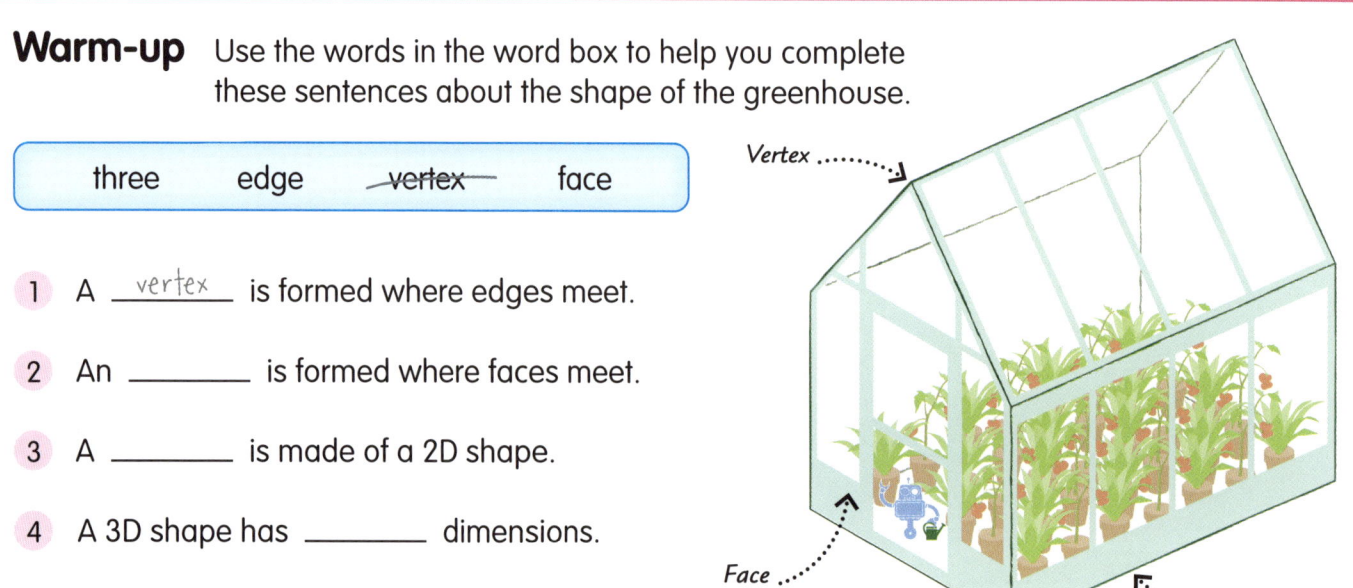

Warm-up Use the words in the word box to help you complete these sentences about the shape of the greenhouse.

three edge ~~vertex~~ face

1 A vertex is formed where edges meet.

2 An ________ is formed where faces meet.

3 A ________ is made of a 2D shape.

4 A 3D shape has ________ dimensions.

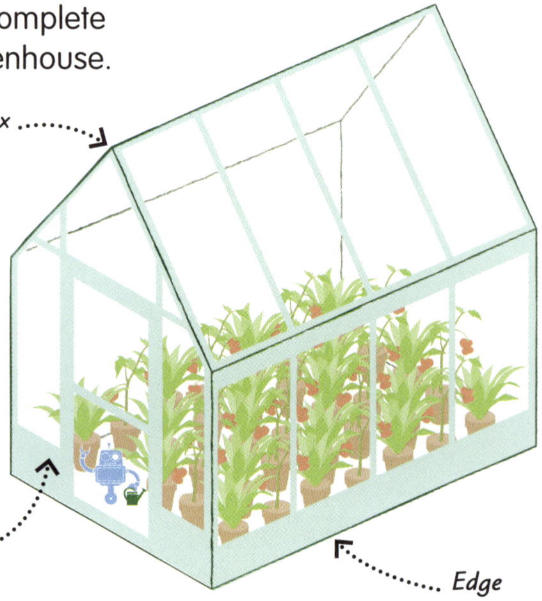

1 Use the words in the word box to help you label the features of these 3D shapes.

width ~~height~~ length edge vertex face

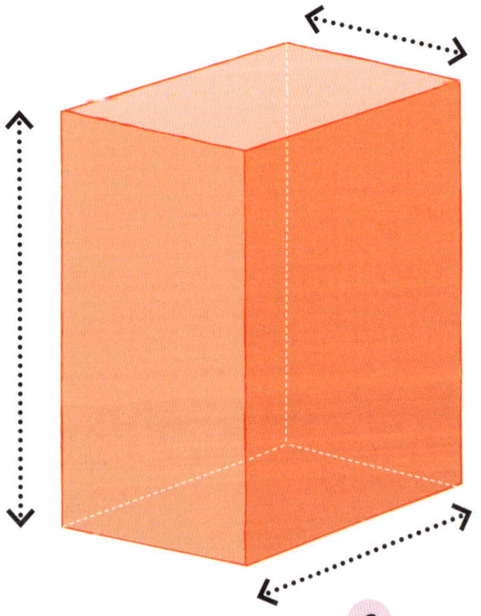

a height

b ________

c ________

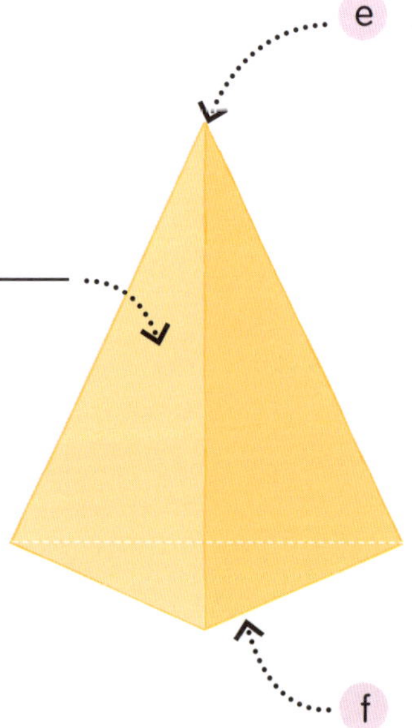

d ________

e ________

f ________

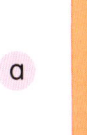

2 Fill in how many faces each of these 3D shapes has.

a  This shape has _3_ faces.

b 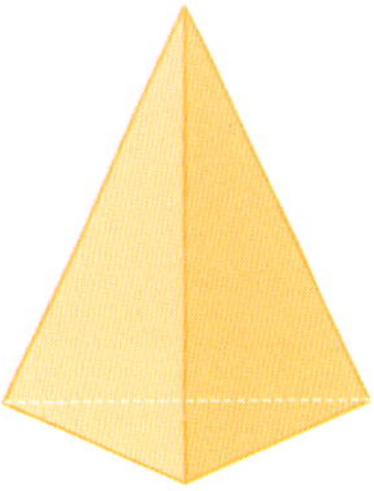 This shape has ____ faces.

c 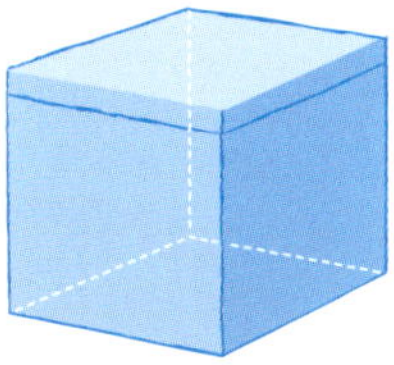 This shape has ____ faces.

d 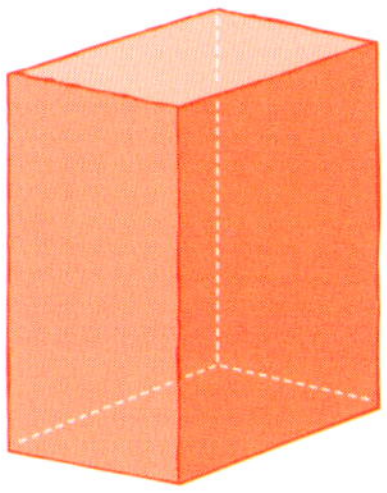 This shape has ____ faces.

3 Fill in how many edges each of these 3D shapes has.

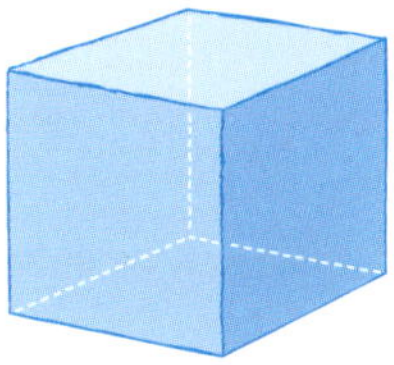

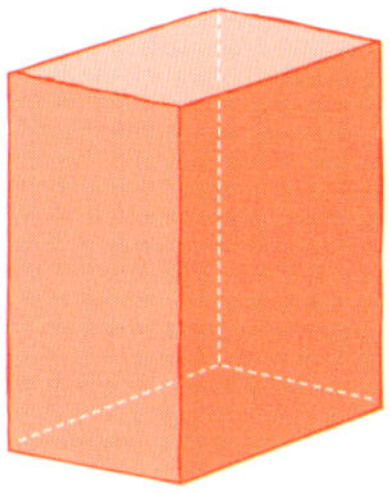

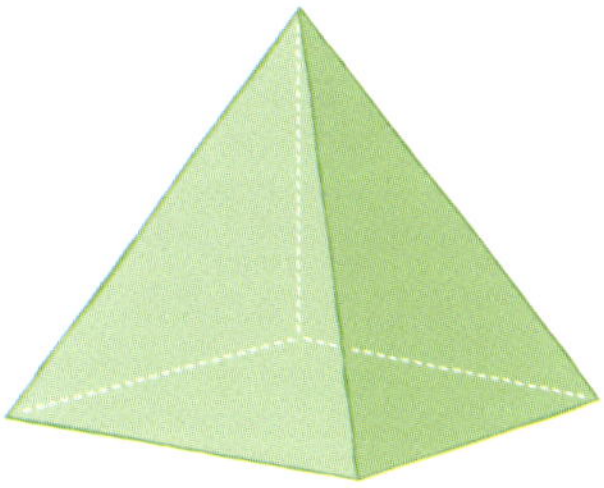

a This shape has _12_ edges.

b This shape has ____ edges.

c This shape has ____ edges.

d This shape has ____ edges.

4 Fill in the name of each of these shapes to match the descriptions below.

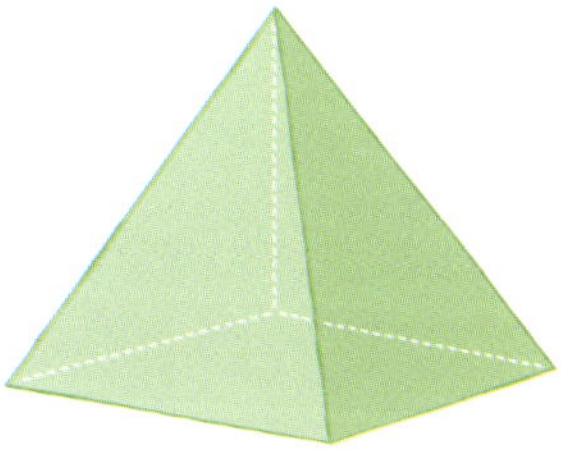

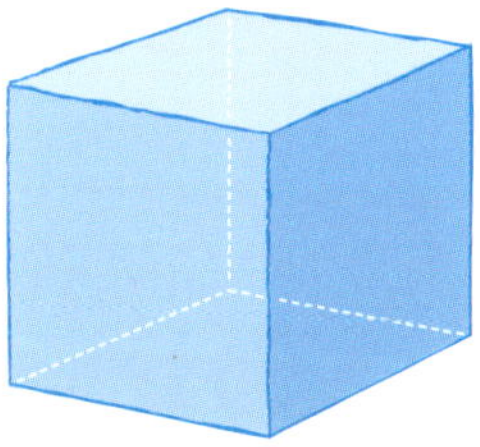

a A prism with circular bases.

a cylinder

b A 3D shape with a square base and four triangular sides that meet at a common point.

____

c A prism with a square base and six square faces.

____

Pages 222–223

Types of 3D shape

3D objects can be any shape or size. They have faces that are 2D shapes, for example a square-based pyramid has four triangle faces and one square face.

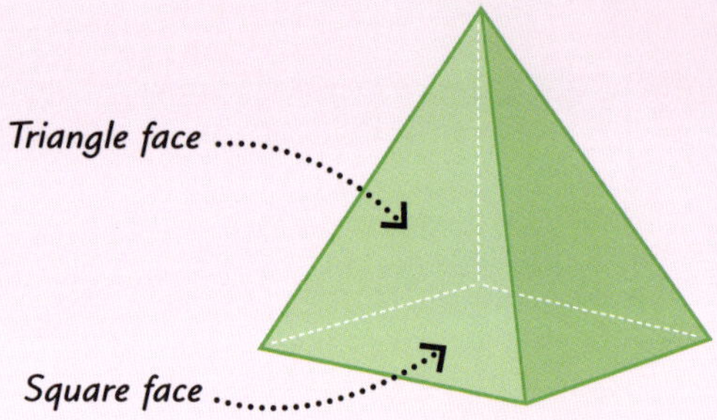

Warm-up Draw lines to match each 3D shape with the correct label.

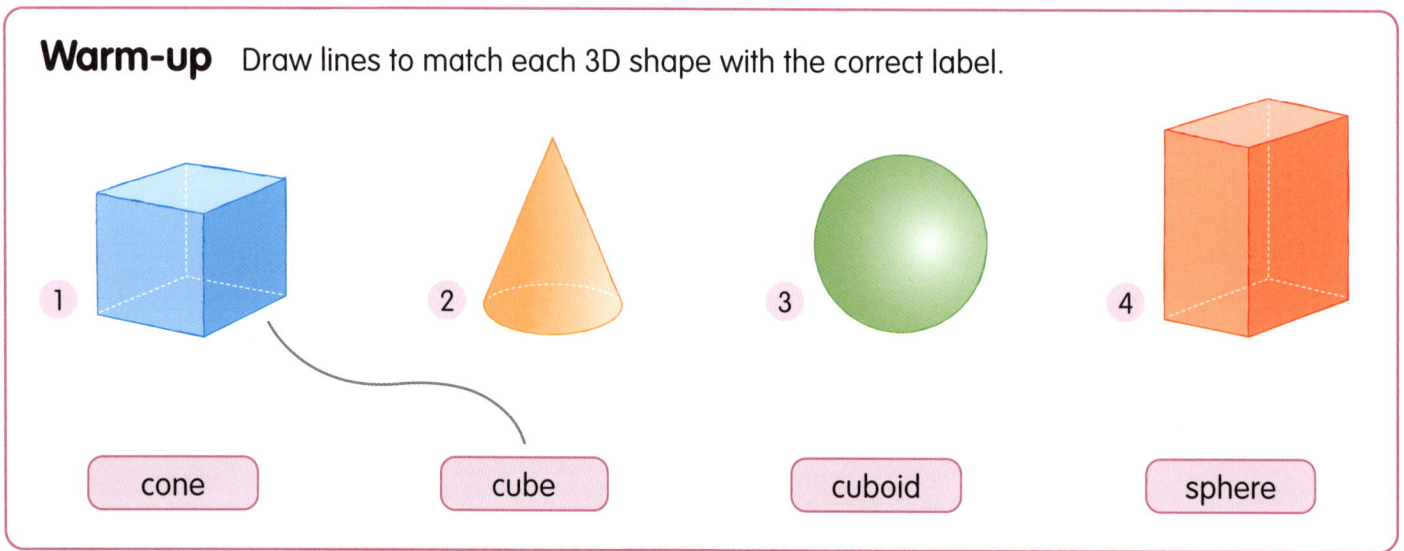

1 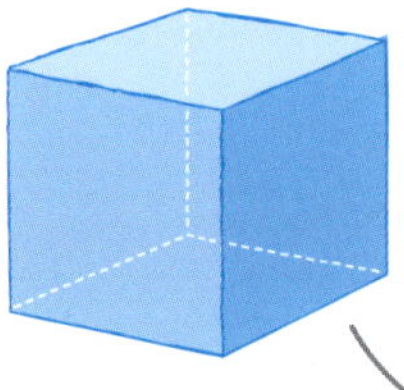

2 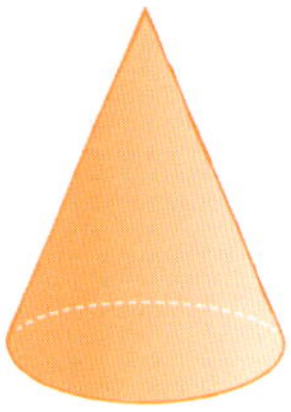

3 

4 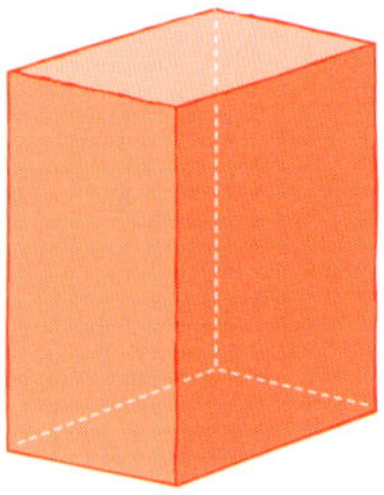

cone

cube

cuboid

sphere

1 Use the words in the word box to help you label these regular polyhedrons.

tetrahedron ~~octahedron~~ cube dodecahedron icosahedron

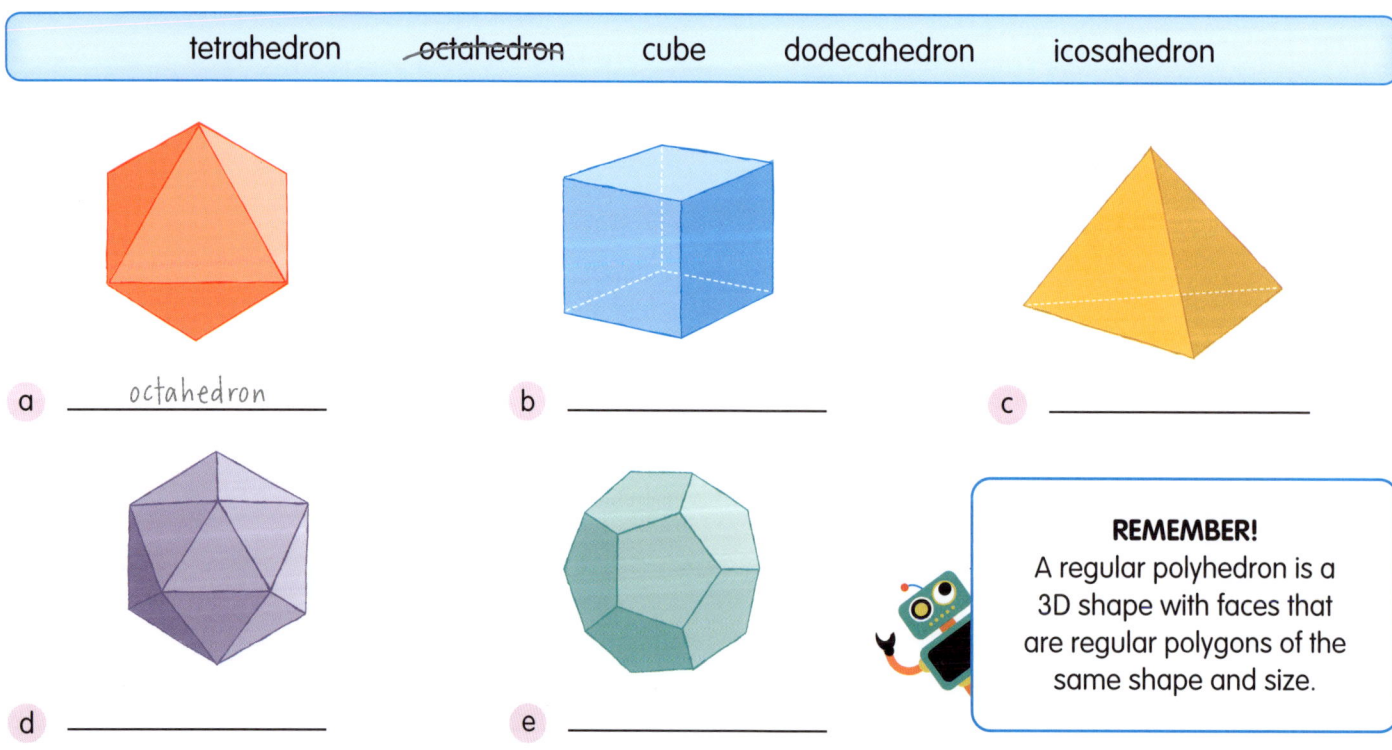

a octahedron

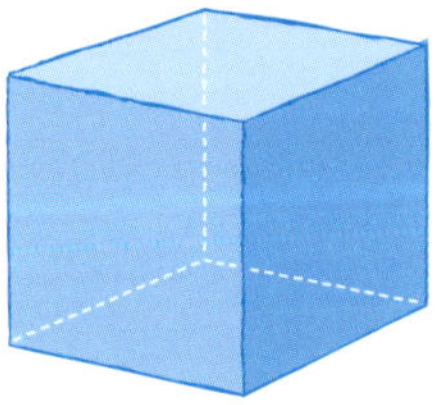

b ____________

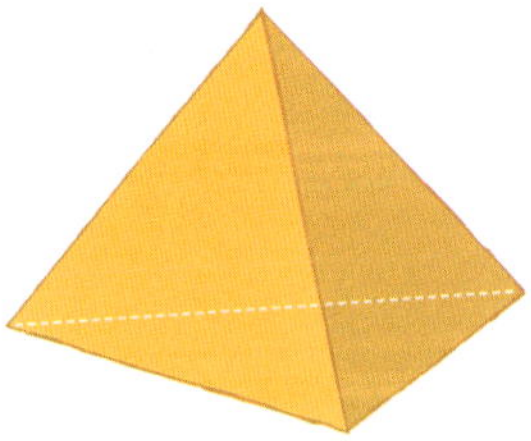

c ____________

d ____________

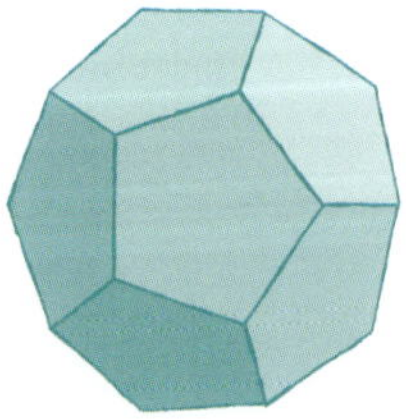

e ____________

REMEMBER!
A regular polyhedron is a 3D shape with faces that are regular polygons of the same shape and size.

2 Complete the sentences to describe these 3D shapes.

a This shape is a cube.

It has 6 faces, 12 edges,

and 8 vertices.

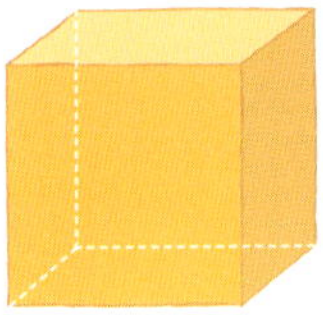

b This shape is a ______.

It has ___ faces, ___ edges,

and ___ vertices.

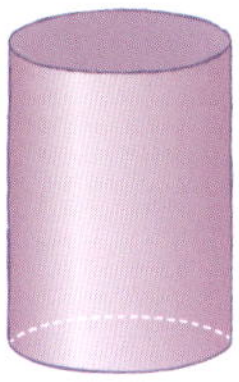

c This shape is a ______.

It has ___ faces, ___ edges,

and ___ vertices.

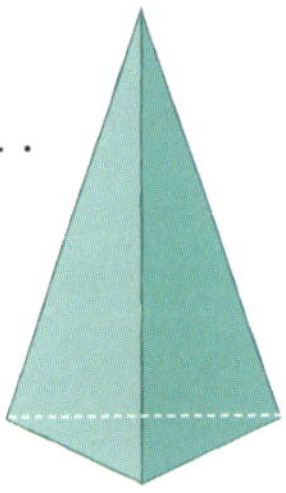

d This shape is a ______.

It has ___ faces, ___ edges,

and ___ vertices.

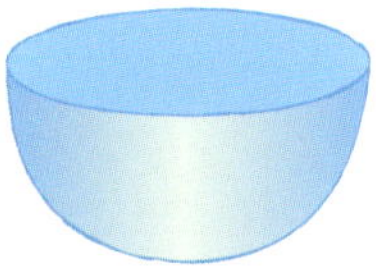

e This shape is a ______.

It has ___ faces, ___ edges,

and ___ vertices.

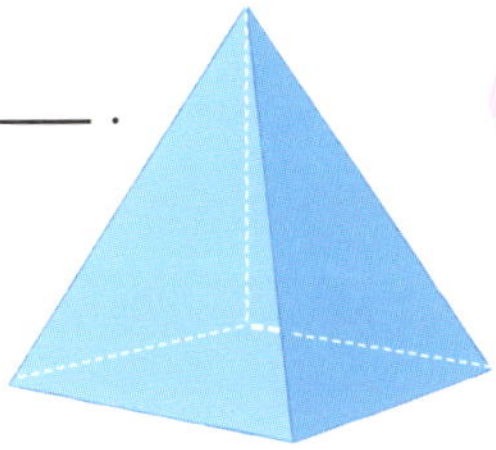

f This shape is a ______.

It has ___ faces, ___ edges,

and ___ vertices.

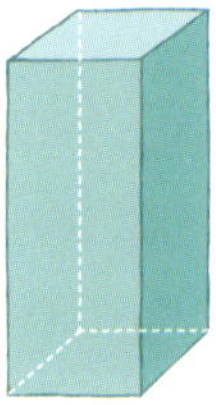

MATHS IN CONTEXT

Paint a shape

Mia has been making art by painting one face of a 3D shape, then pressing that face onto paper. Fill in which 3D shape or shapes could have made each of the prints below.

1. cube
square-based pyramid
______

2. ______

3. ______

4. ______

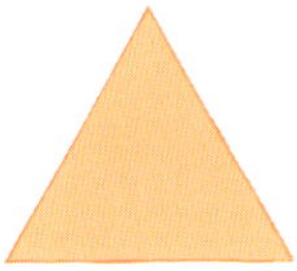

5. ______

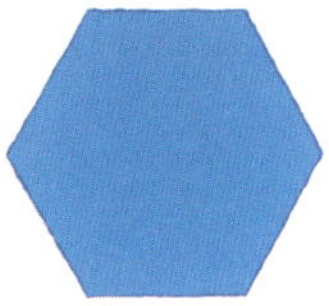

6. ______

Pages 224–225

Prisms

A prism is a type of 3D shape. The two ends of a prism are the same shape and size, and all of its faces are flat. Every prism is the same size and shape all the way along its length.

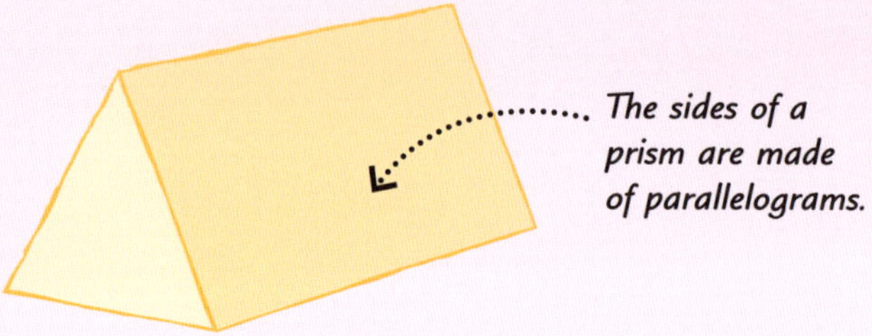
The sides of a prism are made of parallelograms.

Triangular prism

Warm-up Draw a cross through each shape below that is not a prism.

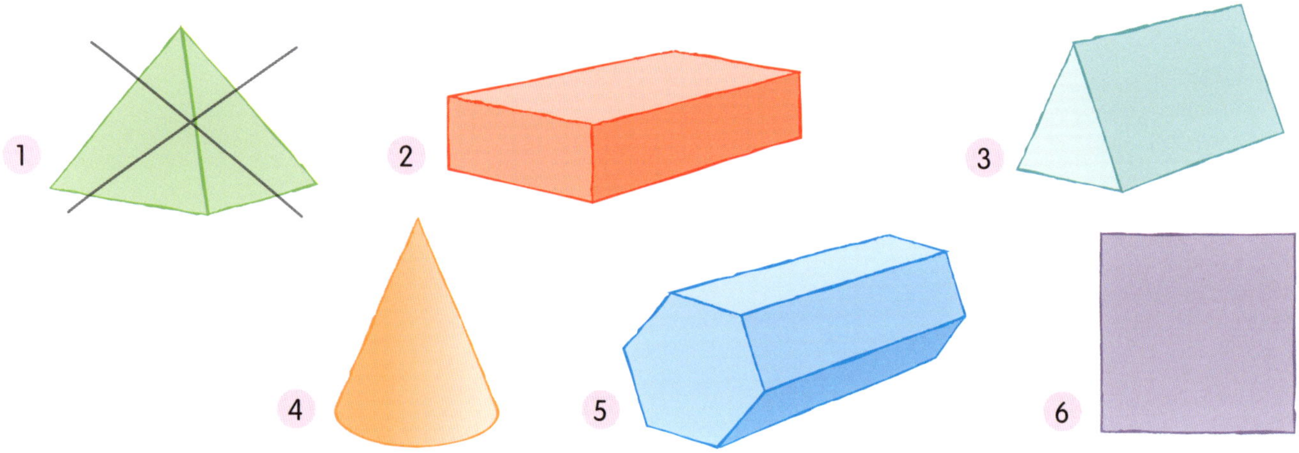
1
2
3
4
5
6

1 Draw a circle around all twelve of the prisms in this picture.

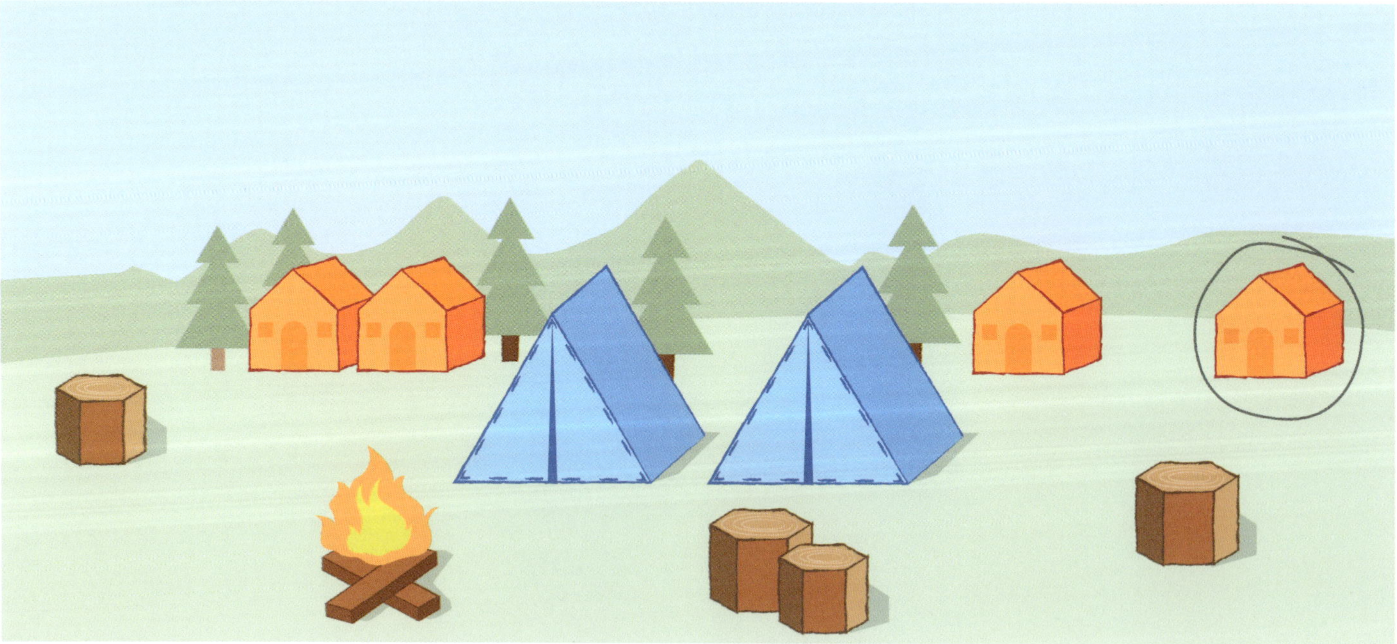

2 Complete these sentences about prisms.

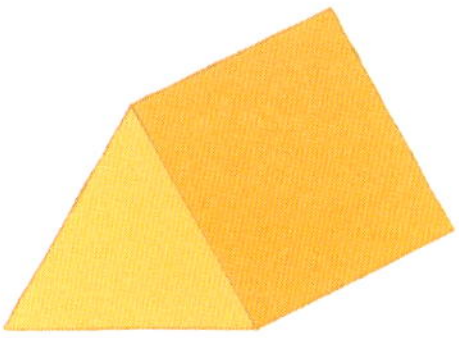

a This prism has

5 faces, 9 edges,

and 6 vertices.

b This prism has

___ faces, ___ edges,

and ___ vertices.

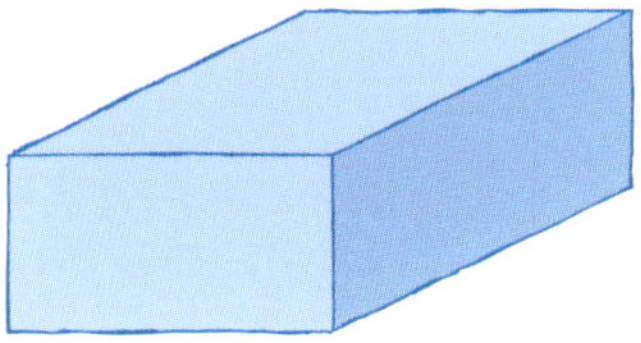

c This prism has

___ faces, ___ edges,

and ___ vertices.

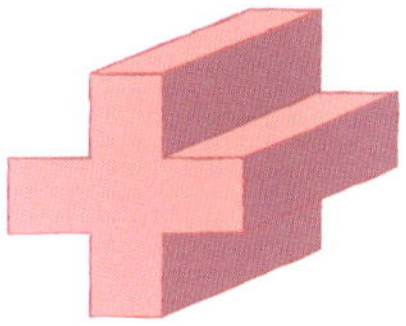

d This prism has

___ faces, ___ edges,

and ___ vertices.

e This prism has

___ faces, ___ edges,

and ___ vertices.

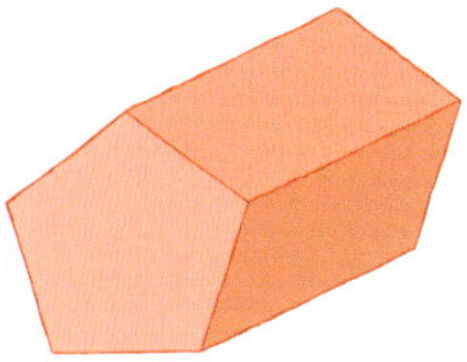

f This prism has

___ faces, ___ edges,

and ___ vertices.

3 Draw lines to match each cross-section with the prism it has come from. Then draw lines to match each prism with its name.

a 

b 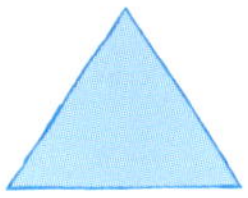

c 

d 

e 

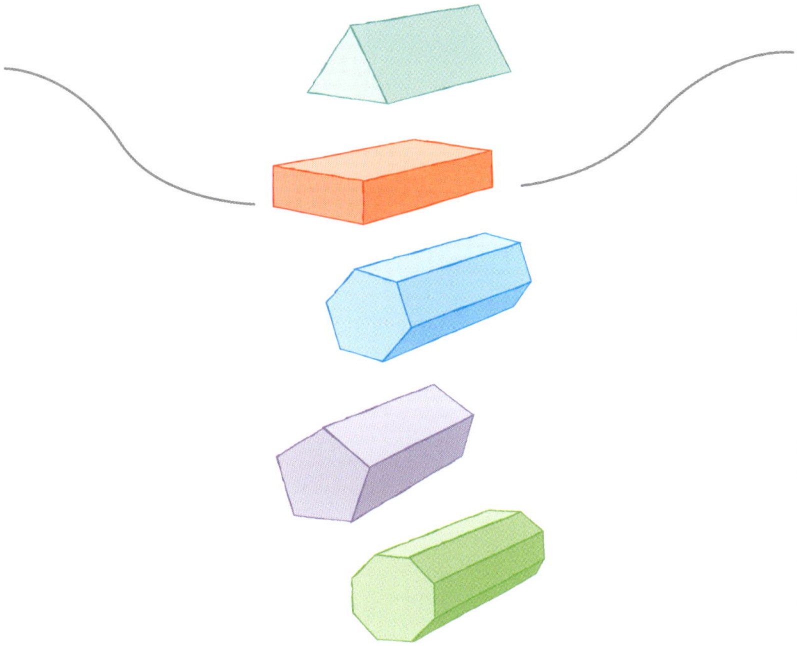

cuboid

pentagonal prism

triangular prism

octagonal prism

hexagonal prism

Pages 226–227

Angles

An angle is a measure of the amount of turn (or rotation) from one direction to another. It is also the difference in direction between two lines meeting at a point.

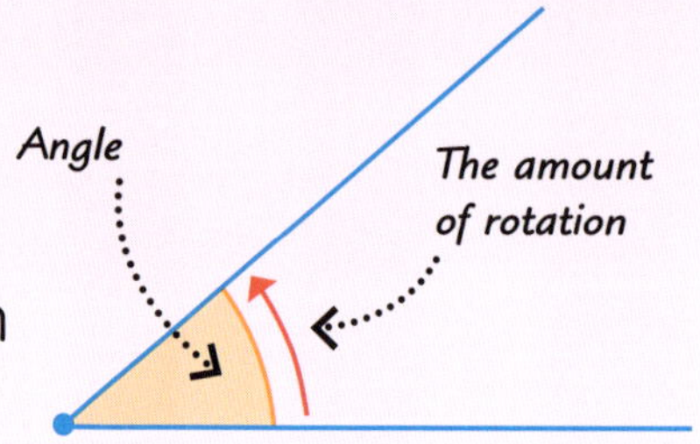

REMEMBER!
Angles are formed whenever two or more straight lines meet or cross over each other.

Warm-up Fill in how many angles there are in each of these diagrams.

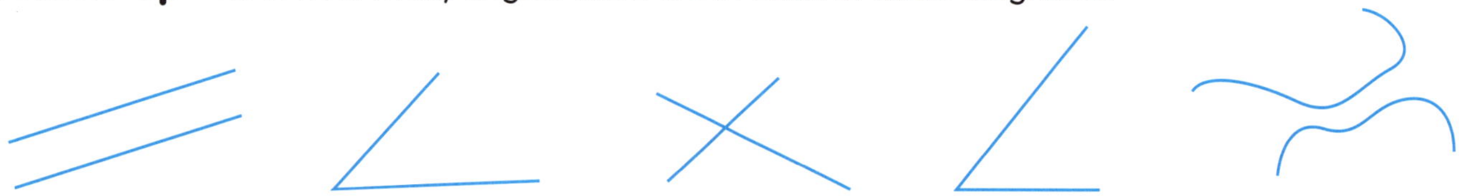

1 0   2 ____   3 ____   4 ____   5 ____

1 Colour in the largest angle on each diagram.

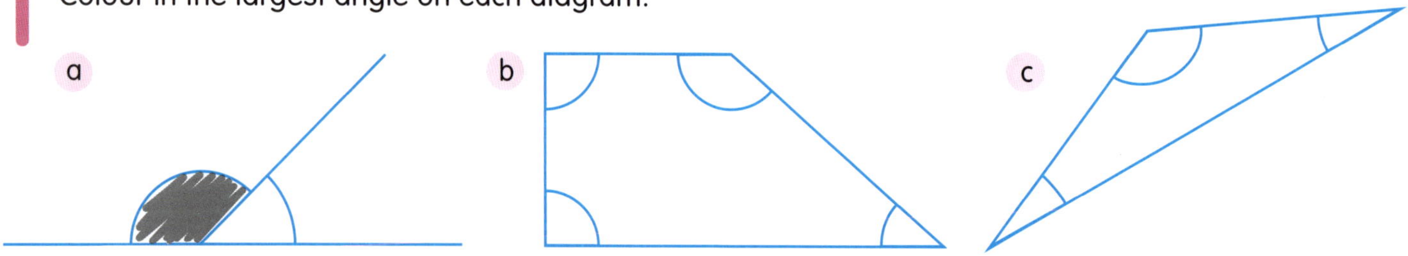

2 Compare the sizes of these pairs of angles by writing less than (<), greater than (>), or equal to (=).

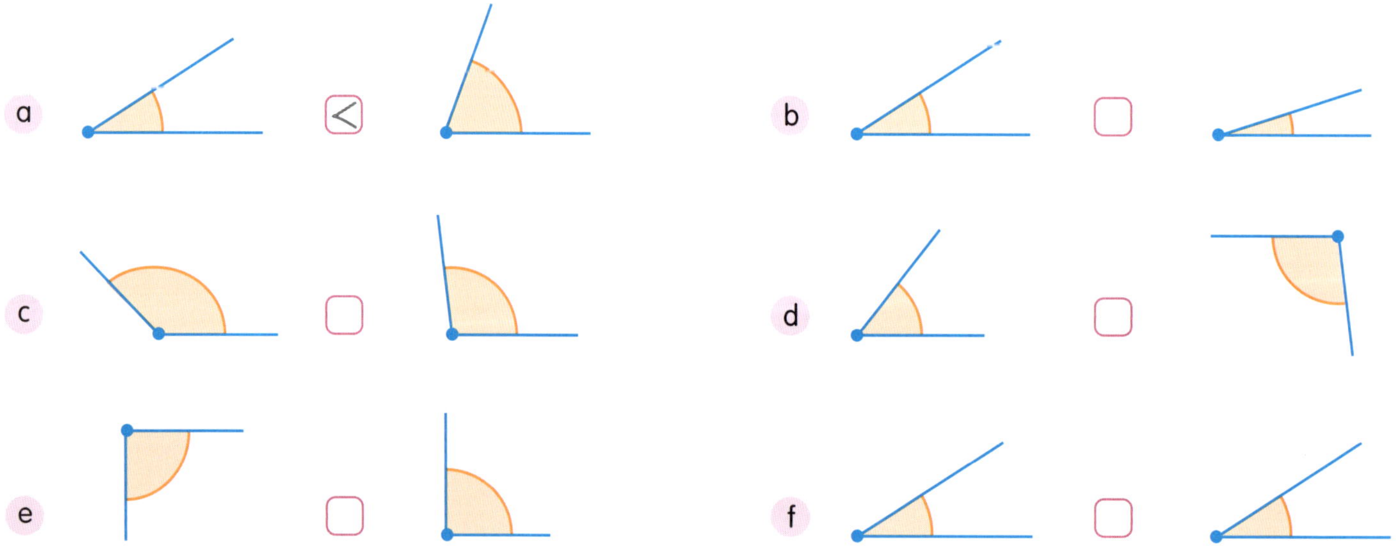

Page 230

Degrees

We use units called degrees to measure angles. Degrees describe precisely how far something has turned around a fixed point. The symbol for degrees is a small circle, like this: °.

REMEMBER!
In a full circle, or a full turn, there are 360 degrees (360°).

Warm-up Use a protractor to measure the size of each of these angles.

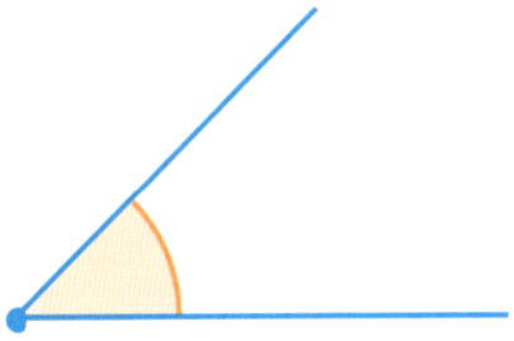

1 45°

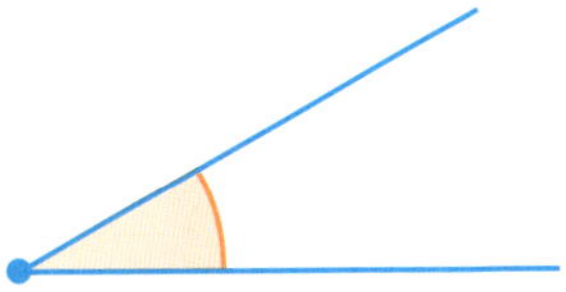

2 ____

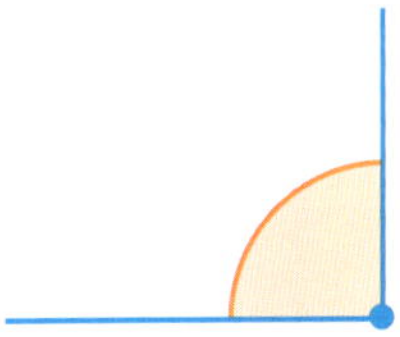

3 ____

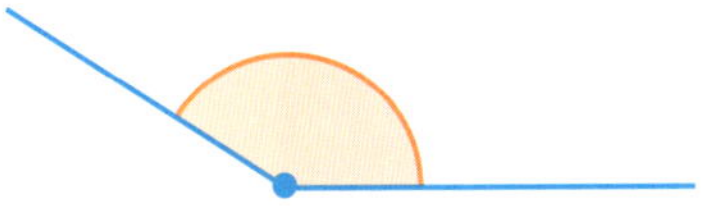

4 ____

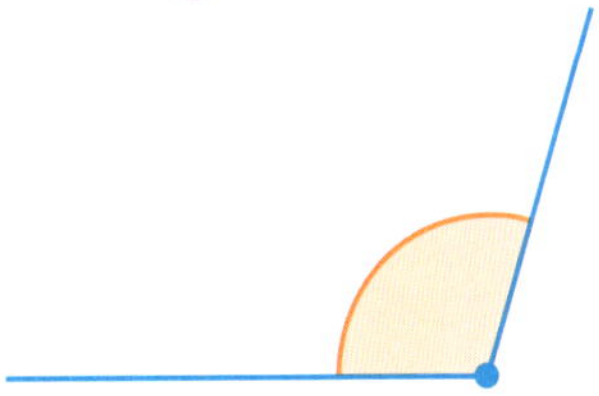

5 ____

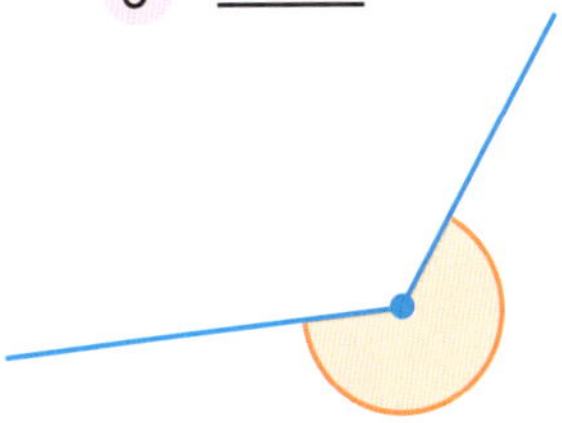

6 ____

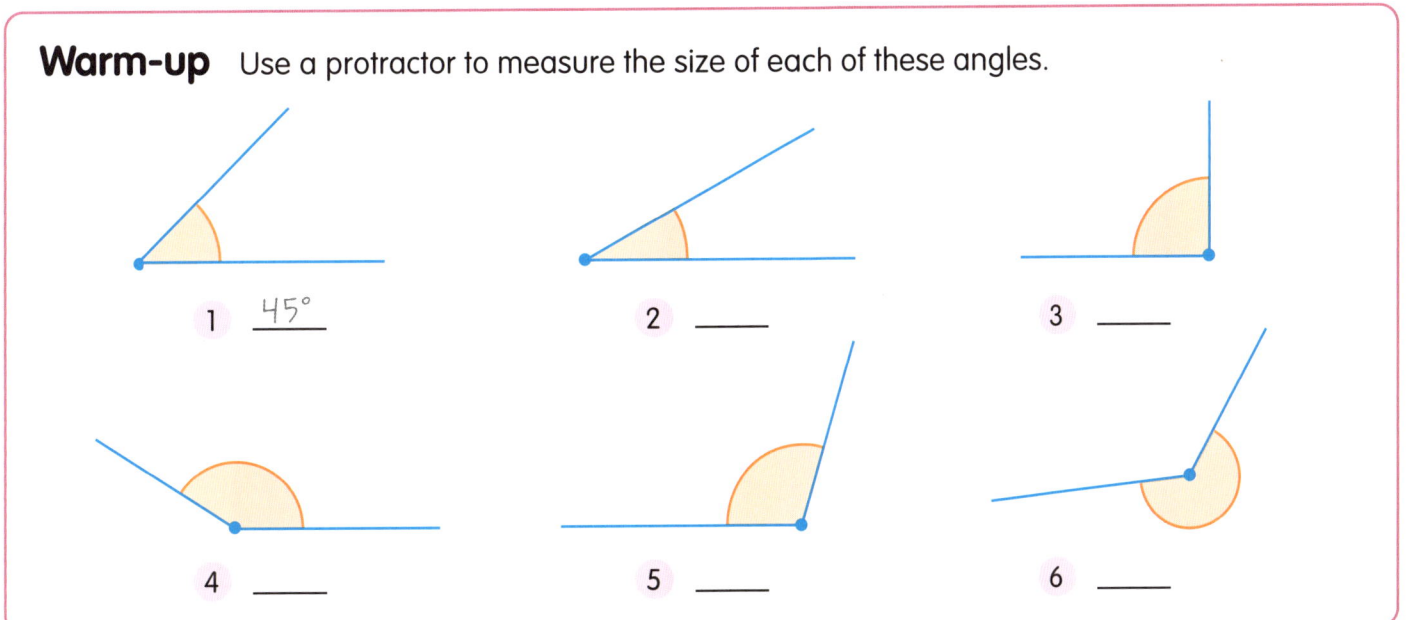

1 Use a protractor and a ruler to draw each of these angles.

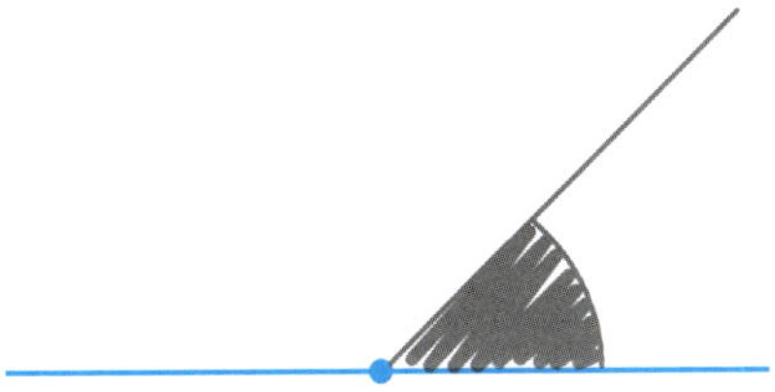

a This angle is 45°.

b This angle is 100°.

c This angle is 135°.

d This angle is 28°.

e This angle is 65°.

f This angle is 70°.

Page 231

Right angles

A right angle is a quarter turn of a circle, and it measures exactly 90°. Four right angles (4 x 90°) make up a full circle (360°).

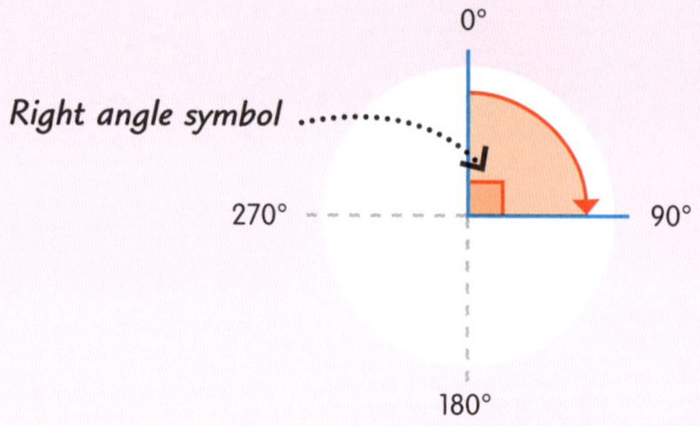

Warm-up Draw the right angle symbol onto each right angle in these drawings.

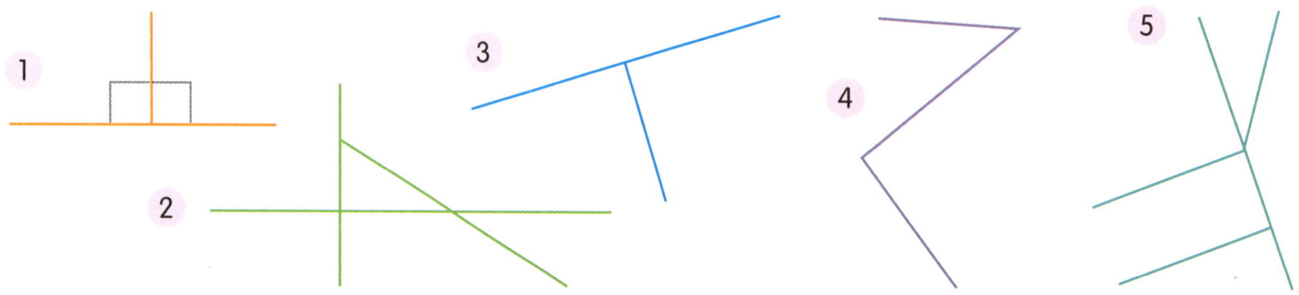

1

Use numbers to complete these sentences about different angles and turns.

a A quarter turn is equal to _1_ right angle(s).

b A half turn is equal to __ right angle(s).

c A three-quarter turn is equal to __ right angle(s).

d A full turn is equal to __ right angle(s).

2

Draw lines to match each angle with the correct degree.

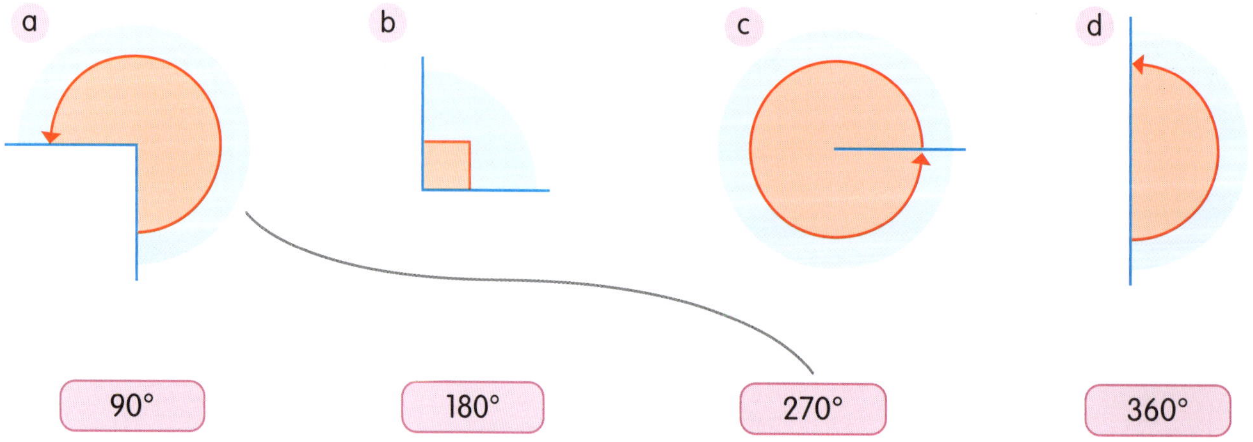

3

Read these descriptions, then draw shapes to match them.
The right angles should be inside the shape.

a A shape that has exactly 2 right angles.

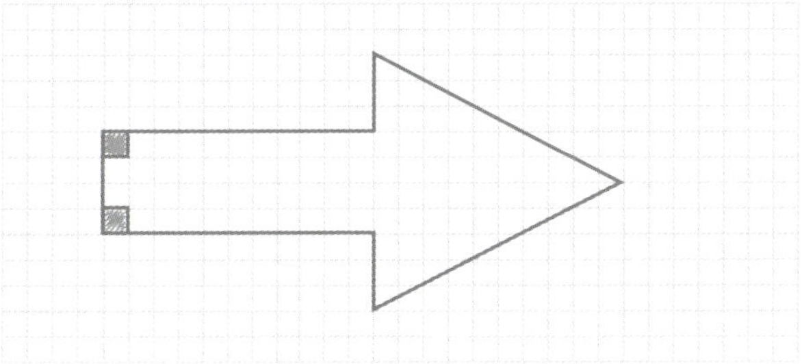

b A shape that has exactly 0 right angles.

c A shape that has exactly 4 right angles.

d A shape that has exactly 3 right angles.

e A shape that has exactly 1 right angle.

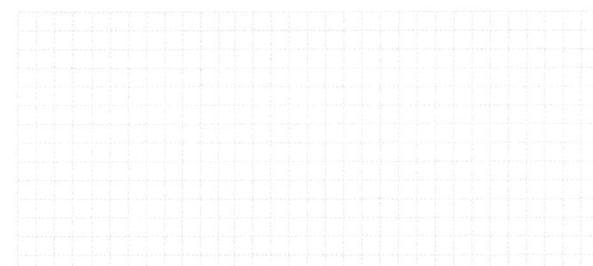

f A shape that has exactly 6 right angles.

MATHS IN CONTEXT

How many angles?

Dan and his family have just moved into a new house. Write down how many right angles you can see in this picture of Dan's new house and the tree. It might help to draw them on so you don't lose count.

I can see ______ right angles in the picture.

Page 232

Types of angle

Different types of angles are named according to their size.

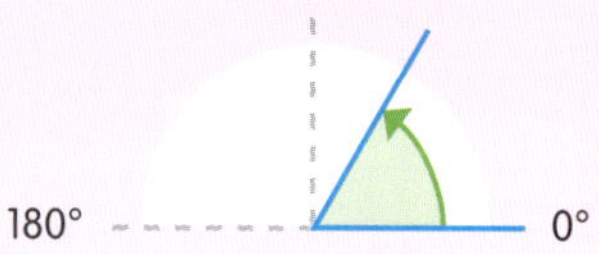

An acute angle is less than 90°.

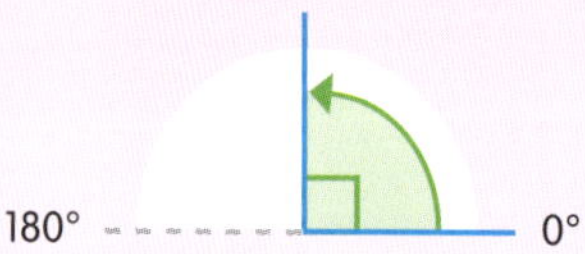

A right angle is exactly 90°.

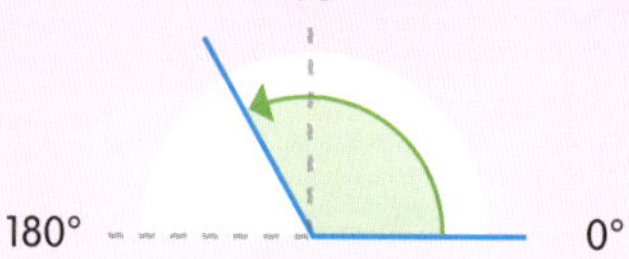

An obtuse angle is more than 90° but less than 180°.

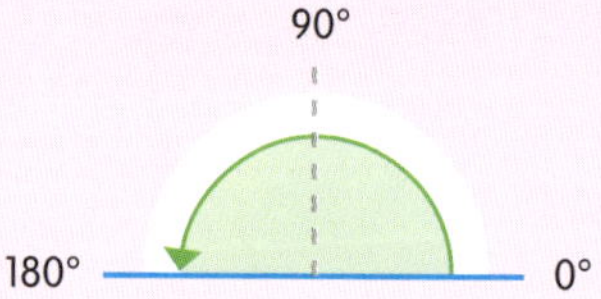

A straight angle is exactly 180°.

Warm-up Draw lines to match each angle with the correct label.

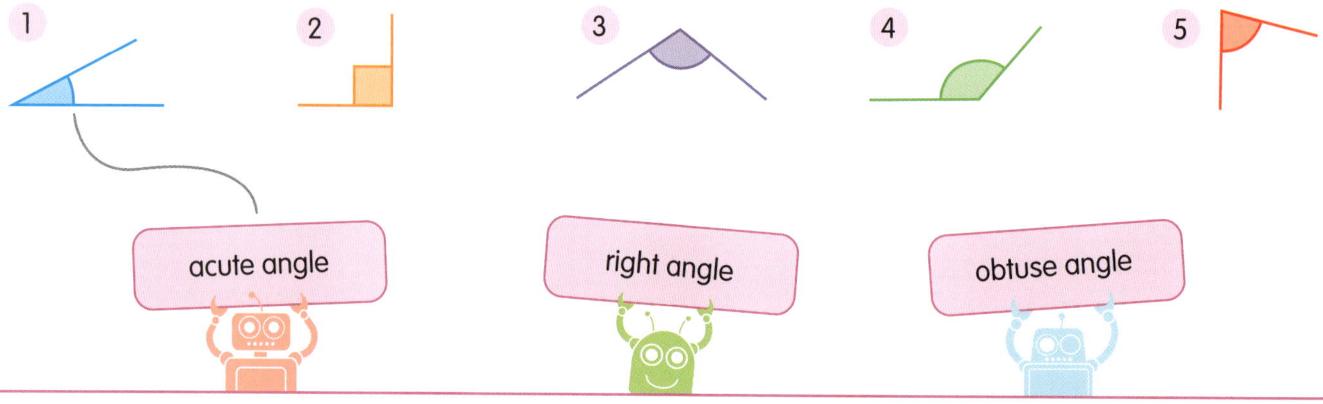

1

Fill in which type of angle has been created by the hands of each clock.

a an acute angle

b ____________ angle

c ____________ angle

d ____________ angle

e ____________ angle

f ____________ angle

2

Use the words in the word box to help you complete these sentences. You will need to use some words twice.

an acute angle	an obtuse angle	a straight angle

a An angle that measures 67° is an acute angle .

b An angle that measures 12° is ________________ .

c An angle that measures 180° is ________________ .

d An angle that measures 91° is ________________ .

e An angle that measures 160° is ________________ .

f An angle that measures 47° is ________________ .

3

Tick the boxes to say if each statement is always true, sometimes true, or never true.

	Always true	Sometimes true	Never true
a An acute angle has a greater turn than an obtuse angle.			✓
b An obtuse angle has a greater turn than a right angle.			
c A straight line is an obtuse angle.			
d If you put two acute angles together, you will have an obtuse angle.			
e If you put four acute angles together, you will have an obtuse angle.			
f If you halve an obtuse angle, you will end up with an acute angle.			

4

Use the key to help you draw in the angles inside the shapes in this picture.

Key

- Acute angle
- Obtuse angle
- Right angle

Pages 233

Coordinates

Coordinates help us to describe where a point or place is on a map or a grid. Coordinates come in pairs, to tell us how far along and up or down the point is.

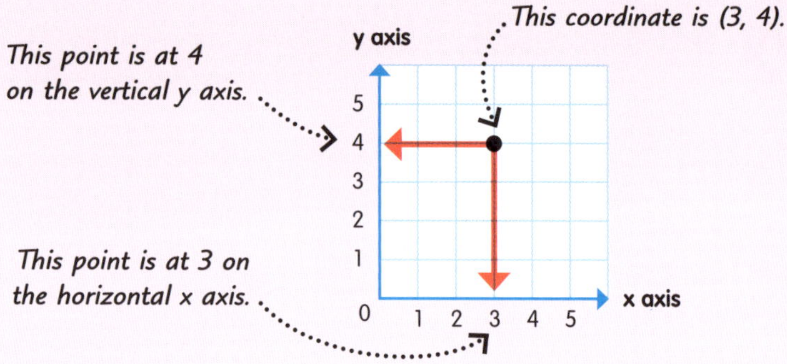

Warm-up

Find the coordinates of each of these points.

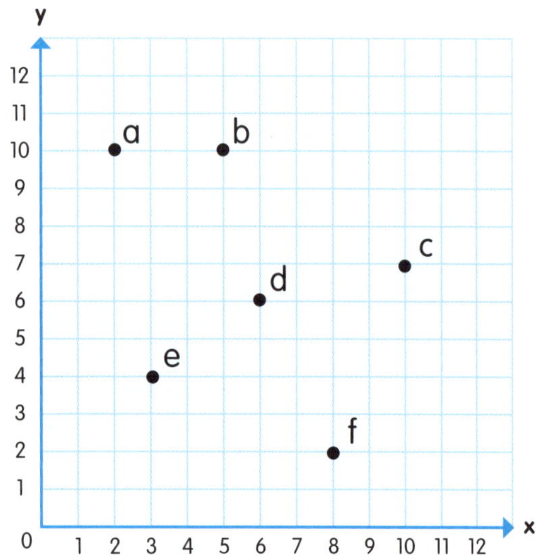

1 Point a = (2 , 10)

2 Point b = (__ , __)

3 Point c = (__ , __)

4 Point d = (__ , __)

5 Point e = (__ , __)

6 Point f = (__ , __)

REMEMBER!
The x coordinate is always written before the y coordinate.

1

Plot these coordinates onto the grid, to find out where the pirates have buried their stolen treasure.

a A sack of coins is at (4, 6).

b A chest of gems is at (6, 4).

c A hoard of silver is at (9, 2).

d A bag of jewels is at (9, 7).

e A pile of treasure is at (7, 8).

f A casket of pearls is at (8, 11).

g A heap of gold is at (10, 12).

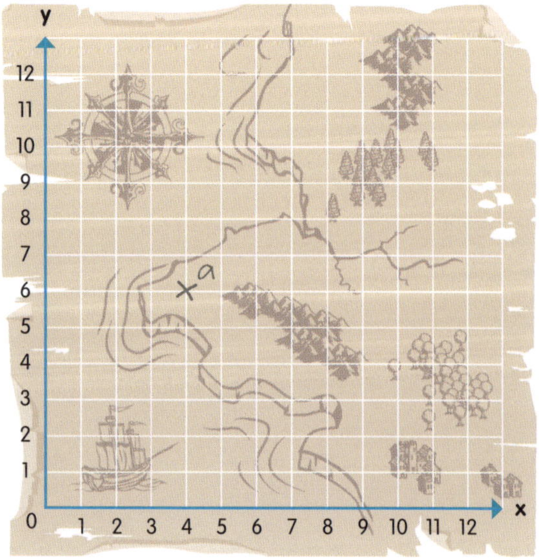

2

Plot these coordinates onto the grids, then join each set of dots to make a shape. Under each grid fill in which shape you have drawn.

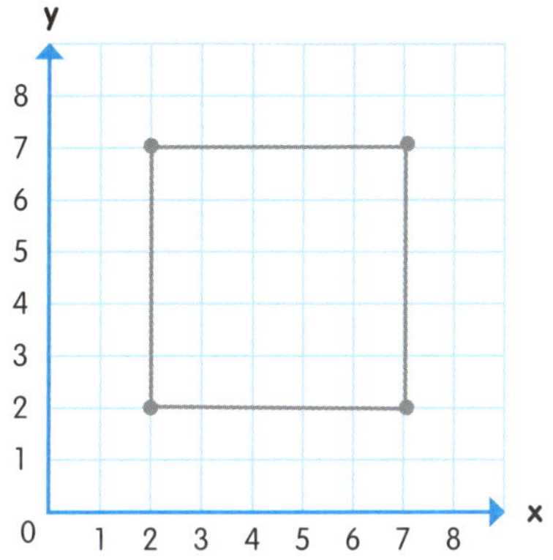

(2, 2) (2, 7) (7, 2) (7, 7)

a The shape is _a square_.

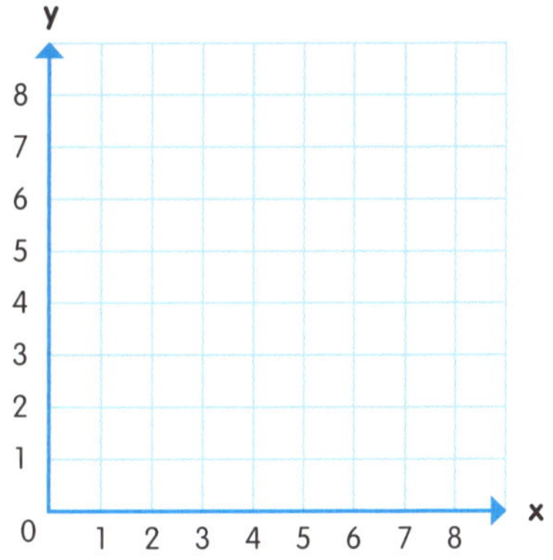

(1, 3) (1, 7) (8, 3) (8, 7)

b The shape is ______________.

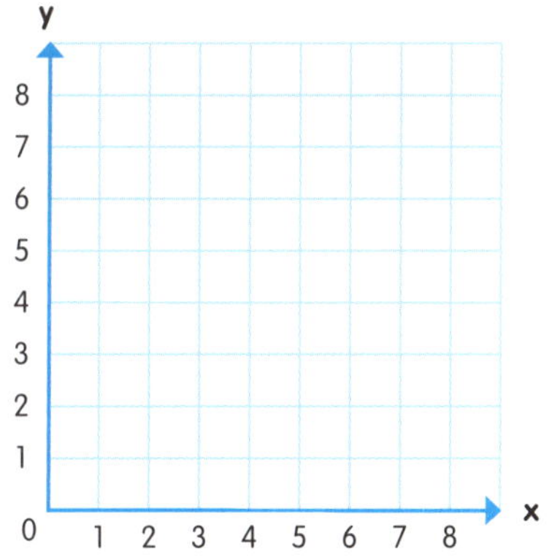

(3, 2) (5, 4) (7, 2)

c The shape is ______________.

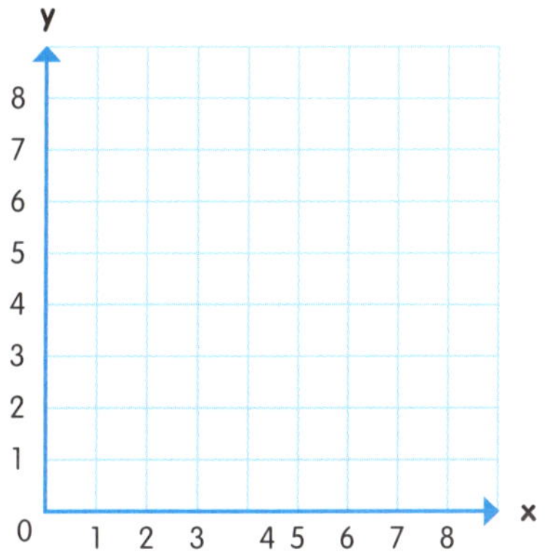

(1, 4) (3, 6) (5, 6) (7, 4)

d The shape is ______________.

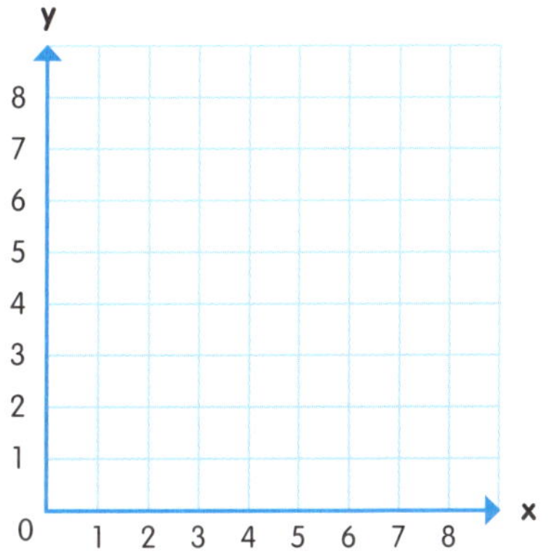

(3, 3) (3, 4) (4, 5) (5, 4) (5, 3) (4, 2)

e The shape is ______________.

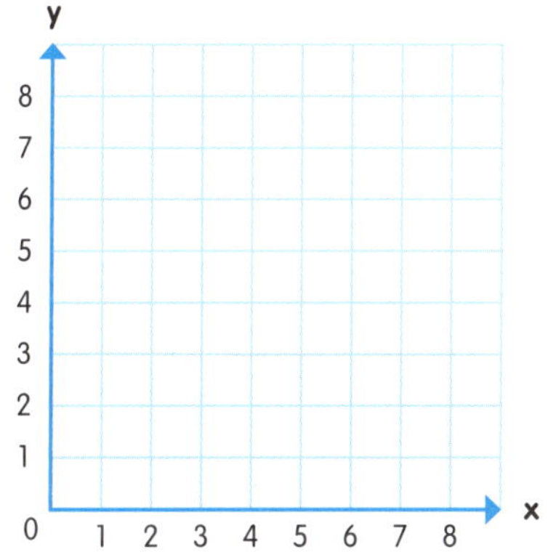

(1, 4) (3, 6) (4, 7) (6, 5) (7, 4)

f The shape is ______________.

3

Some of the coordinates below have been written incorrectly. Circle the ones that are wrong.

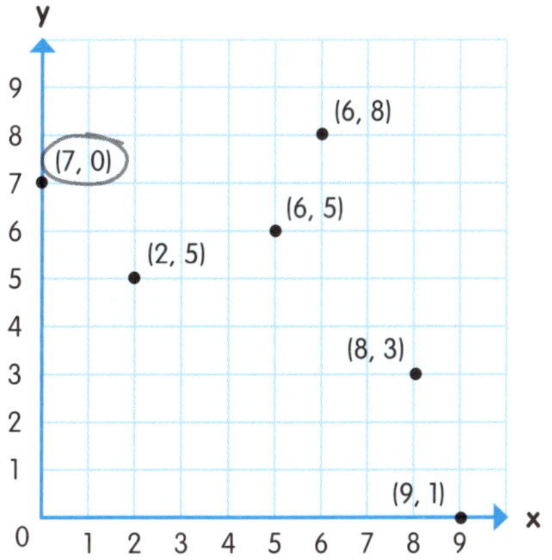

MATHS IN CONTEXT

Plot a pentagon

Ian wants to draw a pentagon on this grid. Work out one set of coordinates that he could use.

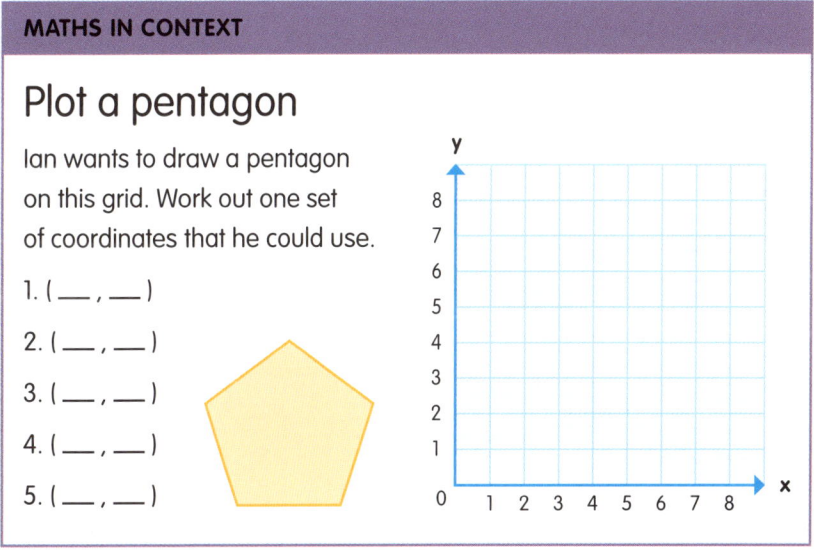

1. (__ , __)
2. (__ , __)
3. (__ , __)
4. (__ , __)
5. (__ , __)

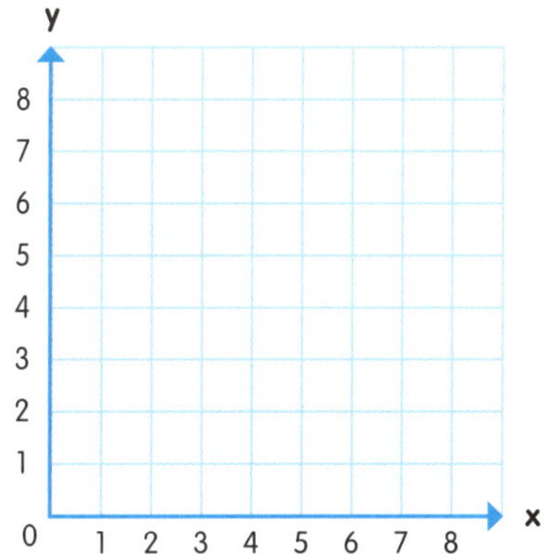

Page 248

Position and direction

We can use a grid and coordinates to describe the position of a point or place on a map. When using maps, coordinates describe a specific square on the map, not a point.

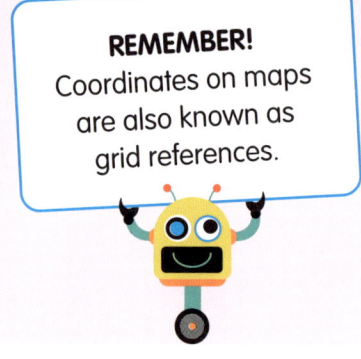

REMEMBER!
Coordinates on maps are also known as grid references.

Warm-up

Look at this map of a theme park. Fill in the coordinates of each of these objects.

1. The duck pond D3
2. The rollercoaster entrance ____
3. The bouncy castle ____
4. Somewhere to buy an ice cream ____
5. The helter-skelter entrance ____
6. The sheep ____

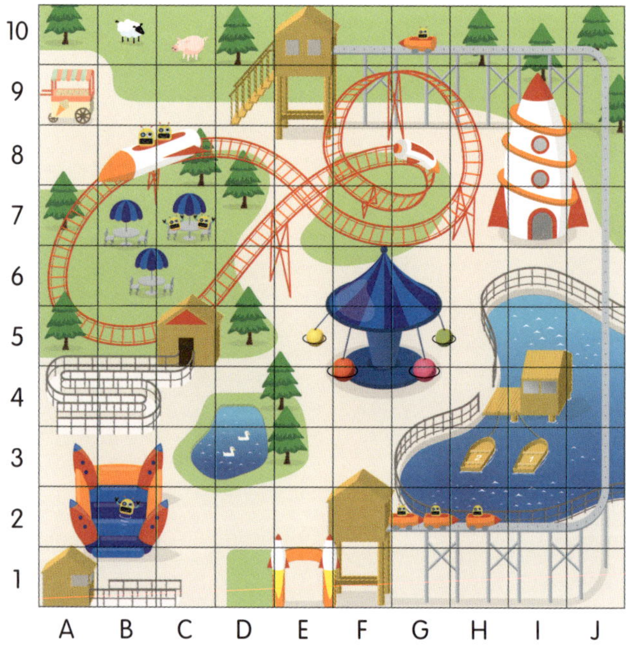

1

Use this map of a farmyard to fill in the position of each of these animals with the correct coordinates.

a. Cow K5
b. Sheep ____
c. Horse ____
d. Chicken ____
e. Dog ____
f. Cat ____
g. Goat ____

2 Some children have flown to different countries on holiday. Fill in the coordinates below for the cities each child took off from and landed in.

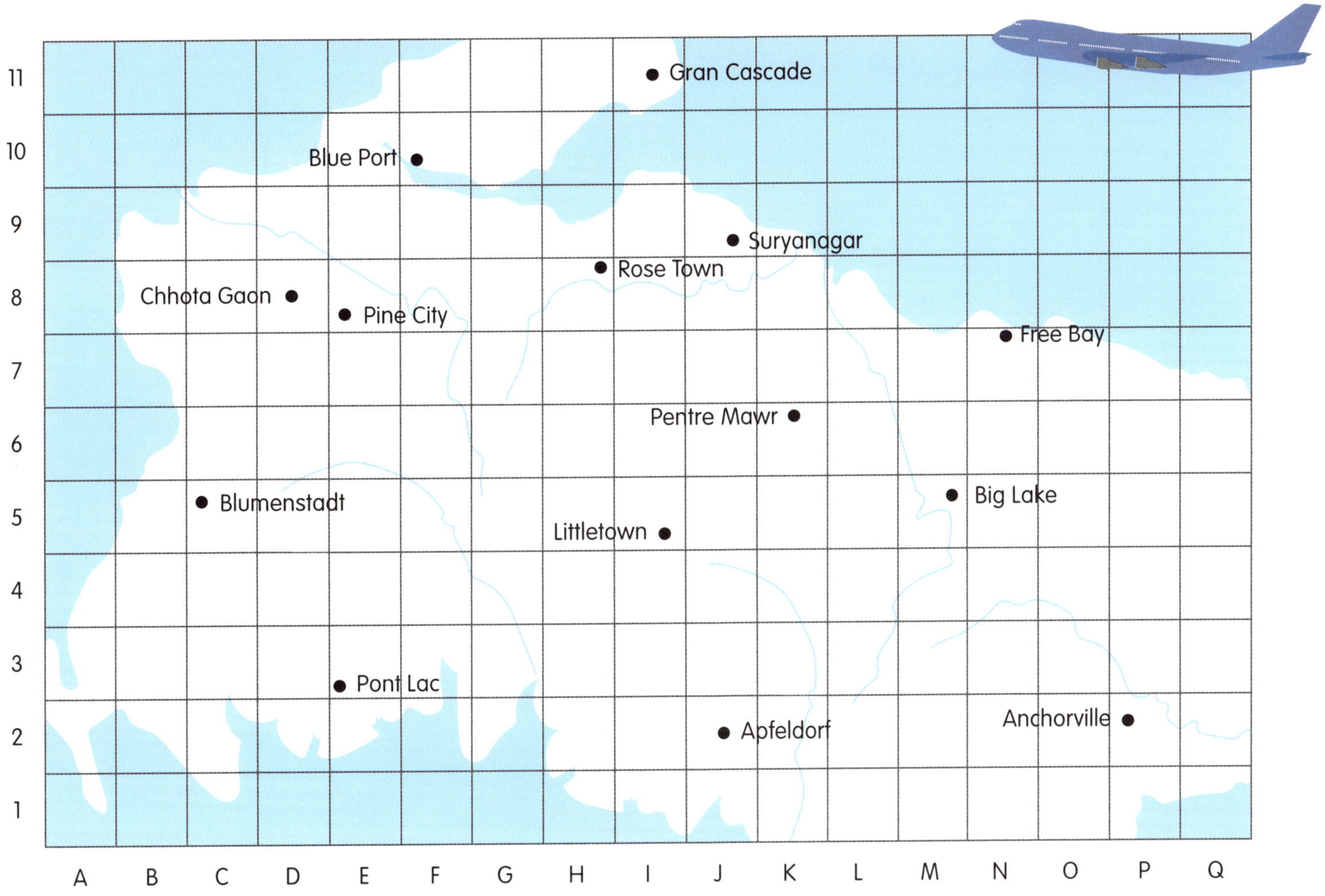

a Ella took off from Big Lake and landed in Apfeldorf. She took off from M5 and landed in J2.

b Jasper took off from Littletown and landed in Pentre Mawr. He took off from ____ and landed in ____.

c Marcus took off from Pine City and landed in Rose Town. He took off from ____ and landed in ____.

d Marat took off from Chhota Gaon and landed in Blue Port. He took off from ____ and landed in ____.

e Nala took off from Gran Cascade and landed in Free Bay. She took off from ____ and landed in ____.

f Ana took off from Suryanagar and landed in Anchorville. She took off from ____ and landed in ____.

g Nico took off from Blumenstadt and landed in Pont Lac. He took off from ____ and landed in ____.

h Andrea took off from Blue Port and landed in Free Bay. She took off from ____ and landed in ____.

Pages 252–253

Compass directions

We can use a compass to help us find a location or to help us move in a particular direction. A compass has a pointer that always shows the direction of north.

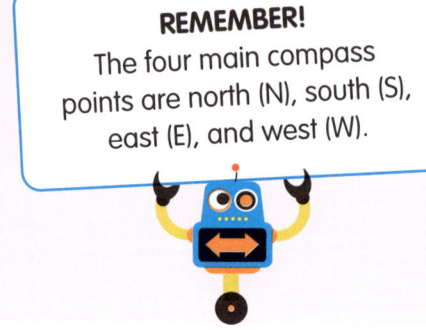

REMEMBER!
The four main compass points are north (N), south (S), east (E), and west (W).

Warm-up Fill in the labels to show the compass directions.

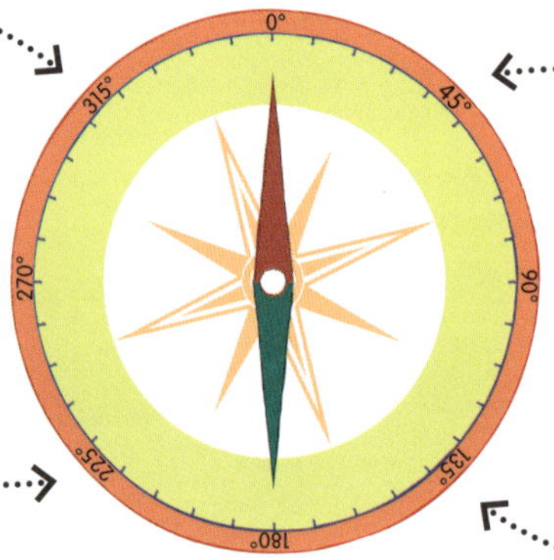

1 northwest

2 ________

3 ________

4 ________

5 ________

6 ________

7 ________

8 ________

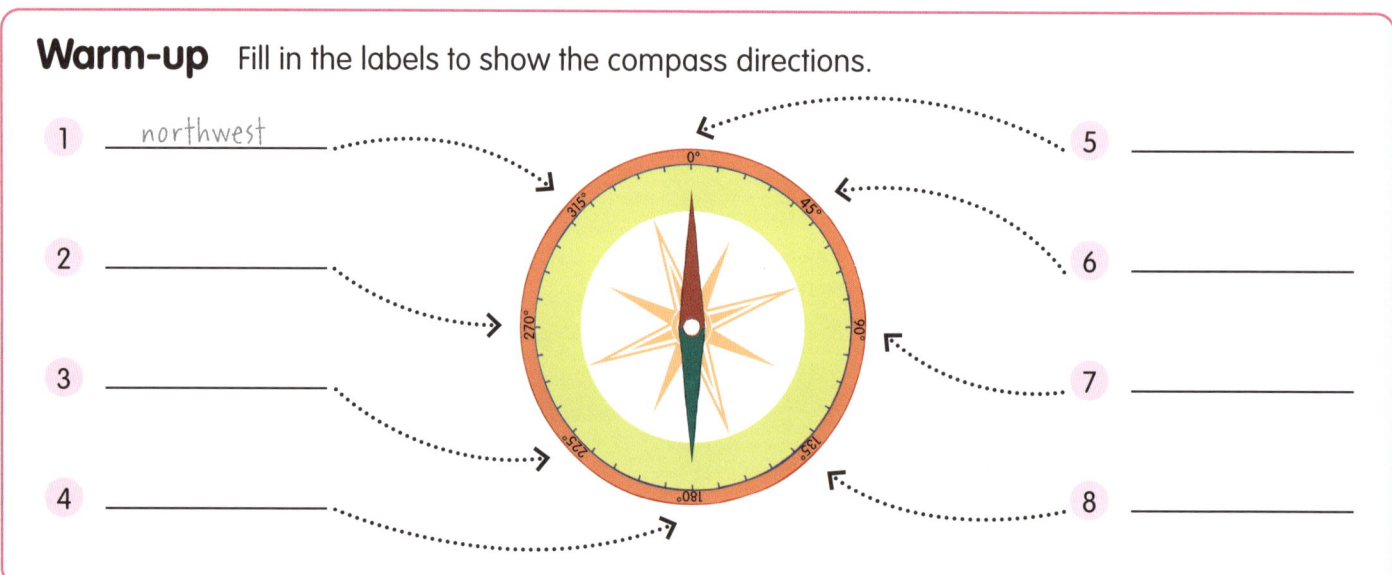

1 A robot is travelling around an island. Work out which direction the robot has travelled in.

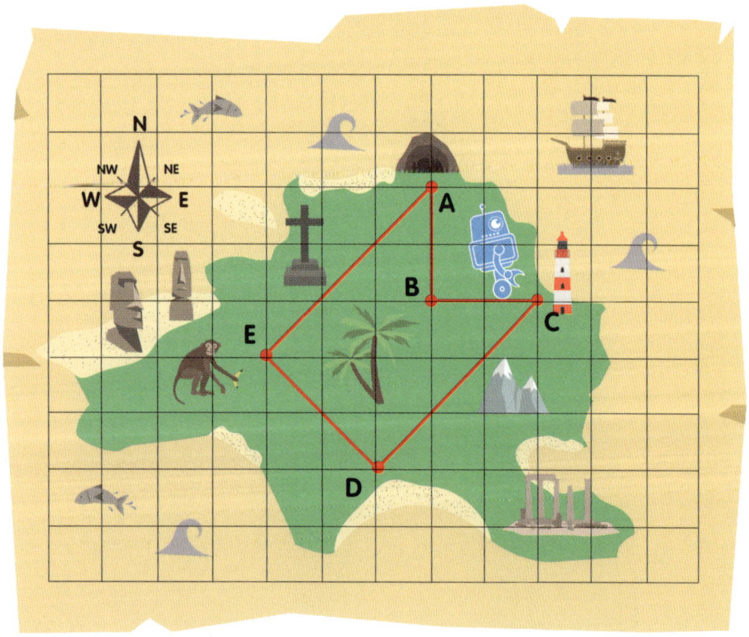

a From point A to point B, the direction the robot travelled in was south.

b From point B to point C, the direction the robot travelled in was ________.

c From point C to point D, the direction the robot travelled in was ________.

d From point D to point E, the direction the robot travelled in was ________.

e From point E to point A, the direction the robot travelled in was ________.

2 A bird is flying around a campsite. Use the sentences below to help you add each letter to the map to show the bird's route.

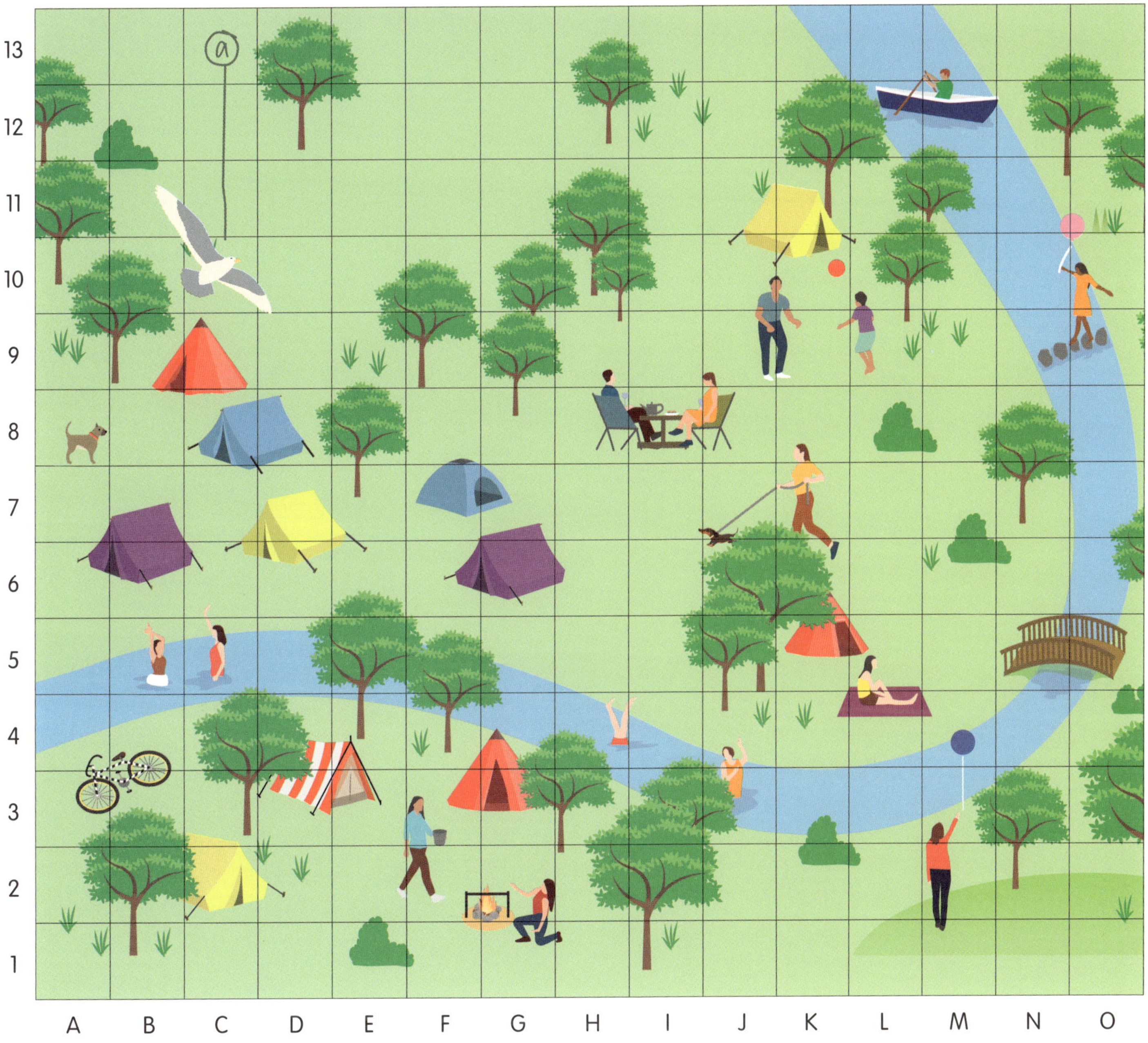

a The bird travels north for 3 squares.

b The bird then travels east for 5 squares.

c The bird then travels south for 4 squares.

d The bird then travels west for 2 squares.

e The bird then travels southwest for 3 squares.

f The bird then travels south for 5 squares.

g The bird then travels northeast for 7 squares.

h Finally, the bird travels east for 4 squares.

Pages 254–255

Reflective symmetry

If you can divide a shape into two identical halves that fit exactly onto each other, then the shape has reflective symmetry. A shape can have more than one line of reflective symmetry.

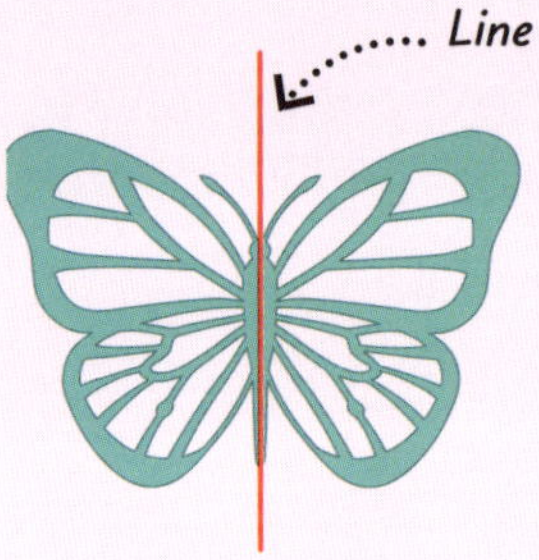

This shape has one line of reflective symmetry.

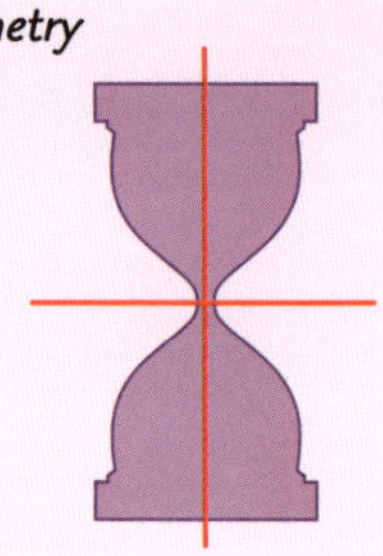

This shape has two lines of reflective symmetry.

Warm-up Colour in the shapes below that have at least one line of reflective symmetry.

1 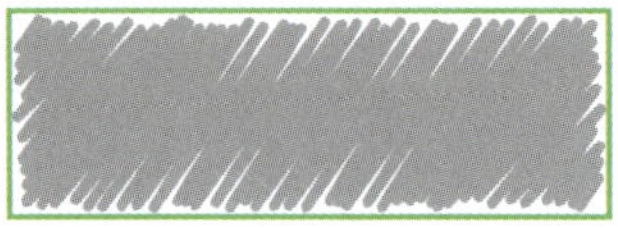

2 

3 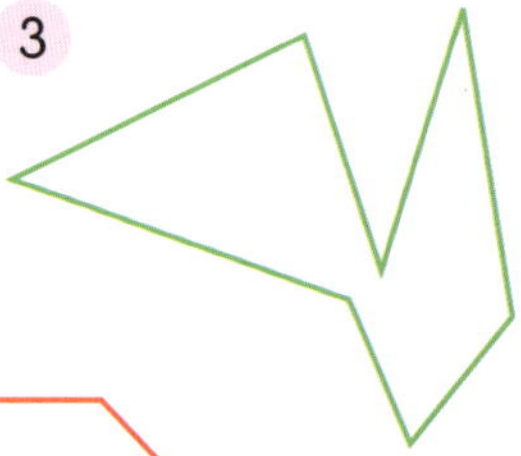

4 

5 

6 

7 

8 

9 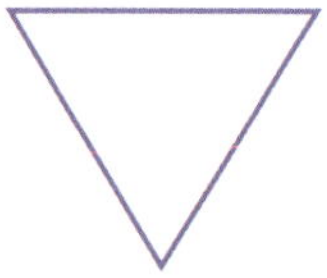

10 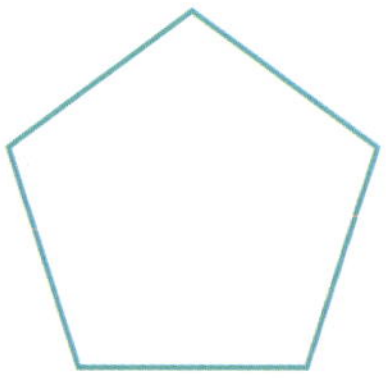

11 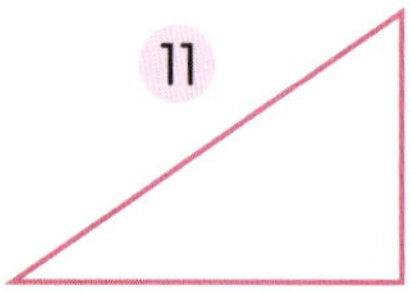

1 Draw all the lines of reflective symmetry onto each of these shapes.

a 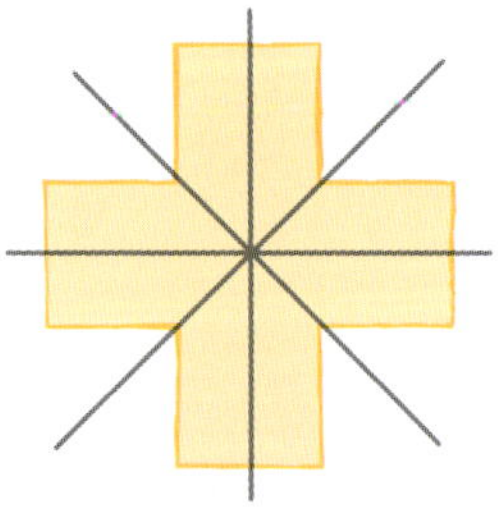

b 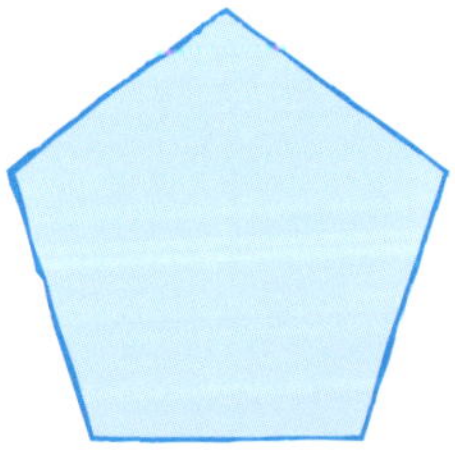

c  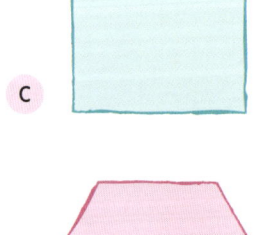

d 

e 

f 

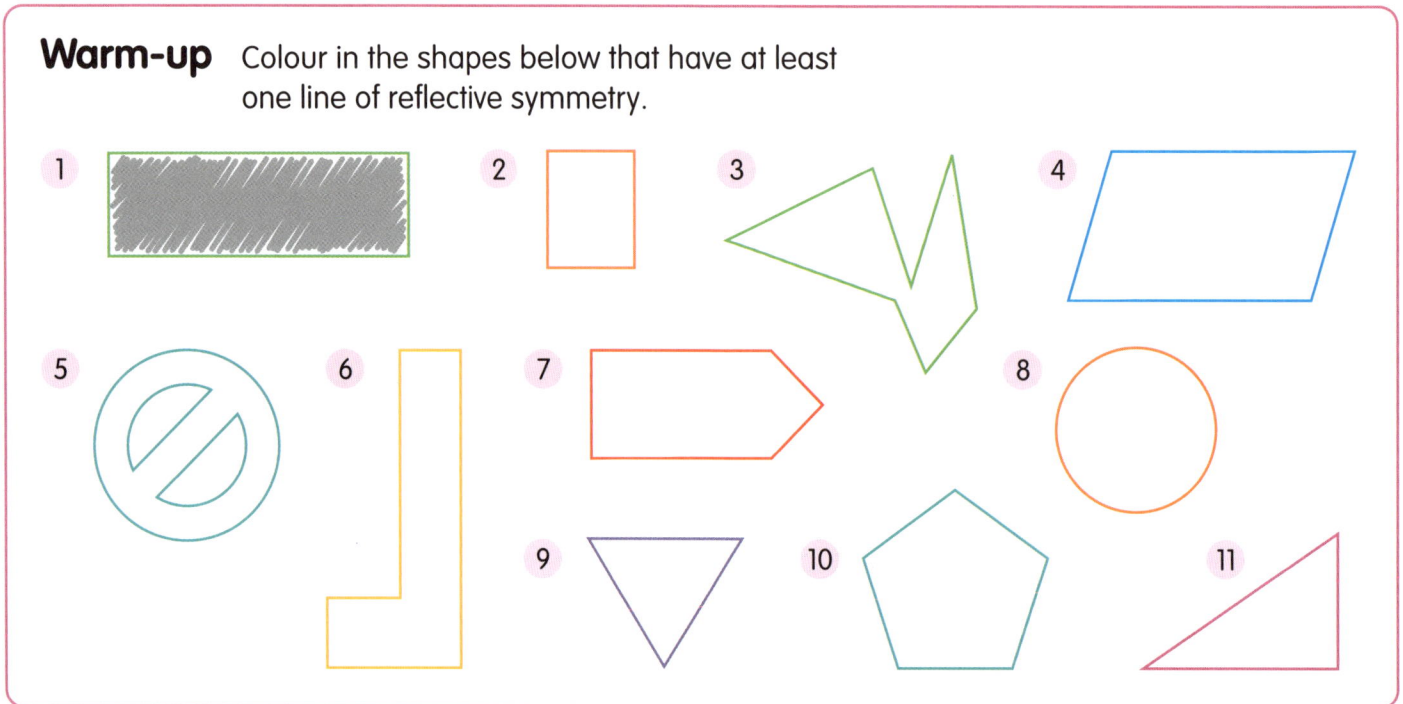

g 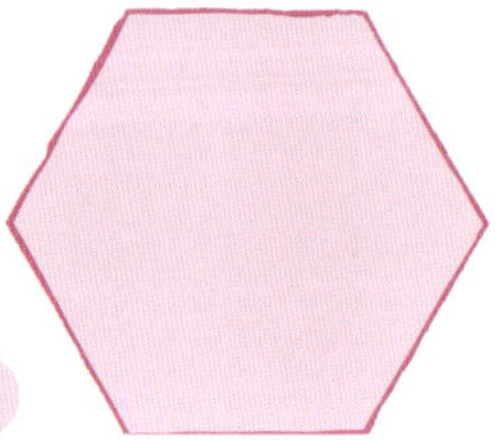

h 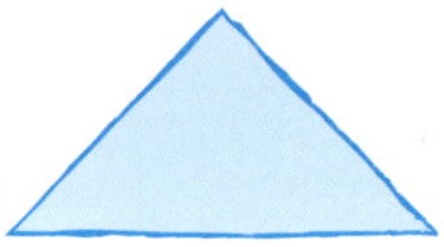

2 Draw in the missing half of each shape, then fill in how many lines of symmetry it has.

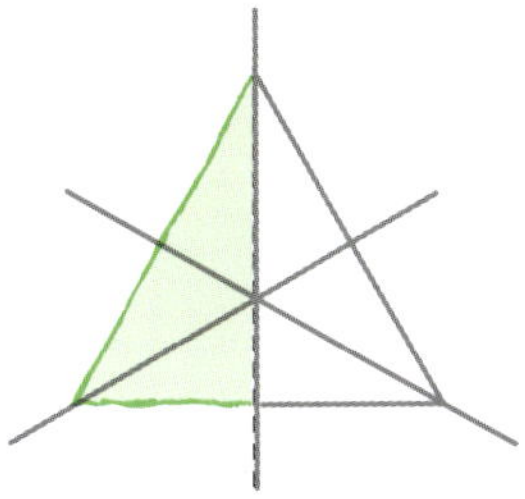

a 3 line(s) of symmetry

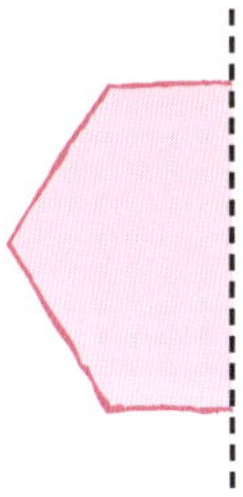

b ___ line(s) of symmetry

c ___ line(s) of symmetry

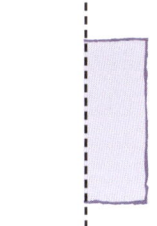

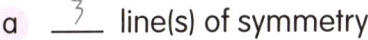

d ___ line(s) of symmetry

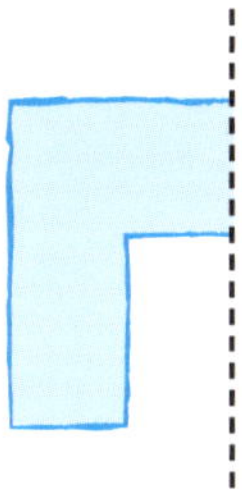

e ___ line(s) of symmetry

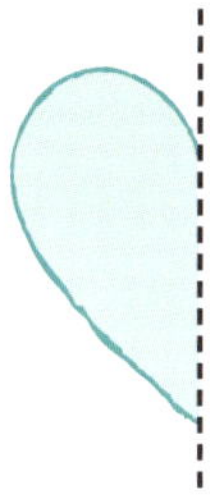

f ___ line(s) of symmetry

3 Have a look at the letters of the alphabet below, then place each letter in its correct box.

A B C D E F G H I J K L M N O P Q R S T U V W X Y Z

a no lines of symmetry

b one line of symmetry

A

c two or more lines of symmetry

Pages 256–257

Tally marks

Tally marks are used to count quickly when we collect data. Each tally mark is a line that represents one thing counted.

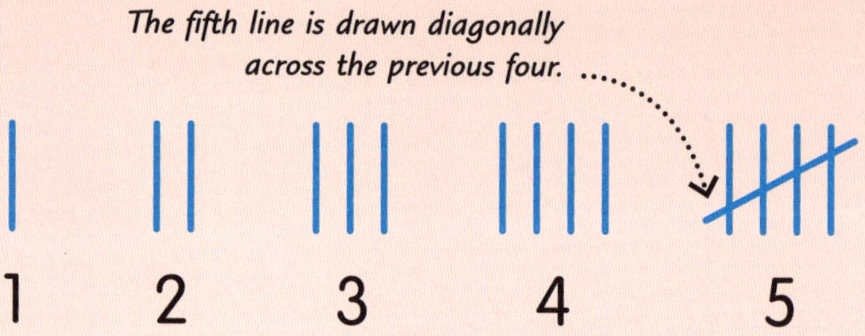
The fifth line is drawn diagonally across the previous four.
1
2
3
4
5

Warm-up Draw lines to match each set of tally marks with the correct number.

1
2
3
4
5
6
7
8

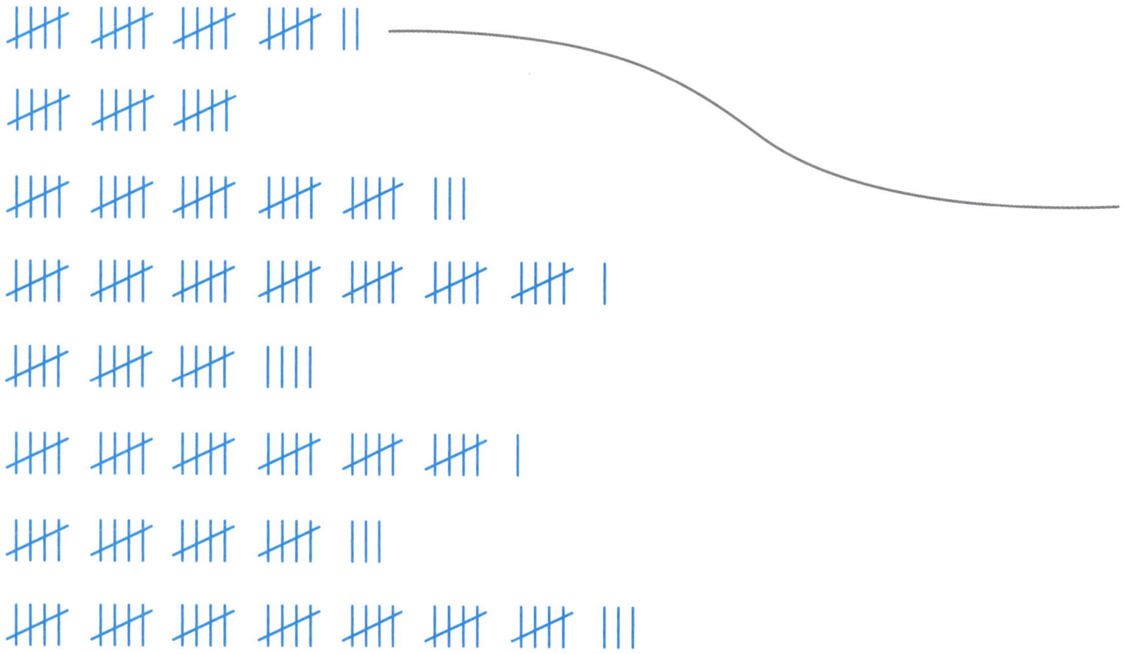

28
19
22
38
31
15
23
36

1 Draw tally marks for each of the following numbers.

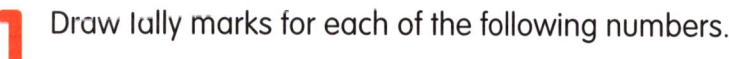

a 25 

b 29 ____________________

c 11 ____________________

d 14 ____________________

e 17 ____________________

f 7 ____________________

g 9 ____________________

h 22 ____________________

i 13 ____________________

j 4 ____________________

2 Use tally marks to record how many fish of each kind there are in the aquarium.

Fish		Tally
a		𝍸 𝍸 |
b		
c		
d		
e		
f	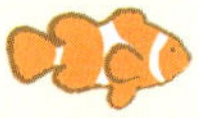	
g		

3 Class 4 carried out a survey about the birds they saw in a park. Complete the tally chart to show their findings.

Child A: "I counted 3 starlings, 2 blackbirds, 2 robins, 4 pigeons, and 1 woodpecker."

Child B: "I counted 5 pigeons, 6 blackbirds, 12 ducks, 1 heron, 2 starlings, and 1 robin."

Child C: "I counted 2 ducks, 1 robin, 4 starlings, 7 pigeons, and 1 crow."

Bird	Child A	Child B	Child C
a Starlings	|||		
b Blackbirds			
c Robins			
d Pigeons			
e Woodpeckers			
f Ducks			
g Herons			
h Crows			

MATHS IN CONTEXT

Car count

Count how many cars with these colours you see in an hour. Which colour was the most popular?

Blue	Red	Black	White

Page 270

Frequency tables

A frequency table is a way to summarize a set of data. It shows you exactly how many times each number, event, or item occurs in the data.

REMEMBER!
The frequency of something is how often it happens.

Warm-up Eighty children voted for their favourite big cat. Count the tally marks to find out the total votes for each cat.

Favourite	Tally	Frequency
1 Cheetah	卌 卌 卌 |	16
2 Jaguar	卌 卌	
3 Leopard	卌 卌 ||	
4 Lion	卌 卌 卌 卌 |||	
5 Tiger	卌 卌 卌 ||||	

1 Complete this frequency table about how many children visited a toy shop on each day of the week. Then use the table to help you circle the correct answer to each question.

Days of the week	Boys	Girls	Total
a Sunday	35	59	94
b Monday		16	34
c Tuesday		11	21
d Wednesday	19		52
e Thursday	42	49	
f Friday	52		104
g Saturday	63	84	

h The greatest number of children visited the store on:
Thursday / **Friday** / **Saturday**

i There were more boys than girls in the store on:
Saturday / **Sunday** / **Monday**

j The fewest number of children visited the store on:
Monday / **Tuesday** / **Wednesday**

k A total of 251 children visited on Friday and:
Saturday / **Sunday** / **Monday**

2

At school, 120 children voted for their favourite author. They put the results in a frequency table. Look at the data, then read the statements about it and circle true (T) or false (F) for each.

Author	Number of votes
Roald Dahl	16
Michael Morpurgo	14
Philip Pullman	19
J K Rowling	26
David Walliams	23
Jacqueline Wilson	22

a Michael Morpurgo has more votes than David Walliams. T / F

b Jaqueline Wilson has three more votes than Philip Pullman. T / F

c Roald Dahl is in third place. T / F

d Philip Pullman has 16 votes. T / F

e David Walliams is in second place. T / F

3

Class 2 carried out a survey of the traffic passing their school. Use the information from their written report to help you fill in the table below.

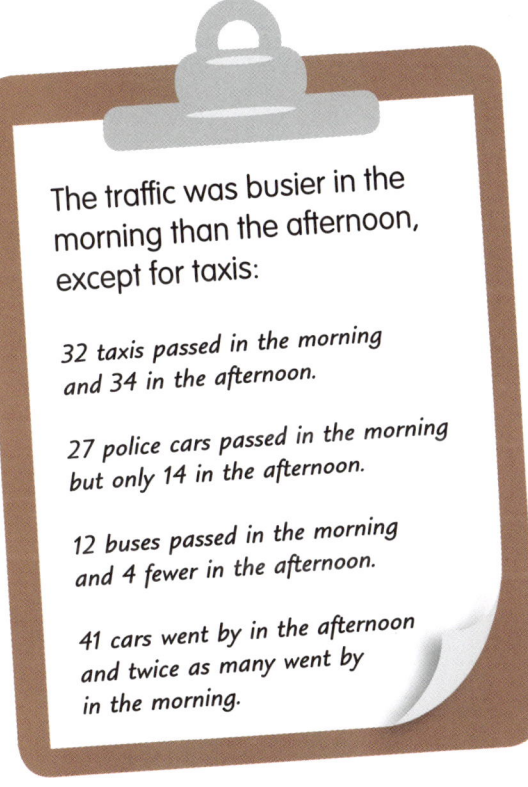

The traffic was busier in the morning than the afternoon, except for taxis:

32 taxis passed in the morning and 34 in the afternoon.

27 police cars passed in the morning but only 14 in the afternoon.

12 buses passed in the morning and 4 fewer in the afternoon.

41 cars went by in the afternoon and twice as many went by in the morning.

	Morning	Afternoon	Total
a 			
b 	32		
c 			
d 			

Page 271

Data handling

"Data" means information. Data handling is collecting, organizing, displaying, and interpreting or explaining information. Data is often collected when carrying out a survey or by having a vote.

REMEMBER!
Data handling is also called statistics.

Warm-up Draw lines to match each heading with the correct type of data below.

1	2	3	4	5	6
Children's exam results	School attendance over a year	Heights of children	Number of brothers and sisters	Volume of water drunk by children in a day	Distance walked by children in a week

130 cm	190 days	78%	8 km	1	1500 ml
138 cm	181 days	92%	10 km	3	1700 ml
128 cm	188 days	59%	7 km	0	2000 ml
135 cm	179 days	64%	15 km	1	1800 ml

1 Look at this data about the fruit in children's lunchboxes, then make a tally for each fruit and find its frequency.

REMEMBER!
It may help to cross out each piece of fruit as you make your tally.

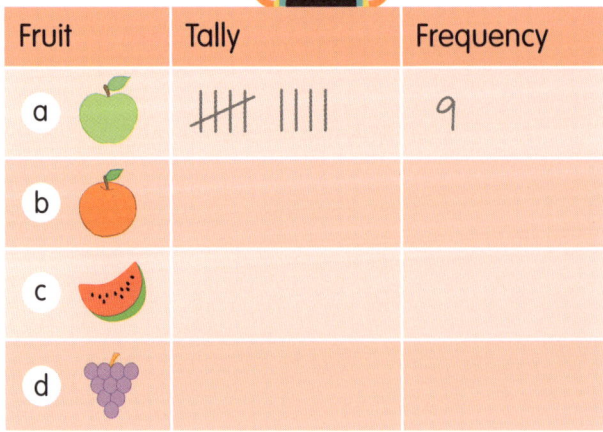

Fruit	Tally	Frequency
a (apple)	~~||||~~ ||||	9
b (orange)		
c (watermelon)		
d (grapes)		

2 Data can be sorted in different ways depending on what is being explained or investigated. Complete the frequency tables for these shapes.

a Sorted by shape

3 sides ________
4 sides ________

b Sorted by colour

Green ________
Yellow ________

c Sorted by size

Big ________
Small ________

3 Each of the 35 children in Class 4 has chosen their favourite colour. Complete the bar chart using the data below.

Colour	Frequency
Red	11
Green	9
Blue	7
Pink	6
Purple	2

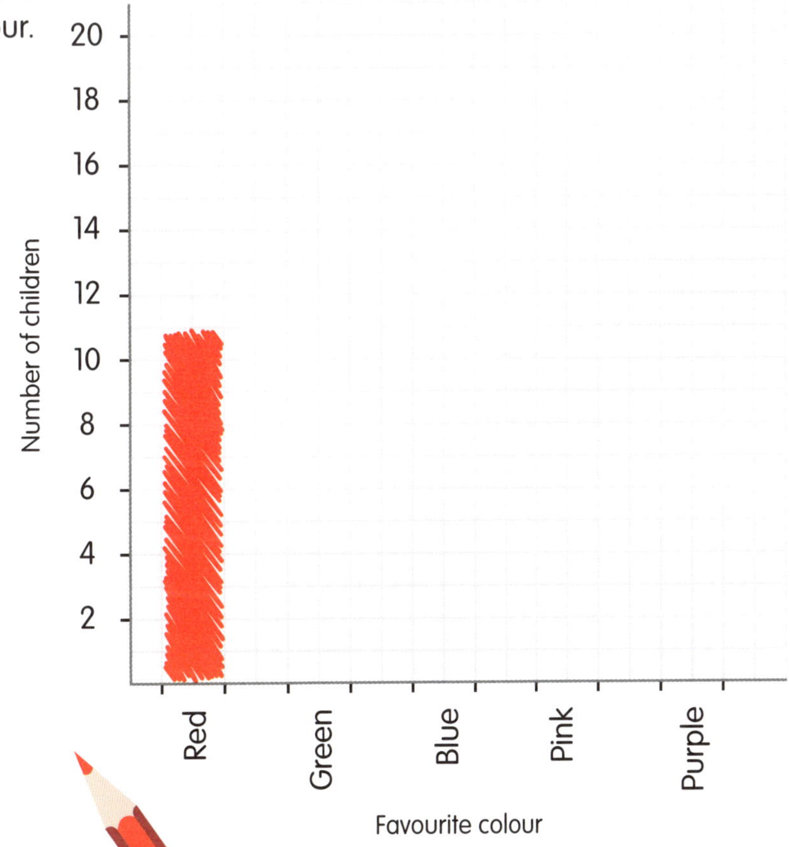

Pages 268–269

Carroll diagrams

A Carroll diagram can be used to sort data, such as numbers or objects, using conditions called criteria. Data is sorted into categories contained within boxes in the diagram.

DID YOU KNOW?
Carroll diagrams are named after Lewis Carroll, the author of *Alice in Wonderland*, who was also a mathematician.

Warm-up Use the words in the word box to help you fill in this Carroll diagram.

worm chicken dolphin ~~crab~~ cat snail fish ~~octopus~~

	Has legs	Does not have legs
Lives in the sea	crab, octopus	
Does not live in the sea		

1

One number in each box of this Carroll diagram is in the wrong place.
Cross out the incorrect numbers and write them in their correct places.

	Divisible by 9	Not divisible by 9
Odd numbers	45 63 27 ~~90~~ 81 ___	79 11 56 23 57 ___
Even numbers	72 54 36 18 44 90	12 49 26 16 62 ___

2

Fill in these numbers in the correct box of the Carroll diagram below.

~~2~~ 5 7 9 11 14 18 23 27 28 33 35 41 42 46 49

	Divisible by 7	Not divisible by 7
Prime number		2
Not a prime number		

3 Fill in this Carroll diagram by putting these capital letters into the correct boxes. It may help to cross them out as you go.

~~A~~ B C D E F G H I J K L M N
O P Q R S T U V W X Y Z

	Made of only straight lines	Not made of only straight lines
Vowels	A	
Not vowels		

4 These shapes have been sorted into a Carroll diagram. Look at them carefully, then fill in what the criteria are.

	______________	______________
______________		
______________		

MATHS IN CONTEXT

Sort your clothes

Choose some of your clothes to sort using a Carroll diagram. How will you sort them – by colour, type of material, whether you can wear them indoors or out, at night or during the day?

Label the Carroll diagram and fill it in.

Pages 272–273

Venn diagrams

A Venn diagram sorts data into circles, which overlap to show what is similar about the data. Data that does not fit into any of the circles is written outside the diagram.

The overlap of circles is called an intersection. Data in the intersection belongs to both sets.

Data written here belongs to all three sets.

Data that is not part of any set can sit outside the diagram.

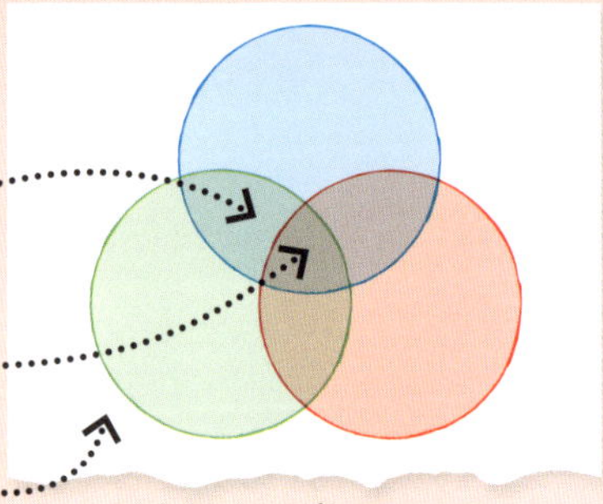

A Venn diagram

Warm-up Add the items from the word box into the correct places in this Venn diagram.

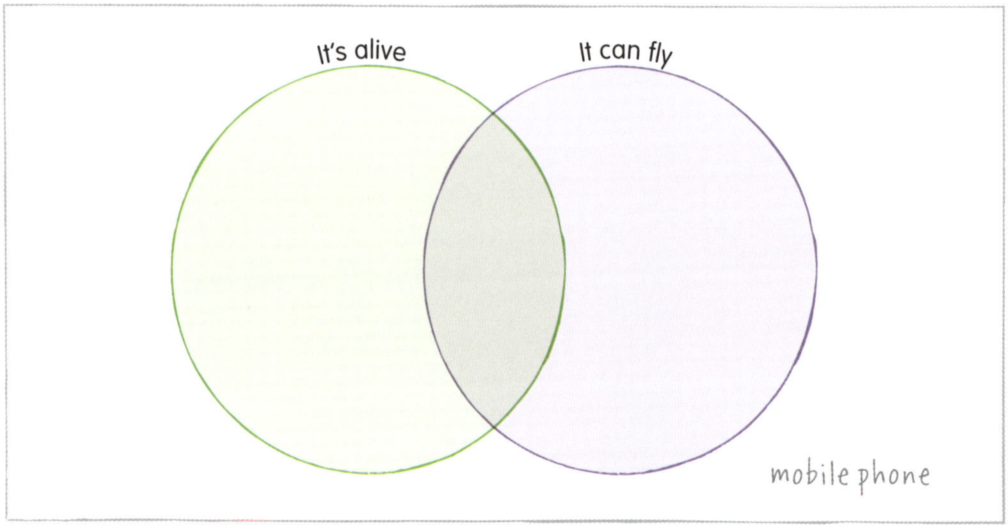

~~mobile phone~~
robin
plane
scissors
penguin
eagle
ant
parrot
drone

1 This Carroll diagram shows whether a group of children can swim, cycle, or do both. Fill in the same information into the Venn diagram.

	Cycles	Cannot cycle
Swims	Cindy	Eli
	Arif	Bob
Cannot swim	Dani	Finn
	Hassan	Grant

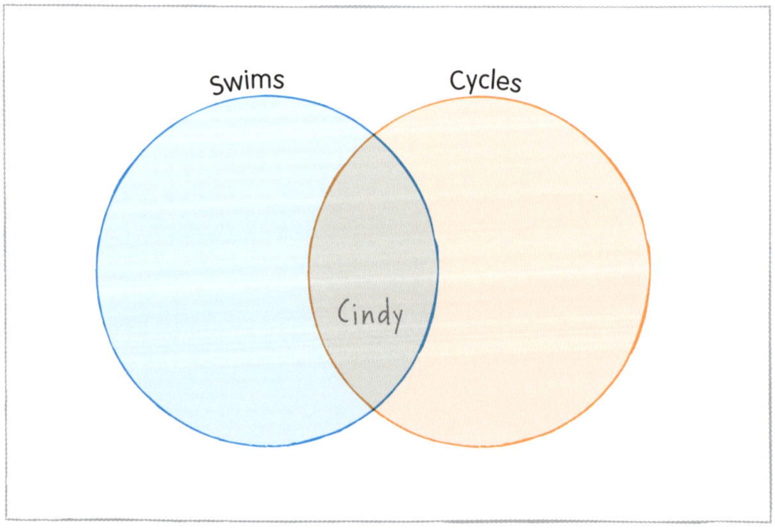

2 Use the Venn diagram to help you answer these questions.

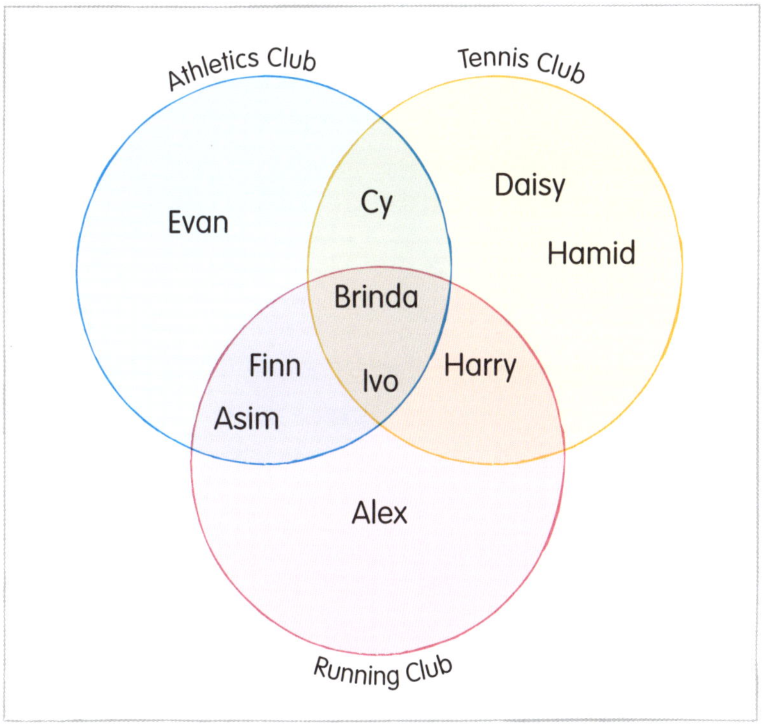

a Who goes only to the athletics and running clubs? Asim and Finn

b Who goes only to the tennis club? ______

c Who goes to all three clubs? ______

d Who goes only to the tennis and running clubs? ______

e Katy joins the running and tennis clubs, Dev joins the running club, and Mo joins all three clubs. Add their names in the correct places on the diagram.

3 Use this Venn diagram to help you circle the correct answer to each statement.

a	The number of red shapes is	8	12 (circled)	20
b	The total number of shapes with more than four sides is	14	18	10
c	The number of shapes that are red and have more than four sides is	7	12	17
d	The number of shapes that are not red and have four sides is	10	13	14
e	The total number of shapes is	39	45	58
f	The number of red shapes that have four sides or less is	5	52	25
g	The number of shapes that are green and have more than four sides is	6	10	2

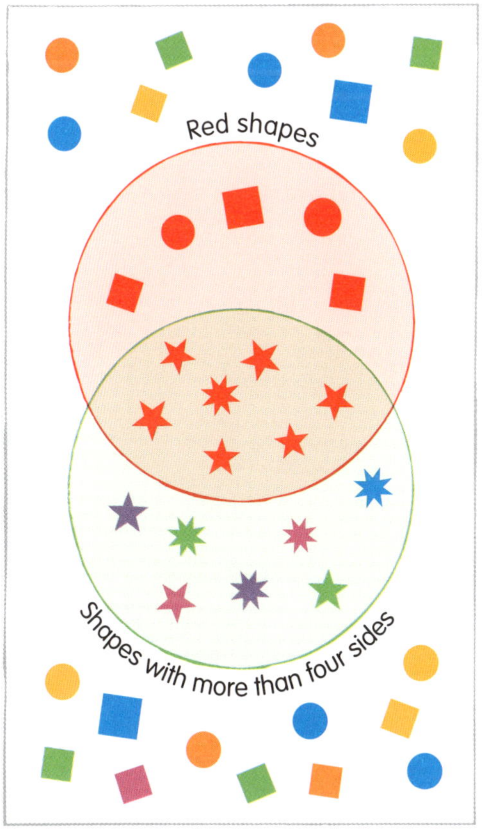

Pages 274–275

Pictograms

In a pictogram, data is represented by small pictures or symbols. A key is used to show how many things each picture or symbol represents.

REMEMBER!
In a pictogram, pictures are usually arranged in rows or columns.

Warm-up

This pictogram shows children's hat choices. Read the statements about the pictogram, then circle true (T) or false (F) for each.

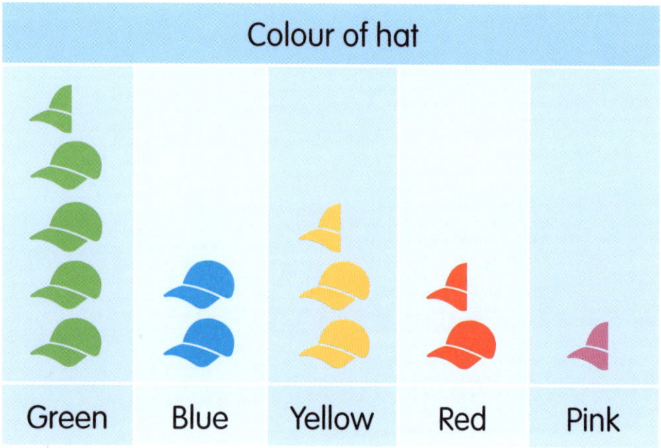

Key  = 2 children

1. Two children chose a red hat. T / F
2. Four children chose a blue hat. T / F
3. Ten children chose a green hat. T / F
4. Only one child chose a pink hat. T / F

1

Look at the pictogram, then fill in the gaps to complete the sentences below.

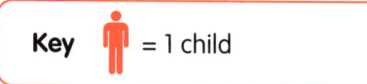

Key  = 1 child

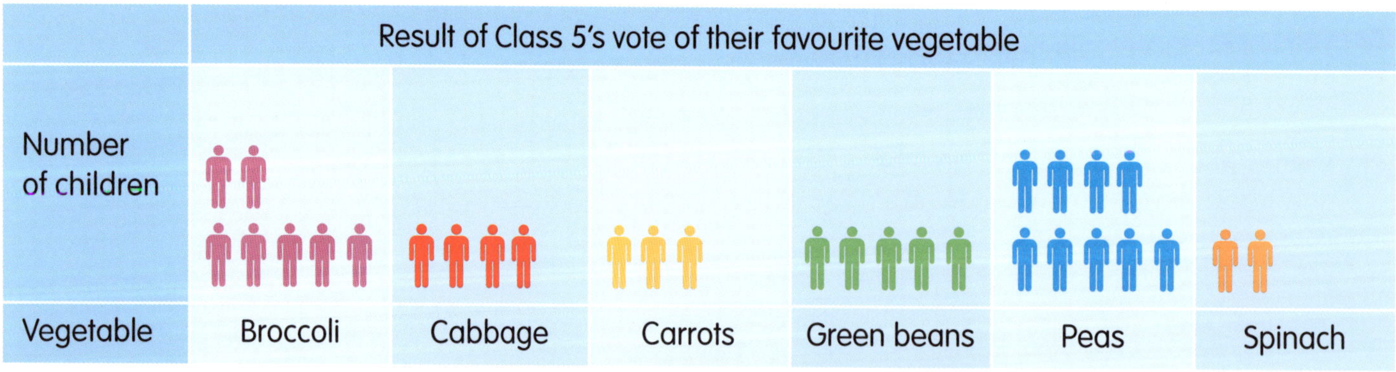

a. Four children chose cabbage .

b. Class 5's favourite vegetable is ____________ .

c. ____ children chose broccoli as their favourite.

d. The least popular vegetable is ____________ .

e. Two more children chose ____________ than green beans.

f. The difference between the votes for carrots and spinach is ____ .

2 This pictogram shows the number of meals that takeaway restaurants prepared during one lunchtime. Use the data to help you complete the frequency table.

Key ● = 4 meals

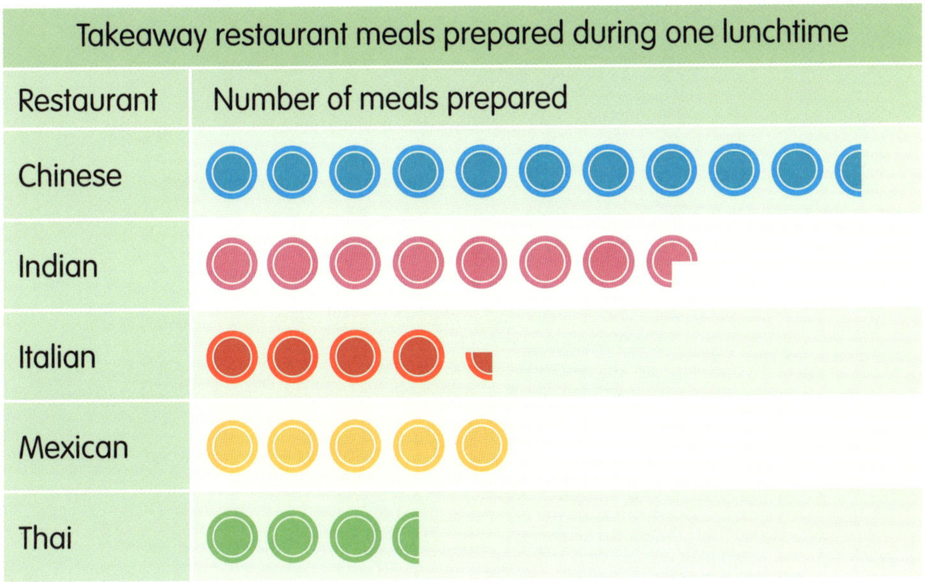

Frequency table	
Restaurant	Frequency
Chinese	42
Indian	
Italian	
Mexican	
Thai	

3 Sami drew a pictogram about the books that he read in one year. Use the data from his pictogram to help you complete his essay on the right.

Key ▮ = 2 books

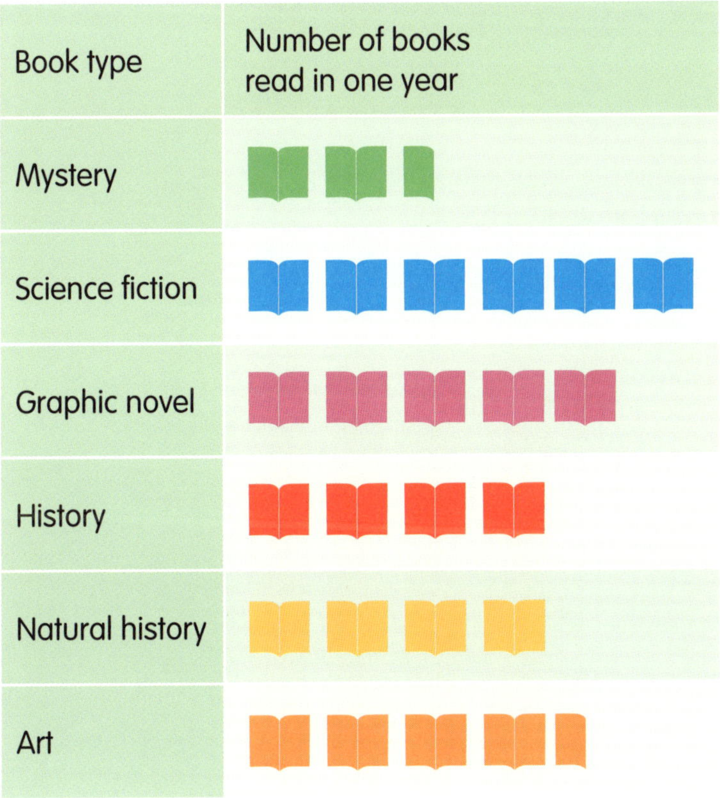

I read one book each week, so I read 52 books in total. My favourite type was ________, and I read ____ books of this type. My least favourite type was ________, and I only read ____ books of this type. I read ____ graphic novels. These were closely followed by ________, scoring just one fewer. I read ____ natural history books, and the same number of ________ books.

Block graphs

A block graph uses square blocks to represent each item of data. The blocks are stacked in columns. You can tell how much data is shown by the height of each column.

REMEMBER!
Gaps should be left between each of the columns on a block graph.

Warm-up Answer the questions about the data shown in this block graph.

Children's choice of ice creams

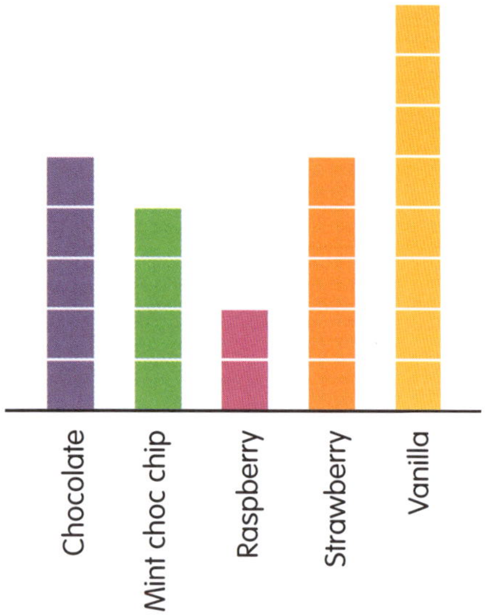

1. Which flavour was chosen by four children?
   mint choc chip
2. Which was the most popular flavour?
   ____
3. Which was the least popular flavour?
   ____
4. Which flavours were chosen by five children?
   ____

1 Some children drew a block graph to show which animals they saw at the farm. Use the information in the graph to fill in the gaps in the sentences below.

Animals on farm

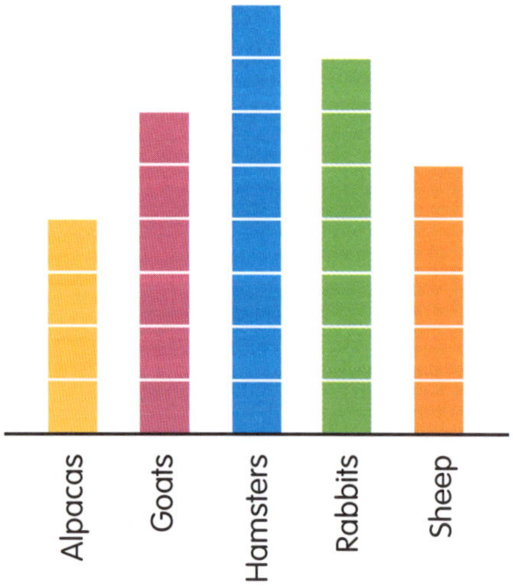

a. Total number of goats and sheep 11 .
b. Total number of rabbits and hamsters ____ .
c. There are ______ more hamsters than sheep.
d. There are two fewer ________ than goats.
e. There are ____ sheep at the farm.

2 Children were given a variety of soups to choose from. Draw a block chart to show how many children chose each flavour.

Soup flavour	Frequency
Chicken	5
Lentil	3
Leek and potato	6
Tomato	7
Vegetable	2

Children's choice of soups

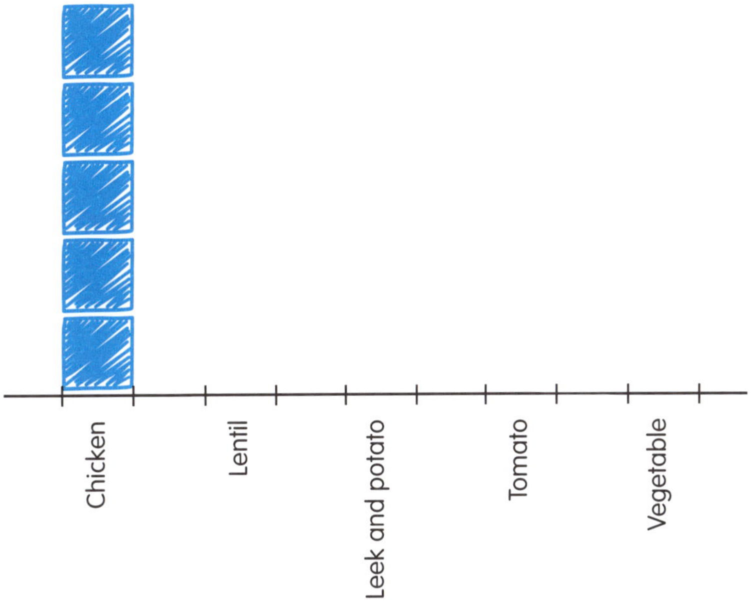

3 Class 3 have drawn a block graph to show the different languages they speak. Tick the statements that are true.

Languages spoken

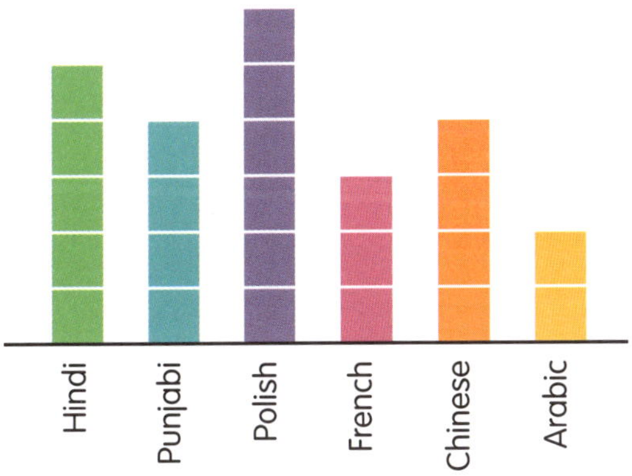

a One more child speaks Hindi than Punjabi. ☑

b Two children speak French. ☐

c The most common language spoken is Polish. ☐

d The total number of children that speak either Punjabi or Hindi is nine. ☐

e Three children speak Chinese. ☐

f Two children speak Arabic. ☐

g The total number of children that speak either French or Polish is nine. ☐

Page 284

Bar charts

In a bar chart, groups of data are represented by bars or columns. The size of each bar shows the frequency of the data.

REMEMBER!
The bars in a bar chart should all be the same width, and should be separated by gaps.

Warm-up

This bar chart shows data about children's favourite musical instruments. Use the bar chart to help you fill in the frequency table.

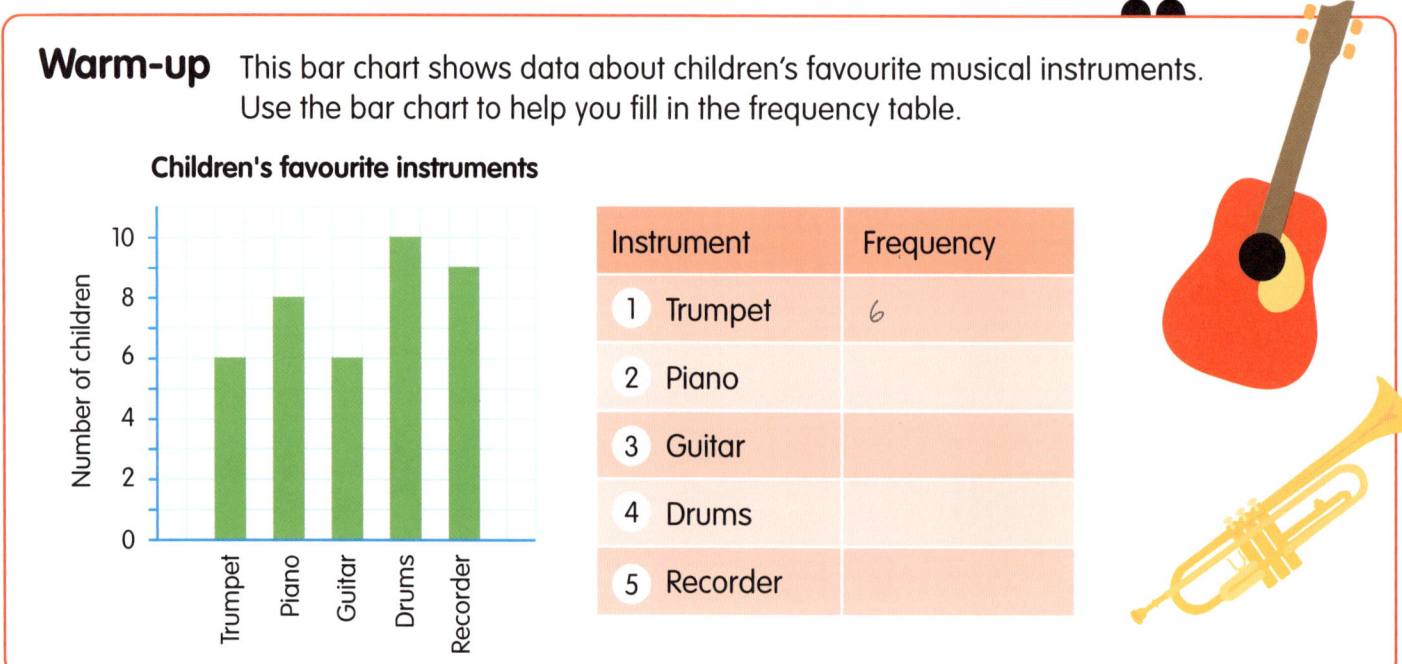

Children's favourite instruments

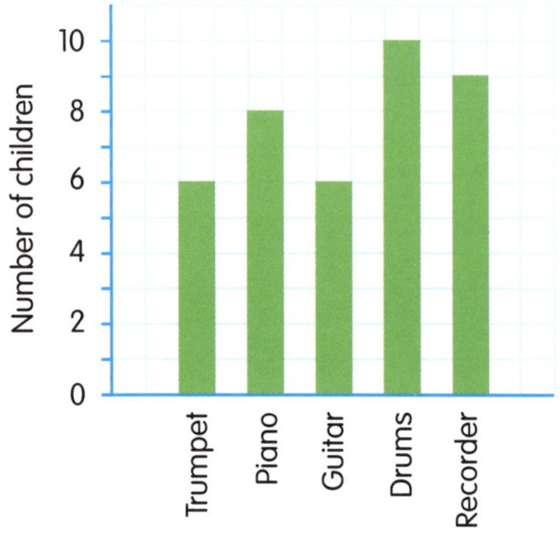

Instrument	Frequency
1 Trumpet	6
2 Piano	
3 Guitar	
4 Drums	
5 Recorder	

1 Year 4 voted for their favourite type of TV programme. They then drew a bar chart to show the results. Use the bar chart to help you circle the correct answer to each statement.

Children's favourite TV programmes

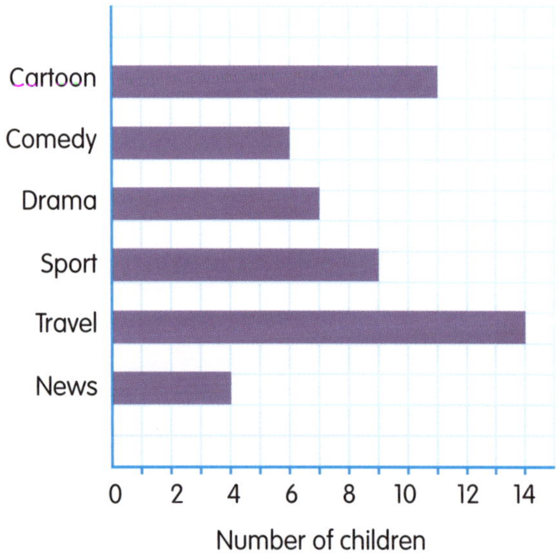

a The total number of votes for sport and news — 9 12 (13)

b The number of votes for comedy — 3 4 6

c The number of votes for news — 4 6 8

d The difference between comedy and cartoon — 5 7 9

e The number of votes for drama — 5 6 7

f The number of votes for travel — 12 14 5

2 Year 5 children gave talks on famous people. The school then voted for their favourite talk. Complete the bar chart using the information from the frequency table.

Famous People	Frequency
Florence Nightingale	9
Nelson Mandela	11
Charles Darwin	8
Mahatma Gandhi	9
Harriet Tubman	5
Martin Luther King	14

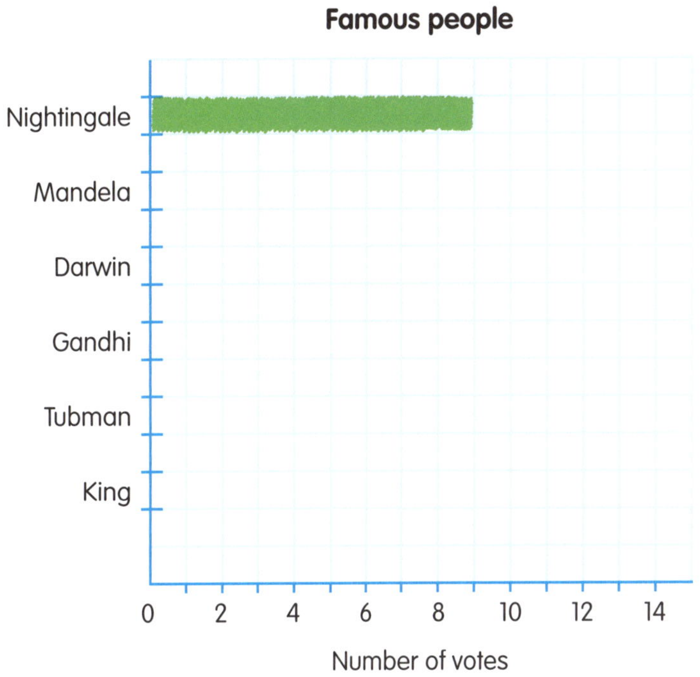

3 Two children counted the punctuation marks in a short story, then wrote their findings in a frequency table. Use the frequency table to help you fill in the missing parts of the bar chart.

Type of punctuation mark	Frequency
Full stop	59
Comma	45
Exclamation mark	15
Question mark	12

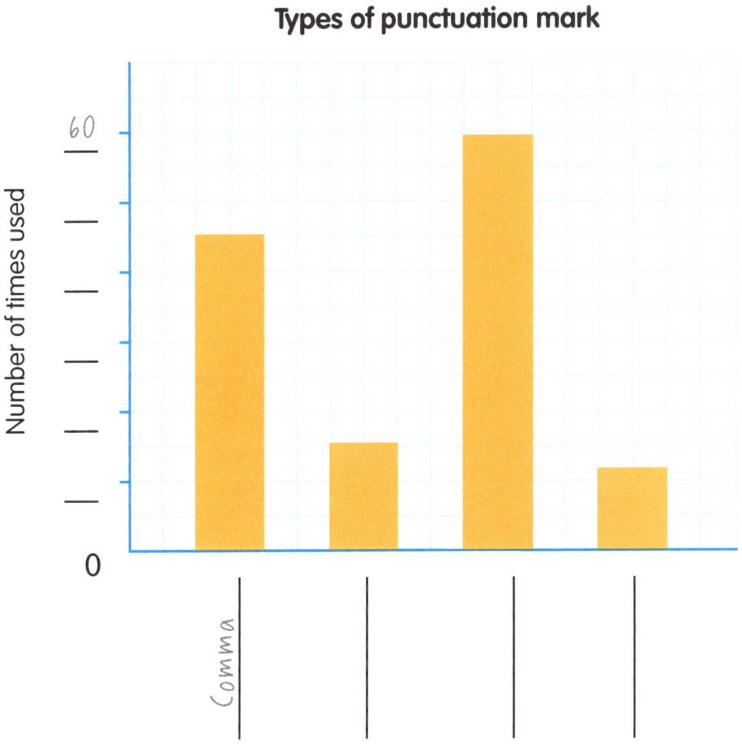

Page 285

Answers

6–7 Number symbols

Warm-up

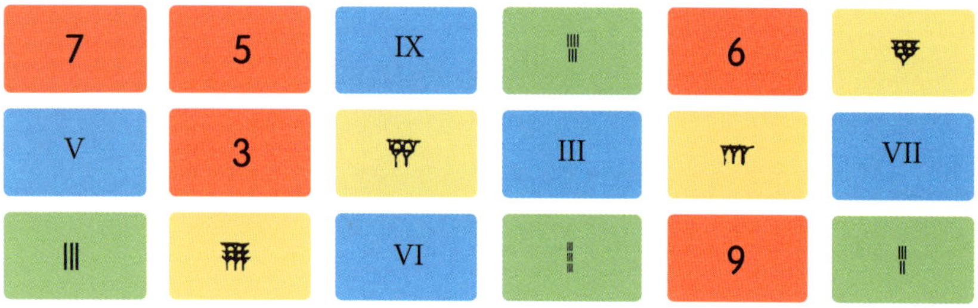

1. a 4 b 2 c 8 d 5 e 8 f 9 g 9 h 9

2. a 2000 – MM
   b 7 – VII
   c 99 – XCIX
   d 38 – XXXVIII
   e 550 – DL
   f 19 – XIX
   g 333 – CCCXXXIII
   h 170 – CLXX
   i 54 – LIV
   j 459 – CDLIX

Maths in context

1 MMXVI – 2016
2 MMXX – 2020
3 MMIX – 2009
4 MMXVII – 2017

8–9 Place value

Warm-up

1 3 2 2 3 5 4 7 5 8 6 4 7 2 8 9

1. a 4 thousands 5 hundreds 6 tens 7 ones
   b 0 thousands 0 hundreds 9 tens 8 ones
   c 2 thousands 4 hundreds 2 tens 5 ones
   d 0 thousands 8 hundreds 9 tens 7 ones
   e 3 thousands 7 hundreds 7 tens 4 ones
   f 0 thousands 7 hundreds 9 tens 8 ones

2. a 5000 b 50 c 5 d 500

3. a 3278 b 4398 c 6485 d 9364 e 3612 f 7840 g 5734 h 2529

4. In any order:

a	b	c	d
4237	1439	37	31

e	f	g	h	i	j
830	380	9370	5322	340	2380

10–11 Sequences and patterns

Warm-up

1 17, 19 2 14, 15 3 29, 35 4 32, 39

1. a –3: 9, 6 b –4: 12, 8 c –1: 17, 16 d –5: 71, 66 e –6: 81, 75 f –2: 19, 17

2. a 28, 32; The pattern is +4 each time
   b 54, 64; The pattern is +10 each time
   c 42, 49; The pattern is +7 each time
   d 19, 22; The pattern is +3 each time

3. Learner's own answers.

4. a +3, –1, +3, –1: 8, 11, 10, 13, 12
   b +8, –3, +8, –3: 5, 13, 10, 18, 15
   c +5, –2, +5, –2: 4, 9, 7, 12, 10
   d –5, +4, –5, +4: 20, 15, 19, 14, 18

12–13 Positive and negative numbers

Warm-up

1 –1, 0, 1 2 –8, –6, –5, –4 3 0, 2, 3, 4 4 –6, –5, –3, –2, –1

1. a –2 b 0 c –5 d –3

2. a 5, 4, 3, 2, 1, 0
   b 9, 8, 7, 6, 5, 4
   c 3, 2, 1, 0, –1, –2
   d 1, 0, –1, –2, –3, –4
   e 12, 11, 10, 9, 8, 7
   f 7, 6, 5, 4, 3, 2

3. a 10, 8, 6, 4, 2, 0
   b 4, 2, 0, –2, –4, –6
   c 3, 1, –1, –3, –5, –7
   d 1, –1, –3, –5, –7, –9
   e 7, 5, 3, 1, –1, –3
   f 9, 7, 5, 3, 1, –1

4. a 5 b 6 c 4

Maths in context

1 It was 9°C warmer at 10am than 4am.
2 It was 8°C cooler at 8pm than at midday.
3 It was 7°C warmer in Norway than in Greenland.

14–15 Comparing numbers

Warm-up

1 350 2 989 3 828 4 1127 5 408 6 2674 7 531 8 822

1. a > b < c > d > e = f < g <

2. a 10 > 8 b 12 = 12 c 4 < 7 d 6 < 13 e 14 > 4 f 9 > 8

3. a 6538 = 6538
   b 3269 > 3268
   c 4971 < 4973

16–17 Ordering numbers

Warm-up

1 12345, 23451, 31245, 43215, 45123, 54321
2 2679, 2769, 6792, 7629, 9672, 9762
3 2958, 2985, 5289, 5298, 5928, 8259
4 3497, 4379, 4397, 4739, 4793, 4937

1. a 487, 567, 568, 578, 587
   b 127, 237, 712, 732, 777
   c 12, 123, 289, 1243, 1289
   d 64, 465, 1465, 4065, 6540
   e 409, 419, 420, 490, 491

2. Learner's own answers.
Suggestions include:
a 4701, 4589, 4569, 4568
b 5993, 5983, 4956, 3956
c 1556, 1526, 1439, 1438
d 8923, 8877, 8787, 7778
e 4124, 4122, 3245, 2345
f 5822, 5802, 5011, 5001
g 5945, 5689, 4999, 4043
h 9966, 9866, 9676, 8877

3. a Colby b Elliot c Josh
d Naziah e Evie f Grace

Maths in context
1 Chennai 2 Durban 3 Shanghai
4 Bangkok

18 **Estimating**

Warm-up
1 Learner's own estimate, actual number is 23
2 Learner's own estimate, actual number is 14
3 Learner's own estimate, actual number is 30

1. a Learner's own estimate, actual number is 24
b Learner's own estimate, actual number is 37
c Learner's own estimate, actual number is 30

2. a Learner's own estimate, actual number is 30
b Learner's own estimate, actual number is 39

19 **Rounding**

Warm-up
1 240 2 220 3 310 4 270

1. a 561, 555, 559, 558
b 796, 804, 802, 795
c 997, 1001, 995, 1004
d 1495, 1503, 1497

2. a 564
b 555
c 894
d 885
e 1004

20–21 **Fractions**

Warm-up
1 $\frac{1}{4}$ 2 $\frac{1}{5}$ 3 $\frac{3}{5}$

1. a = $\frac{1}{4}$ = 
b = $\frac{1}{2}$ = 
c = $\frac{2}{6}$ = 
d = $\frac{1}{6}$ = 
e = $\frac{1}{5}$ = 
f = $\frac{2}{3}$ = 

2. a $\frac{1}{2}$ b $\frac{3}{4}$ c $\frac{3}{5}$
d $\frac{2}{3}$ e $\frac{1}{6}$ f $\frac{1}{4}$
g $\frac{1}{2}$ h $\frac{4}{5}$

3. a colour in 2 pizza slices 
b colour in 5 pizza slices 
c colour in 3 pizza slices 
d colour in 4 pizza slices 
e colour in 1 pizza slice 
f colour in 1 pizza slice 
g colour in 2 pizza slices 
h colour in 3 pizza slices 

Maths in context
2 slices of cake are left

22–23 **Equivalent fractions**

Warm-up 1 $\frac{4}{8}$ 2 $\frac{4}{12}$ 3 $\frac{2}{5}$

1.
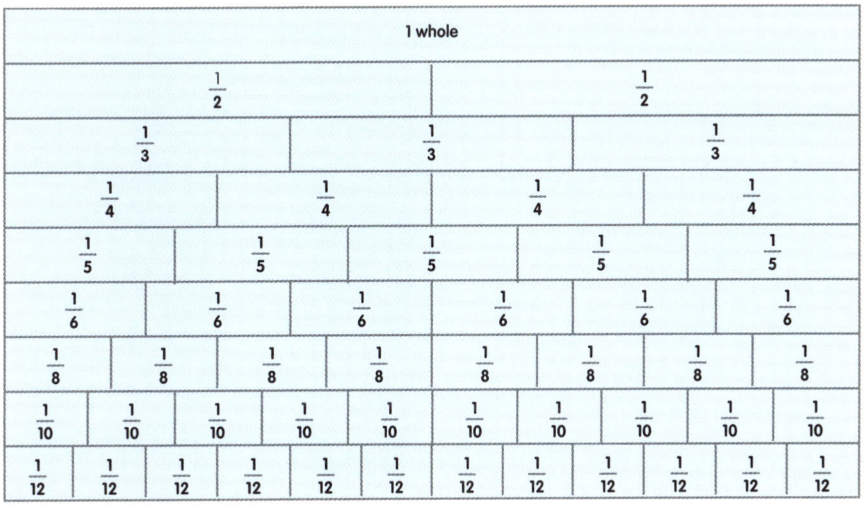
1 whole
1/2 1/2
1/3 1/3 1/3
1/4 1/4 1/4 1/4
1/5 1/5 1/5 1/5 1/5
1/6 1/6 1/6 1/6 1/6 1/6
1/8 1/8 1/8 1/8 1/8 1/8 1/8 1/8
1/10 1/10 1/10 1/10 1/10 1/10 1/10 1/10 1/10 1/10
1/12 1/12 1/12 1/12 1/12 1/12 1/12 1/12 1/12 1/12 1/12 1/12

2. a $\frac{2}{8}$ and $\frac{3}{12}$ b $\frac{4}{6}$ and $\frac{8}{12}$
c $\frac{2}{4}$ and $\frac{4}{8}$ d $\frac{6}{10}$
e $\frac{4}{8}$ and $\frac{6}{12}$ f $\frac{5}{10}$ and $\frac{1}{2}$

3. a $\frac{9}{27}$ b $\frac{3}{15}$ c $\frac{4}{6}$
d $\frac{10}{20}$ e $\frac{12}{16}$ f $\frac{9}{21}$

4. a $\frac{8}{10}$ or any other correct equivalent
b $\frac{16}{48}$ or any other correct equivalent
c $\frac{9}{12}$ or any other correct equivalent
d $\frac{3}{10}$ or any other correct equivalent
e $\frac{6}{9}$ or any other correct equivalent
f $\frac{10}{18}$ or any other correct equivalent
g $\frac{64}{88}$ or any other correct equivalent
h $\frac{33}{36}$ or any other correct equivalent

Maths in context
Rav has eaten more pizza.

24–25 Finding a fraction of an amount

Warm-up
1 4 buckets 2 2 starfish 3 5 shells

1. a 20 b 6 c 12 d 8

2. a 24 b 36 c 25 d 30 e 27 f 5

3. a 10 b 48 c 120 d 64 e 45 f 12 g 30 h 8 i 50 j 36 k 35 l 2 m 10 n 90 o 60

4. Learner's own answers. Suggestions include:

$\frac{1}{3}$ of 90, $\frac{1}{2}$ of 60, $\frac{2}{5}$ of 75, $\frac{5}{6}$ of 36, $\frac{1}{12}$ of 360

26 Comparing fractions with the same denominators

Warm-up
1 $\frac{4}{10}$ 2 $\frac{6}{10}$ 3 $\frac{9}{10}$ 4 $\frac{5}{10}$ 5 $\frac{8}{10}$

1. a $\frac{1}{12}, \frac{3}{12}, \frac{5}{12}, \frac{7}{12}, \frac{9}{12}$
b $\frac{2}{18}, \frac{3}{18}, \frac{4}{18}, \frac{6}{18}, \frac{12}{18}$
c $\frac{1}{20}, \frac{7}{20}, \frac{9}{20}, \frac{17}{20}, \frac{19}{20}$

2. a < b > c > d < e < f < g > h > i > j > k < l > m > n > o < p <

27 Comparing unit fractions

Warm-up
1 $\frac{1}{16}, \frac{1}{9}, \frac{1}{7}, \frac{1}{6}, \frac{1}{2}$
2 $\frac{1}{12}, \frac{1}{8}, \frac{1}{6}, \frac{1}{4}, \frac{1}{3}$

1. a $\frac{1}{3}$ 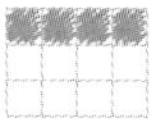 $\frac{1}{4}$ 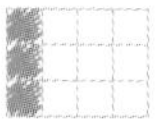
b $\frac{1}{6}$ 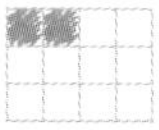 $\frac{1}{12}$ 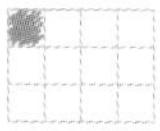
c $\frac{1}{2}$ 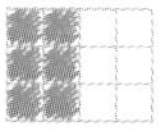 $\frac{1}{4}$ 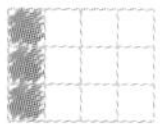
d $\frac{1}{12}$ 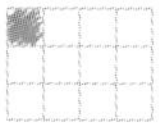 $\frac{1}{2}$ 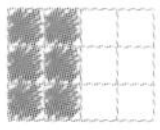
e $\frac{1}{3}$ 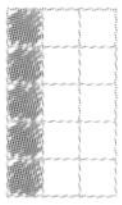 $\frac{1}{5}$ 
f $\frac{1}{6}$  $\frac{1}{2}$ 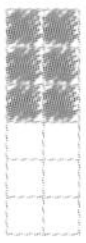

28–29 Addition

Warm-up
1 5 + 3 = 8 2 6 + 5 = 11 3 5 + 3 = 8

1. a 9 b 8 c 12 d 11 e 13 f 15 g 9 h 16

2. a 7 b 5 c 7 d 5 e 15 f 14 g 14

3. Learner's own answers. Suggestions include:
2 + 6 = 8, 1 + 7 = 8, 3 + 5 = 8, 4 + 4 = 8, 0 + 8 = 8

30-31 Addition facts

Warm-up 1 9 2 8 3 7 4 6 5 5 6 4 7 3 8 2 9 1

1. a 1 + 1 = 2 b 2 + 2 = 4 c 3 + 3 = 6 d 4 + 4 = 8 e 5 + 5 = 10 f 6 + 6 = 12 g 7 + 7 = 14 h 8 + 8 = 16 i 9 + 9 = 18 j 10 + 10 = 20

2. 17 + 3, 6 + 14, 14 + 6, 13 + 7, 10 + 10, 9 + 11, 11 + 9, 8 + 12, 5 + 15, 16 + 4, 12 + 8

3. a 70 b 60 c 60 d 40 e 30 f 60 g 60 h 430 i 900 j 100 k 100 l 500

32-33 Adding with a number line

Warm-up 1 11 2 8 3 15

1. a 5 + 3 = 8 b 12 + 8 = 20 c 3 + 13 = 16

2. 12 + 7 = 19, 13 + 5 = 18, 15 + 7 = 22, 11 + 12 = 23, 18 + 6 = 24, 19 + 8 = 27, 21 + 7 = 28

3. a 70 b 80 c 20 d 100

Maths in context
£12 + £4 = £16

34-35 Adding with a number grid

Warm-up
1 65 2 46 3 81

1. a 71 b 50 c 90 d 86 e 72 f 71 g 78 h 90 i 81 j 97

2. a 81 cows
b 39 robots
c 29 kiwis
d 29 coins
e 34 raspberries
f 26 books

3. a 57 b 83 c 29 d 46 e 31 f 92 g 27 h 34

36–37 Partitioning for addition

Warm-up
1 23 + 48 = 71
2 14 + 59 = 73
3 78 + 13 = 91

1. a 46 + 23 = 69
b 54 + 24 = 78
c 39 + 47 = 86

2. a 34 + 33 = 67
b 42 + 37 = 79
c 28 + 38 = 66

3. a 61 pencils
b 83 marbles
c 37 balloons
d 46 yoyos

38–39 **Expanded column addition**

Warm-up
1 791 2 440 3 872 4 990
5 983 6 777

1. a 828 b 913 c 621

2. In any order:
a 57 + 42 = 99
b 57 + 145 = 202
c 57 + 328 = 385
d 42 + 145 = 187
e 42 + 328 = 370
f 145 + 328 = 473

Maths in context
1 225 + 467 = 692 m
2 692 + 342 = 1034 m
3 1034 + 189 = 1223 m

40–41 **Column addition**

Warm-up
1 821 2 742 3 912

1. a 941 b 2036 c 1254 d 2799

2. a 421 cupcakes

$^{1}2$	$^{1}7$	3
1	4	8
4	2	1

b 569 cupcakes

4	2	1
1	4	8
5	6	9

c 806 cupcakes

$^{1}5$	$^{1}6$	9
2	3	7
8	0	6

3. a 1415

	$^{1}8$	$^{1}4$	8
	5	6	7
1	4	1	5

b 2082

$^{1}1$	3	$^{1}2$	4
	7	5	8
2	0	8	2

c 872

$^{1}4$	8	2
3	9	0
8	7	2

d 1823

	$^{1}9$	$^{1}4$	6
	8	7	7
1	8	2	3

e 1378

	7	3	3
	6	4	5
1	3	7	8

f 2198

$^{1}1$	3	$^{1}4$	9
	8	4	9
2	1	9	8

42-43 **Shopkeeper's addition**

Warm-up
1 £10.00 – £6.55 = £3.45
£6.55 + £0.05 = £6.60
£6.60 + £0.40 = £7.00
£7.00 + £3.00 = £10.00
2 £25.00 – £11.23 = £13.77
£11.23 + £0.07 = £11.30
£11.30 + £0.70 = £12.00
£12.00 + £13.00 = £25.00
3 £13.00 – £8.74 = £4.26
£8.74 + £0.06 = £8.80
£8.80 + £0.20 = £9.00
£9.00 + £4.00 = £13.00
4 £7.00 – £3.65 = £3.35
£3.65 + £0.05 = £3.70
£3.70 + £0.30 = £4.00
£4.00 + £3.00 = £7.00

1. a £18.00 – £3.46 = £14.54
b £29.00 – £13.18 = £15.82
c £11.22 – £4.36 = £6.86

2. a £6.25
b £12.39
c £10.62
d £16.57
e £11.12
f £2.47

3. a £10.54
b £14.18
c £6.69
d £9.56
e £2.25

Maths in context £10.49

44-45 **Subtraction**

Warm-up
1 7 – 3 = 4
2 9 – 6 = 3
3 4 – 1 = 3
4 8 – 6 = 2

1. a 4 b 3 c 5 d 1 e 0
f 2 g 7 h 1 i 4

2. a 4 b 5 c 3 d 3 e 6 f 5

Maths in context
1 There will be 3 carrots left.
2 There will be 6 pieces of cucumber left.

46-47 **Subtraction facts**

Warm-up
1 9 2 8 3 7 4 6 5 5 6 4
7 3 8 2 9 1

1. a 10 b 12 c 6 d 1 e 8 f 7
g 14 h 9 i 2 j 5 k 15 l 11
m 4 n 3 o 13

2. a 10 – 6 = 4, 10 – 4 = 6
b 9 – 2 = 7, 9 – 7 = 2
c 15 – 3 = 12, 15 – 12 = 3
d 13 – 8 = 5, 13 – 5 = 8
e 7 – 4 = 3, 7 – 3 = 4
f 20 – 11 = 9, 20 – 9 = 11
g 15 – 10 = 5, 15 – 5 = 10
h 11 – 3 = 8, 11 – 8 = 3

3. a 60 b 50 c 10 d 40 e 30
f 30 g 10 h 10 i 10 j 20
k 40 l 50

48–49 **Subtracting with a number line**

Warm-up
1 58
2 39
3 26
4 13
5 57
6 46

1. a 65 b 283 c 149 d 26
e 109 f 269

2. a 92 g b £69

50-51 Partitioning for subtraction

Warm-up

1 78 – 34 = 44

T	O		T	O		T	O
7	8	–	3	0	=	4	8
4	8	–		4	=	4	4

2 38 – 29 = 9

T	O		T	O		T	O
3	8	–	2	0	=	1	8
1	8	–		9	=		9

3 93 – 47 = 46

T	O		T	O		T	O
9	3	–	4	0	=	5	3
5	3	–		7	=	4	6

4 26 – 19 = 7

T	O		T	O		T	O
2	6	–	1	0	=	1	6
1	6	–		9	=		7

1. a 62
b 59
c 12
d 22

2. a 79 – 16 = 63
b 26 – 18 = 8
c 87 – 38 = 49
d 54 – 34 = 20
e 63 – 45 = 18
f 92 – 28 = 64
g 98 – 89 = 9
h 82 – 71 = 11
i 34 – 14 = 20
j 77 – 18 = 59
k 62 – 22 = 40
l 45 – 29 = 16

3. a 87 – 25 = 62
b 73 – 49 = 24
c 36 – 12 = 24
d 64 – 33 = 31
e 49 – 23 = 26
f 67 – 22 = 45
g 94 – 18 = 76
h 99 – 14 = 85
i 53 – 16 = 37

Maths in context

24 birds were left in the tree.

52–53 Expanded column subtraction

Warm-up

1 316

6	6	4	
3	4	8	
		2	350
	5	0	400
2	0	0	600
	6	4	664
3	1	6	

2 469

7	5	3	
2	8	4	
		6	290
	1	0	300
4	0	0	700
	5	3	753
4	6	9	

3 508

8	2	7	
3	1	9	
		1	320
	8	0	400
4	0	0	800
	2	7	827
5	0	8	

1. a 280

4	5	6	
1	7	6	
		4	180
	2	0	200
2	0	0	400
	5	6	456
2	8	0	

b 145

7	8	7	
6	4	2	
		3	645
		5	650
	5	0	700
	8	7	787
1	4	5	

c 142

4	8	5	
3	4	3	
		2	345
		5	350
	5	0	400
	8	5	485
1	4	2	

2. a 433 g

7	5	7	
3	2	4	
		6	330
	7	0	400
3	0	0	700
	5	7	757
4	3	3	

b £215

8	7	2	
6	5	7	
		3	660
	4	0	700
1	0	0	800
	7	2	872
2	1	5	

c 244

5	7	6	
3	3	2	
		8	340
	6	0	400
1	0	0	500
	7	6	576
2	4	4	

d 186 apples

3	7	5	
1	8	9	
		1	190
	1	0	200
1	0	0	300
	7	5	375
1	8	6	

3. a 315 b 293 c 289 d 332
e 392 f 347 g 305 h 393

54–55 Column subtraction

Warm-up

1 504

8	$^{6}\cancel{7}$	$^{1}2$
3	6	8
5	0	4

2 692

$^{8}\cancel{9}$	$^{1}4$	8
2	5	6
6	9	2

3 215

3	$^{3}\cancel{4}$	$^{1}2$
1	2	7
2	1	5

4 267

$^{4}\cancel{5}$	$^{13}\cancel{4}$	$^{1}3$
2	7	6
2	6	7

1. a 221

6	7	8
4	5	7
2	2	1

b 456

$^{8}\cancel{9}$	$^{10}1$	$^{1}3$
4	5	7
4	5	6

c 371

$^{7}\cancel{8}$	$^{1}2$	8
4	5	7
3	7	1

d 65

9	7	8
9	1	3
0	6	5

2. a 88

$^{7}\cancel{8}$	$^{10}\cancel{7}$	$^{1}5$
7	8	7
0	8	8

b 344

$^{4}\cancel{5}$	$^{11}\cancel{2}$	$^{1}3$
1	7	9
3	4	4

c 305

6	$^{0}\cancel{1}$	$^{1}4$
3	0	9
3	0	5

d 178

$^{3}4$	$^{12}3$	$^{1}7$
2	5	9
1	7	8

e 275

$^{7}\cancel{8}$	$^{13}\cancel{4}$	$^{1}3$
5	6	8
2	7	5

f 594

$^{6}\cancel{7}$	$^{10}\cancel{1}$	$^{1}1$
1	1	7
5	9	4

g 4

9	$^{4}\cancel{5}$	$^{1}3$
9	4	9
0	0	4

h 94

$^{3}\cancel{4}$	$^{1}7$	8
3	8	4
0	9	4

i 272

3	9	8
1	2	6
2	7	2

3. a 619

8	$^{6}\cancel{7}$	$^{1}6$
2	5	7
6	1	9

b 198

$^{5}\cancel{6}$	$^{16}\cancel{7}$	$^{1}3$
4	7	5
1	9	8

c 305

4	$^{5}\cancel{6}$	$^{1}3$
1	5	8
3	0	5

d 454

$^{8}\cancel{9}$	$^{1}3$	7
4	8	3
4	5	4

e 156

6	7	7
5	2	1
1	5	6

f 289

$^{3}\cancel{4}$	$^{1}\cancel{2}$	9
1	4	0
2	8	9

g 636

7	$^{8}\cancel{9}$	$^{1}4$
1	5	8
6	3	6

h 189

$^{5}\cancel{6}$	$^{16}\cancel{7}$	$^{1}4$
4	8	5
1	8	9

56–57 **Multiplication**

Warm-up

1 5 + 5 + 5 = 5 x 3 = 15
2 4 + 4 + 4 = 4 x 3 = 12
3 6 + 6 + 6 + 6 = 6 x 4 = 24
4 4 + 4 + 4 + 4 = 4 x 4 = 16

1. a 4 + 4 + 4 = 12 therefore 4 x 3 = 12
b 5 + 5 + 5 + 5 = 20 therefore 5 x 4 = 20
c 3 + 3 = 6 therefore 3 x 2 = 6

2. a 3 x 3 = 9

b 7 x 2 = 14

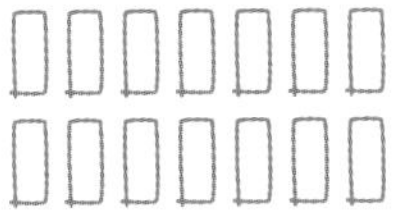

c 3 x 4 = 12

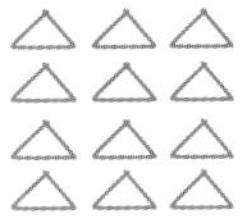

d 6 x 3 = 18

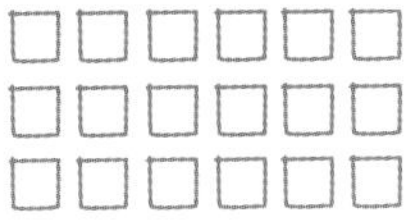

3. a 4 x 3 = 3 + 3 + 3 + 3
b 3 x 6 = 6 + 6 + 6
c 2 x 8 = 8 + 8
d 8 x 3 = 3 + 3 + 3 + 3 + 3 + 3 + 3 + 3
e 2 x 10 = 2 + 2
f 10 x 3 = 3 + 3 + 3 + 3 + 3 + 3 + 3 + 3 + 3 + 3

58–59 **Counting in multiples**

Warm-up

1
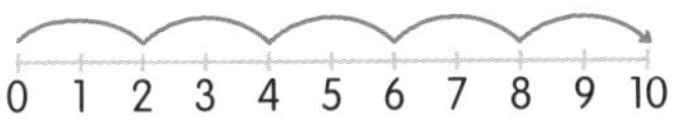

2
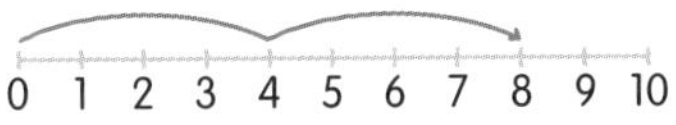

3
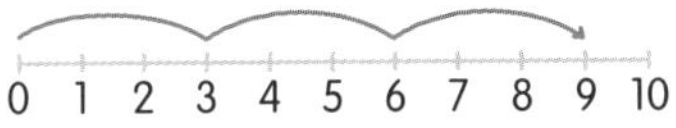

4
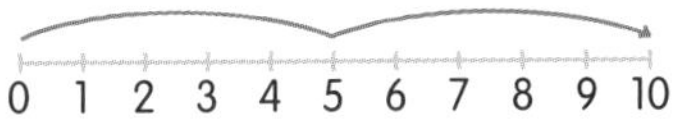

1. a 5 x 4 = 20
b 5 x 5 = 25
c 4 x 6 = 24

2. a 5 x 6 = 30 pens
b 5 x 7 = 35 lessons
c 3 x 8 = 24 balls
d 9 x 8 = 72 pencils

60–61 **Multiplication tables**

Warm-up

1 6x table	2 7x table	3 12x table
6 x 0 = 0	7 x 0 = 0	12 x 0 = 0
6 x 1 = 6	7 x 1 = 7	12 x 1 = 12
6 x 2 = 12	7 x 2 = 14	12 x 2 = 24
6 x 3 = 18	7 x 3 = 21	12 x 3 = 36
6 x 4 = 24	7 x 4 = 28	12 x 4 = 48
6 x 5 = 30	7 x 5 = 35	12 x 5 = 60
6 x 6 = 36	7 x 6 = 42	12 x 6 = 72
6 x 7 = 42	7 x 7 = 49	12 x 7 = 84
6 x 8 = 48	7 x 8 = 56	12 x 8 = 96
6 x 9 = 54	7 x 9 = 63	12 x 9 = 108
6 x 10 = 60	7 x 10 = 70	12 x 10 = 120
6 x 11 = 66	7 x 11 = 77	12 x 11 = 132
6 x 12 = 72	7 x 12 = 84	12 x 12 = 144

1. a 3 x 8 = 24 b 11 x 5 = 55
c 6 x 9 = 54 d 10 x 4 = 40
e 2 x 1 = 2 f 4 x 7 = 28
g 7 x 8 = 56 h 12 x 11 = 132

2. a 4 x 9 = 36 raspberries
b 3 x 5 = 15 bananas
c 8 x 8 = 64 leaves
d 5 x 11 = 55 kiwis
e 3 x 12 = 36 avocados
f 6 x 7 = 42 slices

3. a 77 b 12 c 60 d 48 e 0
f 18 g 60 h 10

Maths in context 72 + 77 = 149 pencils

62–63 **The multiplication grid**

Warm-up

x	1	2	3	4	5	6	7	8	9	10	11	12
1	1	2	3	4	5	6	7	8	9	10	11	12
2	2	4	6	8	10	12	14	16	18	20	22	24
3	3	6	9	12	15	18	21	24	27	30	33	36
4	4	8	12	16	20	24	28	32	36	40	44	48
5	5	10	15	20	25	30	35	40	45	50	55	60
6	6	12	18	24	30	36	42	48	54	60	66	72
7	7	14	21	28	35	42	49	56	63	70	77	84
8	8	16	24	32	40	48	56	64	72	80	88	96
9	9	18	27	36	45	54	63	72	81	90	99	108
10	10	20	30	40	50	60	70	80	90	100	110	120
11	11	22	33	44	55	66	77	88	99	110	121	132
12	12	24	36	48	60	72	84	96	108	120	132	144

1. a 24 b 25 c 70 d 33
e 3 f 18 g 108 h 60

2. a 2 b 4 c 7 d 12
e 9 f 8 g 56 h 36

3. a 9 x 5 = 45 p
b 12 x 7 = 84 cherries
c 3 x 8 = 24 carrots

Maths in context

7 x 4 = 28, 3 x 9 = 27
so Mia has the greater number of stickers.

64–65 **Multiplication patterns and strategies**

Warm-up

Suggested examples:

1 4 x 2 = 4 + 4 = 8
2 6 x 4 = 6 x 2 x 2 = 12 x 2 = 24
3 8 x 5 = 8 x 10 ÷ 2 = 40
4 7 x 9 = 7 x 10 – 7 = 70 – 7 = 63
5 9 x 11 = 99
6 6 x 12 = 6 x 10 + 6 x 2 = 60 + 12 = 72

1. a 12 x 2 = 24 because 12 + 12 = 24
b 7 x 4 = 28 because double 7 = 14 and double 14 = 28
c 5 x 12 = 60 because 10 x 12 = 120 and half of 120 = 60
d 8 x 9 = 72 because 10 x 8 = 80 and 80 – 8 = 72

2. a 4 x 3 = 12
I solved this by doubling 3, then doubling the answer again
b 6 x 12 = 72
I solved this by multiplying the original number by 10, then again by 2, and finally adding the two answers
c 2 x 9 = 18
I solved this by multiplying the original number by 10 and then subtracting the original number
d 7 x 4 = 12
I solved this by doubling the number and then doubling again
e 5 x 7 = 35
I solved this by multiplying by 10 then halving the result
f 8 x 12 = 96
I solved this by multiplying the original number by 10, then again by 2, and finally adding the two answers

3. a 42 b 65 c 180 d 56 e 90
f 64 g 216

66–67 **Expanded short multiplication**

Warm-up

1

	8	7	6
			3
		1	8
	2	1	0
2	4	0	0
2	6	2	8

2

	4	5	7
			4
		2	8
	2	0	0
1	6	0	0
1	8	2	8

3

	1	2	0
			9
			0
	1	8	0
	9	0	0
1	0	8	0

4

	3	7	2
			6
		1	2
	4	2	0
1	8	0	0
2	2	3	2

5

	5	2	6
			8
		4	8
	1	6	0
4	0	0	0
4	2	0	8

6

	2	8	4
			5
		2	0
	4	0	0
1	0	0	0
1	4	2	0

7

	9	5	1
			7
			7
	3	5	0
6	3	0	0
6	6	5	7

8

	6	0	7
			2
		1	4
		0	0
1	2	0	0
1	2	1	4

9

	7	6	4
			9
		3	6
	5	4	0
6	3	0	0
6	8	7	6

1. a

	7	5	3
			5
		1	5
	2	5	0
3	5	0	0
3	7	6	5

b

	3	6	4
			9
		3	6
	5	4	0
2	7	0	0
3	2	7	6

c

	4	5	2
			7
		1	4
	3	5	0
2	8	0	0
3	1	6	4

2. a

	1	3	2
			7
		1	4
	2	1	0
	7	0	0
	9	2	4

b

	2	8	7
			5
		3	5
	4	0	0
1	0	0	0
1	4	3	5

c

	3	5	7
			8
		5	6
	4	0	0
2	4	0	0
2	8	5	6

d

	1	2	9
			9
		8	1
	1	8	0
	9	0	0
1	1	6	1

68–69 **Short multiplication**

Warm-up

1

	^{2}5	^{2}6	8
			3
1	7	0	4

2

	^{1}8	^{1}4	3
			4
3	3	7	2

3

	^{2}3	^{3}4	7
			5
1	7	3	5

1. a 3420 b 2562 c 5904 d 3483

2. a 680 minutes b 1169 grams
c 2070 grapes

	^{1}1	^{3}3	6
			5
	6	8	0

	^{4}1	^{4}6	7
			7
1	1	6	9

	^{2}3	^{3}4	5
			6
2	0	7	0

3. a

	^{3}8	^{2}6	4
			6
5	1	8	4

b

	^{7}5	^{5}8	6
			9
5	2	7	4

c

	^{4}9	^{3}5	4
			8
7	6	3	2

d

	9	4	3
			2
1	8	8	6

e

	^{5}8	^{4}7	6
			7
6	1	3	2

f

	^{3}5	^{6}3	7
			9
4	8	3	3

g

	^{3}8	^{4}6	9
			5
4	3	4	5

h

	^{4}4	^{1}7	2
			6
2	8	3	2

i

	^{1}5	^{2}3	6
			4
2	1	4	4

70–71 **Division**

Warm-up

1 4 groups; 8 ÷ 2 = 4
2 6 groups; 12 ÷ 2 = 6
3 5 groups; 10 ÷ 2 = 5

Maths in context

8 packs; there will be 2 balls extra, 10 pairs of rackets

1. a 20 ÷ 5 = 4 = 16 ÷ 4
b 16 ÷ 2 = 8 = 32 ÷ 4
c 9 ÷ 3 = 3 = 27 ÷ 9
d 21 ÷ 3 = 7 = 42 ÷ 6
e 50 ÷ 10 = 5 = 40 ÷ 8
f 24 ÷ 4 = 6 = 48 ÷ 8

2. a 12, 3 b 15, 5 c 20, 5 d 16, 8
e 10, 5 f 16, 4 g 27, 9 h 24, 6
i 21, 7 j 9, 3 k 40, 8

3. a 4 r1 b 2 r2 c 2 r2
d 5 r1 e 2 f 2 r2

72–73 **Dividing with multiples**

Warm-up

1 8 2 8 3 3

1. a 10 r2 b 12 r1

2. Calculations that are wrong:
46 ÷ 5 = 9, 74 ÷ 4 = 19,
56 ÷ 6 = 9, 36 ÷ 3 = 11.
Corrected calculations:
a 46 ÷ 5 = 9 remainder 1
b 74 ÷ 4 = 18 remainder 2
c 56 ÷ 6 = 9 remainder 2
d 36 ÷ 3 = 12

3. a 22 boxes b 9 taxis c 26 bags

74-57 **Division tables**

Warm-up

1 6÷ table	2 9÷ table	3 12÷ table
6 ÷ 6 = 1	9 ÷ 9 = 1	12 ÷ 12 = 1
12 ÷ 6 = 2	18 ÷ 9 = 2	24 ÷ 12 = 2
18 ÷ 6 = 3	27 ÷ 9 = 3	36 ÷ 12 = 3
24 ÷ 6 = 4	36 ÷ 9 = 4	48 ÷ 12 = 4
30 ÷ 6 = 5	45 ÷ 9 = 5	60 ÷ 12 = 5
36 ÷ 6 = 6	54 ÷ 9 = 6	72 ÷ 12 = 6
42 ÷ 6 = 7	63 ÷ 9 = 7	84 ÷ 12 = 7
48 ÷ 6 = 8	72 ÷ 9 = 8	96 ÷ 12 = 8
54 ÷ 6 = 9	81 ÷ 9 = 9	108 ÷ 12 = 9
60 ÷ 6 = 10	90 ÷ 9 = 10	120 ÷ 12 = 10
66 ÷ 6 = 11	99 ÷ 9 = 11	132 ÷ 12 = 11
72 ÷ 6 = 12	108 ÷ 9 = 12	144 ÷ 12 = 12

1. a 8 ÷ 4 = 2 b 77 ÷ 7 = 11
c 72 ÷ 12 = 6 d 15 ÷ 3 = 5
e 24 ÷ 6 = 4 f 60 ÷ 5 = 12
g 24 ÷ 8 = 3 h 35 ÷ 5 = 7

2. a 48 ÷ 8 = 6 bales
b 108 ÷ 9 = 12 sweets
c 144 ÷ 12 = 12 rows
d 20 ÷ 4 = 5 balloons
e 49 ÷ 7 = 7 bananas
f 18 ÷ 6 = 3 yoyos

3. a 6 b 4 c 9 d 7 e 9
f 11 g 12 h 5

Maths in context 1 8 cakes 2 11 cakes

76-77 **The division grid**

Warm-up

1 12 2 9 3 11 4 7
5 8 6 9 7 7 8 8 9 8 10 11
11 12 12 9

1. a 8 b 6 c 7 d 11 e 54
f 18 g 36 h 12

2. a 88 ÷ 8 = 11 b 48 ÷ 6 = 8
c 27 ÷ 9 = 3 d 48 ÷ 12 = 4
e 24 ÷ 4 = 6 f 30 ÷ 6 = 5
g 108 ÷ 12 = 9 h 56 ÷ 7 = 8

3. a 18 ÷ 3 = 6 tins
b 55 ÷ 5 = 11 coins
c 48 ÷ 4 = 12 chickens
d 56 ÷ 8 = 7 chocolates
e 108 ÷ 9 = 12 pages

78–79 **Partitioning for division**

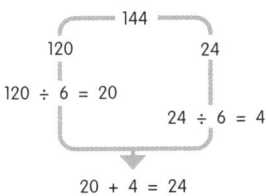

Warm-up

1 144 ÷ 6 = 24

144
120 | 24
120 ÷ 6 = 20
24 ÷ 6 = 4
20 + 4 = 24

2 170 ÷ 5 = 34

170
150 | 20
150 ÷ 5 = 30
20 ÷ 5 = 4
30 + 4 = 34

3 126 ÷ 3 = 42

126
120 | 6
120 ÷ 3 = 40
6 ÷ 3 = 2
40 + 2 = 42

4 264 ÷ 8 = 33

264
240 | 24
240 ÷ 8 = 30
24 ÷ 8 = 3
30 + 3 = 33

(or alternative steps which result in the correct answers)

1. a 176 ÷ 8 = 22 pages

176
160 | 16
160 ÷ 8 = 20
16 ÷ 8 = 2
20 + 2 = 22

b 189 ÷ 7 = 27 packs

189
175 | 24
175 ÷ 7 = 25
14 ÷ 7 = 2
25 + 2 = 27

c 207 ÷ 9 = 23 balls

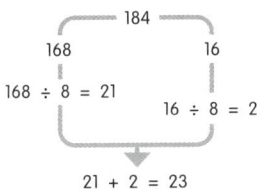

207
189 | 18
189 ÷ 9 = 21
18 ÷ 9 = 2
21 + 2 = 23

d 184 ÷ 8 = 23 shelves

184
168 | 16
168 ÷ 8 = 21
16 ÷ 8 = 2
21 + 2 = 23

(or alternative steps which result in the correct answers)

80–81 **Expanded short division**

Warm-up

1 115 ÷ 5 = 23

		2	3	
5	1	1	5	
−		5	0	(10 x 5)
		6	5	
−		5	0	(10 x 5)
		1	5	
−		1	5	(3 x 5)
			0	23

2 111 ÷ 3 =37

		3	7	
3	1	1	1	
−		6	0	(20 x 3)
		5	1	
−		3	0	(10 x 3)
		2	1	
−		0	0	(7 x 3)
			0	37

(or alternative steps which result in the correct answer)

3 384 ÷ 6 = 64

		6	4	
6	3	8	4	
−	1	2	0	(20 x 6)
	2	6	4	
−	1	2	0	(20 x 6)
	1	4	4	
−		0	0	(24 x 6)
			0	64

(or alternative steps which result in the correct answer)

1. a 128 ÷ 3 = 42 r2

		4	2 r 2	
3	1	2	8	
−		6	0	(20 x 3)
		6	8	
−		6	0	(20 x 3)
			8	
−			6	(2 x 3)
			2	42

b 273 ÷ 5 = 54 r3

		5	4 r 3	
5	2	7	3	
−	1	5	0	(30 x 5)
	1	2	3	
−	1	0	0	(20 x 5)
		2	3	
−		2	0	(4 x 5)
			3	54

c 345 ÷ 6 = 55 r3

		5	7 r 3	
6	3	4	5	
−	2	4	0	(40 x 6)
	1	0	5	
−		9	0	(15 x 6)
		1	5	
−		1	2	(2 x 6)
			3	55

2. a 115 r2 b 116 r4 c 111 r5

3. a 524 ÷ 6 = 87 remainder 2
b 203 ÷ 3 = 67 remainder 2
c 452 ÷ 7 = 64 remainder 4
d 349 ÷ 5 = 69 remainder 4

82–83 **Short division**

Warm-up

1

		4	3
6	2	$^{2}5$	$^{1}8$

2

		2	8
9	2	$^{5}5$	$^{7}2$

3

		8	4
4	3	$^{3}3$	$^{1}6$

4

		7	9
5	3	$^{3}9$	$^{4}5$

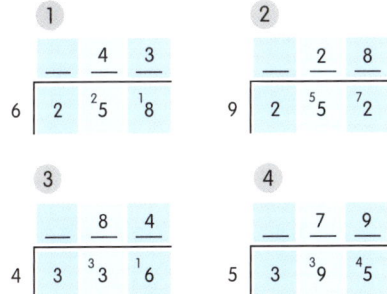

1. a 36 b 28 c 85 d 59 e 43

2. a 90 r3 b 123 r1 c 43 r2
d 77 r7 e 38 r4 f 53 r2

3. a = b < c < d > e = f <
g > h > i < j < k = l <

Maths in context

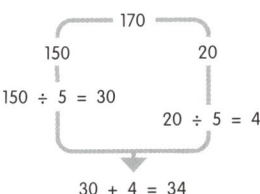

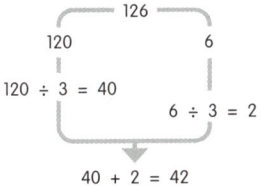

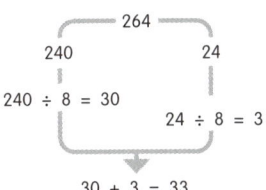

1 0 cm 2 2 cm 3 1 cm 4 5 cm

84–85 **Arithmetic laws**

Warm-up

1 3 x 4 = 12 2 2 x 3 = 6

3 5 x 3 = 15 4 6 x 3 = 18

1. a 4 x 6 = 24, 6 x 4 = 24
b 1 x 2 = 2, 2 x 1 = 2
c 6 x 7 = 42, 7 x 6 = 42
d 4 x 9 = 36, 9 x 4 = 36
e 9 x 1 = 9, 1 x 9 = 9
f 3 x 5 = 15, 5 x 3 = 15
g 5 x 6 = 30, 6 x 5 = 30
h 7 x 8 = 56, 8 x 7 = 56
i 8 x 3 = 24, 3 x 8 = 24
j 9 x 6 = 54, 6 x 9 = 54

2.
a 15 x 6 = (10 x 6) + (5 x 6) = 60 + 30 = 90
b 24 x 5 = (20 x 5) + (4 x 5) = 100 + 20 = 120
c 13 x 9 = (10 x 9) + (3 x 9) = 90 + 27 = 117
d 18 x 4 = (10 x 4) + (8 x 4) = 40 + 32 = 72
e 21 x 2 = (20 x 2) + (1 x 2) = 40 + 2 = 42
f 27 x 8 = (20 x 8) + (7 x 8) = 160 + 56 = 216
g 36 x 3 = (30 x 3) + (6 x 3) = 90 + 18 = 108
h 46 x 8 = (40 x 8) + (6 x 8) = 320 + 48 = 368

3. a 8 x 4 = 32 using the commutative law is the same as 4 x 8 = 32
b 27 x 3 = 81 using the commutative law is the same as 3 x 27 = 81
c 7 x 6 = 42 using the commutative law is the same as 6 x 7 = 42
d 2 x 9 = 18 using the commutative law is the same as 9 x 2 =18
e 19 x 7 = 133 using the distributive law is the same as (10 x 7) + (9 x 7) = 133
f 22 x 4 = 88 using the distributive law is the same as (20 x 4) + (2 x 4) = 88
g 12 x 4 = 48 using the distributive law is the same as (10 x 4) + (2 x 4) = 48
h 9 x 8 = 72 using the commutative law is the same as 8 x 9 = 72
i 28 x 9 = 252 using the distributive law is the same as (20 x 9) + (8 x 9) = 252

86–87 **Length**

Warm-up
1 14 cm 2 6 cm 3 5 cm 4 3 cm
5 2 cm

1. a mm b cm or m c m d m
e km f km

2. a 200 cm b 26 cm c 1.3 m
d 170 mm e 4 cm f 7000 mm
g 280 mm h 38 m

3. 3 mm, 380 mm, 320 cm, 380 cm, 34 m

4. 3 m = 300 cm,
3 cm = 30 mm,
90 mm = 9 cm,
800 cm = 8 m,
900 cm = 9 m,
800 mm = 80 cm,
400 cm = 4 m,
24 cm = 240 mm,
7000 mm = 7 m,
200 cm = 2 m

88–89 **Perimeter**

Warm-up
1 3 + 3 + 3 + 3 = 12 cm
2 2 + 2 + 2 + 2 +2 = 10 cm
3 5 + 3 + 4 = 12 cm

1. a 5 + 3 + 5 + 3 = 16 m
b 12 + 7 + 12 + 7 = 38 m
c 5 + 8 + 8 = 21 m

2. a 5 cm + 5 cm + 5 cm + 5 cm = 20 cm
b 10 cm + 10 cm + 10 cm = 30 cm
c 40 cm + 6 cm + 40 cm + 6 cm = 92 cm
d 12 cm + 8 cm + 12 cm + 8 cm = 40 cm

3. (in any order)
a 1 m and 11 m
b 2 m and 10 m
c 3 m and 9 m
d 4 m and 8 m
e 5 m and 7 m
f 6 m and 6 m
g 7 m and 5 m
h 8 m and 4 m
i 9 m and 3 m
j 10 m and 2 m
k 11 m and 1 m

90–91 **Area**

Warm-up
1 12 cm^2 2 16 cm^2 3 9 cm^2 4 20 cm^2

1. a 10 cm^2 b 9 cm^2 c 11 cm^2
d 7 cm^2 e 6 cm^2 f 8 cm^2

2. a blue tiles: 4 squares,
red tiles: 6 squares, white tiles: 8 squares
b blue tiles: 2 squares,
red tiles: 4 squares, white tiles: 12 squares
c blue tiles: 2 squares,
red tiles: 2 squares, white tiles: 14 squares
d blue tiles: 2 squares,
red tiles: 12 squares, white tiles: 4 squares
e blue tiles: 4 squares,
red tiles: 4 squares, white tiles: 10 squares
f blue tiles: 7 squares,
red tiles: 7 squares, white tiles: 4 squares

3. Learner draws shapes that each have an area of 6 cm^2.

92–93 **Estimating area**

Warm-up
1 11 m^2 2 10 m^2 3 8 m^2 4 10 m^2

1. a 12 cm^2 b 9 cm^2 c 9 cm^2
d 16 cm^2 e 9 cm^2 f 19 cm^2
g 7 cm^2 h 13 cm^2

2. a Learner either draws paint splodge covering 20 full squares, or a combination of full and partial squares as per the method taught
b Learner either draws paint splodge covering 19 full squares, or a combination of full and partial squares as per the method taught
c Learner either draws paint splodge covering 28 full squares, or a combination of full and partial squares as per the method taught
d Learner either draws paint splodge covering 13 full squares, or a combination of full and partial squares as per the method taught

3. a 14 m^2
b 22 m^2
c 55 m^2
d 21 m^2

94 Capacity

Warm-up
1 1250 ml 2 150 ml 3 200 ml 4 1.5 l

1. a saucepan: 4 b egg cup: 1 c drinking glass: 2 d fish tank: 6 e bucket: 5 f mug: 3

95 Volume

Warm-up
1 50 ml 2 80 ml 3 20 ml 4 400 ml 5 550 ml

1. a b c

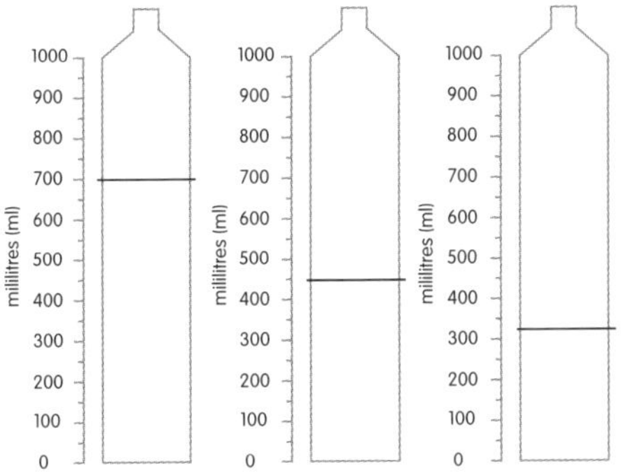

Maths in context (in any order)
1 12 teaspoons and 0 tablespoons
2 9 teaspoons and 1 tablespoon
3 6 teaspoons and 2 tablespoons
4 3 teaspoons and 3 tablespoons
5 0 teaspoons and 4 tablespoons

96–97 Mass

Warm-up
1 150 g 2 5 g 3 4.5 kg 4 6 tonnes

1. a 1 pencil, 2 cake, 3 laptop, 4 car, 5 elephant b 1 feather, 2 pencil sharpener, 3 fox, 4 car, 5 bus c 1 tennis ball, 2 banana, 3 trumpet, 4 motorbike, 5 whale d 1 bird, 2 apple, 3 football, 4 tiger, 5 car

2. a tiger = 200 kg
b five paperclips = 5 g
c rhino = 2 tonnes
d potato = 110 g
e horse = 850 kg
f butterfly = 1 mg
g swan = 12 kg
h house = 150 tonnes

Maths in context Learners own answers.

98–99 Calculating with mass

Warm-up
1 36 kg 2 20 kg 3 28 kg 4 22 kg 5 39 kg

1. a 3012 g b 458 g c 7999 g d 13.458 kg

2. a 4 small weights or 2 medium weights = 200 g
b 2 small weights or 1 medium weight = 100 g
c 1 big weight and 5 medium weights = 1.5 kg
d 8 small weights or 4 medium weights = 400 g
e 7 small weights or 3 medium plus 1 small weight = 350 g
f 1 big weight plus 2 medium weights and 1 small weight = 1250 g

3. a 3100 g b 707 g c 3350 g d 63 g

100–101 Telling the time

Warm-up
1 7 o'clock
2 10 o'clock
3 half past 10
4 half past 12
5 half past 1

1. a quarter past 1 b quarter to 7 c quarter past 8 d quarter to 1 e quarter past 7 f quarter to 8

2.

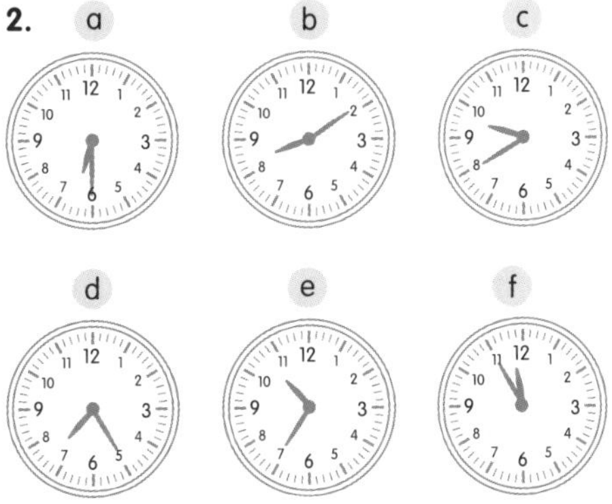

3. a 1 b 4 c 5 d 8 e 2 f 7 g 6 h 3

102–103 Calculating with time

Warm-up
1 48 minutes 2 70 minutes 3 50 minutes 4 85 minutes 5 45 minutes 6 80 minutes

1. a Mia 20 minutes b Kaya 30 minutes c Evie 40 minutes d Josh 70 minutes e Abbas 70 minutes f Tam 25 minutes

2. a 9:20 b 10:05 c 11:50 d 16:55 e 20:20 f 23:39 g 21:48 h 23:39

Maths in context
1 7:40 am 2 25 minutes 3 110 minutes 4 3:20 pm 5 4:50 pm

104–105 Dates

Warm-up
1 7, 365 2 366 3 52 4 12, 28, 31

1. a 28 days: February
b 30 days: April, June, September, November
c 31 days: January, March, May, July, August, October, December

2. a 31 b Friday c 5 d Wednesday e Thursday f 4 g Monday h Monday

3. a February b June c October d October & January e April & June

Maths in context 1 21 2 56 days 3 2 weeks 4 84 months

106–107 Money

Warm-up 1 3 2 1 3 2 4 4 5 5

1. a £3.95 b £6.25 c £5.64 d £10.20

2. a < b < c > d > e = f >

3. a £4.50 b 305p c £8.25 d 325p e 560p f £12.50 g 1060p h 1200p i 286p j £6.01 k 194p l £17.61 m £2.87 n 1819p

4. a £6.65 = £2 + £3 + £1.65
b £10.01 = £4.30 + £5.11 + 60p
c £4.20 = £3 + 80p + 40p

108–109 **Using money**

Warm-up
1 92p 2 £1.25 3 £1.64 4 £3.17

1. a £3.92
b £1.99
c £4.46
d £6.74

2. a £3.50 < £3.62
b £8.80 < £10.00
c £6.90 > £4.85
d £15.45 = £ 15.45

Maths in context answers include:
2 x £1, 1 x 50p, 1 x 2p;
1 x £1, 3 x 50p, 2 x 1p; 5 x 50p, 2 x 1p;
1 x £1, 2 x 50p, 2 x 20p, 1 x 10p, 2 x 1p

110 **What is a line?**

Warm-up
1 6 cm 2 8 cm 3 5 cm 4 8 cm

1. a red b green c pink d purple
e yellow f blue

112–113 **Diagonal lines**

Warm-up

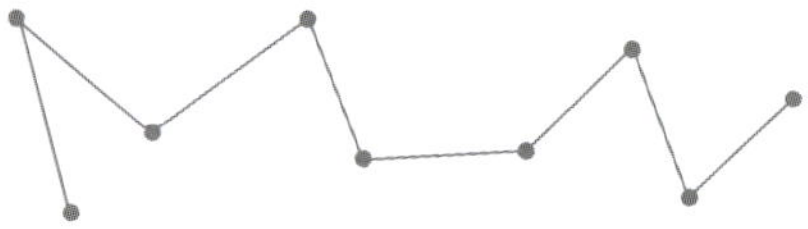

1. a Diagonal lines = 2
Horizontal lines = 1
Vertical lines = 1
b Diagonal lines = 4
Horizontal lines = 2
Vertical lines = 2
c Diagonal lines = 3
Horizontal lines = 3
Vertical lines = 4
d Diagonal lines = 7
Horizontal lines = 4
Vertical lines = 4
e Diagonal lines = 2
Horizontal lines = 2
Vertical lines = 2

2. Suggested answer for c and d

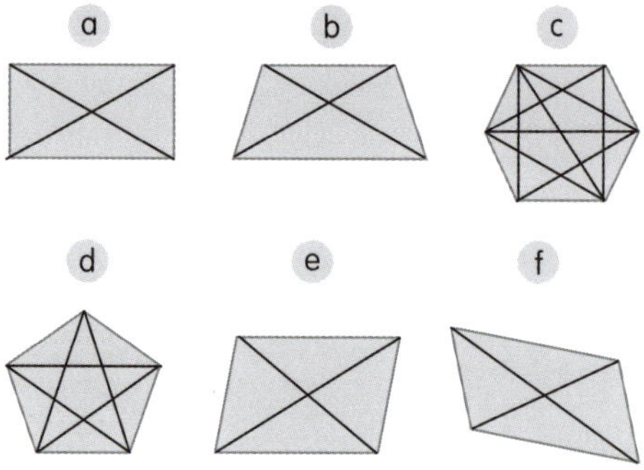

3. a > b = c > d < e > f <

111 **Horizontal and vertical lines**

Warm-up
1

2

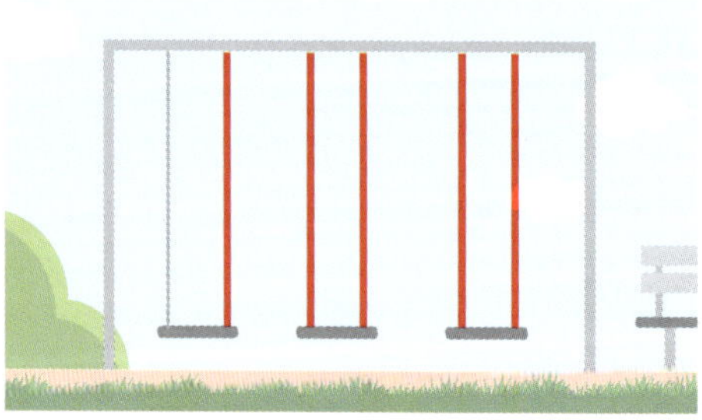

1.

There are 17 vertical lines and 14 horizontal lines.

114 **Parallel lines**

Warm-up 1 ✓ 3 ✓ 5 ✓ 6 ✓

1. Learner draws a line parallel to each of the six lines.

2. a 0 b 2 c 0 d 2

115 **Perpendicular lines**

Warm-up
Suggestions include:

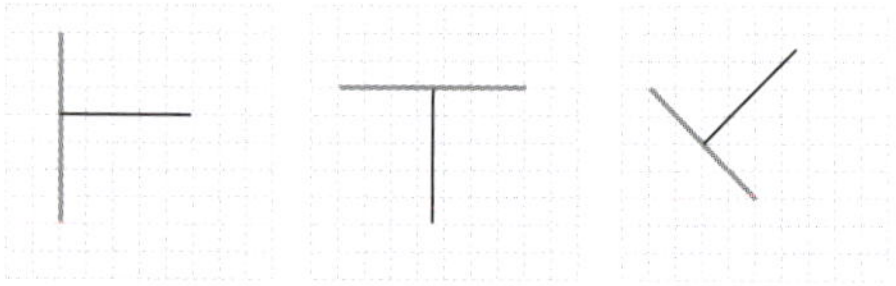

1. Coloured in shapes a b and d.

2.

Learner draws a house using at least five pairs of perpendicular lines.

116–117 **2D shapes**

Warm-up
1 ✓ 4 ✓ 5 ✓

1.

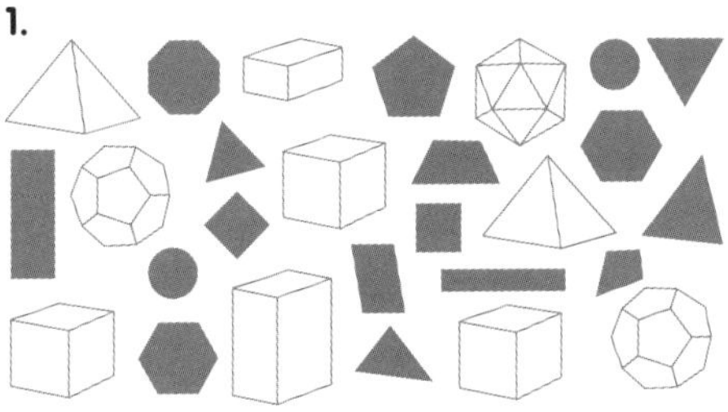

There are 17 2D shapes.

2. a This shape has 4 sides, 2 pairs of parallel lines, and 4 pairs of perpendicular lines
b This shape has 6 sides, 1 pair of parallel lines, and 0 pairs of perpendicular lines
c This shape has 6 sides, 3 pairs of parallel lines, and 0 pairs of perpendicular lines
d This shape has 4 sides, 0 pairs of parallel lines, and 0 pairs of perpendicular lines

3. a Learner draws a square
b Learner draws an equilateral or isosceles triangle
c Learner draws a rectangle
d Learner draws a hexagon

118–119 **Regular and irregular polygons**

Warm-up
1 blue 2 blue 3 red 4 blue 5 red

1. a This shape is a regular polygon with 6 sides
b This shape is a regular polygon with 4 sides
c This shape is a regular polygon with 8 sides
d This shape is an irregular polygon with 4 sides
e This shape is an irregular polygon with 3 sides
f This shape is an irregular polygon with 11 sides
g This shape is a regular polygon with 5 sides
h This shape is an irregular polygon with 7 sides

2. a Learner draws a regular octagon
b Learner draws an irregular octagon
c Learner draws an equilateral triangle
d Learner draws a scalene triangle (where all the sides are different lengths) or an isosceles triangle
e Learner draws a regular pentagon
f Learner draws an irregular pentagon
g Learner draws a square
h Learner draws an irregular quadrilateral

120–121 **Triangles**

Warm-up
1 apex 2 side 3 vertex 4 base 5 equilateral triangle

1. a Equilateral triangle
b Isosceles triangle
c Scalene triangle
d Equilateral triangle
e Right-angled triangle
f Scalene triangle
g Right-angled triangle
h Isosceles triangle

2. a blue b yellow c yellow d red e red f blue g red h blue i yellow

3. Learner's own answers.

122–123 **Quadrilaterals**

Warm-up
1 ✓ 2 ✓ 4 ✓ 5 ✓ 7 ✓ 9 ✓

1. There are 14 quadrilaterals in this picture: 5 red stripes, 1 bucket, 2 sandcastles, 2 flagpoles on the sandcastles, 1 rug, 2 purple ships, 1 big flagpole.

2. a kite
b rhombus
c parallelogram
d rectangle
e square
f trapezium

3. Learner's own answers.

124–125 **Naming polygons**

Warm-up
1 pentagon 2 square 3 nonagon 4 octagon 5 heptagon 6 equilateral triangle 7 decagon 8 hexagon

1. a 4 sides b an octagon c 12 angles d 20 sides and 20 angles e a decagon

2. Learner's own answers.

3. a regular quadrilateral
b regular hexagon
c irregular quadrilateral
d irregular nonagon
e regular heptagon
f regular octagon

126–127 **3D shapes**

Warm-up
1 vertex 2 edge 3 face 4 three

1. a height b width c length d face e vertex f edge

2. a 3 b 4 c 6 d 6

3. a 12 b 12 c 8 d 2

4. a a cylinder b a square-based pyramid c a cube

128–129 **Types of 3D shape**

Warm-up
1 cube 2 cone 3 sphere 4 cuboid

1. a octahedron
b cube
c tetrahedron
d icosahedron
e dodecahedron

2. a This shape is a cube. It has 6 faces, 12 edges and 8 vertices
b This shape is a cylinder. It has 3 faces, 2 edges and 0 vertices
c This shape is a triangular-based pyramid. It has 4 faces, 6 edges and 4 vertices
d This shape is a hemisphere. It has 2 faces, 1 edge and 0 vertices
e This shape is a square-based pyramid. It has 5 faces, 8 edges and 5 vertices
f This shape is a cuboid. It has 6 faces, 12 edges and 8 vertices

Maths in context

1 cube, square-based pyramid
2 cuboid 3 hemisphere, cylinder, cone
4 pentagonal prism, dodecahedron
5 triangular-based pyramid, square-based pyramid, tetrahedron
6 hexagonal prism

130–131 Prisms

Warm-up

1 ✕ 4 ✕ 6 ✕

1.

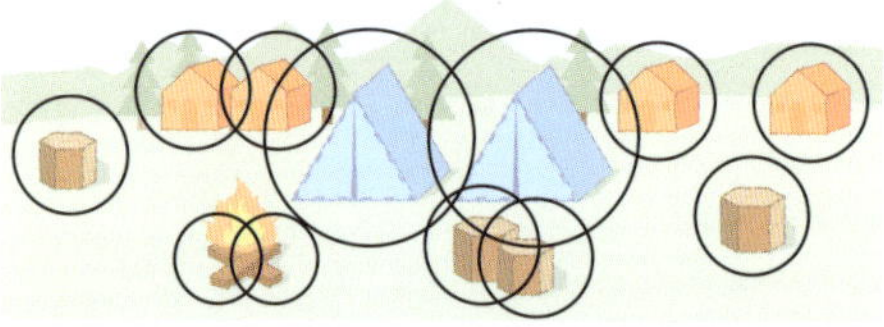

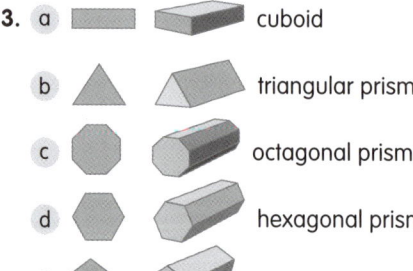

2. a This prism has 5 faces, 9 edges and 6 vertices
b This prism has 12 faces, 30 edges and 20 vertices
c This prism has 6 faces, 12 edges and 8 vertices
d This prism has 14 faces, 36 edges and 24 vertices
e This prism has 5 faces, 9 edges and 6 vertices
f This prism has 7 faces, 15 edges, and 10 vertices

3. a  cuboid
b  triangular prism
c 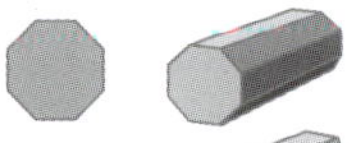 octagonal prism
d 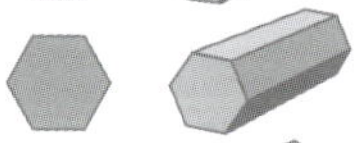 hexagonal prism
e  pentagonal prism

132 Angles

Warm-up

1 0 2 1 3 4 4 1 5 0

1.

a
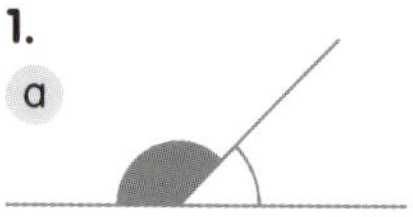

b
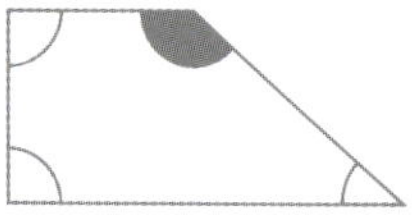

c
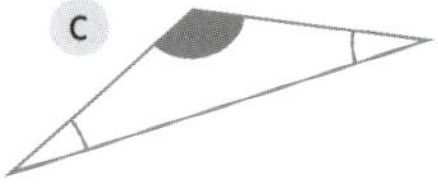

2. a < b > c > d < e = f =

133 Degrees

Warm-up

1 45° 2 23° 3 90° 4 135°
5 100° 6 200°

1. a
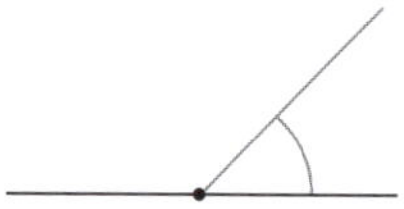

b
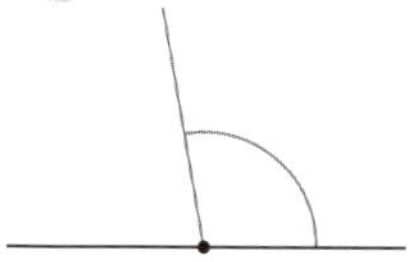

c
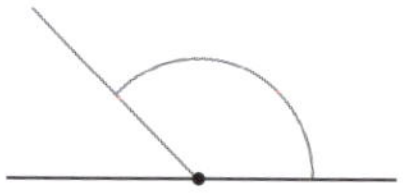

d

e
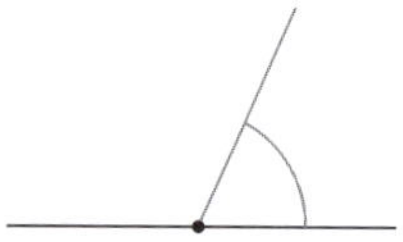

f
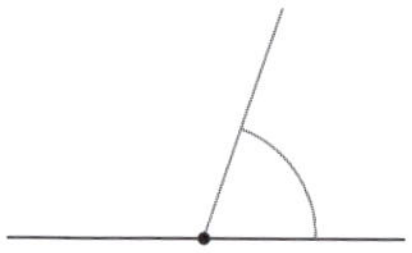

134–135 Right angles

Warm-up

1
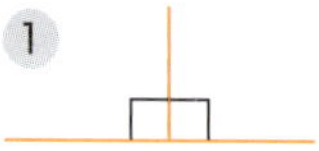

2
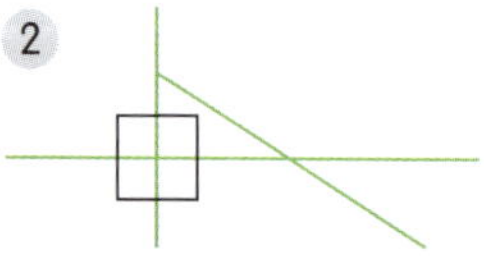

3
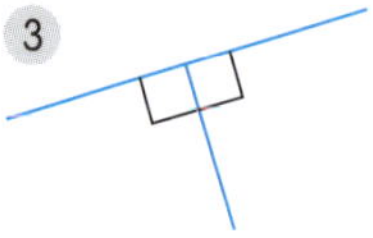

4
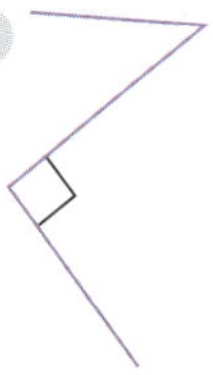

5
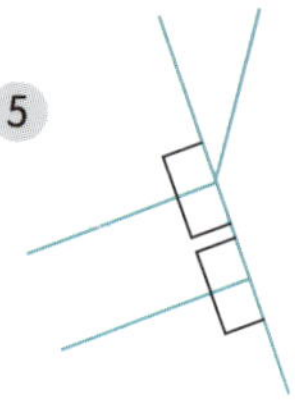

1. a 1 b 2 c 3 d 4

2. a 270° b 90° c 360° d 180°

3. Learner's own answers

Maths in context

I can see 50 right angles in the picture.

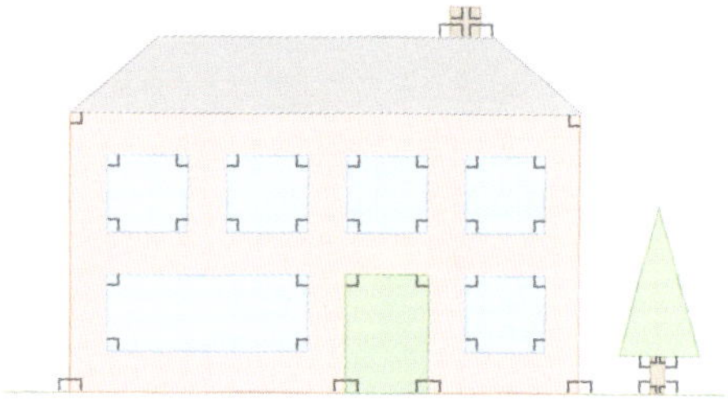

136–137 Types of angle

Warm-up

1 acute angle 2 right angle
3 obtuse angle 4 obtuse angle
5 acute angle

1. a an acute b an obtuse
c a right d a right
e an acute f an obtuse

2. a an acute angle b an acute angle
c a straight angle d an obtuse angle
e an obtuse angle f an acute angle

3. a never true b always true
c never true d sometimes true
e sometimes true f always true

4.

138–139 **Coordinates**

Warm-up

1 (2,10)
2 (5,10)
3 (10,7)
4 (6,6)
5 (3,4)
6 (8,2)

1.

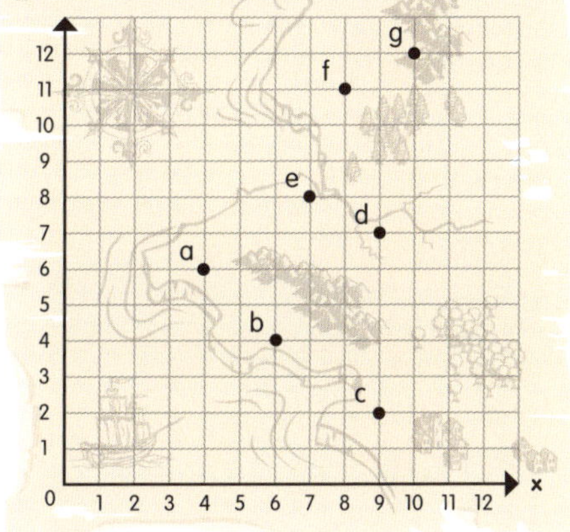

2. a a square
b a rectangle
c an isosceles triangle
d a trapezium
e a hexagon
f a triangle

3. The wrong coordinates are (7,0) (6,5) (9,1).

Maths in context Learner's own answer. Coordinates should draw a pentagon.

140–141 **Position and direction**

Warm-up

1 D3 2 C5 3 B2 4 A9
5 I7 6 B10

1. a K5 b G3 c L3 d C4
e H1 f C6 g B3

2. a M5 and landed in J2
b I5 and landed in K6
c E8 and landed in H8
d D8 and landed in G10
e I11 and landed in N7
f J9 and landed in P2
g C5 and landed in E3
h F10 and landed in N7

142–143 **Compass directions**

Warm-up

1 northwest 2 west 3 southwest
4 south 5 north 6 northeast
7 east 8 southeast

1. a south b east c southwest
d northwest e northeast

2. a C13 b H13 c H9 d F9
e C6 f C1 g J8 h N8

144–145 **Reflective symmetry**

Warm-up 1 2 5 7 8 9 10

1.

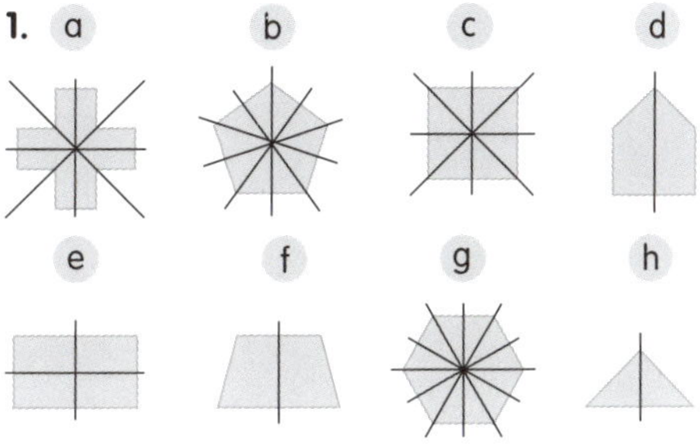

2.

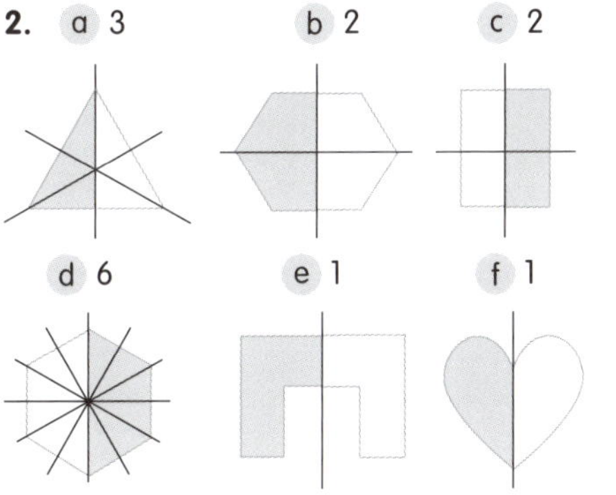

3. a no lines of symmetry:
B F G J L N P Q R S Z
b 1 line of symmetry:
A C D E K M T U V W Y
c 2 or more lines of symmetry H I O X

146–147 **Tally marks**

Warm-up

1 22 2 15 3 28 4 36 5 19
6 31 7 23 8 38

1. a 卌 卌 卌 卌 卌
b 卌 卌 卌 卌 卌 ||||
c 卌 卌 |
d 卌 卌 ||||
e 卌 卌 卌 ||
f 卌 ||
g 卌 ||||
h 卌 卌 卌 卌 ||
i 卌 卌 |||
j ||||

2. a 卌 卌 |
b 卌
c ||||
d 卌 卌
e 卌 ||
f 卌 |
g |||

3. a Starlings 卌 ||||
b Blackbirds 卌 |||
c Robins ||||
d Pigeons 卌 卌 卌 |
e Woodpeckers |
f Ducks 卌 卌 ||||
g Herons |
h Crows |

148–149 **Frequency tables**

Warm-up

1 Cheetah 16 2 Jaguar 10
3 Leopard 12 4 Lion 23 5 Tiger 19

1. a 59 b 18 c 10 d 33 e 91
f 52 g 147 h Saturday i Monday
j Tuesday k Saturday

2. a F b T c F d F e T

3. a 82, 41, 123 b 32, 34, 66
c 27, 14, 41 d 12, 8, 20

150–151 **Data handling**

Warm-up

1 78%, 92%, 59%, 64%
2 190 days, 181 days, 188 days, 179 days
3 130 cm, 138 cm, 128 cm, 135 cm
4 1, 3, 0, 1
5 1500 ml, 1700 ml, 2000 ml, 1800 ml
6 8 km, 10 km, 7 km, 15 km

1. a 卌 ||||, 9 b 卌 ||, 7 c 卌 卌 |, 11
d 卌 |, 6

2. a 3 sides – 13, 4 sides – 12
b Green – 11, Yellow – 14
c Big – 10, Small – 15

3.

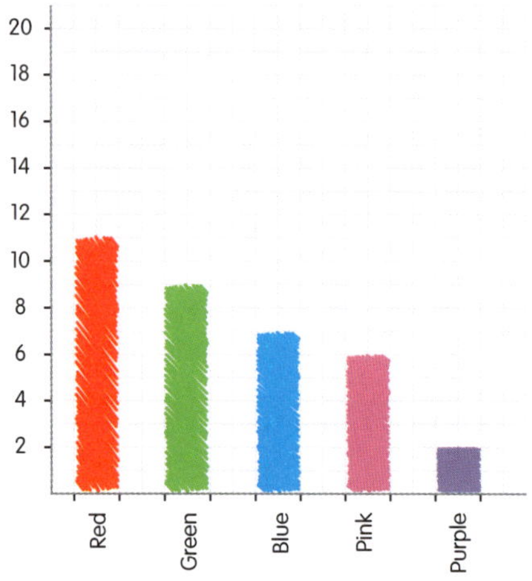

152–153 Carroll diagrams

Warm-up

	Has legs	Does not have legs
Lives in the sea	crab, octopus	dolphin, fish
Does not live in the sea	chicken, cat	worm, snail

1.

	Divisible by 9	Not divisible by 9
Odd numbers	45, 63, 27, ~~90~~, 81	79, 11, ~~56~~, 23, 57, 49
Even numbers	72, 54, 36, 18, ~~44~~, 90	12, ~~49~~, 26, 16, 62, 56, 44

2.

	Divisible by 7	Not divisible by 7
Prime number	7	2, 5, 11, 23, 41
Not a prime number	14, 28, 35, 42, 49	9, 18, 27, 33, 46

3.

	Made of only straight lines	Not made of only straight lines
Vowels	A, E, I	O, U
Not vowels	F, H, K, L, M, N, T, V, W, X, Y, Z	B, C, D, G, J, P, Q, R, S

4.

	Has right angles	Does not have right angles
Is a 2D shape		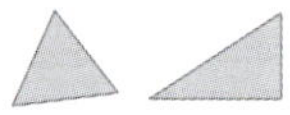
Is not a 2D shape		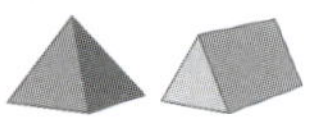

154–155 Venn diagrams

Warm-up

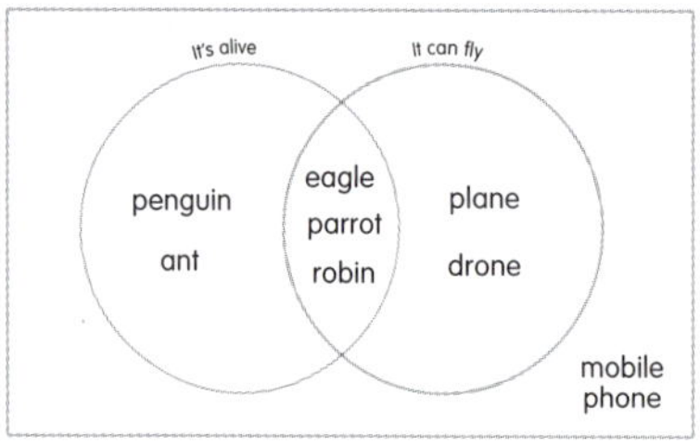

1.

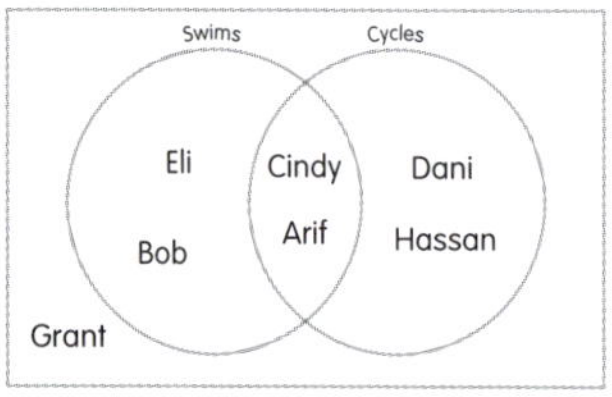

2. a Asim and Finn b Daisy and Hamid
c Brinda and Ivo d Harry

e

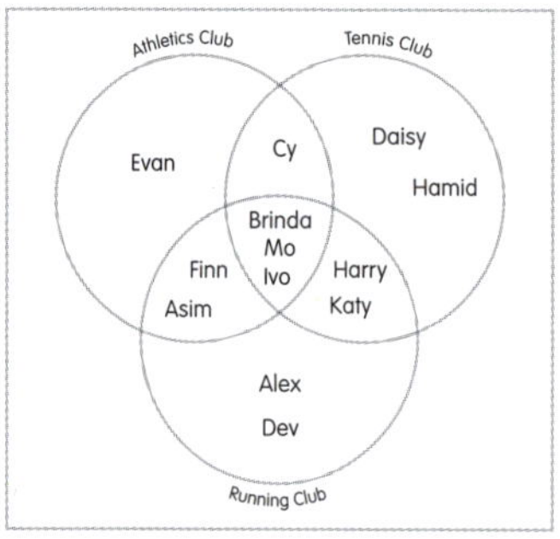

3. a 12 b 14 c 7 d 10 e 39
f 5 g 2

156–157 Pictograms

Warm-up

1 F 2 T 3 F 4 T

1. a cabbage b peas c 7
d spinach e broccoli f 1

2. Chinese 42, Indian 31, Italian 17, Mexican 20, Thai 14

3. I read one book each week, so I read 52 books in total. My favourite type was science fiction, and I read 12 books of this type. My least favourite type was mystery, and I only read 5 books of this type. I read 10 graphic novels. These were closely followed by art, scoring just one fewer. I read 8 natural history books, and the same number of history books.

158–159 Block graphs

Warm-up

1 mint choc chip 2 vanilla 3 raspberry 4 strawberry

1. a 11 b 15 c 3 d alpacas e 5

2.

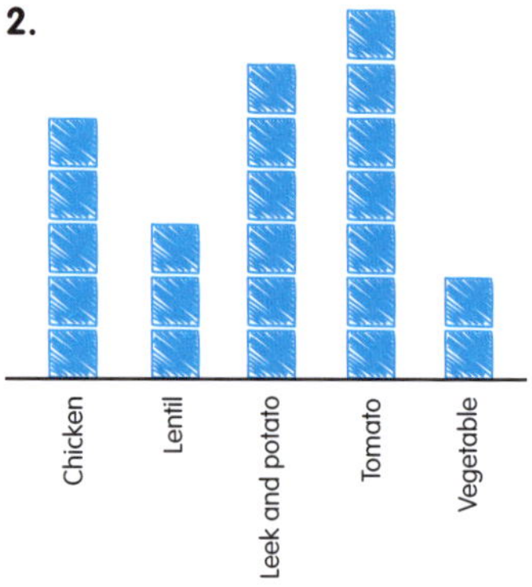

3. a ✓ c ✓ d ✓ f ✓ g ✓

160–161 Bar charts

Warm-up

1 Trumpet 6 2 Piano 8 3 Guitar 6
4 Drums 10 5 Recorder 9

1. a 13 b 6 c 4 d 5 e 7 f 14

2.

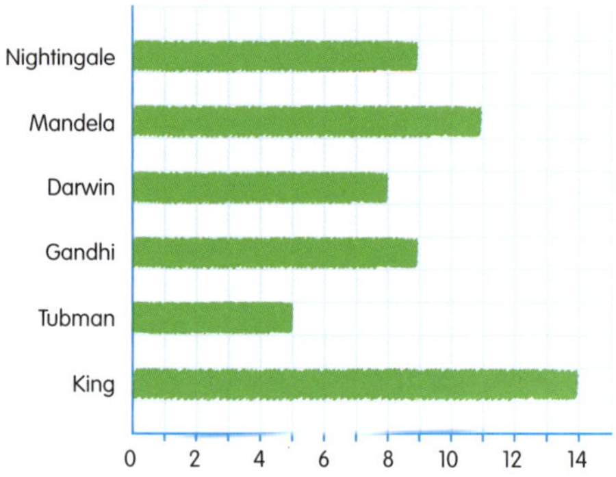

3.

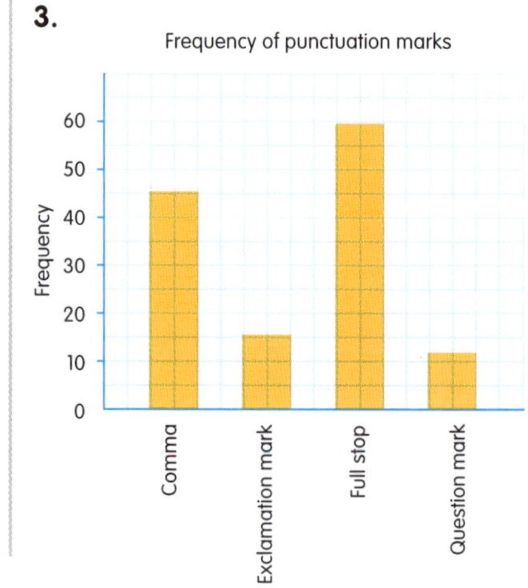